Literary Fat Ladies

Literary Fat Ladies

RHETORIC, GENDER, PROPERTY

Patricia Parker

METHUEN
London and New York

First published in 1987 by
Methuen & Co. Ltd
11 New Fetter Lane, London EC4P 4EE

Published in the USA by
Methuen & Co.
in association with Methuen, Inc.
29 West 35th Street, New York NY 10001

Printed in Great Britain by
Biddles Ltd, Guildford
and King's Lynn

British Library Cataloguing in Publication Data
Parker, Patricia
Literary fat ladies: rhetoric, gender, property.
1. Literature——History and criticism
I. Title
809   PN523
ISBN 0–416–91600–7
ISBN 0–416–91610–7 Pbk

Library of Congress Cataloging in Publication Data
Parker, Patricia A., 1946–
Literary fat ladies.
Includes index.
1. Women in literature.   2. Power (Social sciences) in
literature.   3. Property in literature.   I. Title.
PN56.5.W64P37 1987   809′.9352042   87–11295
ISBN 0–416–91600–7
ISBN 0–416–91610–4 (pbk.)

For

*Jacqueline and Joshua,
Pauline and Alex*

Contents

Acknowledgments

This book could not have been written without the support of others. I am grateful to the Killam Program of the Canada Council, together with the Social Sciences and Humanities Research Council of Canada, for grants which enabled its research and writing, and to the generosity of Victoria College and the University of Toronto for leave in order to finish it; to Bliss Carnochan and the Stanford Humanities Center, René Girard and the Program of Interdisciplinary Research, and John Bender and David Wellbery of the Committee on Comparative Literature at Stanford for hospitality and support during its completion; to the librarians of the Huntington, Folger, Houghton, Pratt and Newberry Libraries for their good nature; to Jean Wilson, Margaret Burgess, Timothy J. Hampton, Mary Jean Corbett and Eileen Reeves for their assistance; to Janice Price, Graham Bradbury and the Methuen editorial staff for their manifold labors; and to Cheryl Davis, John Freccero, Thomas Grey, Ann Kirkland, Rachel Jacoff, Peter Heyworth, and Jon and Lily Lomberg for friendship and support at its various stages.

Writing is, paradoxically, both a solitary and a collective enterprise. My students through the years, at the University of East Africa, at Toronto and at Stanford, enabled much of the formulation of the book's concerns. I would like particularly to honour Kesi Rajabu and, in memoriam, the fierce intelligence of Katherine Alderdice. It is also a pleasure to be able to thank friends and interlocuters who helped shape its direction or entered into discussion of particular issues: Jonathan Arac, Ian Balfour, Terry Castle, Eleanor Cook, Dennis Costa, Deborah Esch, Margaret Ferguson, Mary Jacobus, Ann Rosalind Jones, L. Brown Kennedy, Maureen Quilligan, David Quint, Barbara Mowat, Peter Nesselroth, Mary Nyquist, Julian Patrick, David Riggs, Aubrey Rosenberg and Peter Stallybrass.

I am indebted, beyond thanks, to the love of those who have been with the book from the sidelines, and to early influences on its direction: to the continual gift of Jackie and Joshua, who have grown over the years of its writing from cheerful obliviousness to competitors for computer time; to

Pauline Hill, for her unstinting support, pioneering courage, and punning mother tongue; to Alex Hill for his critical intelligence and Irish vernacular; and to David Hill, for his patient ear. Finally, and long overdue, I owe a debt to the people of Tanzania, for an influence whose imperatives begin their only partial fulfillment here.

Parts of this book reproduce material from previously published essays, here reprinted by permission of the original publishers:

"The Metaphorical Plot," from David S. Miall, ed., *Metaphor: Problems and Perspectives* (Harvester and Humanities Presses, 1982).

"Anagogic Metaphor: Breaking Down the Wall of Partition," from Eleanor Cook *et al.*, eds, *Centre and Labyrinth: Essays in Honour of Northrop Frye* (Toronto: University of Toronto Press, 1983).

"The (Self-)Identity of the Literary Text: Property, Propriety, Proper Place and Proper Name in *Wuthering Heights*," from Mario J. Valdés and Owen Miller, eds, *Identity of the Literary Text* (Toronto: University of Toronto Press, 1985).

"Suspended Instruments: Lyric and Power in the Bower of Bliss," in Marjorie Garber, ed., *Cannibals, Witches, and Divorce: Estranging the Renaissance*, Selected Papers from the English Institute, 1985 (Baltimore and London: The Johns Hopkins University Press, 1987).

1

Retrospective Introduction

The present Introduction, like all Introductions, is retrospective: it looks back over and offers some conclusions from what is about to follow. But it is even more so because the studies in this book, focused on questions of rhetoric, gender and property, have been the work of several years, through stages of development both in my own thinking and in the direction of literary theory and criticism. The oldest, "The Metaphorical Plot"—first published in an interdisciplinary collection on metaphor—contains the germ of the subsequent direction of the investigations here, and two of the links in the subtitle, between rhetoric and property. Extended into a reading of a particular text, it led, in the second-written essay—an analysis of *Wuthering Heights* for a symposium on the identity of the literary text—into more detailed interrogation of the relation between the unsettling mobility of tropes such as metaphor and the boundary markers of private property.

Neither of these earliest studies directly engages the third term—gender—except in elliptical observations in the latter on the forms of exchange marked through women's changing proper names or in the function of the housekeeper narrator of Brontë's novel to provide a story for the pleasure of a master—a function as "gossip" which would link her to the other gossips featured elsewhere in this book. The more recent pieces, however—beginning with the title essay, "Literary Fat Ladies and the Generation of the Text"—move explicitly toward questions of gender and genre as well as of property, and the entanglements of rhetorical questions with questions of ideological framing and political consequence. A common focus of these studies is the link between the categories of rhetoric and discourse and questions of gender and ideology, the importance of rhetoric not just as a system of tropes but as a motivated discourse.

The individual essays proceed as follows, with the first two introducing questions of rhetoric and gender on the one hand and rhetoric and property on the other. The title essay explores the link between the amplification of discourse and the expansive textual figure of the "fat lady," both within the Renaissance and beyond, into more modern instances, including James's Fanny Assingham and Joyce's Molly Bloom. "The Metaphorical Plot" surveys the plots at work within ostensibly neutral neoclassical, Romantic and contemporary conceptions of metaphor and the labor of metaphor within particular literary plots. Its aim is not—as with so many recent studies of this trope of tropes—to put forward a single view from among the multitude of possibilities; but rather to examine some of the most influential descriptions of metaphor and the plots they have generated, including the often unacknowledged *mythoi* of recent critical theory. Because of the occasion of its writing, its survey is necessarily telescopic and partial; a fuller study of metaphorical plots, of which this essay is only a preliminary sketch, would have to include, among other things, the tradition of Vico and the primacy of the metaphorical. But its original purpose, within a group of essays by philosophers, psycholinguists and others, was to give a sense of *mythos* or emplotment to a field of inquiry in which characterizations of metaphor proceed so often blind to the figures which structure the discussion itself.

The second group of essays addresses questions of genre and gender, of rhetorical play on the figures of rhetoric, and the relation between the limiting structures of discourse and questions of social and political control. "Suspended Instruments: Lyric and Power in the Bower of Bliss" seeks to relate the structure of subject male and dominant female in a central episode of Spenser's *Faerie Queene* to the insights and methods of so-called "new-historicist" study of literary text and social text, including the ambivalent figuring of Elizabeth as Spenser's reigning queen, but to do so within the specific context of gender and lyric forms. "Transfigurations: Shakespeare and Rhetoric" sets out to demonstrate, by analysis of paronomastic play on tropes such as "The Doublet" and "The Preposterous," the crucial importance of the lexicon and structures of rhetoric for the interpretation of Shakespeare. Its more elliptical engagement of the relation of such rhetorical tropes and plotting to questions of gender and social ordering is taken up explicitly in its companion essay, "Motivated Rhetorics: Gender, Order, Rule," which looks at ways in which what presents itself as a study of language or logic quickly becomes implicated in questions of social and political control. The instances here of the gendering of rhetorical figures, including metaphor, extend the discussion of the earlier "Metaphorical Plot"; its concern with wayward women and wayward tropes leads finally to *A Midsummer Night's Dream*, a central text within the ongoing feminist debate over Shakespeare.

The next two essays take up differently the relation between structures of discourse and structures of property. "Rhetorics of Property: Exploration, Inventory, Blazon" juxtaposes three traditionally separate domains —the descriptive display of a woman's body; discovery and exploration narratives of a feminized New World; and descriptions of landscape and "prospect" at the culmination of two centuries of British empire—in order to elicit the historically influential links between rhetorical invention and economic inventory, between the possessive display of the female body and the progressive enclosure of land. "The (Self-) Identity of the Literary Text" deals with the relation between property, propriety, proper place and proper name in *Wuthering Heights*, in order to suggest why this novel has attracted formalist and Marxist critic alike.

The last essay in the book is its longest one: "Coming Second: Woman's Place." It had its beginning years ago in a fascination with the echoes of the creation of Eve at the very moment when Rousseau creates "Woman" as a companion for his Emile, and, more generally, with the frequency of a structure in which the narrative of a woman comes only belatedly or supplementarily. It starts from two influential paradigms for this progression—the story of the creation of Adam first in Genesis 2, and the Aristotelian conception of the female as imperfect or botched male—and extends its study of female secondariness into the instabilities of sequence in Milton, Rousseau and Freud.

Each of the studies here has been written for a different occasion, the most recent—"Motivated Rhetorics," "Rhetorics of Property" and "Coming Second"—for the Gauss Seminars at Princeton. They are intended as essays in the older sense of attempts rather than inclusive or conclusive statements, and in the newer sense of interventions in the current state of literary criticism and theory. Because of their originally occasional nature and the requirement that each essay be complete in itself, some overlap in their references is unavoidable and has not been completely excised. The brief illustration from *Wuthering Heights* in "The Metaphorical Plot" is extended in the later, more detailed exploration of that novel in "The (Self-)Identity of the Literary Text," in ways that I hope might indicate why theoretical inquiry into the control of a trope such as metaphor is bound to lead into the textual question of a masterable "identity." Similarly, rhetorical tropes and categories which link the organization of society to the regulation of discourse appear recontextualized in several of these studies, at different refractive angles, as does recourse to the language of *copia* and of sexual or rhetorical "opening." "Increase and multiply," for example—the principle of textual, bodily and generational increase in "Literary Fat Ladies" and in the later discussions of rhetoric in Shakespeare—returns in relation to the emergence of a language of commodity in "Rhetorics of Property." The turn here to the more concrete senses of "increase" makes explicit a continuing argument of these investigations—the implication of the rhetorical in the economic —and links it to the consequences as well as the historical background of the separation of rhetoric from something now called "economics."

The essays have in common a number of connecting links: the textual figure of the fat lady in particular literary texts and the description in one

New World narrative of the "large" and "heavy" body of Maryland displayed to her exploiters; the misogynist topos of women's endless talkativeness and its counterpart in a vagrant female sexuality; the resilient masculinist paradigm of women's erotic delay or holding off, a topos still operative in the text of psychoanalysis; the relation between narrative as a form of overcoming an enchantress in romance and the function of a specifically narrative *telos* in the plotting of sexual difference in Milton, Rousseau or Freud. There are also a number of continuing concerns. One is with structures of linearity and sequence: the Genesis narrative of male and female; Shakespeare's exploitation of models of the sequitur, or of cause and effect; and, at a later stage of the same print culture, the preposterous narrative of *Wuthering Heights*. Another is with the interplay between rhetorical tropes or textual figures and the generation of characters and plots. This is reflected in the focus, in these studies, on small textual elements in order to approach larger ones, or on apparently utterly marginal characters like "Will Page" in *The Merry Wives of Windsor* or the *Henriad*'s "old Double."

A major argument of the essays is also the importance in all three of the terms of the subtitle—rhetoric, gender and property—of the overriding notion of place, and proper place: this includes the topographical resonance of the rhetorical *topos*, the conception of tropes of reversal, transport or exchange as moving words from their proper place, and the influential Aristotelian and biblical traditions of the proper place of women. It is the underlying notion of place and the conception of metaphor as "alien" or dwelling in "a borrowed home," which might be seen to be at work not just in a novel like Emily Brontë's but in the whole tradition of the gothic, whose plots are so frequently dependent on the intrusion of an alien and the usurpation of a house.

Part of what underlies these studies, finally, is a statement about the continuation of the categories and organizing structures of a more self-conscious rhetorical tradition well beyond its apogee in the Renaissance, even beyond the disparaging of rhetoric and trope which accompanied the consolidation of the civil state in the era of Hobbes and Locke. The tradition of the "partition" of discourse is in need of excavation if we are to read the extensive and punning exploitation of such rhetorical terms in Shakespeare, Ben Jonson and other Renaissance writers. But it was still being perpetuated—along with neoclassical notions of the impropriety of metaphor—in as influential an eighteenth-century text as Hugh Blair's *Lectures on Rhetoric and Belles Lettres*, whose chapter on the art of partition in sermon discourse outlines the principle Emily Brontë as a preacher's daughter would have known in its practice if not in its theory, the one which informs the proliferating partitions of a sermon in a nightmare chapter of *Wuthering Heights*. The juxtaposition of texts in "Rhetorics of Property" also depends on the conviction that the apparent

effacing of "painted rhetoric" in Baconian science and subsequent strictures against tropes masked what was a continuation and recontextualizing of terms and structures simultaneously rhetorical and economic, as
well as the subtle gendering of a whole rhetorical tradition.

The essays do not attempt to apply contemporary theory, including
theories of rhetoric such as Barthes' or de Man's, to the different focus of
much older texts; but rather, deliberately, to stay within the problematics
of rhetoric at work in specific texts and traditions of decorum, governance
and disposition. If at points this more particular study begins to recall
certain contemporary theories, we need to remember that much of the
continental theory that has had such an impact in the past two decades is
informed by an education which included classical rhetoric: the texts
which Shakespeare, or Hugh Blair, knew well in their originals or in
redactions, have come back through a French door so to speak. My own
bias is that if we were to attend to this largely forgotten language even in
modern texts which so clearly advertise their relation to it—Joyce's
Ulysses, say—we would be better readers of contemporary as well as of
more remote texts.

The theoretical apparatus of these essays (as with the use of Foucault
and Derrida to approach the structures of *Wuthering Heights*) is a largely
heuristic one. When "Suspended Instruments" was first delivered as an
English Institute talk, one of its hearers remarked that its use of Laura
Mulvey on the male gaze worked much better for Spenser than for cinema,
where its legitimacy has been much debated. This may be because the
powerful scopic drive she describes is already long a feature of literary
romance and Petrarchan lyric. The evocation of the romance paradigms at
work behind Lacan's movement from the "Imaginary" to the "Symbolic,"
the name of the Father and the Law, is also not to apply a post-Freudian
psychoanalytic terminology to an older Renaissance text, but to suggest
the culturally loaded paradigms informing the work of Lacan himself,
whose complex relation to the question of gender, and to courtly romance,
the recently appearing Seminars are just beginning to suggest. Similarly,
the placing of Freud at the end of "Coming Second" and at the end of this
book, is to suggest that a figure read more frequently as the beginning of a
certain history might, with a shift of historical punctuation, be read as well
against the background of one.

I have used contemporary theoretical formulations heuristically partly
to indicate how critical practices generally considered in isolation, or as
mutually exclusive, necessarily meet over problems such as property, the
institution and instability of gender hierarchies, or the ideologically charged
rhetorical instruction which enjoyed such a dramatic rise in England in the
sixteenth century. The evocation of both Macherey and Derrida at the end
of "Motivated Rhetorics" summons names often wielded by opposing
camps: yet the discourse of rhetoric and the decorum of tropes in the

Renaissance calls out for an analysis which attends not only to the surpluses and reserves of language but to its specific historical status as a political instrument. Similarly, the discussion of *Wuthering Heights* in "The (Self-)Identity of the Literary Text" brings both Foucault and Derrida to bear on the consideration of a text which anticipates the twinned questions of the "ghost" and the "proper" which have preoccupied so much continental theory and narratology. I have drawn on Foucault's early description of the classical or Enlightenment *episteme* in dealing with property in relation to this text, and on Derrida and Blanchot to raise the question of its "self-identity," because of the limitations of older Marxist notions of representation which would ask only how such a novel "reflected" property laws and practices in its day and, in its need to stabilize the text in order to answer that question, would elide its fissures and formal complexities. It is not that the relation of the novel to those laws and practices is unimportant or that it has been more than superficially dealt with in earlier treatments of the subject; but rather that "property" is also an epistemological and ideological question affecting both "real" property and the other senses of the term which Brontë's novel so powerfully evokes.

The essays draw more than once upon Foucault: on the notion of the *episteme* with regard to *Wuthering Heights*, and on the relation between power and the circulation of a discourse in "Motivated Rhetorics" and the discussion of exploration, landscape and *blazon* in "Rhetorics of Property." But again they do so with an implicit revision and critique, especially of the epistemics of *Les Mots et les choses*. Foucault's commitment to ruptures or breaks requires him in his early writing to characterize, preposterously, a prior Renaissance *episteme* based on resemblance and metaphor from the perspective of a classical or Enlightenment difference from it, and to do so in ways that make it only too easy for scholars more faithful to the Renaissance to recognize the distortions of this characterization and hence to reject Foucauldian analysis more generally. What the Renaissance models of linearity and the "rule of reason" treated in "Motivated Rhetorics" make clear is that what Foucault identifies as the linearity of a later "classical" discourse—from Hobbes to Locke and into the eighteenth century—is an intensification of something already present in the Renaissance and already related to the controlling of linguistic tropes. From this perspective, one link between the sixteenth-century models of linearity and consequence in "Motivated Rhetorics" and the beginning, with Locke, in "The (Self-)Identity of the Literary Text" would be the Hobbes of the *Leviathan*, whose preoccupation with the control of tropes such as metaphor and with the linear "chain of discourse" marks the culmination of earlier Renaissance models of linearity, and the intensified expunging of tropic ambiguities in the service of a new science and an even greater consolidation of civic power.

The relation between the text of something called (for better or for worse) "literature" and something called (for better and for worse) "theory" is anything but a *sens unique*. The upsetting of proper place and linearity in Brontë's novel comes more than a century before contemporary writing like Luce Irigaray's on the patriarchal orders of linearity, property, and proper name, as it does before Derrida's treatment of the "ghost" which haunts any notion of the "proper." But to juxtapose all three might suggest the possibility of a kind of feminist inquiry which would not be dependent on artificially isolating female characters from the narrative and rhetorical forms in which they appear. The Derridean logic of the supplement, taken up in the more recent analyses of Sarah Kofman and others, already, as Kofman's own subtle allusiveness suggests, has its anticipation in the secondary creation of the female in Genesis. "Literary Fat Ladies and the Generation of the Text" alludes at its end to the affinities between the language of the rhetorical tradition it foregrounds and French feminist celebration of "écriture feminine": the literary texts it treats already long anticipate Cixous and Irigaray on the female body, female tongue and phallic "point."

The texts treated in what follows include Genesis and Milton; Spenser's *Faerie Queene* and Rousseau's *Emile*; textual bodies and their loquacious counterparts in Shakespeare, in Jonson's *Bartholomew Fair*, in the era of "feminized" novels like *Pamela* and *Clarissa*, and in more modern instances from Dickens, James, Joyce and Beckett; a number of Shakespeare plays—*Othello, Hamlet, The Comedy of Errors, A Midsummer Night's Dream*, the *Henriad, The Merry Wives of Windsor* and others less extensively; the inventory of a woman's body in *Cymbeline*, New World narratives like George Alsop's *Character of the Province of Mary-Land*, and eighteenth-century descriptions of landscape and property; Brontë's *Wuthering Heights* and Freud's texts on female sexuality, including *On Narcissism* and *The Taboo of Virginity*. The book's title—"Literary Fat Ladies"—is used, in the terms of the Irigarayan epigraph of the title essay, "mimetically": to "make 'visible,' by an effect of playful repetition, what was supposed to remain invisible," "to convert a form of subordination into an affirmation, and thus to begin to thwart it." The cover illustration —Eve's passing from patriarch to Patriarch—is of one of its recurrent fat ladies, the ongoing representative woman of Western culture, original garrulous female and translative detour. The essays as a whole figure constructions of gender in relation both to the rhetorical tradition and to discourses of property. The concern with rhetoric throughout is in the conviction that only taking it seriously can make us better formalist readers of texts in a wide variety of periods; but that it is precisely such a concern with language and its ordering structures which might lead us to re-pose the question of moving beyond formalism, differently.

2

Literary Fat Ladies
and the Generation of the Text

> To play with mimesis is thus, for a woman, to try to recover the place of
> her exploitation by discourse, without allowing herself to be simply
> reduced to it. It means to resubmit herself—inasmuch as she is on the
> side of the "perceptible," of "matter"—to "ideas," in particular to ideas
> about herself that are elaborated in/by a masculine logic, but so as to
> make "visible," by an effect of playful repetition, what was supposed to
> remain invisible: the cover-up of a possible operation of the feminine in
> language.... One must assume the feminine role deliberately, which
> means already to convert a form of subordination into an affirmation,
> and thus to begin to thwart it.
>
> (Luce Irigaray)

Much of this essay will have to do with walls or partitions; so we begin
with a rhetorical partition, a division of the subject into parts. The first,
which might be called "The Body in Question," comes in several sections
and is perhaps appropriately by far the largest. The concluding will be a
kind of appendage under the rubric of "The Genitive, or Jinny's Case" and
"The Vocative, or the Story of O." The Postscript—which goes beyond
the Renaissance instances primarily foregrounded here—takes this story
into the subsequent history of linkages between female copia, of body and
of word, and the copiousness of texts.

First, the question of "fat ladies." We will begin with a woman called
Rahab, the redeemed harlot of Jericho from the biblical Old Testament.
No record of the conquest of Jericho by Joshua (whom, in Milton's words,
the Gentiles Jesus call) indicates that she was physically fat. She was simply
the harlot associated with the walls at the entrance to the Promised Land.
Her name in Hebrew, however, means "wide" or "broad."[1] Her conversion from the heathen to the Israelite cause involves a turning from letting
in men to letting in men—a prelude to the final act of the story in which, as
the song goes, the walls come tumbling down. As a figure thus associated

both with walls and with discrimination, with taking in the *right* men, she becomes in the biblical tradition of which she is a part a principal Old Testament figure for the Church. The Church figured as female is that other redeemed harlot who in the space between the First and Second Coming of another Joshua, Christ—that is, between the disappearance and final triumphant return of the Master of Creation, Time and History —expands or dilates in order, so to speak, to take in more members, before that ultimate apocalyptic end. One of the iconographic embodiments of this female figure—ambiguously recalling both Mary the Mother and the harlot Mary Magdalene—is the figure most often called *Mater Misericordiae* and pictured as opening her cloak wide enough to encompass the gathered members of the Church or the Body of Christ.

The name of Rahab in Hebrew ("broad, wide") was translated into Latin by the Church Fathers as *dilatio* or dilation, and her opening and expansion in that crucial meantime or threshold period before Apocalypse became known technically as the "dilation of Christendome," a phrase used repeatedly by St Thomas More and others in the Renaissance for the period of spreading or widening through the "dilation of the Word," the crucial activity of that interim of deferred Judgment or Second Coming in which a promised end is yet postponed. "Dilate" comes to us from the same Latin root as Derrida's "différance" and involves—commonly throughout Renaissance usage in several languages—that term's curious combination of difference and deferral, dilation, expansion, or dispersal in space but also postponement in time. The dilation of Rahab or of the Church, then, involves symbolically two orifices: expansion to take in a multiplicity of members (as in Donne's sexual pun in the Sonnet on the Church as she who is—he is addressing Christ her Master—"most trew, and pleasing to thee, then / When she's embrac'd and open to most men"); and the propagation, through the mouth, of the Word, again an activity not unexpectedly linked with a Church figured as symbolically female, since one of the oldest topoi of misogyny is the fabled inability of women to keep that particular orifice shut. There is, as Lee Patterson has recently reminded us, at least one recorded instance of the view that Christ revealed himself to women immediately after his Resurrection because he knew that women would spread the word.[2]

This particular figure—of Rahab, understood as dilation, expansion, and deferral, and used as a figure for the space and time of language, discourse, and history before a Master's apocalyptic return—is the figurative fat lady who first interested me when I started to think about romance and about its characteristic association with such dilation or potential vagrancy (or often simply its dilatory refusal to come to a "point").[3] But it was only much later that I began to discover how pervasive and multivalent this entire complex of "dilation" in the Renaissance actually was and how frequently associated with figures of the feminine. This is a link which arises out of romance itself. Spenser used the term "dilate" both for the dilation of history before its deferred apocalyptic (or "sabbath") ending and for the activity of narrating or telling tales, including by implication the dilatory expansion of his own poem; but he also associates this expansion with a dangerous female temptress or enchantress in a canto which is perhaps not by accident the fattest, most dilated canto in the entire poem—a dilation specifically linked with the "gate" of a "Dame" called "Excesse" ("No gate, but like one, being goodly dight / With boughes and braunches, which did broad dilate / Their clasping armes, in wanton wreathings intricate," *The Faerie Queene*, II.xii.53–5). Overcoming this temptress and the dilated body of the text in question becomes the quest of the knight of Temperance, in a version of what Marvell calls the contest between Resolved Soul—here, the male knight—and the potentially distracting ensnarements of Created Pleasure, the bower of Acrasia. His project, we might say, is to bring this dilated "matter" (with the possibility of a pun on both *materia* and *mater* as in Hamlet's "Now, mother, what's the matter?") to a "point." Though this knight does not use his sword, the word "point" (which designates in so many Renaissance English puns at once "end," sword, and their phallic counterpart) is Spenser's own in the very canto opening which projects the knight's victory over this "matter" in advance even of his setting out ("And this brave knight ... / Now comes to *point* of that same perilous sted, / Where Pleasure dwelles in sensual delights," II.xii.1–3). The subtext for the whole is Odysseus' victory over the feminine enticements and enchantments of Circe, pointedly, in that dilated and dilatory text, with his sword; and the victory which in the *Odyssey* only proleptically prefigures the homecoming or closure of the entire narrative is here only too easily converted into a figure for this canto's ending, the coming to a point of another strikingly dilated text.

This association of the dilation of romance narrative with the figure or body of a female enchantress is, moreover, extended in the debate over romance itself as a Circean, female (or even effeminate) form, particularly in the later stages of the Renaissance. Thomas Nashe's *Anatomy of Absurdity* (1589), for instance, combined a satire on women and those who praised them with an attack on the authors of romance. Both were conceived of as potentially corrupting, or leading astray, the will, as making it into a kind of Prodigal Son who might never return to his father.[4] The very popularity of the story of the Prodigal Son in Elizabethan England—of his errancy and prodigality but also of his eventual, repentant return—became, as Richard Helgerson points out, a chief exemplum for the potential vagrancy of the literary activity itself, and of the suspect effeminacy of poets. When Sir Philip Sidney replies to the attacks on romance, as on poetry, in his celebrated *Defence*, by saying that "he knows men that even with the reading of *Amadis de gaule* ... have found their hearts moved to the exercise of courtesie, liberalitie, and especially courage," he uses the word "men" pointedly as a counter to the attackers' association of poetry with the feminine.[5] The polemic against the Italianization of Englishmen in the work of one of these opponents of romance—Roger Ascham's *The Schoolmaster* (1570), which follows the model of Vives in its attack and characterizes romances as nothing but bold bawdry—is, in fact, inseparable from a polemic against the romance's corrupting and enervating effect, with the implication that the reader of such texts is cast as an endangered Odysseus whose only moly is a humanist countertraining in virtue and in more canonical reading—the preoccupation, precisely, of the schoolmaster.

Certainly it is this plot of reformation or return from such enchantments—or a turning away from them to something higher or more serious—which is the burden of the figure of the Prodigal Son in which one Elizabethan reader casts himself. John Harington, translator of Ariosto's *Orlando furioso*, first finds in Ariosto's portrayal of Rogero's enticement by the Circe-like Alcina (a source for Spenser's Acrasia) "the very picture of the Prodigal Son spoken of in the scripture, given over to all unthriftiness, all looseness of life and conversation," and then discerns a link between such prodigal vagrancy and his own pursuits. He writes as follows of coming to the place in his translation of the *Furioso* where Melissa reproves Rogero for his dalliance with Alcina (for which the model is Mercury's reproof of Aeneas for his dalliance with Dido rather than getting on with the higher task of establishing the Roman empire): "straight I began to think that my tutor, a grave and learned man, and one of very austere life, might say to me in like sort,'Was it for this that I read Aristotle and Plato to you and instructed you so carefully both in Greek and Latin, to have you now become a translator of Italian toys?'"[6] Such indulgence in romance was a form of dilatoriness or dalliance, preventing all such latter-day Aeneases from getting on with the business more proper to them.

Just as important a preface to our subject—and to the role of particular dilated female bodies in particular Renaissance texts—are a number of influential subtexts that a Renaissance poet or playwright would have inherited for the narrative topos of overcoming a female enchantress or obstacle en route to completion and ending. Here, where such female figures are linked with a threat to the execution of closure or accomplishment, the appropriate motto would seem to be not *Cherchez la femme*—or a certain way of understanding the question "Is there a woman in this text?"—but rather what we might dub *Ecrasez la femme*, ways of mastering or controlling the implicitly female, and perhaps hence wayward, body of the text itself.[7] The first of these subtexts—already suggested in the opening reference to Rahab, the redeemed harlot whose name is *dilatio* and who stands as a figure for the dilated space of deferred judgment and ending—is the Bible, which is filled with figures for the space and time of

such extension (the forty-day space between the announcement of judgment and its execution in the stories of Noah's Flood or Jonah's mission to
Nineveh; the space of respite or temporary reprieve from death granted to
Hezekiah; the holding back of time itself in the staying of the sun in
Joshua, and so on). The reprieve granted to Adam and Eve, the "remnant"
of Noah and his family after the almost final closure of the Flood—these
and other such reprieves extend both text and time, widening or increasing
the space between beginning and end which in Genesis threatens to be very
contracted indeed. A structure of deferral inhabits even the Bible's own
end or last word, the Book of Apocalypse or Revelation. There, ending is
linked to the stripping or overcoming of a female figure, the Whore of
Babylon, by the now at last returned Master, Christ. But the final lines end
in the still-deferred and still-anticipatory mode of an apostrophe, invocation, or vocative, "Even so, come, Lord Jesus" (Revelation 22), a retreat
from a vision of Ending into the ambiguous space before that ending (the
model, perhaps, of a similar retreat at the end of Spenser's *Faerie Queene*).
What looks like *the* end is, in this quintessential book of endings, presented
as still put off or deferred, still yet to come. The New Testament, like the
Old, however, is filled with warnings that this deferral of ending must not
lull its hearers into the assumption that the promised end will never come.
The crucial thing about deferral in its biblical context, then, is that its days
are finally numbered, that all time is ultimately borrowed time. The
structure of deferred ending remains resolutely teleological—waiting for
the return of a delayed but finally coming Master.

The second major subtext for the association of specifically female
figures with such dilation or delay is the *Odyssey* already referred to,
where Calypso, the enchantress at whose dwelling we first glimpse the
latent hero, has a name which means "covering," the very opposite of apocalypse or uncovering, and where Odysseus' mastery of Circe with his
sword may be by implication a sort of narratively retroactive liberation
from the covering and latency of Calypso's cave, just as it is an anticipation
of homecoming to Penelope.[8] Penelope herself, keeping her suitors suspended by the stratagem of weaving and unweaving, while the suitors act
like swine, is clearly a subtler or displaced counterpart of Circe, whose
spells turn men *into* swine. It is perhaps no accident, then, that subsequent
tradition tended to conflate or confuse these three female figures—
Calypso, Circe, Penelope—since bringing the story to its ending here
involves overcoming the implicitly female body of the romance narrative
itself. We might remember, by way of parenthesis, that in Roland Barthes
the properly narrative desire to reach an ending and the properly hermeneutic desire to penetrate a text's meaning are countered by the desire to
linger or dilate. In Ariosto's *Orlando furioso*, a Renaissance text remarkable for its metafictional sophistication in these matters, one of the
principal figures for ending is the overcoming of an enchantress who

recalls both Circe and the Whore of Babylon; stripping her bare is termed "reading her pages" in the way they should be read.[9]

It is easy to move from this second subtext to the third—Virgil's influential *Aeneid*—because it is the latter's combination of Odyssean or romance dilatoriness with Iliadic or epic haste which makes it the progenitor of so many Renaissance hybrids, or epic-romances. Virgil's poem, moreover, seems almost to be commenting, in what we would now call self-reflexive fashion, on the differing tendencies and gender associations of both epic and romance: the resolutely teleological drive of epic in its repeated injunctions to "break off delay" (*rumpe moras*) and the Odyssean or romance delaying tactics which make it the long poem it is and which disrupt or postpone the end promised from the beginning. Once again, it is the female figures—Dido, Allecto, Amata, Juno (and their agents)—who are the chief perpetrators of delay and even of obstructionism in relation to the master or imperial project of the completion of the text. Jupiter, the text's meta-authorial presence, is also the guarantor or at least the Olympic patron of ultimate closure. By making the *Aeneid* a principal subtext of his romance *Cymbeline*, Shakespeare provides an implicit reading of Virgil's poem in precisely such terms. In *Cymbeline* the Queen, like Juno in the *Aeneid*, can delay the fated ending but cannot indefinitely forestall or finally alter it; and a character representing Jupiter descends from the meta-authorial skies in that play's final act to announce why the promised ending has been so long deferred, which is to say, in view of this romance play's massively complicated movement to its own point of revelation or recognition scene, why the play itself has lasted as long as it has.

These influential texts—and their female obstructors—already, then, forge a link between such female figures and the extension or dilation of the text in order to defer its end or "point." But the even more specific link we need to explore before moving on to particular dilated *bodies* in a number of Renaissance and other texts is the rhetorical tradition of the dilation of discourse, and specifically its dilation through "partition," through the multiplication of partitions or rhetorical dividing walls. It is this towards which we need to turn before focusing on the identification of such dilation with corpulent bodies of various kinds, and the significance of their appearance in particular texts.

Erasmus's *De Copia* is here the readiest source not just for this rhetorical tradition but for its dual concerns. The preoccupation of this massively influential text is not only how to expand a discourse—to make its "matter" or *materia* respond to the rhetorical counterpart of the command to Adam and Eve to "increase and multiply"— but also how to control that expansion, to keep dilation from getting out of bounds, a concern repeated in the countless Renaissance rhetorical handbooks which both teach their pupils how to amplify and repeatedly warn them against the intimately related vice of "Excesse" (the same name, we might remember, as Spenser's dilating "Dame"). Dilation, then, is always something to be kept within the horizon of ending, mastery, and control, and the "matter" is always to be varied within certain formal guidelines or rules.

The rhetorical figure of walls or partitions, from that part of Cicero's *Topics* where a discussion of physical "walls" is juxtaposed with a definition of oratorical "partition," involves the dividing of a discourse, like a body, into "members"—a tradition which Shakespeare reveals he knows only too well when, in the Pyramus and Thisbe play of *A Midsummer Night's Dream*, he has Demetrius punningly call the mechanical playing the character of Wall the "wittiest partition that ever I heard discourse" (V.i.161–8).[10] In the related art of preaching, the principal method of proceeding was to divide and open up a closed or difficult scriptural text so that it might "increase and multiply," be dilated upon by the preacher so as to dilate and spread abroad the Word. In the words of Donne, summing up the entire tradition of the *ars praedicandi*, "Through partition or division, the Word of God is made a Sermon, that is, a Text is dilated, diffused into a Sermon." And this rhetorical dilation by partition was to be used by preachers of the Word in precisely that period of the "dilation of Christendome" before Apocalypse, before the final apocalyptic end both of that "wall of partition" spoken of in Ephesians (2:14) and of discourse itself.[11]

This tradition of rhetorical *dilatio*—with its references to the "swelling" style or its relation to the verbal "interlarding" produced through an excessive application of the principle of "increase"—provides its own links between fat bodies and discoursing "at large," between the size of a discourse and the question of body size. Ascham's *Schoolmaster* treats of the use of "epitome" in reducing the inflated bulk of an oration through the example of the need to put an "overfat" and "fleshy" style on a diet, as Cicero himself did in order to rid himself of "grossness." Though fat is not gendered as female in this passage from Ascham, it most definitely is in anti-Ciceronian contrastings of a more effeminate Ciceronian or Asiatic style—linked with "bignesse" as well as prodigality—to the more virile Attic. Erasmus's *Ciceronianus* (1528) speaks of seeking in vain in Ciceronian eloquence for something "masculine" and of his own desire for a "more masculine" style. Ciceronian copia in these discussions is both effeminate and the style of a more prodigal youth, to be outgrown once one had become a man: "I used to imitate [Cicero]," writes Lipsius; "but I have become a man, and my tastes have changed. Asiatic feasts have ceased to please me; I prefer the Attic." A similar contrast, with the appropriate shift of symbolic locus, informs the opposition of fat and effeminating Egypt to lean and virile Rome in Shakespeare's *Antony and Cleopatra*.[12]

This specifically rhetorical tradition of amplified textuality and dilated middles is joined by and easily combined with a whole host of other resonances of "dilation" in the Renaissance, which we can only briefly touch on here, but must at least mention, since they too figure frequently in the imaging of postponed ending or "increase" in the texts of our exemplary fat ladies. One is the Neoplatonic tradition of *dilatio* as the dilation or Emanation of Being, its procession out from and its crucial return to the Source or One. For not only is this one Western example among many of what Derrida repeatedly wants to distinguish from "différance" (since deferral or dilation in this tradition is contained within the horizon of ending, a simple detour between Origin and End); it also provides Spenser with the crucial authority for the final "putting downe" of the upstart Goddess Mutabilitie (as well as the specter of endlessness, perhaps) by Jupiter's female agent Nature, who has clearly been reading her Ficino. A second, related meaning is as a synonym for temporality, for the mediate or earthly as distinguished from the eternal, simultaneous, or immediate— hence the easy identification of dilation, as of the female, with the body of both time and the world, or creation itself. A third is the sense of dilation as the puffing up of pride, as in the warning in an English translation of Erasmus's *Adages* that "we dylate not our selves beyond our condition and state," or the "dilation" of Satan, progenitor of sin, in Milton's *Paradise Lost* ("Collecting all his might dilated stood"; IV.986).[13]

Still another use of "dilation" occurs in the context of propagation or generation, the postponing of death through natural increase, one of the principal arguments against the premature closure of virginity and a meaning crucial to the potential identification of the rhetorical tradition of "increase and multiply" with the more fruitful dilation of another kind of "fat lady"—the pregnant female body, promising even as it contains and postpones the appearance of an "issue." The generational joins the rhetorical and hermeneutic here through the fact that the command to "increase and multiply" which stands behind this kind of dilation ("Two joyned can themselves dilate") has its rhetorical counterpart in the tradition of the copia of discourse. Augustine in the *Confessions* has a whole chapter devoted to "increase and multiply" (XIII.xxiv) in the sense of the interpreter's opening and fruitful extension of a closed or hermetic scriptural text, what the rhetorical tradition would call "dilating or enlarging of a matter by interpretation." But this "matter" and its enlarging also easily joined with *mater*. Obstetrical descriptions in the Renaissance frequently start with a reminder of the divine command to "increase and multiply" and see the "mouth" of the *matrix* or womb as "an orifice at the entrance into the which may be dilated and shut." Dilation as the "opening" of a closed text to make it "increase and multiply" and to transform its brevity into a discourse "at large," then, joins dilation as both sexual and obstetrical "opening" and the production of generational increase.[14]

There are, to complete this Renaissance catalogue, two other signal contexts for dilation, which in fact often appear together as figures for the postponed ending of a text. The first is the judicial one—the tradition of Essoins or "dilatory pleas" which Hamlet, in a play very much concerned with postponement or deferral, calls "the law's delay," a means of putting off judgment or execution. Hamlet's complaint against the "law's delay" comes in the middle of the very soliloquy of hesitation or doubt ("To be or not to be"), with both its "consummation / Devoutly to be wish'd" and its hesitation to rush to that conclusion. And "dilatory pleas" as a means of putting off an ending easily participate in a crossing of legal with other contexts of judgment or consummation. At the end of Chaucer's *Canterbury Tales*, for example, the Parson, speaking of the apocalyptic "day of doom," describes it as that one "juggement" before which "there availeth noon essoin," a reminder that, in the biblical tradition out of which he speaks, dilation as delay is circumscribed finally by a telos, that the putting off of ending here is finally only temporary. The appearance of such a reference in the Parson's Tale (which has been frequently described as the *Tales'* culminating Book of Apocalypse or Revelation) may suggest retrospectively that all of the impressive *copia* or "God's plenty" of *The Canterbury Tales* up to that ending has been a form of "essoin" or "dilatory plea," including the text of that female figure, the Wife of Bath, whose copious discourse or dilated textual body puts off the Parson's concluding text, who announces "My joly *body* shall a tale tell," whose motto is "increase and multiply," and who herself turns to her own quite different purposes the sermon art of the dilation of discourse. As one recent reading of this excessive "Dame" puts it, Alisoun of Bath ameliorates the harsh polarizations of apocalyptic judgment and eschatology and opens up a space of dilation in which what we have come to call literature can have its place. Her "increase," however, is verbal rather than generational, and from this more judgmental perspective, as a form of sterility or fruitless activity, it is finally preempted by the teleological framework in which there is no—or no longer—"essoin."[15]

The final context for "dilation" is an erotic one within a specific masculinist tradition—the putting off of coitus or consummation which Andreas Capellanus describes as a feminine strategy in the art of love, a purportedly female plot in which holding a suitor at a distance creates the tension of a space between as well as an intervening time. By the time of Eve's "sweet reluctant amorous delay" in Book IV of *Paradise Lost*, "dilation" in this sense was almost a *terminus technicus* for the erotics of prolongation, a tradition still current in Addison's reference to "women of dilatory Tempers, who are for spinning out the Time of Courtship." Its focus on the hymen as a dividing wall or partition, moreover, made it easily conflatable with both the rhetorical tradition of the dilation of discourse by "partition" and the intervening "partition wall" of Ephesians

2. This amorous dilation is a frequent part of the plot of wooing or courtship in Shakespeare, in examples almost too numerous to name. But this plot of feminine dilation or delay is rarely linked, by critics of Shakespeare, with the temporal and rhetorical dilation of the plays themselves, though in *A Midsummer Night's Dream* (to take just one example) the erotic consummation promised in the play's opening scene is deferred for a time and space which coincides with that of the play as a whole and which is achieved only when a "partition" or wall associated both with the hymen and with the rhetorical "partition of discourse" is finally put "down,"[16] just as in *The Comedy of Errors* the wall of partition which prolongs the play's various romance-like "errors" by delaying the final recognition scene is associated with the intervening body of a much-dilated female.

*

This brings us, then, to our first Renaissance "fat lady," the comically dilated body of the kitchen wench in *The Comedy of Errors*, the early play of Shakespeare that is most closely allied to romance. This play extraordinarily combines the dilation of discourse through partition with the figure of Apocalypse (and what delays it) from Ephesians 2, where the coming of Christ breaks down the "wall of partition" between men, anticipating the final, apocalyptic removal of all walls or partitions. It is, indeed, set in Ephesus. The *Comedy* begins with a dilation or deferral of judgment and execution: Egeon, asked to "dilate at full" (I.i.122) the narrative of his life, is granted a temporary reprieve from "doom" (I.i.2) which then becomes the whole space and time of "error" in the play itself, culminating in an extraordinary concentration of allusions to the biblical Apocalypse, to the end, that is to say, of this meantime space of deferral, or *dilatio patriae*. The whole of the play, then, becomes an analogue of a space of dilation which does, however, finally come to an end.

In the play's own middle (the third act out of five), we encounter a wall of partition, which keeps the sets of twins from precipitating too early that final recognition scene and thus putting an end to the errors prematurely at that point. The figure who guards this wall and keeps the partition intact is a wondrous fat lady, the opposite (if we might exploit the play's own highly concentrated biblical echoes) of "Knock, and it shall be opened unto you." She is so fat that she is spherical, like the globe itself: "I could find out countries in her," says Dromio (III.ii.114–15), as he proceeds to do just that. And she is described in a pun which connects "grease" and "grace"—a tradition that seems to have as one of its origins commentaries such as St Bonaventure's on that "grace" which dilates the heart as "oil" dilates the flesh and that is still going strong as an all too easy English-Irish pun in the washerwomen scene of Joyce's *Finnegans Wake*.[17] This "wench" is "swart" like the Bride in the biblical Song of Songs, and decked

with comic versions of the precious stones of the New Jerusalem whose
Master is to return to his betrothed in the Book of Apocalypse. Her
description, in fact, ambiguously combines both female versions of the
world at once, recalling both the Whore of Babylon and the redeemed
harlot, Rahab, and the Church: the phrase applied to her ("a very reverent
body," one of whom it is not permitted to speak without saying "Sir-
reverence") nicely applies to both Church and whore. This Circean
"witch" (III.ii.144), however, is also, as the scene puts it, a "wondrous fat
marriage." We are reminded that she too awaits the return of her betrothed—an event that will occur with the final return of a figure called
earlier, in a clear echo of the New Testament passages on the delay of
Apocalypse, a "tardy master" who is "at hand" but not yet come (II.i.44).
This female "mountain of mad flesh" (IV.iv.154) appears in the midst of a
comedy which is itself a "farce" in the etymological sense of fattened or
"stuffed." But if her dilated body stands in some sense as a figure for the
dilation (and "errors") of The Comedy of Errors, she is finally to be
referred to her proper Master, or returned "betrothed." Perhaps significantly, then, this fat lady (variously called Luce/loose/"light" and Nell/an-
ell) never clearly appears on stage or is permitted, in propria persona, to
speak: she is only described in her globe-like rotundity. We might remember in this regard that the other text from Ephesians that is crucial to
this play set in Ephesus is "Wives submit unto your husbands," the text of
the proper hierarchy of female and male. For the play includes not just
echoes of this Pauline and other New Testament passages on that end and
marriage, including the apocalyptic marriage which will put an end to
error or "harlotry," but repeated play on the proverbial Latin tag respice
finem, or "look to the End," as it moves from this dilated female figure and
her "partition wall" to its own ending.

    The question of "fine" or end also dominates our second fat lady—the
figure of the pregnant woman, that visually dilated mater whom Lisa
Jardine has linked, in her massiveness of body or "grossesse," not just with
copious fertility but with a threatening female sexuality as well.[18] Here we
might consider two Shakespearean instances, both in relation to the
question of closure. One is the pregnant "gossip" and votaress whose
swelling body, "rich" with its contents, is described by Titania in A
Midsummer Night's Dream:

              Full often hath she gossip'd by my side,
              And sat with me on Neptune's yellow sands,
              Marking th'embarked traders on the flood;
              When we have laugh'd to see the sails conceive
              And grow big-bellied with the wanton wind;
              Which she, with pretty and with swimming gait,
              Following (her womb then rich with my young squire),
              Would imitate, and sail upon the land

> To fetch me trifles, and return again,
> As from a voyage, rich with merchandise.
> But she, being mortal, of that boy did die.   (II.i.125–35)

The passage presents, in C. L. Barber's phrase, a picture of a female-centered world, of "women who gossip alone, apart from men and feeling now no need of them, rejoicing in their own special part of life's power." The pregnant votaress is almost literally an image of dilation or swelling (in the sense, at least, of "Women grow by men," as the Nurse puts it in *Romeo and Juliet*, I.iii.95). And the "grand" style associated with rhetorical dilation or "swelling" is described by Quintilian in precisely the image used here of swelling sails ("Greek keels, even the little ones, know well their ports; let ours usually travel under fuller sails, with a stronger breeze swelling our canvas").[19] But the votaress is also an image of that dilation as only temporary, ending in an "issue" like all pregnancy or "travail," and in her case even more definitively, in death. In this regard, she figures by metonymy much of what happens to the female—as to a temporary dilation and delay—in *A Midsummer Night's Dream*, which begins with the deferral of consummation, deviates into a topsy-turvy middle space of female rebellion, and ends with the proper marital hierarchy. For the child she bears in her own "big-bellied" body is the changeling which will finally be taken away from Titania when that unruly and separatist female—holding off from her own master's bed—is finally mastered by Oberon and this "issue" passes from the world of the mother to that of the father.[20] What, then, in Barber's phrase, might have seemed an autonomous female-centered world turns out to have been only a dilative detour en route to that end, like pregnancy itself in the patriarchal economy enunciated by Theseus in which it is the father who provides the imprinting form ("To you your father should be as a god; / One that compos'd your beauties; yea, and one / To whom you are but as a form in wax, / By him imprinted," I.i.47–50). Like the dilative copia of the entire play, ending when the hymen or partition preserving another kind of female separateness is finally "down," the swelling of the pregnant or "big-bellied" votaress is only *pro tempore*.

The other Shakespearean "fat lady" in this regard—as a dilative means to a patriarchal end—might be the "Doctor She" of *All's Well That Ends Well*, a play whose teleological title belies the fact that it too depends upon extension and delay, upon the opening of a space both for a female plot and for what its character of "Parolles" ("many words" rather than one) calls a "more *spacious* ceremony" and "more *dilated* farewell" (II.i.50–7). The play right from its beginning links the generative imperative to "increase and multiply"—the generation of issue through the inflation or "blowing up" of virgins (I.i.119 ff.)—with the putting off of ending through the increase of a copious supply of intermediate words (II.ii.). Making the champion of the former and representative of the latter kind of "increase" or "blowing up" the character of Parolles or "words" draws attention to the extending of the play itself, which depends not only on such intermediate *paroles* but on the "putting off" of erotic consummation (II.iv.43; IV.ii.34; V.iii.212–17) and on a series of such displacing fare- wells. The fact that the play does finally reach an end, if a famously problematic one, provides in gross a repetition of the structure of that smaller scene within it devoted to the theme of "putting off" through words (II.ii), which ends with "things may serve long, but not serve ever" (II.ii.58–9).

The space opened up to "increase" between the heavy sense of ending at the beginning of *All's Well* and its final end or "fine" is the space of a particular female plot: the working of Helena, the heroine and "Doctor She" whose conversion of her husband's seemingly final "sentence" or doom (III.ii.61) into her own version of "increase and multiply" in the bed-trick finally makes her pregnant according to the demand. In the language of the whole comic scene on "putting off"—which finally, however, does come to an end—Helena's accomplishment of this "increase" and her pregnancy as the answer to the play's concluding riddles makes her its female embodiment of that "bountiful answer that fits all questions" (II.ii.15) or that "answer of most monstrous size that must fit all demands" (II.ii.32–3). Her dilated body—"blown up" on the same night as the merely inflated or puffed-up Parolles is deflated or blown down—is the fulfillment of the whole opening exchange between them on the subject of "increase." But, even in a play which seems to give a space to the achievement of a woman whose pregnancy is the sign of her triumph and achievement, this very "increase" has again to do with the production of an "issue," and with the winning of a recalcitrant husband, to whom the heroine then willingly submits. His noble family expands or extends itself just far enough to contain the exogamous detour her inclusion represents.

The other obvious Shakespearean "fat lady" is ostensibly no lady at all —old Jack Falstaff, whose corpulence, in the *Henriad*, in some sense embodies Prince Hal's delay, a Prodigal Son plot in which the completed movement of reformation and return to the father takes not one but two long and prodigally copious plays to effect. This "hill of flesh" (*1H4*, II.iv.243) "lards the lean earth as he walks along" (*1H4*, II.ii.109). But he is even more tellingly imaged in the series of hierarchized oppositions we have already encountered. His fat body is specifically a "*globe* of sinful continents" (*2H4*, II.iv.285). The second and completing half of the two plays also evokes in both comic and more serious contexts that "Jordan" to be crossed before entrance into the Promised Land, before its own culminating "Jerusalem." It is, we remember, the Chief Justice, represent- ative of both the father and the Law he evades, who warns Falstaff that his "waste"—manifested in his expanding waist—is "great" (*2H4*, I.ii.141). And the Hal who from the beginning of the two extended plays forecasts to the audience that his own tarrying and prodigality, with this "fat rogue" and the other "tattered prodigals," will be of only a "holiday" or temporary nature, ends that promise of reformation with an echo of the text in Ephesians on redeeming the time ("Redeeming time when men think least I will"; *1H4*, I.ii.217), leaving Falstaff with the other "Ephesians" or "boon companions" as the counterpart of the unredeemed Ephesus before the "partition" between Old and New is crossed.[21]

Falstaff in these plays, as Hal puts it, is "my sweet creature of bumbast" (*1H4*, II.iv.327) in both punning senses—the padding that stuffs a body out and its verbal equivalent. His fat is linked not just with "harlotry" (*2H4*, II.iv.41)—including perhaps that of Mistress Quickly's malapropped "harlotry players"(*1H4*, II.iv.395)—but with verbal *copia* as well, with that "throng of words" (*2H4*, II.i.112) which, even in these two prodigally copious plays, "cannot," as Falstaff says of himself, "last forever" (*2H4*, I.ii.214). Falstaff's own decision to repent his wasted life (with more punning on his expanded waist or girth) is, we might note, accompanied by references to his dwindling size, as if this movement to closure, reformation, and repentance involved a literal relation between the body of this prodigal play and its physically fat emblem (*1H4*, III.iii.1–2: "Bardolph, am I not fall'n away vilely since this last action? Do I not bate? Do I not dwindle?").

Falstaff himself is, of course, not a woman but a man. But he actually appears as a fat lady in *The Merry Wives of Windsor*. When he does, in a scene of transvestitism which perhaps suggests what Fal-staff has all along been missing, explicit embodiment is given to his effeminate associations throughout the other plays in which he figures. Here, as a "fat woman," he takes refuge in the chamber associated with an "Ephesian" Host (IV.v.18) and "painted about with the story of the Prodigal" (IV.v.7–8). And the play links references to "Fat Falstaff" with figures of "mirth ... so larded with ... matter" and of recounting "at large" (IV.vi.14–18). In *Henry IV, Parts 1* and *2*, fat itself is compared to the image of the pregnant earth, filled with wind (Falstaff punningly attributes his great size to his "sighs" or wind). Falstaff's fat is repeatedly associated with the copiousness or dilation of discourse, with avoiding the summons of the law through various counterparts of the "dilatory plea," and with the wombs and tongues of women ("I have a whole school of tongues in this belly of mine, and not a tongue of them all speaks any other word but my name. . . . My womb, my womb, my womb undoes me"; *2H4*, IV.iii.18–23).

But his expanded "waste" is a womb which in a sense never delivers the "issue" and which is therefore left behind in what, after all, is the drama of a return to the father, or genealogical succession. Falstaff's belly full of tongues links him, as do his tavern hostesses, Mistress Quickly and Doll Tearsheet, with the proverbially unstoppable female tongue. But Hal, in his only temporary prodigality and delay, merely "studies his companions /

Like a strange tongue," in order to master or "gain the language," so, "like gross terms" (with Falstaff visibly the grossest), he can "cast" them "off" in "the perfectness of time" (*2H4*, IV.iv.68–78).[22] If, in seasonal terms, Falstaff's fatness suggests the autumnal plenty of "martlemas" before the coming of winter (*2H4*, II.ii.97), in genealogical and political terms, he is, together with the languages or "tongues" to be gained by the young prince, finally a sign of the prodigiousness and teleology of mastery. Though technically androgynous, Falstaff ends up, in this movement to kingship which banishes and effectively "kills" him, subject to that law of categorization in which, in relation to the exclusively male, even the androgyne remains on the side of the female. And "banish plump Jack, and banish all the world" (*1H4*, II.iv.479–80) leaves fat Falstaff, in relation to the fabled leanness of a king descended from a "John of *Gaunt*," in the same textual space, so to speak, in this movement to ending, as that of the globular Nell in *The Comedy of Errors*.

As the "fat woman of Brainford" (*Wives*, IV.ii.75), Falstaff is not only a harlot or "quean" but a Circean "witch" as well (IV.ii.172). The fact, however, that this figure associated both with "fat" and with a Ciceronian *copia* of words is not actually female but effeminized male is in itself revealing. The gendered oppositions at work here—the ones that produced another Renaissance text entitled "Women are words, men deeds," which goes on to treat not of wordy women but of the monstrous third possibility of wordy men, including by implication what Greene called the "babbling" of poets—are by no means stable.[23] The opposition male/female often masks anxieties surrounding the figure of the feminized or effeminate male, just as in the misogynist diatribes against the female tongue the generative power inhabiting and generating the very discourse of misogyny often becomes the female loquacity which is its animating subject.

Male anxiety about the feminization of the verbal body and *copia* of a text which delays arrival at its own point or ending is by no means restricted to the images hovering around the figure of the fat, and transvestite, Falstaff. Dilatory, fat Falstaff, that "globe of sinful continents," and Hamlet, that "distracted globe," both appear in plays whose evocations of Apocalypse call to mind the end of the "globe" itself. Critics recoil, as Maurice Charney observes, from the notion of a corpulent Hamlet, though the slender Burbage who had earlier played Prince Hal was considerably fatter by the time he played the Prince of Denmark, and though there may be more than sweat, inactivity, or indolence involved in Gertrude's reference to her disturbingly prodigal son as "fat, and scant of breath" (V.ii.287 ff.) in the duelling scene. To propose the soliloquizing prince as a fat *lady* would presumably be even more repugnant. Yet some of the same figures—including the traditional association between wordiness and idleness, or the meaning of *dilatio* as melancholic *tarditas*—are clearly operating in this other play in the Shakespeare canon which matches the *Henriad* for sheer copiousness and length, and in which fat is associated explicitly with delay ("the fat weed / That roots itself in ease on Lethe wharf," I.v.32–3 ff).[24] Hamlet compares his own delay and Polonius- or Osric-like wordiness to the impotence and proverbial wordiness of the harlot or whore in one of the many soliloquies castigating himself for "tardiness" (III.iv.106) in bringing his task to completion ("I ... / Must like a whore unpack my heart with words, / And fall a-cursing like a very drab," II.ii.583–6). We might also remember that it is the impotent Polonius who ironically utters the anti-Ciceronian formula "Brevity is the soul of wit" in a scene where he is incapable of bringing his narrative to a point or "consequence" (II.i.51); or that the kind of effeminate wordiness associated with the courtier Osric is in a similar context in the *Henriad* specifically referred to as indulgence in "holiday and *lady* terms" (*1H4*, I.iii.46).

In the traditional opposition of genders in which "Women are words, men deeds," Hamlet's comparison of his verbal and deedless delay to the impotent anger of a "drab" sets up a link between his entire period of inactivity and delay and womanish wordiness, in contrast to such one-dimensional emblems of masculinity as Laertes and the aptly named Fort-in-bras. It may be such subtle linkages within the play that Joyce picked up when he incorporated into *Ulysses* the theory that Hamlet was in fact a woman as well as a production of the play with an actress in the role, or that still enable it to be a question, in contemporary productions, of whether Hamlet is predominantly masculine or feminine—Richard Burton's virile or John Neville's effeminate prince. In a plot movement which recasts the political teleology of the *Henriad* in a more tragic key, the Hamlet who can in his delaying phase only like a "whore" unpack his heart with words incorporates ultimately both dilatory Falstaff and the leaner Hal, who in his movement to kingship asserts control over the tongues and styles he has mastered. For at the point of the famous turn in the later play when the Prince of Denmark tells of his revised commission, sending Rosencrantz and Guildenstern to their deaths under the king's seal, there are brought into focus three such purposeful and end-directed messages: the "dilated articles" (I.ii.38) of the reigning king's earlier commission sent to put an "end" to a troublesome business (II.ii.85); that same Claudius's second commission to the King of England "*Larded* with many several sorts of reasons" (V.ii.20) but controlled by the telos of a particular message or point; and finally, in a marked turn from his earlier delay, the revised commission in which Hamlet too now masters the techniques of dilation used to "interlard" a more pointed purpose or end (V.ii.38–43)—an act which prompts Horatio's ambiguous "Why, what a king is this!" (V.ii.62).[25] Undirected and pointless dilation, without "consequence"—the feminized Hamlet impotent to do more than utter "words, words, words." (II.ii.192)—yields finally, that is to say, to a sense of an ending which gives us in the emblematic form of a duelling scene the literal and fatal "point" which puts an end to all.

There is one final fat lady we will consider here, not from Shakespeare, but rather from Ben Jonson. Jonson signals his own familiarity with the tradition of rhetorical dilation and its link with the extending of time in an evocatively bad pun in the Cary-Morison Ode, about a character whose life was simply undistinguished temporization or prolongation ("What did this stirrer," he asks, but *"die late?"*).[26] The Jonsonian fat lady I wish to exhibit is the pig woman Ursula from *Bartholomew Fair* (1614), who stands in some sense as a symbol for the fatness of the Fair and its fabled "enormities," and thus also by extension for the world, and whose associations with swine make her part of the sisterhood of Circe (as well as another instance of the prodigality of the Prodigal Son). As the School-master in this play says to the play's own Prodigal Son, who only too enthusiastically would get lost in the Fair's "enormities," this fat woman is "all vanity": "The fleshly woman (which you call Ursula) is above all to be avoided, having the marks upon her of the three enemies of man, the world as being in the Fair; the devil, as being in the fire; and the flesh, as being herself" (III.vi.30–3). She is not only fat but perpetually in heat, and her body seems to image not just this gross animal sexuality, but its female original in Eve. "I am all fire and fat," she herself is made to say; "I shall e'en melt away to the first woman, a rib again" (II.ii.46–8)—as if she were a kind of latter-day, much-expanded version of the initial "enormity" brought into the world by Adam's rib and dilated through the principle of "increase and multiply," which also applies (as Donne notes in one of his sermons) to sin, or the body of Leviathan. Like Falstaff, indeed, she is very like a whale ("They'll kill the poor whale and make oil of her"; II.v.114– 15).[27]

Ursula's enormity thus makes her a principal target of the judgment in this play of a character fittingly called "Adam" Overdo, whose first name links him explicitly to the founding father, and who, like Christ, promises to appear at the Second Coming, in a version of the Last Judgment. Her booth at the fair—"the very womb and bed of enormity"—recalls the traditional stage entrance to Hell in the Moralities. The "pig" she is coterminous with revives an ancient slang term in Latin and in Greek for the female genitals. As the "sow of enormity" (V.vi.51) in a play full of gaps and holes, she is "the celebrant of the open orifice," both gaping mouth and womb.[28] Her grossness is more than once an object of misogynist fantasy, of the fear that in this "quagmire" or "bog" a man "might sink ... and be drowned a week, ere any friend he had could find where he were" (II.v.83–5). In a play whose copia is generated by the increase and multiplication of vernaculars or mother tongues, the implicit "Hail Ursula full of grease" which hovers around the figure of this "mother," whose pigs are symbols not just of female sexuality but of birth, makes her, as a daughter of Eve, a kind of profane or "harlot" counterpart to Eve's corrective, Mother of God. As with Shakespeare's Nell, her grease punningly echoes grace (there is, indeed, another female character in the play whose name *is* "Grace" and who is Adam's to bestow), and as with Nell her dilation is linked with the dilation, or copiousness, of discourse: her language is said to be "greasier" than her pigs. She is, however, also joined in this by her overbearing judges, and their own tendency to verbal dilation or rhetorical amplitude—by the Schoolmaster's bloated speech, filled with classic instances of *amplificatio*; by Rabbi Busy, whose repetitious rhetoric evokes the notorious dilation of the often seemingly endless Puritan sermon; and by Adam "Overdo" himself, whose oratorical style, with his fatuously rotund circumlocutions, explicitly recalls all of the traditional excesses of rhetorical amplitude.[29] This Jonsonian fat lady, that is, appears in a play whose own verbal copia is generated from representatives of both the *ars praedicandi* and the Ciceronian rhetorical tradition.

In a sense, neither fat Ursula nor her attackers in this play (who also include the figure of Puritan attackers on the "enormities" of the plays and the stage) emerges unscathed. But what is interesting here, again, is that the fat lady in question is brought under control as the play itself proceeds—a movement associated explicitly with the shrinking of Ursula's body size (as in "I'll stay the end of her now; I know she cannot last long; I find by her similes she wanes apace," II.v.122–3). Like the greatly expanded body of the play itself—generated in characteristically ambivalent Jonsonian fashion by the puffing up of pride, as by variations on the refrain of increase and "multiply ye," and an extremely varied yet masterfully controlled matter or *materia*—this particular *mater* ("mother of the pigs," "mother of the bodies," and "Body of the Fair") cannot last forever. Reminiscent both of Virgil's female discord Allecto and of the fat *Mère* of Mardi Gras or "Fat Tuesday" before it yields to the leanness of Lent,[30] this carnivalesque Discordia, large as the play itself, yields ultimately to a more austere shaping; and a "Jordan" of passing—like Falstaff's, a pisspot—is once again associated with her dwindling.

Rabbi Busy, in the end, is finally put down by the puppet Dionysius, whose name recalls the patron of theaters. The extreme representative of Puritan opposition to the theaters is put in his place by a puppet in a gesture which seems a kind of grotesque version of the biblical prophecy that in the Apocalypse or final Recognition Scene of history there will be neither male nor female, whatever the more hierarchical relation of the sexes in the meantime ("It is your old stale argument against the players, but it will not hold against the puppets; for we have neither male nor female amongst us," V.vi.88–90). Dionysius pulls up his garments to reveal that puppets are innocent because they are sexless, a transformation into the language of gender of Sir Philip Sidney's earlier defense of poetry as that which neither "affirmeth" nor "lieth." And yet Ursula herself, whatever carnivalesque overturning she has occasioned, is finally subordinated within a hierarchy which still ends with an "Adam," even though he has been counseled to leave his other name of "Overdo," and to invite one and all to a slightly more chastened feast, neither the leanness of the Puritan nor the enormity of the Fair. In the Apocalypse there may be neither male nor female, but here the hierarchy of the middle or mean-time is one that is only too familiar: the play's *copia* is controlled, at last, and it ends with an address to the judgment and authority of the king, ruler and patriarch at once.

*

One of the chief concerns of the tradition that portrays women as unflappable talkers is how to master or contain such feminine mouthing. In the different terms we have traced, this control of female speech resembles the provision of shaping and closure to the potentially endless movement of dilation or, in the specific case of the fat lady who is the only temporarily dilated, pregnant woman, the production of an issue within a patriarchal economy of increase. The supposed copiousness of the female tongue, epitomized in the admission of Shakespeare's Rosalind ("I am a woman ... I must speak"),[31] or in the open mouth of Mopsa in Sidney's *Arcadia* ("her mouth O heav'nly wide!"), has its textual counterpart in the danger of losing the thread of a discourse and never being able to finish what was begun, the specter of endlessness or inability to come to a point which hovers around the edges of all these characterizations of a female speech as "penelopes webb ... [that] never makes an end."[32] A Renaissance text actually called *Penelope's Web*,[33] by Robert Greene, is literally generated out of the "prattle" of Penelope's garrulous Nurse and her maids ("setting their hands to the Web, and their eares to hir talke," p.62) as their nightly untwisting of this famous unfinished textile makes the labor of weaving potentially "endlesse" (p.194) and defers indefinitely the moment of choosing among the suitors. Their "endlesse Web" is finally abandoned only at the point of the return of the absent master Ulysses, when their "discourse" is at the same time "broken off" (p. 233) and when, in dialectical fashion, the "foolish prattle" (p.208) or female chatter which had provided up to this point the generative power of the text is ended on the night dedicated to the wifely virtue of "Silence."

Female speech or mouthing, however, is not only in this misogynist tradition the representative of the infuriating opposite of Silence but—as with the two orifices with which we began—inseparable from the vice opposed to the corresponding virtue of Chastity, as both are ranged against Obedience. Not only is the link between garrulity and unbridled sexuality expressed in such utterances as the husband's complaining "I could neither governe her tongue, nor——" in the anonymous *Curtaine*

Figure 1   Scold's Bridle

Lecture (1637) devoted to the fabled talkativeness of women; but the extremes of the effort of containment are traceable in such instances as the figure of *Garrulitas* in emblem books like Alciati's or Whitney's (the violated Procne/Philomel seen as a woman who, even with her tongue cut out, managed somehow to tell her tale),[34] or the instrument of containment and discipline known as the brank or "Scold's Bridle" (figure 1), quite clearly, in what it encloses and restricts, a kind of chastity belt for the tongue.

It is this question—of a feminine speech potentially out of control, and of a linking of these two female orifices—which brings us finally to our last partition: the question of the Genitive or "Jinny's case" and the Vocative, or the story of "O," the figure whose shape brings us back full circle to the fat ladies of our title. Both figures—genitive and vocative—are suggested by a single scene from Shakespeare's *Merry Wives of Windsor* (IV.i), the same play in which Falstaff appears as a fat woman and is roundly cast out. It is a strange (and to the rest of the play seemingly irrelevant) scene of grammatical instruction, in which the mother of a schoolboy asks that her son be put through his lessons by the schoolmaster; and it is an exchange in which it is very much a question of the relation between humanism (with its pedagogical economy of men and boys)[35] and an extravagantly errant female speech, the female in question here being that seemingly irrepressible producer of malapropisms, Mistress Quickly, a garrulous old woman and the play's principal go-between.

The subject of "case" is present in this scene throughout, as one would expect in a lesson on grammar,[36] but "Jinny's case" occurs only when Mistress Quickly gives evidence of a particularly improper misunderstanding of the lesson she witnesses from the outside. "What is your

genitive case plural, William?" asks the schoolmaster, and William duti-
fully replies, in the lesson's properly catechistic mode, "Genitive case ...
horum, harum, horum" (IV.i.59–61). "Vengeance of Jinny's case! Fie on
her!" breaks in Mistress Quickly. "Never name her, child, if she be a
whore." "Genitive case," in Quickly's mistranslation, slides into "Jinny's
case," the case of the "Virginia"/"Jinny"/"Jenny" who is the feminine
counterpart of "Jack," simply the stock name of the female. And "case"
clearly (here, as elsewhere in Shakespeare, or in Freud, in the "Theme of
the Three Caskets," or in female "cases" of various kinds) is the code term
for female genitalia, as in our contemporary slang phrase "the family
jewels." "Case" is also linked elsewhere in Shakespeare with the legal case,
as when Cloten in *Cymbeline*, mounting his attack on the seemingly
inviolate Imogen, determines "I will make / One of her women lawyer to
me, for / I yet not understand the case myself" (II.iii.73–5). In other
words, in order finally to under-stand that case (a familiar enough pun in
Shakespeare's bawdy), he will find himself a female go-between, thus
opening up a space or plot which might link the pursuit of such a "case" to
the legal and erotic language of the dilatory plea.

   "Case," however, is also never far from the question of romance, in a
literary as well as an erotic sense; and when we come upon the observation, in Helgerson's *Elizabethan Prodigals*, that "Humanism inhabited the
masculine and misogynistic world of school and state; romance 'had
rather to be shut in a lady's casket,'"[37] we might begin to see some link
between Quickly's errors and the characteristic errancy of romance as the
humanists' particular version of Pandora's Box. We have already remarked the tension between humanism and the enticements both of
women and of romance. Both work directly on the will, leading a young
man into wanton living. It may be no accident, then, that the schoolboy in
this very scene from *Merry Wives* bears Shakespeare's own name of "Will"
(indeed, in a play which calls attention elsewhere to textuality, "Will Page");
for the school here is on a holiday, and the boy in this impromptu scene of
masterly instruction is, one senses, very much a potential Prodigal Son.
The focus of the lesson is the humanist pedagogical method of a fixed
system of translation—out of Latin into English and then from English
back into Latin again (it is, indeed, her inability to comprehend the Latin
of the lesson that leads to Mistress Quickly's errant "Jinny's case").[38] But
when "will" appears earlier in this same play, not as proper name but as
the potentially vagrant faculty itself, it is also in a context of translation:
"He hath studied her will, and translated her will—out of honesty into
English" (I.iii.49–50). It is English, the vernacular or "mother" tongue,
which here (outrageously, as the vehicle of Mistress Quickly) tempts Will
into a kind of lazy vagrancy, into a prodigality of synonyms or sideways
sliding from English to yet more English (synonyms being also one of the
principal means of verbal dilation), in lines in which Will is only at the

schoolmaster's sharp reproof brought back to Latin or the *sermo patrius*. "What is *lapis*, William?" asks the schoolmaster, expecting the dutiful return of the translated back into its paternal origin or father tongue. "A pebble," replies William, sliding laterally out of honesty into the sexual double entendre which is the province of the untutored Mistress Quickly herself.

"Jinny's case," nowhere mentioned in the humanist grammars, is thus in some sense here the "mother tongue." Mistress Quickly's case—described elsewhere as "so openly known to the world" (*2H4*, II.i.31)—is generative, through both the vagaries of her indefatigable mouth and her uneducated female ear. Indeed, Jinny's case (to adopt a punning line from *Cymbeline*) is to have a "vice" (but also, punningly, a potentially different "voice") in her "ear," which interrupts or transforms the message, just as Quickly, ignorant of the master tongue, can only mangle or deform it.

"Jinny's case," in this scene from *Merry Wives*, would thus appear to be subversive of the entire system of instruction, a dangerous supplement to the closed humanist economy of "translation." And yet, like the genitive case itself, it remains enclitic or dependent on something else. The genitive (despite or perhaps because of its associations with both gender and the generative) is always grammatically related to another, "as source, possessor, or the like," says the *OED*.[39] And the case of Jinny here (*horum, harum, horum*) is also to belong to another. Mistress Quickly both interrupts and ultimately defers to the Master. When Quickly herself pronounces "Vengeance of Jinny's case!" it is not clear—precisely because of the ambiguous grammatical construction—whether this vengeance is a vengeance of Jinny's case *on* something else or a plague on Jinny's own case. In the familiar misogynist tradition with which we began, the genitive/generative space of female speech or loquaciousness is traditionally often simply nagging, or at least some form of pursuit of a "master" ear, and like the dilation of textuality is still from this perspective dependent on that end. Thomas Greene points out, in an essay which argues against the anachronistic reading of an endless Derridean "différance" into Renaissance texts, that it is precisely dilation or dissemination *without* return to a source which haunted Erasmus and the humanists who followed his magisterial example.[40] Copia is to be controlled, and one wonders if this final closing of the case, so to speak, might relate as well to the enclosure of the dilated textual bodies we have had occasion to treat. "Jinny's case" is always possessed by something it depends upon; and old woman Quickly remains throughout not just a deviant and loquaciously digressive female but (like the character who is literally a "Page" in this play) simply an instrument or go-between.

This brings us finally to the story of "O," which appears in this same scene of Quickly's aberrant translations, and which as a figure of both open mouth and open female "case" already appears in the mouth of Quickly's counterpart, the garrulous Nurse of *Romeo and Juliet* ("O, he is even in my mistress' case, / Just in her case. . . . / Stand up, stand up, stand, and you be a man. / For Juliet's sake, for her sake, rise and stand; / Why should you fall into so deep an O?"; III.iii.84–90). The story of "O" in Shakespeare, as in other Renaissance texts, is one which includes both a round space (like the world) and a zero or nothing—including that "nothing" which lies "between maid's legs," as Hamlet puts it (*Hamlet*, III.ii.119–21). "What is the focative case, William?" asks the old schoolmaster in the scene of instruction from *Merry Wives*, thus by his own Welshing of English sliding into the vernacular as into the obscene. "O—*vocativo*, O," replies William, hesitatingly suspended for lack of an immediate answer in the father tongue—only to be reminded by this parody humanist that "focative is *caret*." "*Caret*" in this mangled Latin means "is missing." But Quickly's ear hears the everyday garden-variety "carrot" and hastens to pronounce it a "good root," obscenely transferring the Latin "is missing" into the slang for penis, but also echoing an earlier scene when the Latin *pauca verba* (or "few words") is also translated into the vegetative tongue, as "Good worts" (I.i.121). If "few words" are valued as "good words," then the feminine mouth which produces by contrast a throng of words is the kind of copiousness produced by this "nothing," the copious "O" produced by that female deficiency or lack.

The sexual double entendres for what is missing here are clearly too tangled for the present occasion to follow through to their enticing conclusions, but in the context William's "O" is not only an unwitting *example* of the vocative, and clearly related somehow to the female space designated throughout as "oman" (rather than as "woman"), but also schoolboy Will Page's hesitation or delaying of the required answer: "O" here, that is to say, designates (and unwittingly fills by embodying) that seemingly empty space of stalling for time with a figure ("O") which elsewhere in Shakespeare variously figures the globe (this "little O, th' earth," in *Antony and Cleopatra*), a "nothing" or cipher (in *King Lear*), and the space of playing, the round globe of the stage itself (as in the "wooden O" of the Prologue to *Henry V*).

The vocative, or apostrophe, remarks Jonathan Culler in the course of a well-known essay on the subject, is associated with mouthing and with voice (and with poetry itself, perhaps, as in Auden's "poetry is / A way of happening, a mouth").[41] But it is also frequently a subject of embarrassment, a temporary turning from which one might want to turn away in turn. "Apostrophes are forbidden on the funicular," writes Wallace Stevens, in a line Culler uses for the epigraph for his essay, presumably because there is, on the funicular, no turning back. "Apostrophes are vorbidden in the vernacular," we might malaprop this line, falling in with the errant language of Mistress Quickly. The figure of "O" which figures the open mouth or the voice—the figure of the vocative which Culler describes as so frequently "repressed or excluded"—may be our final mouthy fat lady, at least in a story of "O" in which that space finally does come to an ending. The Page, as we noted, is one of the several bearers of messages, or go-betweens, in *Merry Wives*, a play which repeatedly calls attention to textuality and puns on the name of the veiled Mistress Page.[42] And the schoolboy *Will* Page, after all, in this scene—when temporarily caught out, at a loss to finish the lesson of the Master—produces in embarrassment a stalling "O," whose principal invocation or call is a call for (more) time.

Postscriptum

Since [women] have such a copia verborum, or plenty of words, it is a pity they should not put it to some use.

(Addison, 1713)

Censor the body and you censor breath and speech at the same time . . . More body, hence more writing.

(Hélène Cixous)

In the texts we have looked at, the dilation and control of a copiousness figured as female might at the highest level of generalization be seen as the gendered counterpart of what Steven Mullaney and other recent interpreters of representation in the Renaissance have characterized as a "rehearsal"—an allowed expansion or proliferation of the alien, multi-form, and multilingual in order finally to dramatize the very process of its containment, the limiting structures of authority and control.[43] Each of the texts we have seen would need, in a more detailed treatment than is possible here, to be situated in its own historical specificity in order to gauge the politics as well as the gender politics negotiated through this textual body's figurings and refigurings. Certainly by the time of Donne's version of Rahab as the Church who is "open" to most men, or Jonson's richly ambivalent generation of the "enormities" of the Fair and its enormous female emblem, we can begin to see at work a specifically post-Reformation shifting of the ambivalences of this female figure toward the type of the Whore of Babylon that in another contemporary version of the Protestant imagination created the very unreverent body, as well as "enormity," of a pregnant female Pope, the Whore of Babylon made palpable and present in the flesh.[44]

To follow through the reasons for the shifting relation between such textual bodies and the generation, and body, of a given text would take more space and more specific historical investigation than the present context allows. But we might do worse than to stay a bit longer within the textual traces of this figure and the complex of "dilation" we have remarked. In the oral form in which this essay was first presented, its aligning of fat female bodies, or female loquacity, with fatty texts elicited a series of instances of such an alignment in periods later than the Renaissance, including the punning "fluent mundo"—world and mouth or *Mund*—of the "Fat girl, terrestrial" who appears as muse-figure in that very unapocalyptic (or "eucalyptic") poet Wallace Stevens, producer of the hyperbolically redundant "Fat! Fat! Fat! Fat!" Others included the fat lady at the end of Salinger's *Franny and Zooey*, and the one in the story by Flannery O'Connor significantly called "Revelation," whose name is "Ruby," who tends an "old sow" in a "pig parlor," and who hears from "Mary Grace" that she is both "saved" and "from hell."[45]

It is also striking to turn from the texts and tradition we have traced to recent French discussions of *écriture féminine*, which reproduce the misogynist topoi of unending female speech and multiple "tongues" in a celebratory and, as Elaine Showalter puts it, "utopian" mode, or to encounter the multiple "O's" in Monique Wittig's *Les Guérillères* or the description of women's speech, in Luce Irigaray, as "dilatable."[46] The rhetorical tradition of dilation here outlined is one on the whole forgotten to us, though when Roland Barthes wrote of the extending strategies of the classical novel he had recourse to the figure of the narrative's dilatory and dilated "espace dilatoire"—perhaps self-consciously, considering that he also wrote a much lesser-known "Aide-mémoire" to the terminology of ancient rhetoric, including *partitio* and *divisio*. The tradition of narrative romance, developing into the novel, gave us after all Richardson's *Pamela*, a "dilated novel" in the sense of the shorter novella form extended, and a heroine whose seductive disclosures and prodigious textuality recontextualize the stereotypical female case in which the "Closets of Womens thoughts are always open; and the depth of their hearts [provided with] a string that reacheth to their Tongues," whatever other case may temporarily be closed.[47] We might remember that Richardson's heroine derives her name from the same *Arcadia* as the one which gives us the "O" of Mopsa's mouth, its orality recast in a more contemporary written mode.

It is certainly remarkable how much of the tradition we have traced through the Renaissance survives into later periods, after the apparent eclipsing of a more self-conscious rhetorical tradition. Pope, whose *Dunciad* provides extraordinary instances of this continuance, speaks elsewhere of *amplificatio* as the "spinning wheel" of bathos, in a distant echo of the feminine distaff of Penelope. Fielding, that novelist who swallowed earlier romance tradition virtually whole, devotes a prominent chapter of *Joseph Andrews* to the question "Of Divisions in Authors," noting that "common readers imagine, that by this art of dividing, we mean only to *swell* our works to a much larger *bulk* than they would otherwise be extended to." He remarks its use not only in Homer and Virgil but also in Milton, who "went originally no farther than ten [books]; 'till being *puffed up* by the praise of his friends, he put himself on the same footing with the Roman poet." The instance makes explicit an alignment between the puffing up of pride and the puffing up of texts which Milton himself may be more subtly noting in linking the "dilation" of Satan with the rhetorical dilation of his own epic, product of the desire for fame, that last infirmity of noble minds. In another direction, we might ponder the fact that Mary Shelley, in writing of the monstrous and out-of-control in *Frankenstein*, reflects upon how she came to "dilate upon so very hideous an idea," or consider the figure of the tale-telling housekeeper of the gothic *Melmoth the Wanderer* (1820), a "witch" or "Sibyl" whose body seems to increase in size with her incredible tale ("when interrogated on the subject of the story, she rose at once into consequence,—her figure seemed *frightfully dilated, like that of Virgil's Alecto*, who exchanges in a moment the appearance of a feeble old woman for that of a menacing fury").[48]

The underground link between sexual opening and the opening of a closed or difficult text also continues well beyond the Renaissance, in texts such as an early eighteenth-century one which introduces its explication and dilation of a scriptural verse with "Now to draw our Discourse to a Head, after we have thus *opened the Case*." A virulent piece of misogyny roughly contemporary with it provides in a single paragraph a truly extraordinary concentration of the entire complex we have outlined—including the opening of a text and the open "O" of vagina and mouth—in a satire against women which begins with one "whose Sins are as big as her body":

> My Lady F ... one whose *Proportion* puts us in Mind of her *Excellencies*, and he who means to *board* her must put off his Doublet and *Swim*, its being of the same *Size* with a *Fish-Pond*. Yet it is *ten* to *one* if he escape *sinking*; since she is somewhat of Kin to *Goodwin Sands*, having swallow'd up Abundance of whole Families. ... It is a very hard Matter to know, whether she be a Lady, or a *Leviathan*. Sure no *Weapon* but that of a *Goliah* can *fit* her. ... And he who will *please* her ... must convert a *Weaver's Beam* into a *D–l–e* [Dildoe]. ... I believe the *Parson* too is puzzled; to interpret the barrenness of My Lady S——. She gives him the *opening* of many a hard *Text*. ... Her *Mouth*, like *Mopsa's*, is O *Heavenly wide*; ... her *Tail* being of the same *Size*.[49]

Changes in the semiotics of body size are subtly tied to other economies and exigencies of representation, including those linked to the shifting figure of the body politic, as recent work on the body and its representations has made clear.[50] But as part of the continuation of this assimilation of body and text, we need to remark how persistent is the link between textuality and female bodies, whether fat or talkative or both. Though the texts we have considered are male-authored ones, the collocation seems to depend not so much on that fact as on the existence and adoption of a form which involves a combination and double movement of textual expansion with closure or "point."[51] A text like Ann Radcliffe's *Mysteries of Udolpho*, for example, depends for its considerable size not only on the garrulity of its lower-class women but also on the separation of the heroine from their hysteria and pointlessness. Jane Austen's *Emma* might similarly be read in a way which would take David Miller's category of the "narratable" in Austen even more specifically back through questions of gender and the female tongue, beginning with the relation between the unbearable loquacity and diffusiveness of Miss Bates and the trajectory which takes Emma through so much "error" or wandering to the trad-itional marital end. We might also consider the talkative and ample Flora Finching of Dickens's *Little Dorrit*, whose prattle never leads anywhere, or the simultaneously loquacious and fat gossip-writer Henrietta Stackpole of Henry James's *Portrait of a Lady*. James would provide a particularly telling study in this regard, perhaps nowhere more importantly than in *The Golden Bowl*. For that late novel features both the full-figured Fanny Assingham, whose "amplitude of person" is matched by a verbal ampli-tude which generates so much of the text, and her husband, whose "leanness of person" is joined by a dislike of "waste" and who "edit[s], for economy" the "play" of his wife's mind as he does her redundancies— avatars together, perhaps, of the particularly Jamesian project of bringing the more undisciplined form of the novel, that "loose baggy monster," under greater control.

There are many directions this complex would lead to, including, closer to the present, the "overfed" and "flabby" mother of John Osborne's *Look Back in Anger* or the overweight "Mom" of Philip Wylie's immensely popular *Generation of Vipers*, "all tongue and teat and razzmatazz"— both contemporary novels which reproduce the topoi of more ancient misogynist tradition. Or the female "Mouth" of Beckett's *Not I*, one of the many late Beckett texts preoccupied with the postponing of ending. The anxieties of effeminization we have traced, together with the motive of controlling the female tongue, would also take us to Freud and the text of psychoanalysis—the "talking cure" named and generated through the historic case of the multilingual "Anna O." But perhaps the text that comes most easily to mind is the one generated by yet another Penelope, the rambling and unpointed monologue of Joyce's Molly Bloom. The refusal of closure in "Penelope," *Ulysses'* open-ended ending, seems to reflect Joyce's overall refusal of closure, what Ernst Bloch, in a passage full of anxieties of form equal to the anxiety critics have felt before Molly's sexual and verbal openness or the effeminacy of Bloom ("the new womanly man"), characterizes negatively as "a mouth without Ego, drinking, babbling, pouring it out."[52] The unpointed monologue of the figure who makes her appearance in "Notes and Early Drafts" as a *perragorda* or "fat bitch" continually both evokes and postpones images of the Last Judgment, in ways that prefigure the never accomplished "Bockalips" and recurrent Scheherazade of *Finnegans Wake*. "Stately plump" and garrulously evasive of narrative point (though not, in Joyce's patriarchal economy, of phallic ones), this modernist Penelope might image the way that wayward women and wayward and copiously fattened texts continue to figure and refigure each other still.

[handwritten note:] good on textuality + female bodies — gross fat ladies & narration dilatio romance

3

The Metaphorical Plot

The Proper Place

Property was thus appalled
That the self was not the same;
Single nature's double name
Neither two nor one was called.
        (Shakespeare, "The Phoenix and the Turtle")

One of the remarkable features of classical writing on metaphor is the dominance of the notion of "place"—of territory already staked out, of the tropological as inseparable from the topological—and thus also of "property," or of a place where a word properly belongs. The development after Aristotle of the links between proper place, property, *sens propre*, and "propriety" may be perceived retrospectively *in nuce* in the famous Aristotelian definition: "Metaphor consists in giving the thing a name that belongs to something else; the transference being either from genus to species, or from species to genus, or from species to species, or on grounds of analogy."[1] The *phora* of the Aristotelian *epiphora* or "transfer" is, as Paul Ricœur remarks, a "change with respect to location,"[2] a crossing of predetermined boundaries, and this "substitution view" of metaphor involves a conception of words as what a character in *Great Expectations* calls "portable property," as "goods" which can be moved or "transported." Joined to this idea of boundary-crossing is Aristotle's notion of the transposition of an "alien" (*allotrios*), a "name that belongs to something else," and one which differs from "ordinary" or "current" (*kurion*) usage. Metaphor, as Ricœur points out, is "doubly alien": it is a name that belongs elsewhere and one which takes the place of the word which "belongs."[3] *Allotrios* encompasses, in a single term, the notions of deviation, borrowing, and the "in place of" of substitution.

    This sense of a transfer which is not quite proper, of a substitution which is also a displacement, increases in Cicero: "A metaphor is a short form of simile, contracted into one word; this word is put in a position not belonging to it as if it were its own place [*in alieno loco tanquam in suo positum*], and if it is recognizable it gives pleasure, but if it contains no similarity it is rejected. *Alienus* in Cicero can simply mean "other," but, as the description continues, "substitution" and "transfer" begin to suggest usurpation, or appropriation; and what seems to be a straightforward illustration of the trope generates a kind of plot, with metaphor as the foreigner or "alien" usurping the place properly occupied by the original term. There is, *pace* Wallace Stevens, no dearth of metaphors for metaphor, and Cicero's description is rich in such potential plots or scenes. The original importation of metaphorical terms was necessitated by *angustia* or lack, but the metaphors (*verbi translatio*) brought in, like "clothing," to fill a need, stayed for the sake of entertainment (*delectatio*). A metaphor can be imported to supply a local need, but, if a word already exists to occupy the place, the "alien" or "translated" term must justify its displacement of the rightful occupant not only by its "resemblance" to it but by its superiority. Even then, however, the *Gastarbeiter* must be as civil as possible, an outsider on its best behavior:

> If one is afraid of the metaphor's appearing a little too harsh, it should be softened down with a word of introduction [*mollienda est praeposito saepe verbo*]. . . . In fact the metaphor ought to have an apologetic air, so as to look as if it had entered a place that does not belong to it with a proper introduction [*ut deducta esse in alienum locum*], not taken it by storm, and as if it had come with permission, not forced its way in [*non vi venisse videatur*].[4]

The Ciceronian emphasis on place and on the decorum or propriety governing changes of place continues in Quintilian, who defines a "trope" as the alteration of a word from its "proper" meaning to "another" and goes on to describe metaphor—the Greek word he translates as *translatio*—in terms of the potentially "improper" (*improprium*) or "out of place": a noun or a verb "is transferred from the place to which it properly belongs to another where there is either no literal ('proper') term or the transferred is better than the literal" (*ex loco in quo proprium est, in eum in quo aut proprium deest aut translatum proprio melius est*), as either "clearer" or more "decorative"; when "it secures none of these results," however, the "metaphor will be out of place."[5] Once again, as in Cicero, the prepositions suggest both movement and "pre-position," or predetermined placing; and the fusing of the notion of the "proper" with that of "place" inevitably generates a number of plots, with words as "portable property" functioning as Greimasian actants, or "characters."[6] Familiar as we are with the subsequent reverberations of this language, we can discern a number of plots, narratives, or theatrical "scenes" developing through this movement and portability of terms—the proper and metaphorical as "rivals," or as legitimate and bastard brothers, with the metaphorical "alien" as changeling, picaro, or usurper.

Dumarsais's first example of a metaphor, of a word put "in place of" the proper one is: "lying often dresses itself up in the colors of truth" ("le mensonge se pare souvent des couleurs de la vérité"), where, as he puts it, "colors" loses "its proper and primitive signification" ("sa signification propre & primitive") and comes to signify instead external appearances ("les dehors, les apparences"). His example of metaphor, an imposture, comes curiously close to being a figure for it: "likewise we are often the dupe of a specious sincerity [*une sincérité apparente*], and while an imposter only takes on the appearance of a sincere man, we believe that he speaks to us sincerely."[7] The figure of the "impostor" appears as well in Puttenham's description of the "long and perpetuall Metaphore" of "Allegorie," or the "Figure of False Semblant,"[8] the master of illusion and imposture from *Le Roman de la rose*. The "alien" or "translative" nature of metaphor is extended in the *allos* of allegory. And the metaphor put "in place of" is an impostor to be exposed in the appropriate recognition scene.

The *exemplum* of the "impostor" in Dumarsais is followed by an explicit metaphor for metaphor, that of its dwelling in "a borrowed home" ("*il est*, pour ainsi dire, *dans une demeure empruntée*, dit un ancien"), a familiar image of domestication, or of the "naturalizing" of the "alien," which can, however, as easily suggest usurpation or appropriation, a transfer in which the guest becomes host. The link between metaphor and usurpation runs through the most influential definitions,[9] and the "transfer" of *translatio* seems frequently to involve a *trans-passus*, or trespass, an overstepping of bounds which, since Aristotle, has linked it with *superlatio*—hyperbole or "The Over reacher" (Puttenham)—and with a kind of Marlovian overreaching or *hubris*. In Quintilian the rules which define legitimate crossings or displacements sound like a form of social legislation, a carefully controlled plotting of movements into new "houses" or rooms; but the "transfer" or "translation" also includes the possibility of competition for the same place and the threat of expulsion ("For metaphor should always either occupy a place already vacant or if it comes into that of another should be worth more than that which it expels"; VIII.vi.18). In Puttenham's description of "METAPHORA, or the Figure of TRANSPORTE" ("There is a kinde of wresting of a single word from his owne right signification, to another not so naturall, but yet of some affinitie or conveniencie with it," as when a term is "transported from a mans head to a hill or a tree"),[10] "wresting" sounds more like the activity of a press gang, and "transport" like a forceful abduction or unsettling "transportability." The "transfer" of metaphor seems inseparable from a kind of violence or violation. Shakespeare's Viola crosses the boundaries of social and sexual place or identity; but the idea of metaphor itself as "clothing" includes the possibility of a linguistic transvestitism, a violation of boundaries which makes Shakespeare's plots—of changelings, exchangeable twins, disguises, usurpation, illegitimacy—virtual *mises-en-scène* of the activity of tropes, and tempting ground for structuralist "grammars."

The emphasis on place and transgression in the classical view of metaphor explains its obsession with catachresis, or the "figure of abuse," the "forced" transfer which Fontanier, in *Les Figures du discours*, is so careful to distinguish from metaphor's "freedom," a figure whose condemnation by Locke[11] as a merely verbal or monstrous joining, with the grotesque possibility of mistaking a purely verbal entity such as the "centaur" for a natural one, reminds us that the figures of catachresis in Dante—the centaurs and the Minotaur—are the emblems of the circles of *forza*, or violence. It seems finally impossible, however, to separate the use from the abuse of language, and metaphor's own aberrant "couplings" give to its description in Dr Johnson's *Dictionary* ("The application of a word to an use to which, in its original import, it cannot be put") a sense of impropriety bordering on abuse. Metaphor in these discussions is always "on the margins of discourse" (Barbara H. Smith), outside the city walls, and its potential incivility generates concern for its "mastery" (Aristotle), "moderation" (Quintilian), or "proper management" (Blair). But the "rule of metaphor" contains, as an ambiguous genitive, that mastery's threatened opposite, the rule of metaphor as a Lord of Misrule. As Derrida suggests, the "master" of metaphor may himself be "transported."[12]

Paul de Man has described the anxiety which results from the difficulty, in the face of this boundary-crosser, of maintaining even the boundary between "figural" and "proper," and the way in which discussions of the "mastery of metaphor" begin to sound, in the very effort of containment, more "like the plot of a Gothic novel."[13] Classical textbook examples of metaphor—the traditional *pratum ridet*, with its transfer of human laughter to nature—reveal a potential menace within the conception of metaphor as a transfer from place to place. The very idea of "transportability" is a threat to decorum or "decor," a sense that things might not only be "out of place" but out of control. Locke's concern with the movements open to purely verbal entities extends this gothic plot to language, and the idea of metaphor as "alien," as not in its "proper" but in a "borrowed home," raises the question of its movement as a function of the *Unheimlich*, or uncanny.

A brief consideration of *Wuthering Heights*, a novel whose much-discussed violence is very much bound up with metaphor's outrage to "place," "property," and "propriety," may help to suggest why the classical conception of metaphor as "a change with respect to location" should have a gothic extension. The novel is remarkable for its emphasis not only on "right place" (III, 64),[14] property, and "position" (including

the "positions" appropriate to the Sabbath as a fixed place in time, III, 63),
but also on transgression or crossing, from the apprehension of Catherine
and Heathcliff as trespassers on the more civilized Linton residence at
Thrushcross Grange, to the socially regulated exchanges, through
marriage, between the two houses, and the plot founded on the transfer of
property—Heathcliff the alien, outsider, or changeling brought into the
Earnshaw home, given the name of a dead son, regarded by "the young
master" as a "usurper" (IV, 79), and ultimately becoming the new master
of the house. Throughout—spectacularly in Lockwood's dream of the
sermon "divided into *four hundred and ninety* parts," with its "odd
transgressions" assigned the extreme decorum of "different sins on every
occasion" (III, 65)—the very erection of boundaries seems to create the
possibility of "trespass," a crossing more primitive and less defined than
"sin"; and the much-commented-on "amorality" of Brontë's novel may be
the product less of the conduct of its characters than of the working within
it of metaphor as radical boundary-crosser, a trope "beyond good and
evil," an "alien" at work in the novel in a more profound way even than
Heathcliff.

The outrage to "Reason" and "Property" in the poem which serves as
an epigraph to this section is a feature of what Northrop Frye calls radical
or "anagogic" metaphor ("A *is* B"),[15] as in the "one flesh" of Christian
marriage; the poem's "twain" made "one" echoes descriptions of the
Incarnation as the definitive "copula" or "copulacion" and of the breaking down of divisions through the Cross (Ephesians 2:14–15: "For he is
our peace, who hath made both one, and hath broken down the middle
wall of partition between us ... to make in himself of twain one new
man"). *Wuthering Heights* provides a literalizing echo of this "anagogic"
boundary-crossing in the description of the clergyman's "house with two
rooms, threatening speedily to determine into one" (III, 65), and in
Heathcliff's plan to have his coffin and Catherine's opened to one another
("by the time Linton gets to us, he'll not know which is which"; XXIX, 319),
a version of "one flesh" which would make Catherine's defiant "I *am*
Heathcliff" (IX, 122) a macabre fact.

The defiant "I *am* Heathcliff" is metaphor in its radical copular form, a
violation of the law that two bodies cannot occupy the same space at the
same time, but a joining which is perfectly possible as an autonomous
trick, or trope, of language, a possibility which makes metaphor more
repugnant to reason than more distanced and mediated tropes. Catherine's
radical copula is joined in the novel by what Frye calls "literal" metaphor,
parataxis or juxtaposition without predication ("A;B"), a form which,
like "anagogic" metaphor, is less accommodated to logic and plausibility
than the intermediate forms he cites—metaphor as a condensed simile or
analogy.[16] The three names Lockwood finds etched on the window ledge
in his room at the Heights in chapter III—*Catherine Earnshaw, Catherine*

Heathcliff, Catherine Linton—are detached from all predication, but in their concentration provide a rebus or ideogram for the novel's plot, charting from left to right the outlines of the first Catherine's story and, in reverse, the second-generation story of her daughter Cathy.[17] These juxtaposed and disembodied names have an unsettling power of movement ("a glare of white letters started from the dark, as vivid as spectres—the air swarmed with Catherines"), and the knot of names begs "explication," the transformation of the "name repeated in all kinds of characters, large and small" (III, 61) into characters in an explanatory "history." The unfolding of this history by Nelly Dean immediately after this crucial scene—with Lockwood's insistence that she proceed "leisurely" and "minutely" (VII,102)—is the provision of linear, chronological order or sense to almost unbearably condensed connections, a "spacing" or narrative *espacement* accommodated to Lockwood's civilized and "enlightened" mind, and its demand that times and characters have, and keep, their places.

The names in chapter III map a crossing in which one character, in name at least, turns into another, and through the novel both the economy of names and the fact that more than one character can possess the same name begin to make names themselves appear as places, or "houses," to be occupied. The outsider Lockwood's feeling "unmistakably out of place" (II, 56) in the opening chapters results partly from the ambiguity of proper names as indicators of place or property—of who belongs to whom—and of position in the temporal grid of the generations. "Mrs Heathcliff" could be both Heathcliff's wife and his daughter-in-law (II, 55), the "Catherine Linton" of Lockwood's dream (III, 67) either mother or daughter. The inability of words as "portable property" to keep their places has in *Great Expectations* a comic effect—changes from "literal" to "transferred" sense which play havoc with "expectation" ("What's he living on?" "On the second floor"). But in *Wuthering Heights* the transportability and unsettling autonomy of names recalls Locke's horror of the combinations open to purely verbal entities, the nightmarish possibility of words taking on a life of their own, and creates a sense of incestuous coupling which has less to do with the actual relations of the novel's characters than with a promiscuity open to names themselves, crossings not permitted on the novel's more "naturalized" surface.

Nelly's "history" performs its function, and the two characters who could embody the obtrusive "Catherines" are distanced by a generation. But this spectral rising of names detached from persons and their easy combination into a kind of "plot" is too unsettling to master altogether and stands within the novel as a sign of something resistant to logic, chronology, and the sense in both of "proper place." As with Catherine's manuscript diary, in the margins of more "legitimate" texts (III, 62), there is a sense of something operating outside or against the constrictions of the novel's more ordered frame: the novel form itself as a "house" or container cannot fully domesticate the "alien" or *unheimlich* presence of metaphor, a trespass as violent to the linearity of the narrative and orderly succession of "times" as the more obvious violence of the novel's events.

The echo of Job 7 (III, 66) in Lockwood's first dream ("he that goeth down to the grave shall come up no more. He shall return no more to his house, neither shall his place know him any more") has an ironic extension in his second dream, when Lockwood himself tries to keep a ghostly *revenant* from returning to her house, by rubbing her wrist against the broken window pane and piling up books as a dividing wall between them. The very defensiveness of the impulse raises the possibility that the novel's ending with Lockwood's visit to the graves of Catherine and Heathcliff might be part of a desire to preclude any further returns, to be sure that the dead now keep their proper place. The violence of metaphor is joined by the violence of the effort of mastery or containment (Lockwood's name recalling Locke's), of the effort to establish a secure realm of the "proper" set off, or distanced, from more primitive couplings. It is impossible, finally, even to maintain the stable division of "proper" and "metaphorical," since it is as justifiable to describe Lockwood's own turns of speech and defensive gestures as a turning (or "troping") from an unmediated "proper" as it is to contrast the radical copula of metaphor ("I *am* Heathcliff") with more civilized concern for property, propriety, and proper place. The impossibility makes *Wuthering Heights* a crossroads of theories of metaphor—"classical," "Romantic," and (preposterously) "Nietzschean"—and suggests that even the apparently modern notion of a text writing itself, without controlling "subject" or "Master," is, in its sense of the autonomy of language, a profoundly "gothic" one.

The Figure of Transport

Wo gehn wir denn hin? Immer nach Hause.

(Novalis)

A second, and contrasting, aspect of Puttenham's "figure of transporte" is metaphor not as radical identity, appalling to the boundaries of property or proper place, but rather as exile from "Identity," *translatio* as distance or separation. Cicero, seeking to explain why a metaphorical term might be preferred even when a proper one exists, points to the delight of having one's thoughts led to something "other" (*alio ducitur*) without actually going "astray,"[18] and this controlled and even delightful "wandering" is cited often in the rhetorical handbooks. In a theological context, however, the deviance or wandering of metaphor makes it the emblem of the errancy of all language, less *a* transgression than sign of *the* transgression, of the act through which man became an "alien" and his language grew "as double as his Mind" (Marvell, "The Mower against Gardens"). In the repeatedly echoed Pauline and Augustinian terms, metaphor, like all "figures," is the sign of exile from God into a "region of unlikeness," of distance from a presence in which the intellect will know "not in part, not in enigma, not through a glass," but "simultaneously, without the succession of times."[19]

Metaphor combines both transport to, or "reaching" (as in McLuhan's "Man's reach must exceed his grasp or what's a metaphor"), and transport from, or "alienation." The emblem of this double nature, the poetic counterpoise to the radical "identity" of "The Phoenix and the Turtle," might be Marvell's "Definition of Love," a poem which suggests, in retrospect, that a good deal of "Petrarchan" poetry might be seen as variations on the "transport" of metaphor, a "reach" which joins but also separates, a balked union, or "turning," which forestalls consummation and thus preserves the "world":

> And yet I quickly might arrive
> Where my extended soul is fixed,
> But Fate does iron wedges drive,
> And always crowds itself betwixt.
>
> For Fate with jealous eye does see
> Two perfect loves; nor lets them close:
> Their union would her ruin be,
> And her tyrannic power depose.
>
> And therefore her decrees of steel
> Us as the distant poles have placed
> (Though Love's whole world on us doth wheel),
> Not by themselves to be embraced:
>
> Unless the giddy heaven fall,
> And earth some new convulsion tear;
> And, us to join, the world should all
> Be cramped into a planisphere.

If metaphor's errancy was a sign of exile, the way back to paradise was to involve removal of this "error," a return to man's proper "home." This errancy turned exodus or *parodos* has its own circular plot: after the Fall into the "Babel" of language, the Bible dramatizes as "history" the reconstitution of the *nom propre*, the end of which is Apocalypse as the Book of the Proper Name. The conception of the "mists" or "Painted Glass" of metaphor and the project of eliminating its "error" united Puritan theology and Baconian science, and gave to both their apocalyptic drive. The search for a universal scientific language was closely connected with nostalgia for the Edenic one; both involved what Derrida has called an "eschatologie du *propre*."[20]

In the tradition of metaphor as exile or distance, the conception of the Greek *metaphora* as *translatio verbi* is inseparable from the notion of history itself as *translatio*—based on the east–west movement of the sun from its source to its "occident"—the "translation" of empire and learning from Greece to Rome to the *Abendland*, a scheme which structures countless European "progress" poems and is still the controlling figure of Hegel's *Philosophy of History*. Metaphor in this scheme shares in the melancholy of what Stevens calls "The Westwardness of Everything" ("Our Stars Come from Ireland"), but is also part of a *felix culpa* or providential "progress": the "plot" in which it is subsumed is one which links history and language to a "transport" which is both exile and return, a foreshadowing of the "Light" or presence from which it is still distanced. It is as *translatio* that the "orbit of the sun" is "the trajectory of metaphor," the heliotropic "turning" of Blake's "Ah! Sun-flower."[21] The figure of transport carries with it a fundamental dualism, the reason why the "vehicle" of I. A. Richards's famous pair is so often misread as "metaphor" and "tenor" as "meaning." The image itself transports an "interactional" theory of metaphor back into the language of portability and place.

The persistence of this *translatio* from medieval historiography to Hegel to Stevens allows us to move elliptically from the older conception of the "wandering" of metaphor to the modern measurement of its "deviation," its "violation" of "the predictable pattern" (Samuel R. Levin) or distance from a rhetorical "zero degree." The older parousial or paradisal impulse has its reflection in modern versions of the desire to purge language of its error, to regain a purity which may be simply that of the object: "We seek / The poem of pure reality, untouched / By trope or deviation, straight to the word, / Straight to the transfixing object" (Stevens, "An Ordinary Evening in New Haven") or, again, "Trace the gold sun about the whitened sky / Without evasion by a single metaphor. / Look at it in its essential barrenness / And say this, this is the centre that I seek" ("Credences of Summer"). Stevens is the exemplary poet of this modern impatience with metaphor, of the desire for the nakedness of the object or of truth—an impulse which is still "apocalyptic" (*apo-calypsis*) if we recall that the opposite of such "un-covering" is conveyed in the name of the enchantress Calypso. But Stevens is also the poet of another tendency, of the recognition that there is no removing this "error" or "covering," that the end of all such stripping is still a "figure":

> On her trip around the world, Nanzia Nunzio
> Confronted Ozymandias. She went
> Alone and like a vestal long-prepared.

> I am the spouse. She took her necklace off
> And laid it in the sand. As I am, I am
> The spouse. She opened her stone-studded belt.
>
> I am the spouse divested of bright gold,
> The spouse beyond emerald or amethyst,
> Beyond the burning body that I bear.
>
> I am the woman stripped more nakedly
> Than nakedness, standing before an inflexible
> Order, saying I am the contemplated spouse
> .   .   .   .
> Then Ozymandias said the spouse, the bride
> Is never naked. A fictive covering
> Weaves always glistening from the heart and mind.
>
>   ("Notes Toward a Supreme Fiction," VIII)

The ambiguities of metaphor as "transport" or *translatio*—of an "errancy" both delightful and lamented, a "distance" which is both freedom and a form of impotence—are all contained within the complex poem Stevens calls "The Motive for Metaphor":

> You like it under the trees in autumn,
> Because everything is half dead.
> The wind moves like a cripple among the leaves
> And repeats words without meaning.
>
> In the same way, you were happy in spring,
> With the half colors of quarter-things,
> The slightly brighter sky, the melting clouds,
> The single bird, the obscure moon—
>
> The obscure moon lighting an obscure world
> Of things that would never be quite expressed,
> Where you yourself were never quite yourself
> And did not want nor have to be,
>
> Desiring the exhilarations of changes:
> The motive for metaphor, shrinking from
> The weight of primary noon,
> The ABC of being,
>
> The ruddy temper, the hammer
> Of red and blue, the hard sound—
> Steel against intimation—the sharp flash,
> The vital, arrogant, fatal, dominant X.

The "motive" here involves a movement of evasion or retreat, a "shrinking from" the shadowless, vertical moment of the sun at "noon," and the speaker's preference for the umbral, lunar ("obscure moon") and oblique, for the freedom from fixed identity ("Where you yourself were never quite yourself / And did not want nor have to be"), is part of a positive "desire." "Exhilarations of changes" seems to link metaphor here to the chromaticism ("seven-colored changes") of Stevens's "Oak Leaves Are Hands," where the copular "is" of metaphor is less an apocalyptic joining than an evasion of all fixities ("Evasive and metamorphid"), and where the "alien" nature of metaphor is its promise of movement to "other" things ("In Hydaspia, by Howzen, / Lived a lady, Lady Lowzen, / For whom what is was other things") and a continual succession of not-quite-proper names or "aliases." This "motive for metaphor" recalls that of one of Stevens's *Adagia* ("Reality is a cliché from which we escape by metaphor"). But the "escape" which makes metaphor, like metamorphosis, a principle of levity ("shrinking from / The weight of primary noon") also, in this "Motive for Metaphor," conveys a sense of weakness or regret, an ambivalence underscored by the syntactic ambiguity of the appositional structure of the final seven lines. The "X" of the poem is "arrogant" and "fatal," but it is also "dominant" and "vital"; and the "shrinking" of metaphor, though part of the desire for "the exhilarations of changes," is also suggestive of the more negative connotations of "half dead," "cripple," and "obscure moon." The "figural" has traditionally been spoken of in shadowy, or lunar, terms as a "foreshadowing" or "adumbration," as distance from the fuller light of "noon." The avoided "X" may be the fixed and unimaginative world of "things as they are," but it also inevitably recalls the "X" who is Alpha and Omega, "noon" as the apocalyptic end of all "figures," a change which would end change and confer final "identity," as opposed to the Shelleyan movement ("motive" / *motus*) of metaphor, a continual discovery of "the before unapprehended relations of things" (Shelley, *A Defence of Poetry*). The possible echo of Shelley's "Ode to the West Wind" in the autumn wind here, moving "like a cripple among the leaves," may also involve an attenuation of the more "exhilarating" Shelleyan claims for the "vitally metaphorical." Metaphor's "transport," its continual movement, may be the promise of continually changing perspectives (a positive conception Shelley did much to found), but it also remains here within a more sobering perspective of *relation*: the metaphor which retreats from the "weight of primary noon," the "vital, arrogant, fatal, dominant X," also remains dominated by that "X," perpetually "referring" to it in the very attitude of retreat. The *translatio* of this modern "Motive for Metaphor" still retains the mark of translation as movement and exile, the freedom or errancy of metaphor still defined by the "X" which is this poem's "end."

The Plot of Metaphor

Annihilating all that's made
To a green thought in a green shade.

(Marvell, "The Garden")

Distinguishable, at least for the moment, from the view of metaphor as "alien" in either sense (as boundary-crosser or as exile) is the conception of metaphor not only as "retreating" but as creating a "retreat"—a plot or space which Ricœur calls "l'espace de la figure." Coleridge, the source of much of this tradition within English criticism, speculated on a "figurative space" which would have "real Being and energy and the active power of figure," and spoke in his analyses of Shakespeare of the poet's creation of a space which invites the reader to enter and co-create, a privileged space which sounds, in Coleridge, much like the secluded plots, bowers, or "retreats" which fill his poetry.[22] After Coleridge, this sense of a creative "plot" continues in Richards's description of metaphorical "interaction," in Wheelwright's emphasis on "semantic tension," in Empson's character-ization of ambiguity as "giving room" for different responses, and in Barfield's notion of "Tarning," a mode of troping used to conceal one meaning in another, in which there should be no obvious or rapid re-turning to "what is meant."[23]

This delaying of the movement towards meaning or object is what Valéry seems to be suggesting in calling metaphors "those stationary movements" ("ces mouvements stationnaires"), or "deviations that enrich" ("les écarts qui enrichissent"), creators of a space of "hésitation" distinct from the kind of language which disappears as soon as its "aim" has been reached, entirely replaced by its "meaning" ("s'évanouit à peine arrivé ... remplacé entièrement et définitivement par son sens").[24] The conception of the interruption of movement towards a simple linear end or straight-forward reference characterizes a number of otherwise divergent critical approaches—Gérard Genette's description of "la figure" as "an inner space [espace intérieur] of language," C.S. Peirce's "interpretant" and Kenneth Burke's "deflection" as subverters of the direct route between sign and meaning, Geoffrey Hartman's idea of a "breathing space," or "etiologic distancing." The "plot" of metaphor, in these terms, recalls that "dialogical" space which Bakhtin opposes to "monologic" and its "ready-made truth," a ludic or "carnival" space of the Excluded Middle in the logical, or monological, world of the tertium non datur.[25]

The writer who has most expressly considered the "plot" of metaphor as the creation of a figurative "space" is Ricœur, who associates it with the shift from the "substitution" to the "interaction" view, where "the bearer of the metaphorical meaning is no longer the word but the sentence as a whole" and where "deviance" involves not lexical transfer but what Jean Cohen calls "semantic impertinence," an unexpected or "impertinent" predication.[26] The figurative plot which the reader, in the familiar spatial metaphor, "enters into" is described by Ricœur as a "*suspension*— or *epoche*—of ordinary descriptive reference" (p.151), a space of "rapprochement" in which "things or ideas which were remote appear now as close," in which the Aristotelian *epiphora* or "transfer" is a "shift in the logical distance, from the far to the near" (p.145).

Poetry abounds in images for the "suspension" Ricœur describes, one of the most fertile being the plot or green space of the creative bower, a retreat from the world of ordinary reference and the scene of fresh creation. The productive shift from "far" to "near" characterizes one of the best-known of poetic green spaces, a *translatio* of the distant Greek "Psyche" to an English poet's "psyche," in which the bower or "fane" of meeting is the metaphorical space of "feigning":

> Yes, I will be thy priest, and build a fane
> In some untrodden region of my mind
> . . . .
> And in the midst of this wide quietness
> A rosy sanctuary will I dress
> With the wreathed trellis of a working brain,
> With buds, and bells, and stars without a name,
> With all the gardener Fancy e'er could feign.

Keats's "Ode to Psyche" gathers up many of the aspects of metaphor's creative "space," including the outsider's desire to penetrate what happens in that scene of "copulation," the mystery of the knot or join which makes metaphor a secular *mysterion*, the source of endless fascination and inquiry. But other Keatsian versions of this suspended "plot" suggest as well the potential dangers of the "retreat." It is perhaps not by accident that a fundamentally Romantic view of metaphor—its space of "interaction"—contains within it the tensions within a major Romantic image, the bower whose "suspension" of ordinary reference may lead to a creative "return," or might simply, as Barthes says of language, "celebrate itself." "Reason," in "The Phoenix and the Turtle," complains that the union of the "twain" leaves "no posterity," that it is barren of consequence for the world from which they retreat. Ricœur too is concerned with the question of metaphor's fertility. The space of "suspension" is only a preliminary bracketing. The "plot" of metaphor as *epoche* is inseparable from the more active sense of "plot" as *mythos*: the "suspension" of reference has only a "mediating role" in the "whole process of reference" (p.151), the conversion of "impertinence" into "new pertinence" (p.144); it is "only the negative condition of a second-order reference, of an indirect reference built on the ruins of the direct reference" (p.151). What happens in poetry is not the suppression of the referential function but rather, as with Jakobson's "split reference," its re-creation. Proponents of the auto-referentiality of language would remain, in Ricœur's terms, caught within a hypostatized "suspension," a charmed plot from which there would be no exit or "issue."

Ricœur's description of the "metaphorical process" is one of the most cogent statements, after Richards, of the productiveness of "tension." But the particular plot he outlines—the transformation of "impertinence" or "incongruence" on one level to "pertinence" and "congruence" on another—is a movement common to a number of poetic theories which appear in other respects to be even antagonistically different. In Michael Riffaterre's description, in *The Semiotics of Poetry*,[27] of the space between the reader's first and second ("truly *hermeneutic*") reading of a literary text, it is "ungrammaticality" which provides the initial impasse or *scandalon* ("The reader's acceptance of the mimesis sets up the grammar as the background from which the ungrammaticalities will thrust themselves forward as stumbling blocks, to be understood on a second level"; p.6), and the role these "ungrammaticalities" ("simply the mimetic face of the semiotic grammaticality") play in the "metamorphosis of what was a signifying complex at a lower level of the text into a signifying unit ... at a higher level of the text" (p.11) strikingly recalls the "semiotics" of older figural treatments of the "letter," of the "stumbling blocks" which initiate conversion to a "higher" level. Riffaterre's description of this process occurs not insignificantly in the midst of a reading of Gautier's "In Deserto," a poem whose details recall the desert of the Exodus; for the semiotic process itself sounds here like a kind of "exodus" or romance quest, with the initial de-viation the prelude to a new cognition (the reader "is first sent off in the wrong direction, he gets lost in his surroundings, so to speak, before he finds out that the landscape here, or the description in general, is a stage set for special effects"; p.7). This "stage," however, is only a first stage, part of the movement of "translation": the reader who successfully negotiates this space is rewarded by what Riffaterre calls an "*epiphany* of the semiosis" (p.12; my italics), a "blaze of revelation" (p.166).

This "revelation" is never final ("each rereading ... forces the reader to undergo again the experience or temptation of a decoding obedient to mimesis, hence to relive the block of distortion"; p.166), but the conversional structure remains: Riffaterre's description of the movement from "ungrammaticality" to "grammaticality" sounds not unlike Ricœur's description of the "*new* predicative meaning" which emerges from the "collapse" of the "literal meaning."[28] The de-viation is only temporary. And the notion of place—of a place for everything, even the seeming misfit—returns in a recuperated form: "The poetic sign has two faces: textually ungrammatical, intertextually grammatical: distorted in the mimesis system, but in the semiotic grid appropriate and rightly placed"

(p. 165). Though the view of metaphor—and metaphorical interaction—as "space" appears very different from the classical sense of "proper place," it too has a sense of "placing," the comprehension of deviance within a larger "plot," or "grid." `

Metaphor is here a "plot" in both senses—a space of disorientation and discovery, and a *mythos* of transformation. Indeed, the description of metaphor in terms of "impertinence," "ungrammaticality," or predicative "deviance" which after a process of transformation becomes "pertinence," "grammaticality," or acceptability at another level begins to sound like the plot of a Shakespearean comedy—an initial challenge to the existing order by a misfit or young impertinent, retreat into a transformative "green space," and the emergence of a "new" order with the former misfit now its ruler (a plot which accounts for both the "rule" of metaphor and its "freshness"). The "plot" of metaphor as creative space is subsumed within the plot of a completed process or comic *Aufhebung*, reintegration at a new level.

The space of "retreat" still has a teleology; and this movement of subordination is one of the ways in which the metaphorical "translation" approaches the metaphysical one.[29] Owen Barfield's very "Coleridgean" concern that the space of "Tarning" should not become an end in itself ("if you set out to say one thing and mean another, you must really mean another, and that other must be worth meaning")[30] recalls the classical Johnsonian one ("The force of metaphors is lost, when the mind, by the mention of particulars, is turned ... more upon that from which the illustration is drawn than that to which it is applied"). The "plot" of metaphor as retreat from ordinary, or former, meaning must not here prevent a return to meaning. We might ask, however, whether the comic or successful romance plot of metaphor is the only one, whether the ludic or "green" space is only a stage in a drama of succession, or whether metaphor remains a permanent Lord of Misrule, a Falstaffian misfit or, like the fool of the tragedies, a perpetual surd element. If we recognize that metaphor is only a *fable* of identity (Frye), must it necessarily be a fable of *identity*?

Metaphor, which for seventeenth-century writers was a sign of paradise lost, is described by Frye as the instrument of anagogy or "return," the "language of identification" through which poetry tries to "lead our imaginations back to the identity figured in the stories of a lost Golden Age, Eden, or Hesperides," a "motive for metaphor" which makes the "story of the loss and regaining of identity" the "framework of all literature."[31] But even in that *Paradise Regained* which is English poetry's most explicit treatment of this plot of return, the "is" of metaphor involves the danger of an aberrant, literalizing or premature identification, and metaphor's apocalyptic "identity" is qualified by the diachronicity of the biblical "type," and its recognition of discontinuity and temporal difference. The Bible presents us, in Frye's words, with "a series of repetitions of what is spiritually the same event" (in Milton's poem the Son "is" Moses, David, Solomon, and Job), but only in the Apocalypse do contiguity and succession drop away. Even in the Book of Apocalypse, metaphor cannot escape being "plotted" or staged: the culture's definitive anagogic text is still a text, and the vision of paradise regained ends even there in the prospective mode of an "Even so, come" (Revelation 22:20).

The radical verticality of metaphor is always, to use Jakobson's terms,[32] "projected on," subjected to or compromised by the horizontal or metonymic. Pure metaphor would be an ultimate "contiguity disorder," or, to adapt Joyce's phrase, an ideal language suffering from an ideal aphasia. Pure verticality can no more exist than the "mountainous coiffures" of Stevens's "Le Monocle de Mon Oncle"(iii) can maintain their composure before the horizontal strain of entropy, or the traditional images of verticality and definitive "translation"—mountain, tower, paradisal ascent—escape altogether the successiveness of syntax. No attempt to isolate the synchronicity of metaphor can be anything more than a *structuralisme pétrifié*.

If we view metaphor as a kind of "plot"—whether as a space of encounter or as a *mythos* with its own "sense of an ending" (Kermode)— we can also see it as a "plot" in the sense of "conspiracy," like the "conspiring" of Season and Sun in Keats's "Autumn Ode," which may simply be the plot of an illusion, or the ambiguous "plot" of the "Ode to a Nightingale" ("some melodious plot / Of beechen green, and shadows numberless") which provides yet another poetic version of the magical green space, or retreat from the world of ordinary reference, but also carries with it hints of something more sinister, of a "transport" and "identity" which may be only that of death. Keats's poem may be an apostrophe less to a poetic bird than to the "Figure of Transport," a trope whose transports Longinus identified with sublimity but which in much "sublime" poetry also involves a fear of verticality. The Romantic poetry which Jakobson associates with the vertical or "metaphoric" axis is also the poetry which provides the most radical critique of metaphor.

The metaphorical "plot" may also include a kind of takeover or compulsion, the element of magical control Christine Brooke-Rose locates in metaphors with the verb "to make,"[33] an aspect which suggests that metaphor may be Moriarty rather than Holmes, with a plot to take over the world. Frye speaks, in a discussion of Stevens's "Motive for Metaphor," of the poet's desire to show us "a world completely absorbed and possessed by the human mind."[34] But Stevens himself maintains a more wary sense of the nearness of a "hypothetical" identity (Frye) to an aberrant one, a "violence from within" which a chilling section of "The Man with the Blue Guitar"(XI) presents as a pathetic, and a dangerous, fallacy:

Slowly the ivy on the stones
Becomes the stones. Women become

The cities, children become the fields
And men in waves become the sea.

It is the chord that falsifies.
The sea returns upon the men.

The fields entrap the children, brick
Is a weed and all the flies are caught.

The "space" of metaphor is, in its traditional descriptions, one whose
break with predetermined meaning invites the reader to participate, an
invitation which makes of metaphor the exemplary *opera aperta*. A
particularly striking metaphor—say, Stevens's "The poem is a pheasant"—
creates the space in which we pause to puzzle over it, to try, by the scheme
of relations outlined in Aristotle or by a less disciplined process of allowing
the mind its play, to uncover the secret of the connection, the knot, or plot,
of the "copulation." Stevens's metaphor not only takes the authoritative,
copular form, but comes from his *Adagia* and has the combination of
ambiguity and authority that we associate with "adages." Metaphors are
"arresting"; they compel as well as invite us to enter their figurative
ground in order to "grasp" them. But it is often difficult, in this process of
"play," for the reader to perceive that he himself has been "grasped," or
"occupied." The copular "is" of metaphor which Ted Cohen (writing in
the tradition of metaphor as interactive "space") describes as creating
"intimacy" may, as he acknowledges, as easily involve "insult," what
Geoffrey Hartman (reflecting on Freud and Derrida) calls a "*scene of
nomination*," a combination of nominative and "accusative" which not
only "grounds," but entraps. Metaphor both opens up and forecloses. Its
"radically perspectival" aspect (Wheelwright)—its creation of "perspective
by incongruity" (Burke)—can also be a more daemonic "perspectivism,"
and what Max Black calls a "filter" may become what a powerful A. R.
Ammons poem calls a "Laser," a "focused beam" which "folds all energy
in," and, "filling all space," subverts the mind's efforts to "dream of
diversity," to "cast a new direction, / any direction" ("Laser").[35]
    The multiplicity of plots contained within metaphor—transference,
transport, transgression, alienation, impropriety, identity—suggests why
metaphor can be at work in so many genres not just as figure of speech or
rhetorical ornament but as structuring principle. The diversity of metaphorical "plots" also accounts for divergences within the field of literary
criticism,—between, for example, Frye's "comic" or "romance" bias
towards anagogic metaphor and Paul de Man's post-Nietzschean sense of
the potential violence and aberration of figures, of "the error of identifying
what cannot be identified"; between Ricœur's emphasis on the "mediating"

role of metaphor and Barthes's semiotician's emphasis on its celebration of itself; between Barfield's concern for the movement towards meaning and a "deconstructive" questioning of whether the plot of metaphor is a teleological one or whether this "end," like the idea of the "proper," is a projection of metaphor itself, whether metaphorical errancy has a place of rest, of subordination within a hierarchy of discourse or of reference, or whether it *is* its movement, part of a perpetual regression or signifying "chain."[36] Metaphor has not yet been mastered by a single "translation." *Meta-pherein*: figure of transport *and* exile, evasion *and* transformation, deviation *and* copulation, identity *and* transgression, without necessary direction, or *sens*.

4

Suspended Instruments: Lyric and Power in the Bower of Bliss

In the midst of the Bower of Bliss, the culminating episode of Guyon's quest in Book II of *The Faerie Queene*, the Elfin knight and his Palmer guide gain a sight of the Bower's reigning Enchantress and Verdant, her male victim:

> His warlike armes, the idle instruments
> 　Of sleeping praise, were hong upon a tree,
> 　And his brave shield, full of old moniments,
> 　Was fowly ra'st, that none the signes might see;
> 　Ne for them, ne for honour cared hee,
> 　Ne ought, that did to his advauncement tend,
> 　But in lewd loves, and wastfull luxuree,
> 　His dayes, his goods, his bodie he did spend:
> O horrible enchantment, that him so did blend.
>
> 　　　　　　　　　　　　　　　　　　　(II.xii.80)[1]

The immediate resonance of these "idle instruments / Of sleeping praise," suspended or "hong" upon a tree, is the iconography of Venus and Mars—with Verdant lying like the disarmed warrior in the lap of his paramour before Vulcan, the formerly impotent voyeur husband, rushes in upon them with his crafty "net." The suspension or hanging of these instruments reiterates the suspensions of the Bower itself, and the hovering of Acrasia as she cannibalistically "pastures" her eyes upon her powerless subject. But the instruments hung upon a tree also recall a very different and specifically lyric context—one that will lead us toward the various strains of lyricism that cross in this crucial Spenserian scene. This context is the suspended song and suspended lyric instruments of the haunting Psalm 137:

> By the rivers of Babel we sate, and there we wept, when we remembered Zion.
> We hanged our harpes upon the willowes in the middes thereof.
> When thei that led us captives required of us songs and mirth, when we had hanged up our harpes, saying, Sing us one of the songs of Zion.

How shall we sing, said we, a song of the Lord in a strange land?
If I forget thee, O Jerusalem, may my right hand forget to play.
If I do not remember thee, let my tongue cleve to the rofe of my
mouth....
O daughter of Babel, worthie to be destroied, blessed shal he be [who]
rewardeth thee, as thou hast served us.
Blessed shal be he that taketh and dasheth thy children against the
stones.[2]

That this biblical lyric of lament should sound in the midst of the otherwise
euphonious and *carpe diem* lyricism of the Bower of Bliss—filled with
songs and lyric traditions of its own—should not, on reflection, be
surprising. The psalm sings of abandoned instruments in Babylonian exile
and captivity: Verdant's instruments are suspended on the tree of a
"Witch" only too easily assimilated to Babylon and its famous Whore.
Calvin, in his gloss on the psalm, speaks of its Babylon as a *locus amoenus*
very much like the Bower of Bliss—as a "fair and fertile" place "with
charms which could corrupt effeminate minds" and "tempt them to
forget their native inheritance." Augustine speaks of its "Babylon" as the
pleasures of this world and of the "willows" on which its lyric instruments
are hung as ultimately barren rather than fruitful trees—an emblem of
barrenness in the midst of apparent fertility that repeats the biblical
dynamic of Spenser's principal subtext, the Garden of Armida in Tasso
which stands upon a Dead Sea.[3] The invocation of the psalm not to
forget—or to be punished with speechlessness and forcibly suspended
song as a result—thus joins the Homeric, lotus-eating resonances of this
Spenserian scene, and both figure the necessity of the withheld and vigilant
mind, the reversal of Verdant's suspended instruments, which themselves
provide a sign not of song refused but, more ominously, of song as in some
other sense suspended.

The psalm behind Verdant's suspended instruments, however, also
imports into this private and enclosed erotic scene the powerful political
dimension this psalm has always had for singers conscious of the wider
context of their singing, a resonance that might make it a powerful subtext
for lyric poets in the era of Spenser, subject to a queen who very much
demanded their voices. Hanging up one's instrument stands here as a sign
of resistance, a refusal to hire out one's voice on the part of a people who
otherwise sure can sing and dance. The specifically political force of this
psalm continues in a contemporary reggae version of the impossibility of
singing in Babylon, a version that chillingly suppresses the psalm's own
violent ending—"Blessed shal be he that taketh and dasheth thy children
against the stones"—and ambiguously substitutes for it another very
different psalm text, "May the words of our mouths and the meditations
of our hearts be *acceptable* in thy sight" (my emphasis).

The echo of this psalm's suspended instruments introduces if only elliptically into Spenser's scene the threat of the silencing, controlling, or compromising of song, one that is biblical in its immediate reference but also, in Acrasia's leafy retreat, inevitably evokes a particularly pastoral lyric tension between power and song—that tension that opens Virgil's *Eclogues* with an allusion to the "god" who has given the singer his "ease." Indeed, the other lyric context recalled in the stanza of Verdant's suspended instruments is this specifically pastoral one, hanging up one's instruments being not just the gesture of a Mars-like warrior abandoning the instruments of war, the hanging up of trophies as signs of victory, or the lament of a Dido-like abandoned lover (as in Spenser's "Willow worne of forlorne Paramours" or "Hang my harp on a weeping willow tree"), but also the suspending of instruments on trees in pastoral lyric, a suspension of song that may reflect the suspension Paul Alpers and others find characteristic of pastoral lyric itself.[4] In Sannazaro's *Arcadia*, one of the principal subtexts for Spenser's *Shepheardes Calender,* the hanging of the instrument of Pan upon a tree generates an entire history of pastoral lyric from Theocritus to Virgil and, by implication, to the poet-persona of the *Arcadia* itself.[5] The suspending of Pan's instrument there—in a way suggestive for a Spenserian episode that signals its debts to multiple predecessors—is an emblem of the interval before a new poet takes up these temporarily "idle instruments" and turns them into the instruments of his own potency.

Within this specifically pastoral lyric tradition, Verdant's suspended instruments summon up a Spenserian echo as well, and one intimately bound up with the tensions within Spenser's lyric vocation. Readers of *The Shepheardes Calender* will remember that it opens with Colin Clout, Spenser's own pastoral persona, not just suspending but breaking his pastoral instrument. And it ends with Colin hanging his pipe upon a tree, in a gesture that more than one commentator has linked with a sense of the impotence of song, or the necessary compromising of lyric voice in a political context which would make only too appropriate a conflation of a recall of Psalm 137 with a reminder of Colin's own suspended instrument.[6] *Otium,* or idleness, is traditionally the attraction of pastoral, as it is also of the fatal Bower of Bliss; but the "idleness" of the suspended instruments of Verdant suggests in their echo of Colin's gesture the potential impotence of poetry itself in a state in which it was scorned as a form of effeminacy, or idle "toye," in contrast to more active, imperial pursuits.[7] In this context it was highly problematic whether there was any alternative to the opposed temptations of the idle Phaedria and the industrious Mammon of Book II—an opposition that Blake might later ridicule as a "cloven fiction," but one that continued to dominate a whole post-Spenserian tradition of the potential impotence or irrelevance of the poetic vocation. The Romantics' Aeolian harp, we may remember, is one of the lyric descendants of this suspended instrument.

There is, however, yet another aspect of Verdant's suspended instruments that needs to be explored and, though it will emerge only after a brief excursus, another specifically lyric dimension of this episode and the defeat of its reigning queen. The pervasive phallic symbolism of Guyon's Odyssean journey to the Bower of Bliss makes it impossible to miss the fact that these suspended "instruments" are also clearly *male* instruments and that the impotence their suspension betokens is an impotence that is sexual as well as martial or lyric.[8] A link between the instruments of war and the instruments of virility is, of course, part of the visual cliché of the iconography of Mars and Venus: we think of Botticelli's painting with its wreathed phallic lance, clearly no longer ready for immediate use as an instrument of war, though still serviceable as an instrument of a different kind.

The sense not just of lyric but of sexual contest within the stanza of Verdant's suspended instruments evokes a recall not only of Mars and Venus but of a whole series of subject males and dominating female figures, from Hercules and Omphale to Samson reclining in the lap of that Delilah who deprives him of his strength, a figure of the man dedicated to higher things who cannot, however, ultimately escape the power of women. The link between the latter emblem and Spenser's pair is made even stronger by the fact that Samson in sixteenth-century depictions was also represented as laying aside his warlike instruments. Spenser's scene manages to evoke the iconography of both Virgin Mother with her sleeping infant and the more sinister Pietà, a dead Adonis in the lap of a powerful maternal Venus. The emblem of Samson made impotent in Delilah's lap shares with the tableau of Verdant and Acrasia anxieties of a particularly oral kind, the reduction of the male subject to an infant, or *infans*. Acrasia, like Delilah throughout much of her pictorial history, is not just a temptress but an overpowering mother; and it is in this respect worth citing at least one Renaissance representation of that overpowering. Madlyn Millner Kahr, in *Feminism and Art History*, cites a late sixteenth-century drawing entitled "Allegory of the Power of Woman" (figure 2), which shows in the foreground a woman nursing an infant in one arm, holding a royal scepter and golden chain in the other, and standing on the broken instruments—shield and sword—of male power; in the background are the women who tempted Solomon to idolatry (and hence, ultimately, into Babylon) and Delilah cutting off the hair, and strength, of Samson in her lap.[9]

The underlying threat of the story of Samson's abandoned instruments is, of course, the threat of castration. The hair mentioned in the case of Verdant is the just-beginning hair on his boyish face: if Acrasia is a Delilah, she has only a symbolic need for scissors. But the sense of castration pervades the entire scene, and the unavoidably phallic overtones of Verdant's removed and now useless "instruments" bring to the scene an

Figure 2   Maerten de Vos (?), Allegory of the Power of Woman, late sixteenth-century drawing, formerly in the collection of C. Fairfax Murray. Present location unknown. Reproduced from Norma Broude and Mary D. Garrard (eds), Feminism and Art History *(New York: Harper & Row, 1982), p.137.*

echo of the severed instruments of yet another boy—Attis, who after transgressing the demand of the Great Mother Cybele that he remain forever a boy, in a frenzy castrates himself, thus becoming not just an impotent Adonis to Cybele's Venus but also the prototype of the *Magna Mater's* Galli or eunuch servants. Attis is traditionally represented as an effeminate youth, wearing the distinctive Phrygian cap whose droop, as Neil Hertz has recently reminded us,[10] conveys an equivocal sense of both the possession and the lack of phallic power, as indeed the effeminately dressed porter of the Bower of Bliss wields his "staff" for "more [we may hear "mere"] formalitee" (II.xii.48.9), and reminds us of the Attis-like Aeneas at the court of Dido, another powerful female, his forgetfulness of outside world and higher task the Virgilian counterpart of the dangers of oblivion in Babylon.

The evocation of these pairs of dominant female and subject, even castrated, male in the episode of Verdant's suspended instruments works with other elements of the description to establish the Bower as a predominantly female space—whose enclosures suggest the *hortus conclusus* of the female body—and a place that might excite the knight to forget his own higher purpose, an act of submission that would suspend his "instruments." But the motif of male subjection within at least some of the plots suggested here—the case of Hercules, for example—is one in which the moment of male subjection is only one moment in a larger narrative progression. Though Guyon, unlike his prototype Odysseus, does not use his sword to overcome the Bower's witch, the culminating or phallic narrative "point" (1.7) of his Odyssean journey substitutes, for homecoming to Penelope, the overpowering of a threatening Circe through the potent "vertue" (41.9) of the Palmer's simultaneously phallic and Mosaic staff. Like the staff of Mercury to which it is kin, the staff is able both to recall souls from the symbolic Hades of subjection to female power and also to "rule the *Furyes*, when they most do rage" (41.8), a hint perhaps of the relation between the establishment of civilization and the taming of the female from the story of yet another dangerously powerful queen.

But the echo of Cybele in particular gives a further dimension to this episode's suspended—and (in the case of Guyon) potentially suspended—instruments, both lyric and virile, one that involves not just the episode's narrative progression but a specific form of lyric tradition adumbrated within it. Cybele, the *Magna Mater* of imperial Rome, is one of *The Faerie Queene's* most ubiquitous figures for the presiding patroness of "Troynovaunt" and hence for Elizabeth, the poem's allegorically shadowed queen, who was repeatedly represented (and self-represented) as the great "Mother," and even nursing mother, of her subjects. Virgil's Roman version of the *Magna Mater* carefully removes the more oriental and threatening female aspects of her cult—including the castration of Attis and her subject males. But Spenser's allusions to Cybele include this more ambivalent complex, Cybele's "franticke rites" (I.vi.15) as well as her maternal embodiment of order and civilization.[11] The Cybele–Attis iconography of the Isis Church episode of Book V of *The Faerie Queene,* with its Galli-like priests who "on their mother Earths deare lap did lie" (V.vii.9), links the pair of Great Mother and castrated boy emblematically with the posture of the mother-queen of the Bower of Bliss and the reclining youth who has surrendered his "instruments." But, interestingly enough, the vision at Isis Church also comes within the larger story of the powerful Amazon Radigund's subjection of Artegall, who comes under her control by abandoning his sword (V.v.17), which she then breaks, causing his "warlike armes" to be "hang'd on high," suspended so that they "mote his shame bewray," and forcing him to dress in "womans weedes" (20–2). The echoes of the Verdant–Acrasia scene in Artegall's humiliating subjection to a woman also, however, include a stanza that makes explicit reference to Spenser's ruling queen, the exceptional powerful female dominant over her male subjects.

> Such is the crueltie of womenkynd,
>   When they have shaken off the shamefast band,
>   With which wise Nature did them strongly bynd,
>   T'obay the heasts of mans well ruling hand,
>   That then all rule and reason they withstand,
>   To purchase a licentious libertie.
>   But vertuous women wisely understand,
>   That they were borne to base humilitie,
> Unlesse the heavens them lift to lawful soveraintie.
>
> (V.v.25)

Elizabeth here is so belatedly made an exception to the rule—indeed only in a single concluding alexandrine—that what emerges in the picture of the monstrosity of the subjection of male to female power makes one wonder whether, reading back from this episode to the hints of Attis's severed instruments in the Bower of Bliss, Elizabeth herself is not also "shadowed" in the scene of suspended instruments, evocative both of male "vertue" and of instruments of a more lyric kind.[12]

Recent Spenser criticism has increasingly drawn attention to the relation between the combination of eroticized Virgin and dominating mother in the figure of Acrasia and the typical self-presentation of Spenser's ruling queen.[13] Certainly, the *otium* and debased lyric "toyes" of Acrasia's Bower echo the debased social situation of which Cuddie complains in lamenting the impotence of his own lyric instruments in the "October" eclogue, implying that, at least in part, the predicament of the poet in the age of Elizabeth—his potentially impotent, or suspended, instrument—is that he is subject to powers that necessarily compromise his song. Cuddie's complaint resembles the lyric lament of the Muses themselves in another Spenserian intertext for Verdant's suspended instruments, *The Teares of the Muses*, whose complaint of internal exile (341) and of the "idlenes" and brute sloth (99, 335) of the contemporary English context recall at once the language of the Bower of Bliss and the lament of suspended song in Psalm 137, which might indeed provide its most appropriate lyric epigraph. The episode of Guyon in the Bower has long been interpreted, following Milton, as the drama of an individual trial. But the affinities of its language with a lament published only a year later imports into the Bower itself a suggestion of that contemporary "Babylon" in which the Muses' "sweete instruments" (20) can no longer be heard and are finally broken, replaced instead by vain idle "toyes" (325), a place where it is difficult to distinguish between "Poets" and "Sycophants" (471–2), or to save one's own lyric instruments from a subject's use.[14] Once again, in this lament, Elizabeth is made explicitly an exception, but in a fashion reserved until the end, and in a praise so exceptional that it too seems a second thought (571 ff.)

The iconography of subject male and dominant female in the scene of

Verdant's suspended instruments brings us, then, to the last of the lyric traditions figured in this scene—not just the suspended lyricism of Psalm 137 or the pastoral topos of pipes hung on trees, but also the polarized structure of Petrarchan lyric, itself dependent on the polarity of male subject and elevated female figure, a polarity of which the suspended dyad of the subjected Verdant and dominant Acrasia offers an almost parodic visual emblem. This context for these suspended instruments necessarily returns us to our first—the suspension of song in an alien political context—for in both, as so much of recent Spenser criticism suggests, the relationship of lyric to society, in the terms of Adorno's famous essay, is one that cannot be overlooked.

It has long been recognized that the vogue for Petrarchan lyric in the era of Elizabeth was inseparable from the structure of a politics in which political and erotic codes interpenetrated to a remarkable degree, in which Elizabeth's courtiers related to their queen as Petrarchs to an often cruel mistress, and in which the male poet was "subject" in both the political and in the Petrarchan lyric sense. Petrarchism was not just a lyric but also a dominant cultural form, a politicized lyric structure inscribed within the complex sexual politics of the exceptional rule of a woman in an otherwise overwhelmingly patriarchal culture. Stephen Greenblatt and others have noted the antagonism—or implicit contest of wills—always present within this Petrarchan politics of courtier-lover and tantalizing, dominant, and even cruel mistress.[15] Greenblatt cites the example of Ralegh's playing a frenzied Orlando to Elizabeth's disdainful beloved; and Elizabeth figured as Ariosto's already highly Petrarchanized Angelica, who drives her courtier-knights mad, might also easily be shadowed as a dominating Acrasia artfully orchestrating both her own rival romance and her own Petrarchan poetics. The Bower of Bliss is a threatening female space not just because of its enervating *carmina* and etymologically related "charms" but also in part because, while it arouses hopes of gratification, it does not clearly fulfill them or fulfills them only in an illusory or compromising way; in the stanza of Verdant's suspended instruments, the knight's slumber seems post-coital, but it is not at all clear from the syntax what his share has been in these delights ("There she had him now layd a slombering, / In secret shade, after long wanton ioyes"; 72.5–6). Bacon, for one, could easily assimilate Elizabeth's Petrarchan politics to the arts of "the Queen in the blessed islands . . . who allows of amorous admiration but prohibits desire."[16]

The antagonism within this politicized lyric structure, however, also left the way open for a male remastering of its dominant Petrarchan mistress. As Sir John Harington observed, the queen's male, Petrarch-like subjects could and would themselves make "matter" out of their *Magna Mater*. Her subjects (both in the political and in the erotic sense) could make the queen in turn the "subject" of their verse,[17] just as in the emblem of suspended pastoral instruments which Spenser echoes from Sannazaro, the origin of those instruments is in the death of Syrinx, in the transformed body of that female figure who becomes literally the enabling instrument of pastoral song.

The dynamics of this threatening female dominance and male re-mastery—the narrative dynamism of the overpowering of the Bower's Queen—is, however, already part of the sexual politics of Petrarchan lyric itself. Nancy Vickers, in *Writing and Sexual Difference*, describes the threat of dissolution or dismemberment that haunts the subject–object structure of the Petrarchan poetry of praise, in which the male subject is always potentially an Actaeon, torn apart after his vision of an unattainable Diana.[18] The canto of the Bower of Bliss bears a hint of this potential dismemberment as well as the castration of the male poet-lover in its reference both to Ida (II.xii.52)—sacred to Cybele and her Phrygian rites—and to Rhodope, where Orpheus, the male lyric poet par excellence, not only sang but was undone by women. Its suspended instruments obliquely recall the lyric contests not just between shepherd-singers hanging their pipes upon a tree or between sacred and secular lyric traditions (as is suggested in the echo of Psalm 137 in the midst of the Bower's very different lyricism) but also between male poet and female object of desire in Petrarchan lyric, a relationship of power translatable into both psychological and sociopolitical terms.

The vulnerable, subject status of the male lover within this Petrarchan lyric structure is countered by the mastery of the poet. In Petrarch himself, as Vickers suggests, the poet reverses the dangers of subjection and dismemberment by scattering the body of his mistress across his own *rime sparse* or scattered rhymes. In Spenser, the same stanza as evokes Ida and Rhodope in the Bower of Bliss makes reference to "Thessalian *Tempe*, where of yore / Faire *Daphne Phoebus* hart with love did gore" (4–5). The reference is to the first, or lover, moment of the myth—the victimage of the male subject before a cruel and unattainable mistress. But it inevitably provokes consciousness of its second moment—the transformation of the body of Daphne into a laurel, the triumphant sign of Phoebus' poetic power, the *lauro* that in Petrarchan lyric punningly assimilates the body of *Laura* just as Syrinx becomes in her death (an event that, though it means a loss for her lover, also removes her threat) the instrument of Pan.

The Diana–Actaeon structure of Petrarchan lyric and its underlying dyadic antagonism were clearly part of the Petrarchan politics of a reign in which the Ovidian story had already been assimilated to relationships of power through a play on the Latin words *cervus/servus* ("stag" and "slave") and a comparison of the fate of Actaeon to the perils of life at court.[19] Like the myth of Attis' permanently suspended instruments, the threat of the Actaeon persona of the Petrarchan lyric poet is, once again, castration—a threat that Spenser recalls in the "Some would have gelt him" (VII.vi.50.3) of the story of the Actaeon-like Faunus in the *Cantos of Mutabilitie*. The same threat enters euphemistically into the Bower of Bliss when Guyon's quaintly named "courage cold" (II.xii.68) begins to rise up at the sight of the naked bathing nymphs. The Actaeon–Diana story has been thought to be one of the many myths relating to the incest prohibition, the consequence of a forbidden view of the body of the mother; and certainly Guyon and the Palmer creep somewhat pruriently through the female brush ("couert groues, and thickets close"; 76) to gaze upon the simultaneously erotic and maternal "Witch" of this scene before they destroy it. The infant posture of the sleeping Verdant, together with the echo of the silencing of song from Psalm 137, reflects as well the threat of speechlessness in this Petrarchan structure, as in the Circean metamorphosis of her male victims. Petrarch, the threatened poetic Actaeon of his own canzone 23, can utter his lyrics only because he has an Orpheus-like respite between a forbidden seeing and dismemberment, and through his respite is able to silence rather than be silenced, to scatter the body of Laura rather than be dismembered himself. In Spenser's episode, Verdant's suspended instruments—signs of his status as what Mariann Sanders Regan suggestively calls "Lover infans"[20]—may figure a threat in which the potentially suspended instrument is poetic voice itself.

The split within the male subject of lyric that Regan represents as the split between Lover and Poet is matched in the episode of the Bower of Bliss by the splitting of the male figures of the scene between the subjected and symbolically castrated Verdant—his instruments hung like a sign of victory on Acrasia's tree—and the mastering Guyon, who by implication releases them. Ralegh presented the whole of *The Faerie Queene* not as the more usually cited outdoing of the narrative Ariosto but as an overgoing of the lyric Petrarch, written by a subject of a queen greater than Laura. But to become merely a Petrarch-like lyricist in praise of Elizabeth would be in some sense to become an imitative subject of the queen herself, held within a structure already appropriated as an instrument of power and presented elsewhere in *The Faerie Queene* as both paralyzed and paralyzing. In overgoing Petrarch in a poem that seems to repeat the Petrarchan lyric structure at a higher level, Spenser may also be subtly reversing the relation dictated by his own subject status. A gentleman by education only, himself dependent on the patronage system manipulated by the queen, might well conflate a visual icon reminiscent of a Petrarchan cruel mistress and her paralyzed male subject with echoes of the psalm of suspended instruments and potentially captive as well as captivating song. But, like Petrarch, the poet subject to his mistress is also capable of creating—or decreating—her, and Spenser at the end of Book II gives us an episode whose pervasive echoes of Aeneas at the court of Dido already evoke a text in which this moment of potential suspension is left behind by the narrative itself, and a female ruler is both surpassed and overruled.

Elizabeth was already identified by name with Dido or "Elissa." In the same legend which culminates in the overpowering of Acrasia, the Belphoebe who shadows Spenser's queen in her aspect as unattainable virgin or Petrarchan cruel mistress is introduced in a compound simile (II.iii.31). Its first part ("Such as *Diana* by the sandie shore / Of swift Eurotas . . .") makes her a reminiscence of Dido as she first appeared to the Aeneas she temporarily effeminated and forestalled. Its conclusion, however, compares her to "that famous Queene / Of *Amazons* whom *Pyrrhus* did destroye," an allusion which not only anticipates the Amazonian Radigund who suspends the warlike instruments of Artegall but manages, as Louis Montrose reminds us,[21] to suggest at once an exceptional female power and its destruction or remastery. The destruction of the Bower of Bliss is as violent as the prophesied ending of Psalm 137, with its captive and suspended instruments. Paradoxically, as Stephen Greenblatt and others have observed,[22] the final act of the Knight of Temperance is an act of intemperate violence, destruction of the Bower as a place of dangerous female dominance as well as of a suspect and seductive lyricism. Though the Cave of Mammon in this book is left standing and Verdant is let go with a mere lecture, Acrasia herself is led away in triumph. As with the dyadic antagonism of Petrarchan lyric, there seems to be here, ironically, no temperate middle way, no alternative to the polarity of subject or be subjected.

The lyric appeal of the Bower of Bliss is the isolated moment of its *carpe diem* song and its suspended cynosure. Regan, in *Love Words*, offers a psychologized theory of amorous or Petrarchan lyric in which the "charm" or "spell" that holds the lover resembles the Lacanian Imaginary or Melanie Klein's primal dyad of mother and child. We do not need object-relations theory or Lacanian psychoanalysis to catch the spellbound or oral fix of Verdant in the arms of a maternal Acrasia: indeed, the attempt to apply such contemporary theories to Renaissance texts often simply reveals the bluntness of our own instruments. And yet the simultaneous use and critique of Lacan in a famous essay by Laura Mulvey on the male gaze (in cinema)[23] might provide a suggestive supplement for students of this particular Spenserian episode, undergraduates and overgraduates alike. Mulvey describes the mediatory function of the female—and the threat of castration she represents—in the movement from the mother–child dyad, which Lacan terms the Imaginary, to the realm of the Symbolic, the name of the Father and the Law. The narrative of the overpowering and surpassing of Acrasia uncannily resembles the narrative progression of this Lacanian family romance. The raised and potent Mosaic "staffe" of the Palmer (which makes possible a detour out of this enclosure) evokes both the Law and the Father at once and rescues Guyon as potential second Verdant or arrested boy from the fate of the latter's suspended instruments, from the posture of the speechless *infans* caught within a spellbinding female space.[24] What Mulvey goes on to say of the voyeuristic *scopophilia* of the male gaze recalls much of the striking voyeurism of the visitants who come to destroy the Bower of Bliss, and her description of the two ways of overcoming the threat of castration figured by the female has intriguing resonances both for the defeat of Acrasia and for the representation of Elizabeth, Spenser's Petrarchan mistress-queen. The first way, writes Mulvey, involves turning the dangerous female figure into an image entirely outside the narrative—as, for example, in the cult of the female star, a strategy that might shed light on the cult of Elizabeth as Astraea, or quite literally a "star," transcendent embodiment of all the idealized Stella figures of Petrarchan lyric. This virgin star reigns outside the sublunar system as Gloriana is figured as outside *The Faerie Queene* or Elizabeth presented repeatedly as transcendent exception to the threatening dominant females within it.

The other means of escape from female power and the anxiety of castration, however, is a specifically narrative one, an overcoming through narrative of the "extradiegetic tendencies" of woman as spectacle, whose "visual presence tends to . . . freeze the flow of action in moments of erotic contemplation"—a visual freeze that resembles the moments of paralysis, astonishment, or stonification in Petrarchan lyric as well as the potentially suspending moments of centripetal gaze that A. Bartlett Giamatti and others have described within *The Faerie Queene*.[25] It is, in Mulvey's description, the active male protagonist, the gazer rather than the gazed upon, who neutralizes this dangerous suspension by specifically narrative means, by a reenactment that repeats both the original trauma of the castrating female and the process of her overcoming. The sense of resolute narrative movement and of reenactment as a form of control is conveyed in the canto of Acrasia by the resolutely "forward" movement (II.xii.76.5) of Guyon's quest and by the aura of repetition and even *déjà vu* in its imitation of earlier literary scenes, which suggests that the victory over its threatening female is in a sense already won: Guyon's almost ritual reenactment of Odysseus' resistance to the Sirens suggests that they are by no means as threatening the second time around.[26] In Mulvey's account, in a way reminiscent of Guyon's destruction of the Bower, this narrative process of overcoming is not only voyeuristic but sadistic, its violence a sign simultaneously of the form of the threat and of the imperative of asserting control. In Spenser, the "suspended instruments" of Acrasia's male captives are recovered as the Bower itself is overcome, and as Guyon and his Mosaic guide move forward to the narrative "point" or end of a Book of the Governor in which both a threatening female ruler and her suspect lyricism are finally mastered and surpassed.

Perhaps because of the notorious difficulty of defining it, lyric is frequently described in oppositional terms, by its relation or tension with something else—lyric cynosure as distinct from centrifugal movement, lyric as opposed to epic or narrative, and so on. *The Faerie Queene* seems to be exploring the implications of this opposition in its very form—narrative in its forward, linear quest and yet composed out of lyric stanzas that, like the enchantresses within it, potentially suspend or retard. It would be crude simply to transcode genre into gender here, though much of the history of lyric associates it with the female or the effeminate, and though Spenser's episode contains that confrontation which Horkheimer and Adorno saw as part of a revealing "dialectic of enlightenment" between a questing Odysseus and Sirens evocative of both lyric and threatening female "charm." But Guyon's defeat of Acrasia seems to involve something more than one of the poem's many narrative defeats of a potentially suspended, centripetal, "lyric" space, to be not just, as Greenblatt suggests, a repression of pleasure for the sake of an empire ruled by Elizabeth (who in this reading would be simply *opposed* to Acrasia) but more complexly an overgoing of the potentially paralyzing suspensions—unpleasure as well as pleasure—of a lyric form adapted to the domination of a woman.

Spenser's monarch was ultimately subject not only to the higher patriarchal authority of her God but to the allegorical fashioning of the poet who scattered her dread image into "mirrours more then one" (III. Proem.5.6). The allusive structures and staging of the Bower of Bliss suggest repeatedly that what is at stake within it is a complex hierarchy—the defeat of the Sirens by female Muses who are in turn subject to the authority of Apollo; the subordination, in Renaissance lyric theory, of secular lyric and its motivations to the higher lyricism and higher epideictic object of the Psalms; the surpassing, in Virgilian epic, both of the lesser pastoral genre of the Petrarchan *Shepheardes Calender* and of the power of eros and female rule. Its reticulation of these hierarchies suggests not simply the imperial politics inherited from Virgil and conveyed through the episode's unmistakeable echoes of contemporary colonial enterprise but the subtle gender politics inscribed within the contradictory structure of rule by a Queen whose name recalled not Aeneas but Elissa.

The Palmer's power to defeat all "charmes" gives to this episode a sense, ultimately, of something suspect about all *carmina*, something Protestant as well as male about its anxieties, though the defeat of Acrasia's "subtile web" (77) by the Vulcan-like Palmer's "subtile net" (81) suggests a strategy more complex than simple straightforward "enlightenment," a sense, as Keats put it, that only the poet's fine "spell of words" can rescue from a "dumb" and paralyzing "charm" and, perhaps, from an enchantress. A poem, finally, as dedicated as Spenser's to the polysemous perverse could easily encompass the psychological dynamic of the overpowering of a potentially castrating female, the covert political allegory of the overgoing of a lyricism associated with Elizabeth, and a simultaneously aesthetic and moral uneasiness about the seductiveness of lyric "charm," even if that charm is an inseparable part of the attraction of his own poetry, its own tantalizingly suspending instrument.

5

Transfigurations: Shakespeare and Rhetoric

Hysteron Proteron or the Preposterous

All his successors (gone before him) hath done't: and all his ancestors
(that come after him) may.

(*The Merry Wives of Windsor*)

In the final act of *The Winter's Tale*, the Clown, who is the Shepherd's son
and foster-brother to the newly found Perdita, daughter to a king, remarks
that he and his father are now in a "preposterous estate" (V.ii. 148).[1] The
phrase is routinely glossed as simply a comic malaproprism, fitting enough
for an untutored rustic to speak. What he means, goes the standard gloss,
is that he and his father are now in a "prosperous estate," the correct
phrase to describe their recent and dramatic rise from the lowly status of
shepherds to the state of "gentlemen born" (V.ii.127). "Preposterous
estate" is explained as a simple verbal error for the "prosperous estate" the
Clown really means—an untutored slip of the lip, like Mistress Quickly's
many similar malapropisms or like the repeated verbal slips of the "rude
mechanicals" of *A Midsummer Night's Dream*. We are thus, it seems,
within the familiar realm of Shakespeare's rustic wit, and the comedy here
is a laugh restricted to a single line.

And yet there may be something more than a simple characterological
slip in this "preposterous," and more involved than the comic effect of a
single phrase. For "preposterous" itself is not only a term connoting the
reversal of proper or natural order, a sense in which it appears frequently
in Shakespeare, but also the name of a rhetorical figure or trope—*hysteron
proteron*, routinely Englished in the Renaissance as "The Preposterous."
Puttenham and others described it as a form of verbal reversal, one which
sets "that before which should be behind" (Puttenham) or "that which
ought to be in the first place ... in the second" (Angell Day), a reversal or
exchange of place which is routinely linked with the proverbial putting

of the "cart before the horse." Puttenham, like the other rhetorical authorities of the day, classes it under the general figure of disorder— "*Hyperbaton*, or the Trespasser"—and Peacham, also typically, links it to disruptions in other kinds of order and hierarchy as well. The author of *The Garden of Eloquence* classes it among the "Faults opposed to naturall & necessary order," immediately after a discussion of proper order, sequence, or placing "when the worthiest word is set first, which order is naturall, as when we say: God and man, men and women, Sun and Moone, life and death." *Hysteron proteron* is a preposterous placing, a trespass against "naturall" order insofar as proper syntactical sequence, or the order of the syntagm in Renaissance discourse, was to be the discursive counterpart of proper vertical hierarchy as well.[2]

The Clown's aberrant "preposterous" as a simple mistake for "prosperous" suggests echoes of precisely such a preposterous placing or reversal of natural order—as in the Italian *preposto*, which Florio's *Worlde of Wordes* informs us means "preferred, put before, made chiefe," or "advanced before others," and hence might easily be substituted for *prospero* as "prosperous, thriving . . . luckie, fortunate." The Clown and his father have just, in this last act's festive ending, been raised from low to high by good fortune, by an unlooked-for prosperity which might indeed be said to be "preposterous" even without having anything at all to do with its rhetorical counterpart. And yet there is more to say once we widen our lens beyond the focus of the single phrase. For only lines before the malapropped "preposterous estate" the same Clown remarks, "I was a gentleman born before my father" (V.ii.139), a line which produces rhetorically, by its ambiguous blurring of proper syntactical placement, a comic version of *hysteron proteron*. If the trope itself is understood—in its reversal of proper order—as "unnaturall," this particular comic line produces even further the unnatural or preposterous possibility of a son born before his father, a genealogical *hysteron proteron* not unlike the one Derrida remarks in his analysis of the Freud of *Beyond the Pleasure Principle*, observing a daughter who is in some sense his mother as well.[3]

What looked at first, then, like a simple malapropism on the Clown's part or a restricted verbal quibble on Shakespeare's already starts leading us farther afield, into the verbal reversals or syntactic ambiguities of other nearby lines. But it may also take us beyond this single scene to other preposterous placings in a play whose own ending depends upon a reversal, or to other Shakespeare plays which play with the idea of following and succession, of "naturall" or ordered sequence. Within *The Winter's Tale* itself, such a close juxtaposition of an apparently simply bumbling and mistaken "preposterous" with an actual syntactic analogue of "The Preposterous" or *hysteron proteron* would indeed lead us to other structures of reversal. For these same rustic shepherds are surrounded elsewhere in the play with echoes of Jacob and Esau,[4] the smooth man and hairy man who show up both by name and around the edges of other Shakespearean scenes of firsts and seconds, and their exchange. This particular biblical paradigm of reversal, in which Jacob—the second-born in the order of nature—is given priority over the first, is the model of the reversal of properly sequential or "naturall" order which gives us finally that great biblical *hysteron proteron* in which the second-born of brothers is spiritually first (Exodus 4:22), in which, in the curious riddling form of Matthew 22: 41–6, the Christ of the Gospels is both the "*son* of David" in the order of nature or genealogical line and David's Creator or "Lord," and in which a younger or second Testament is said to have priority over the elder or first.

If we begin to follow out the wider extensions of "The Preposterous" within *The Winter's Tale*, we are also inevitably led beyond the boundaries of this single play to other Shakespeare texts which play upon reversals which are simultaneously rhetorical and genealogical, which upset both the syntactic and the historical line—from Hamlet's ambiguous "that follows not" (II.ii.413) in a play that has very much to do with causal and genealogical sequence, to Slender's pronouncement in *Merry Wives* that "all his successors (gone before him) hath done't; and all his ancestors (that come after him) may" (I.i.14–15). We would also be led to its implications for hierarchies of gender. Reversals in *King Lear*, for example, include not only that line in which it is by no means clear whether the "generation" that the barbarous Scythian is said to eat means his parents or his offspring (I.i.117) but also a plot in which the Lear who ironically in some sense *is* that Scythian is eaten or consumed by "daughters" whom he makes his "mothers," a preposterous reversal which the Fool explicitly allies with the familiar proverbial instancing of *hysteron proteron*, of putting the "cart" before the "horse" (I.iv.223–4).[5]

Geminatio, or the Doublet

My jerkin is a doublet—Well, then, I'll double your folly.
                                                              (*The Two Gentlemen of Verona*)

We might take a second rhetorical example, the case of the trope in which words are repeated with no intervening space between—*epizeuxis* in Greek, *geminatio* in Latin, or in English "the Doublet." *Geminatio verborum* (Cicero, *De oratore*, III.liv.206) comes from *geminus* or "twin" and hence also from the verb *geminare*, "to double." Englished in Thomas Wilson's *Arte of Rhetorique* (1553), such "doublettes" make their appearance "when we rehearse one and the same word twice together," producing the "redoubling of a word" (Angell Day). Just as in Quintilian words may be doubled or twinned (*verba geminantur*) for the purpose of amplification as well as emphasis, so in the English rhetorics "doublettes" or the "oft repeatyng of one worde" not only engages the attention of the hearer but "makes the worde seeme greater," as Wilson puts it. It is a form of increasing *copia*, of making more copious by twinning or doubling.[6]

"Gemination" in English can also denote, however, as the *OED* reminds us, not just the "immediate repetition of a word or phrase . . . for the purpose of rhetorical effect" but, more generally, any kind of doubling, duplication, or repetition. Consequently, this trope easily attaches itself to other kinds of doubling—as, for example, when Fuller's *Pisgah* (1650 edition) explains Christ's putting forth not one but "both his hands" and saying not just "My God" but "My God, my God" as his "claiming by that gemination a double interest in God's fatherly affection" (III.xii.345). Translated in the handbooks of rhetoric as "the Doublet," *geminatio verborum* not only provides a punning counterpart for that "doublet" which is a familiar article of clothing but becomes available as a figure for other kinds of twinning or doubling as well.

Shakespeare, as our epigraph suggests, puns on just this sartorial "doublet" in a play, *The Two Gentlemen of Verona*, which is itself full of various twosomes. He also employs the rhetorical trope of "the Doublet" with truly remarkable frequency, often in contexts which have to do with twins, with duplicates or seconds, or with doubling and duplicity of various kinds, in ways that link the tricks and turns of rhetoric at the local level of the line with the larger structures and plots of the plays themselves. In *The Comedy of Errors*—whose echoes of Jacob and Esau invoke the quintessential biblical *gemini* for its own doubling of rival twins—*geminatio verborum* has its counterpart in the whole play on doubling, twinning, or duplicity in which one twin is so to speak the repetition or "doublet" of the other. The play exploits the full range of verbal and other doublings—Luciana's speech to the wrong or duplicate twin with its "Ill deeds is doubled with an evil word" (III.ii.20); the ironic playing on the citizen twin as "second to none" in the city (V.i.7); or the constant exploitation of amphibology, a form of speech which looks two ways at once. Its increase of *copia* by the further doubling of Plautus's twins is joined by the rhyming form of the couplet or "gemel" and by the multiple play on the double sense or doubling power of signs and words, their potential for "folded meaning" or "deceit" (III.ii.36) and hence for reduplicating "error" as well, just as the duplicating or impostor twin is wrongly taken to be his double before the unrecognized doubling is exposed.

Such twinning is by no means restricted to comic play in Shakespeare: there are other, much darker structural analogues to this trope. Francis Bacon, in his discussion of the "coulers" of rhetoric, observes that "the sting and remorse of the mind accusing it selfe doubleth all adversitie. . . . For if the evill bee in the sence and in the conscience both, there is a *gemination* of it."[7] Bacon goes on to speak of this "gemination" in tragedy in particular: "so the Poets in tragedies doe make the most passionate lamentations, and those that forerunne final dispaire, to be accusing, questioning and torturing of a mans self." Something very much like this "gemination" would seem to govern the whole last speech of Othello, where, after the evocation of the "Turk" who is in some sense his double there, the Venetian Moor, on "smote the Turk," kills not this narrativized other, but himself.

We might consider in an even more detailed way, moreover, the relation of such a verbal or rhetorical form to the problem of seconding or succession in the histories. In what is appropriately called the second part of *Henry IV*, that play's playing on its own doubling or seconding—as well as complementing and completing—relation to an original or first is full of suggestive linkages between the rhetorical "Doublet" or *geminatio verborum* and the larger problem of doubling, seconding, or repetition, including that involved in the genealogical and generational as in the rhetorical line. There would appear to be, that is to say, a link between rhetorical gemination, as a repetition with no intervening space between, and the whole problem of kingly succession which is the larger burden of the *Henriad*, as of the history plays as a whole.

Henry IV, Part 2 opens, in a self-reflexive way not uncommon in the Renaissance, with a play on the doubling or seconding involved in the very idea of a second part, as well as on the potentially treacherous *copia* or increase of the "body" of "Rumour." This second part—as might be expected of an extension which both doubles and completes its counter-part or textual other half—is also literally crammed with rhetorical Doublets, most spectacularly but by no means exclusively in Shallow's "Where's the roll? where's the roll? where's the roll? Let me see, let me see, let me see. So, so, so, so, so, so, so"(III.ii.96–7) or his "Barren, barren, barren, beggars all, beggars all" (V.iii.7). Again, it joins rhetorically with a whole network of other kinds of doubling in a play which repeatedly reiterates the notion of the double. We have, for example, the description of the Archbishop of York as "a man / Who with a double surety binds his followers" (I.i.190–1), in lines which speak of the splitting in two of "body" and "soul" by the divisive power of rebellion, or the description of Falstaff as the "ill angel" (I.ii.164) or daemonic double of Hal, just after lines whose own exploitation of rhetorical *geminatio* ("gravy, gravy, gravy"; I.ii.162) summon up in the attendant doubleness of a pun the gravity of "gravy" and hence of his fat, the gravity which Falstaff as an elder so sorely lacks, and the grave he is headed for. We may remember, in this scene from *Part 2*, those lines in *Part 1* where fat Falstaff, who may be his own double or ghost, is punningly associated with "a double man" (V.iv.138).

Shakespeare's second Henry play, however, also calls attention to the other biblical *gemini* of Cain and Abel in its plot of a divided body politic (I.i.157). The problem of doubling in this second part, which both doubles and brings to an end its predecessor or first, includes the problem of how to put an end to the repetition which is civil war, the successive toppling of pretender kings by pretender kings. This fact brings together the play's political plot line, the threat to Henry IV's own stability ("For he hath found to end one doubt by death / Revives two greater in the heirs of life: / And therefore will he wipe his tables clean / And keep no tell-tale to his memory / That may repeat and history his loss / To new remembrance"; IV.i.197–202), with scenes which at first appear to have nothing to do with it. Act III, for example, opens with a scene whose ending recalls Richard II's prophecy that the Northumberland who helped Henry to his throne would one day challenge it—a doubling or repetition which Henry's very attempt to put down rebellion in this play would bring an end to. The scene concludes with lines on the "doubling" power of that Rumour who spoke the beginning of *Part 2* itself (III.i.97–8: "Rumour doth double, like the voice and echo, / The numbers of the feared"). This first scene, concerned with the repetition or doubling of pretenders, is then followed by a second, comic scene which begins with the rhetorical *epizeuxis* or *geminatio* of Justice Shallow ("Come on, come on, come on: give me your hand, sir, give me your hand, sir"; III.ii.1–2), and which treats of the death ("Jesu, Jesu, dead") of an otherwise utterly gratuitous character who just happens to be named—"old Double."

So much concentrated *geminatio* or wordy repetition occurs in the scene where Falstaff puts off his debt both to the Hostess and to the Law in the form of the Chief Justice ("do me, do me, do me. . . . Wilt thou, wilt thou. . . . Murder! Murder! . . . with her, with her! Hook on, hook on") that it is hard not to come to the conclusion that this trope of amplification by doubling is the rhetorical counterpart of the copious extension produced by such putting off. For part of the death of "old Double," surely, has to do with this play's final repudiation of Falstaff: the first part had already, as we mentioned, linked him with a "double man," and his promise to Shallow that he can still make him "great," even in the very scene of his repudiation and casting out by Hal, is met by Shallow's doubting "I cannot perceive how, unless you give me your *doublet*, and stuff me out with straw" (V.v. 81–2).[8]

The most telling use of the "doublet" in this play, however, links it, as a trope of seconding with no space between its identical repetitions, to the larger problem of Hal's own succession to kingship and his seconding of his father's name. The play's final act gives us both together—rhetorical and generational doublet—in its version of the King's Two Bodies understood not vertically and simultaneously within a single person but succes-

sively within a single family line. "Not Amurath an Amurath succeeds, /
But Harry Harry" (V.ii.48–9) is the formulation of this succeeding of
father by son, king by king; and the former Prince Hal who is here
described as having earlier mocked the workings of his father "in a second
body" (V.ii.90), but who in his invocation of sleep (IV.v.20 ff.) had already
seconded his father's own earlier ode to sleep (III.i.4 ff.), now repeats or
seconds his kingly father's functions, as he does his "father's words"
(V.ii.107). This scene on the succession of this second "Harry" is then
followed by one which gives us, yet again in the mouth of Shallow, a whole
series of rhetorical "Doublets," including "Barren, barren, barren, beggars all, beggars all" and "A good varlet, a good varlet. . . . Now sit down,
now sit down" (V.iii. 7–15).

"Not Amurath an Amurath succeeds, / But Harry Harry" is itself, in its
"Harry Harry," exactly a form of rhetorical *geminatio*, of repetition with
no differentiating space between. And though the context of the line is the
proclamation of a *difference*—this is not Amurath, our king, but English
Harry—the immediate seconding of "Harry Harry" raises more subtly, at
the microlevel of the incessantly reiterated trope, the larger question of
what difference the whole two plays together at this point of succession
may after all have made. *Geminatio*, as we have seen, is a trope of
amplification or *copia*. But *copia* has its double in the phenomenon of
mere "copy" or duplication made even more possible in the Renaissance
by the duplicating power of print, a form of mechanical reproduction that
Shakespeare elsewhere extends to the iterations of generation ("Although
the print be little, the whole matter / And copy of the father"; "She did
print your royal father off, / Conceiving you"; *The Winter's Tale*, II.iii.
99–100 and V.i. 125–6).[9] The "Doublet" or immediate repetition is a form
of such reproduction at the level of the line. One of the questions, then, this
juxtaposition of "Harry" with "Harry" raises is whether this particular
succession will mean a fruitful and copious development (as in "Harry's
dead . . . / But Harry lives, that shall convert those tears / By number into
hours of happiness"; V.ii.59–61) or a simple copy, quotation, or repetition of his father or original. The rhetorical form in which one word or
name immediately "succeeds" another in a scene whose whole context is
kingly succession might lead, that is to say, to the question of precisely
what difference has been made at this end by the whole Prodigal Son
detour of Hal's adolescence, or in other words by the whole first and
second parts of this doubled play. *Part 2*, in which the second Harry finally
does follow the first by ending his period of truancy and becoming king,
both continues on from *Part 1* and seconds or doubles it in succession; but
its induction by "Rumour" recalls Virgil's Fama who starts the second
part of the *Aeneid*, in which it is very much a question whether
or not a second time will be a fruitful development over a first or simply a
repetition or seconding of it in a "second Achilles" and "second Troy."

Sensus Germanus, or the German Sense

> The phrase would be more germane [Q1, "more cosin-german"] to the
> matter if we could carry a cannon by our sides.
>
> *(Hamlet)*

In *The Merry Wives of Windsor,* whose involvement with two wives
should authorize doubling much as the title of *The Two Gentlemen of
Verona* does, the play on "double" and "doublet," as on doubles and
gemini or twins, is extensive. One scene in fact directly links it to the
duplication, or twinning, of a "copy" or "second edition" (*Merry Wives,*
II.i.76), with a recall, once again, of the twins Jacob and Esau. The letter
Falstaff sends to Mistress Page is exactly like, "letter for letter" (II.i.70),
the one he sends to Mistress Ford. And the revelation of this twinning by
the former of the two wives to the other is filled with figures of reduplica-
tion as well as specific invocation of the geminating power of print:

> here's the twin-brother of thy letter; but let thine inherit first, for I
> protest mine never shall. I warrant he hath a thousand of these letters,
> writ with blank space for different names (sure, more!), and these are of
> the second edition. He will print them, out of doubt; for he cares not
> what he puts into the press, when he would put us two. (II.i. 72–9)

Other scenes of *Merry Wives,* such as the one between Shallow and
Slender at the play's beginning, give us more comic versions of *geminatio*
or the "Doublet" (as in Slender's "You'll not confess, you'll not confess,"
followed by Shallow's "'Tis your fault, 'tis your fault"; I.i.92–3). *Gemini*
or twins appear directly in Falstaff's reference to Pistol and Nym
as "a geminy of baboons" (II.ii.8). But perhaps most intriguing of all in this
play is the way in which this "gemini" or *geminus* slides by sound as well as
sense into a whole different complex, ultimately producing an involvement of mysterious "Germans" as well. The notorious boundary-crossing
of sound here becomes the co-conspirator of Shakespeare's fatal Cleopatra,
the pun. For, just as "gemman" was a vulgar sixteenth-century pronunci-
ation of "German," and hence linked by sound to "geminate" or "twin,"
so in the play itself Doctor Caius, the French physician, pronounces
"Germany" as "Jamany" (IV.v.87), not far indeed from that "geminy" of
baboons.

Geminatio verborum is the rhetorical form of the "Doublet," as we have
seen. "Double" in Shakespeare, however, can connote not just twofold or
twinning but also treacherous or duplicitous—as *Henry VIII* makes clear
in its "Say untruths, and be ever double / Both in his words and meaning"
(IV.ii.38–9), as *Twelfth Night* reiterates in its repeated references to
double-dealing in a play of twins (II.iv. 74–5; III.ii.25; V.i.35), or as the

double-meaning of the witches in *Macbeth* only belatedly reveals. Let us slide then from "geminy" to Germany, as *Merry Wives* does, and explore the slightly different case of what Erasmus famously called *sensus germanus*, a term which both he and his critics punningly dubbed "the German sense." *Germanus* in Latin can mean several things—a brother or close kin: an adjective meaning "genuine, real, or true," and the proper noun for a "German."[10] It also has this range of meaning in English, in ways which allow considerable Shakespearean punning and may even help to explain what those mysterious German thieves are doing in *Merry Wives*. The *OED*, for example, citing the *Towneley Mysteries* of 1460 (v.29: "Iacob, that is thyne owne germane brother"), makes it clear that the biblical pair of Jacob and Esau were not just *gemini* or twins but brothers "german." Germane "germans," or "cosin-germans," are everywhere in Shakespeare, as is the generalized sense of "german/germane" as closely related or kin. We have only to look at *Timon of Athens* (IV.iii.340: "Wert thou a leopard, thou wert germane to the lion") or *The Winter's Tale* (IV.iv. 773–5: "Those that are germane to him ... shall all come under the hang man"), or at *Othello*, where "germans" is juxtaposed with "cousins" or kin (I.i.113: "you'll have coursers for cousins, and gennets for germans"). But the Shakespeare canon also plays insistently on the tension between the sense of "german" as "genuine" or "true" and the doubled meaning of "cozen" as both kin and cheating, or cozening.

Erasmus developed the specific sense of "german" or *germanus* as "genuine, faithful, or true" into the notion of the *sensus germanus* for the faithful paraphrase or duplication of an original text in his paraphrases of Scripture. We are told that the method was put forward as a reaction, and alternative, to modes of allegorical commentary which deviated far from—and hence betrayed—the great original or sacred text. For Erasmus, the *sensus germanus* was by contrast a mode of authenticity, and paraphrase a faithful "speaking alongside" the host text. But his opponents satirized him by taking the phrase as meaning "German sense" in reference to his nationality instead; and in a letter of 1523 Erasmus himself plays upon *germanus* in the doubled sense.[11]

This *sensus germanus* or kindred and genuine sense is opposed in Erasmus to the *sensus alienus* or distorted sense which deviates from, and thus betrays, the text's true meaning. As Terence Cave describes it, the "german sense" is a figure of authenticity "by means of which Erasmus attempts to close the fissure between the text and what it signifies, or— more problematically—between the discourse of Scripture and a new discourse seeking to reproduce its sense."[12] The *germanus* or "kindred" sense, then, like the *geminus* or twin, has as its function the faithful duplication of an original, as with the second "letter" described in *Merry Wives* as the "twin-brother" of the first. The "German sense," as "true sense," offers the ideal of an exact paraphrase or transparent translation, a genuine reproduction without distortion, in which the paraphrase or duplicating text would be both "german" and "germane," genuine or true and a faithful brother text, or kin. Yet, as Cave's critique of Erasmus makes clear, wherever there is two-ness rather than singularity, there is the possibility of duplicity. Paraphrase itself, inasmuch as even commentary which goes "alongside" a text also doubles and necessarily deviates from it, may also finally be not just a faithful "cozen-german" but involved in some kind of cozenage as well; its very otherness may involve it, as a process of translation, in the "alienating" or transporting such germaneness would seek to avoid.

Let us return, then, to those mysterious thieving Germans of *Merry Wives*. Shakespeare's own playing on "german" and "germane," in contexts which sometimes also evoke its closeness in sound to "gemmen" or "twin," conveys just such an awareness of the potentially treacherous or cozening "german." In *The Winter's Tale*, the Shepherd and his son are faced with the conflicting demand to be both "german" in the sense of "honest" and "true" and yet not "germane" in the sense of "kin" to Perdita, from whom they need to alienate themselves (IV.iv.773 ff.) when Autolycus reports the king's anger at his son's dalliance with a "shepherd's daughter." Hamlet remarks of Osric's extravagant, metaphorically transported terms that "The phrase would be more germane [or, as the first quarto has it, "more cosin-german"] to the matter if we could carry a cannon by our sides" (V.ii.158–9). And other Shakespearean instances exploit the potential cozenage or cheating of the "cozen-german" as cozening accompaniment or duplicitous duplicate.

The Merry Wives of Windsor itself combines play on "cozen-germans" with a host of verbal echoes which link German or *germanus* with *geminus* or twin, precisely in the context of cozenage of both kinds. Erasmus's much-punned-upon *sensus germanus* or "German sense" represented an attempt by a figure who was both a humanist and an interpreter of sacred text to claim the possibility of an interpretative glossing or translation which would be without error or duplicitous, alienating gap. In *The Merry Wives*, a figure called the "Host" similarly attempts to reconcile what he terms "the terrestrial" and "the celestial"—the warring Doctor and Parson of the play. Their revenge on him is to send those Germans whom he takes to be "honest men" (IV.v.72) but who cheat him and literally translate or alienate, in the sense of "steal," his property—"cozen-germans," as one character puts it, who finally "cozen" or cheat him by their duplicity:

> *Bard.* Out alas, sir, cozenage! mere cozenage.
> *Host.* Where be my horses? . . .
> *Bard.* Run away with the cozeners . . . three German devils, three Doctor Faustuses.

Host. They are gone but to meet the Duke, villain, do not say they be
fled. Germans are honest men.

Enter EVANS

Evans. Where is mine host?
Host. What is the matter, sir?
Evans. Have a care of your entertainments. There is a friend of mine
come to town, tells me there is three cozen-germans that has cozened
all the hosts.   (IV.v. 63–78)

It is immediately after these lines, as the Host, cozened by these honest-
seeming but duplicitous Germans, finds himself "in perplexity and doubtful dilemma" (84–5)—terms which also suggest a difficult two-ness—that
the Doctor pronounces his "Jamany" for "Germany"(87). The play as a
whole repeatedly suggests a link between these cozening Germans and the
idea of *gemini* or twins, from the description of Nym and Pistol (who may
indeed *be* these same cozen-Germans) as a "geminy of baboons" to
Falstaff's two love letters, the second of which is called the "twin-brother"
of the first, in lines which once again recall the biblical paradigm of a
cousining, but also cozening, twin. Divergent possibilities in Shakespeare
rarely simply cancel each other out, and nothing in this association of
sounds and puns removes the possibility that these Germans may also take
us outside the text, to the much-debated contemporary reference to
Germans in general or one Count Mömpelgard in particular.[13] But the
very extent of its paronomastic cousining of Germans and twins suggests
that there is plenty still to be done within the germane senses of the play
itself.

Chiasmus, or the Crossing Scheme

Fixing our eyes on whom our care was fix'd
                                        (*The Comedy of Errors*)

An instance like the "german" from *germanus* might suggest ways in
which wordplay in general in Shakespeare remains still, long after studies
like Mahood's,[14] far from an equal partner in the business of interpretation with the continuing legacy of psychological and other models inherited from a certain reception of nineteenth-century narrative. Other
instances would suggest, even more specifically, the comparative lack of
critical investigation of Shakespeare's extensive play on the terms of
language and discourse, on rhetoric as structure as well as trope. This lack
affects everything, from the larger interpretation of particular scenes—in
which it is often the logic of rhetoric, or of a particular rhetorical turn,

rather than an anachronistic psychologic, which is being dramatized—to the minute particulars of editorial and textual scholarship. Iago's description of Cassio as "A fellow almost damn'd in a fair wife" (*Othello*, I.i.21), to cite just one instance, has given us at the level of a narrowly characterological criticism all of the speculation about a mysterious extratextual "wife" of Cassio or a lapse either on Shakespeare's part or in some aspect of the transmission of the text. Yet we might hear this line, uttered early in the play, not as a referential signal to the existence and subsequent textual effacing of a dramatizable person but rather as a particular verbal form, reminiscent of the proverbial jumping to conclusion that produces something like "Shee is a faire woman: Ergo, shee is unchaste." For in Blundeville's famous *Arte of Logike*, in the same era as the play, this is exactly the example, in the discussion "Of Probable Accidents, Conjectures, Presumptions, Signes, and Circumstances," of what was called an argument by "consequence," a form singularly appropriate to introduce a play in which precisely such jumping to conclusion from conjecture and circumstance is to become the plot of the tragedy itself.[15]

The next two examples, then, will be of interpretative or editorial cruxes and presuppositions in which a cul-de-sac of assumption might be circumvented by recourse to a rhetorical structure, or more widely to the whole discourse and lexicon of rhetoric which Shakespeare exploits so ubiquitously. First, chiasmus, that scheme of exchange or crossing produced, as Scaliger puts it, "when the first element and the fourth, and the second and the third are conjoined, giving a scissor formation in the sentence,"[16] or when some other, looser form of verbal crossing links the first and final word of a single line. In the opening scene of *The Comedy of Errors*, Egeon provides his extended narration of the shipwreck of his family, and of the stratagem employed by him and his wife to save themselves, their twin sons, and the corresponding servant twins from the threat of an "immediate death" (I.i.68) at sea:

> My wife, more careful for the latter-born,
> Had fast'ned him unto a small spare mast,
> Such as sea-faring men provide for storms;
> To him one of the other twins was bound,
> Whilst I had been like heedful of the other.
> The children thus dispos'd, my wife and I,
> *Fixing our eyes on whom our care was fix'd,*
> Fast'ned ourselves at either end the mast.
>
> (I.i.78–85; my italics)

Henry Cuningham and R. A. Foakes, editors of the two Arden editions of the play, assume that there must be an inconsistency in these lines, a mistake or slip of memory on Shakespeare's part.[17] Egeon states here that it was the mother who was "more careful for the latter-born" (78), while he was responsible for the elder, when they bound the sets of twins to the "small spare mast" (79). The Arden editors therefore conclude that he can only be contradicting himself when he says only shortly after, in line 124, that he was subsequently left with the "youngest" rather than the eldest boy after the mast itself was "splitted in the midst" (I.i.103). The assumption comes from their visual construction of the placing of the children on the mast—that each child must have been placed on the same side as the parent "most careful" for him; for this leads to the conclusion that the mother should have been left with the "youngest" and the father with the elder twin when the mast was finally split in two. Hence the conclusion of a slip or mistake.

There is, however, another possibility, one which would not only reveal this relation of elder and younger to be anything but a "mistake" but would also lead us, via a particular rhetorical form, into the larger structures these lines adumbrate within the play as a whole. If we were to take a clue from the rhetorical crossing of a crucial line within this passage— "Fixing our eyes on whom our care was fix'd"—we might catch instead another possible visualization of the scene which would mirror the exchange and crossing this version of chiasmus rhetorically suggests. This would be a placing of the various family parts upon the mast in such a way that it is precisely a crossing which takes place: each parent bound to one end, gazing upon the twin most "cared" for not on the same but on the opposing half. The chiasmus as figure for a crossing both rhetorical and positional would, if taken seriously, elucidate what has been mistakenly assumed to be an oversight or memory slip on Shakespeare's part when Egeon tells his audience that he was left, after the splitting of the mast, with "My youngest boy, and yet my eldest care" (I.i.124), since the child bound by the mother would be on the father's half of the mast, and vice versa.

This chiasmic placing of the family parts, moreover, would not only remove any charge of a memory slip or error, which is only the projection of a particular visual construction of these lines, but would dramatically emblematize the sense of crossing or exchange which dominates the play right from this opening scene. For the repeated rhetorical sense of chiasmus or crossing in the continued phrasing of "youngest boy" and "eldest care" suggests that the very idea of crossing is being emphasized throughout Egeon's speech—an emphasis appropriate in any case to a scene where this father faces death precisely because he has crossed an absolute dividing line between two sides. Within the immediate context of these lines (I.i.78–103), the positioning, in this chiasmic sense, of the family members upon the mast would mean, as we saw, that in the splitting of the mast each parent is severed from the twin he or she had originally been most "careful" for. And the sense of an original crossing, missed if we assume that Shakespeare is simply nodding here, imparts an even greater dramatic tension to the subsequent seeking of one divided half for the other after their "unjust divorce" (I.i.104) at sea.

But there is also in the crossing of "elder" and "younger" here a further resonance, which would connect Egeon's extended and otherwise point-lessly detailed description of the placing on the mast with both the intervening "comedy of errors" and the reappearance of the question of "elder" and "younger" in the play's own closing lines. The detail of lines 78 and 82 ("My wife more careful for the latter-born ... Whilst I had been like heedful of the other") raises there a seemingly gratuitous echo once again of the biblical story of Jacob and Esau, the "younger" and "elder" twins on whose rivalry and birth order so much of subsequent Old Testament history depends. When the question of the birth order of twins resurfaces in the comedy's closing lines, it is between the two adopted twins, the Dromios:

> *Ephesian Dro.* Methinks you are my glass, and not my brother:
>   I see by you I am a sweet-fac'd youth.
>   Will you walk in to see their gossiping?
> *Syracusian Dro.* Not I, sir, you are my elder.
> *Ephesian Dro.* That's a question; how shall we try it?
> *Syracusian Dro.* We'll draw cuts for the senior, till then, lead thou first.
> *Ephesian Dro.* Nay then thus:
>   We came into the world like brother and brother;
>   And now let's go hand in hand, not one before another.
>
> (V.i.418–26)

There are many ways to play these final lines, from the two twins walking "hand in hand" through the door in a way appropriate to a sense of festive comic ending, to something less than the ideal reconciliation the words themselves suggest.[18] But the play's own setting—Ephesus, long linked by commentators to the Ephesus of Paul's New Testament journeys and the Epistle—as well as its two sets of twins, one "alien" and one citizen, recall the "wall of partition" between "stranger" or "alien" Gentile and citizen Jew from Ephesians 2, a division into sides as absolute as that between Syracusian and Ephesian in the *Comedy*'s opening scene. And hence the whole emphasis in the Epistle on the "Cross" (X) which reunites two divided sides, replacing the Old Law's division of Esau and Jacob, Gentile and Jew, by a reconciliation in which both become equally "adopted" sons (Ephesians 1:5). *The Comedy of Errors* begins with the "law" which sets a barrier between Syracuse and Ephesus and condemns Egeon, as the crosser of this dividing line, to "doom." In the intervening "comedy of errors," the exchange of place of "alien" and "citizen" twin is accompanied by more evocations of the smooth man and the hairy man (II.ii.64–109) from the archetypal biblical story of elder and younger twins, whose history, after the initial story in Genesis, does indeed go through various exchanges and crossings in which the elder or the younger is by turns the favored one. By the end of Egeon's one day's respite, and the whole complex comic set of changes and exchanges of place that ensue, the initial "doom" is converted into a "nativity" (V.i.400–6), in final scenes whose biblical echoes call to mind a "redemption" easily combined with the play's own commercial metaphors and the removal of barriers, walls, and partitions by that "Cross" which traditionally puts an end to "Error" itself.

The opening scene's recall of Jacob and Esau, "younger" and "elder" twin, evokes the Old Testament context of the Law and its divisions in the context of the "greater care" of each parent for each twin, just before that crossing on the mast which "Fixing our eyes on whom our care was fix'd" chiasmically suggests. But both the crossing over of sides and positions and the subsequent course of Egeon's narrative already attenuate the Jacob-and-Esau sense of parental preference:

> Our helpful ship was splitted in the midst;
> So that, in this unjust divorce of us,
> Fortune had left to both of us alike
> What to delight in, what to sorrow for.
>
> (I.i.103–6)

The rhetorical crossing of Egeon's lines, the ones the Arden editors take to reveal an error or slip ("My youngest boy, and yet my eldest care, / At eighteen years became inquisitive / After his brother"; I.i.124–6), evokes a brotherly seeking more suggestive of the Joseph than the Jacob narrative, even as the crossing of the boundary by both Egeon and his "wandering" son already anticipates the play's ultimate reunion of divided sides. What a larger criticism of this play would make of its repeated recourse to biblical terms and structures is very much open to debate. But what had been perceived as a contradiction or mistake—the confusion of "elder" and "younger" in its opening scene—is not only not necessarily an oversight but a figure and a crossing crucial to the allusive movement of the play as a whole. The rhetorical crossing of "Fixing our eyes on whom our care was fix'd," if taken seriously within the lines in which it appears,[19] would lead us not just out of an unnecessary assumption of textual mistake or nodding but into something much broader than the single line. Rhetoric here is not just decoration but structural analogue and interpretive tool.

Dilation and Delation by "Circumstance"

The time When? about the sixt hour, when beasts most graze, birds best peck, and men sit down to that nourishment which is called supper: so much for the time When. Now for the ground Which? which, I mean, I walk'd upon: it is ycliped thy park. Then for the place Where?

(*Love's Labour's Lost*)

A rhetorical structure or recourse to the language of rhetoric can, I would argue, very frequently offer clues to problems apparently opaque when approached from a different set of assumptions or editorial biases. Rhetoric and its lexicon can become interpretive tools even at the most basic levels of textual commentary and editing. Here, in relation not just to a trope like *hysteron proteron* or a structure like chiasmus, but rather to the whole tradition of rhetoric and its affiliations, we might take an even more important textual crux in Shakespeare than the one in *The Comedy of Errors*.

In the great Temptation Scene of *Othello*, Iago begins to put the Moor "on the rack" through those pauses, single words, and pregnant phrases which seem to suggest something secret or withheld, the possibility that his ensign "knows more, much more, than he unfolds" (III.iii.243). In the Folio version and all the authoritative texts of the play but one, Othello's response to Iago's technique refers to its "close dilations, working from the heart, / That passion cannot rule"(III.iii.123–4). Editors from Warburton onwards have puzzled over the meaning and import of "dilations" here— some citing one Renaissance meaning ("dilations" as "delays"), others, with Malone, the sense of "dilation" as rhetorical *dilatio* or amplification, and a few choosing to substitute for "close dilations" the single other possible text, "close denotements," found only in the earliest Quarto. Arden editor M. R. Ridley, confessing that, since the Folio phrase "can hardly have been due to a mere blunder," whoever put it there must have "meant something by it" but that he himself has "very little idea what that was," chooses to efface the Folio text altogether, substituting "close denotements" instead on the grounds that to this more neutral phrase at least "no reasonable objection can be made."[20] At this most basic level, a certain interpretive assumption affects even the text that readers of this edition of the play get to see.

But there is another possibility here, one which if followed out might lead us to see in the Folio's "close dilations" an overdetermined or portmanteau phrase which carries the burden of combinations particular to the plot and language of *Othello* as a whole. When Dr Johnson raised his eccentric but to subsequent editors fascinating suggestion—that the Folio's "close dilations" should be read instead as "close delations" or "occult and secret accusations"—it was frequently rejected and has been still, by Ridley himself, on the grounds that there is no evidence of "delation" in its Latin sense of "accusation" in Shakespeare's day. But in fact, as only a cursory glance at the *OED* or at contemporary texts would make clear, such instances abound. "Delate" or "accuse" in Renaissance English usage could not only be, in a variant spelling, identical in appearance and sound to "dilate" or amplify, but was even available for punning links with it (as in Bishop Hall's resonant "dilaters of errors, delators of your brethren," for instance). The Folio's "close dilations," that is to say, would not even need to be amended in its spelling to "close delations," as Johnson supposed, to be capable of suggesting both meanings, amplification and accusation, in the same phrase.[21]

This enigmatic phrase and textual crux, then, might not necessarily lead us to mere puzzlement or a throwing up of hands like Ridley's, nor to the necessity, and all too frequent editorial practice, of choosing one meaning *over* another—a process of elimination which so often presupposes a singularity of one definitive text or reduced authoritative meaning—but rather to the possibility of reading *Othello* more largely in relation to this semantic crossroads and all of the resonances it conjures. It would be just such a combination of amplification and accusation we would encounter in noticing, first of all, that rhetorical dilation is explicitly evoked within the play, and precisely within the context of a judicial accusation, in the central scene in Act I: Othello, accused of "witchcraft" in wooing Desdemona, is summoned before the judicial inquiry of the Venetian Senate and tells of her earlier entreaty ("That I would all my pilgrimage dilate, / Whereof by parcels she had something heard"; I.iii.153–4). His own narrative dilation before the Senate serves, in what has been called the "comic" context of this opening scene, to acquit him of the charge of which he is accused. But his description of Desdemona's "greedy ear" (I.iii.149), hungry to hear more of his discourse, ominously anticipates the play's later tragic turn, when Iago begins to "abuse" Othello's own increasingly insatiable "ear," and the "witching" effect of the ensign's eventual unfolding of what the "close dilations" of the great Temptation Scene have similarly only "in parcels" or in part revealed leads to the "delation" or accusation of Desdemona before *her* judge.

There is, however, even more to this link between rhetorical "dilation" and judicial "delation," a term which would lead us into the crossing of judicial and rhetorical not just in this play but in others as well. In the passage which provides our epigraph here, Armado's dilated or wordy accusation of Costard in *Love's Labour's Lost* proceeds by a detailing of what were known technically as "circumstances," the "who, what, where, why, when" we continue to learn in watered-down form in the continuation of ancient rhetoric into the techniques of modern composition. What we need to know for *Othello* and for the crossing of dilation and delation within it, is that these were the "circumstances" of a judicial accusation as well, part of what we still call "circumstantial evidence" offered to a judge when there is no direct or "ocular proof." Rhetorical dilation and judicial delation, that is to say, shared the same rhetorical form, detailing through the "circumstances," a combination which the bombast or verbal amplification of Armado's accusation exactly provides, but in a comic mode. *Othello* not only alludes self-consciously to the whole rhetorical tradition of "dilation" in Othello's description of his wooing, but increasingly brings to mind these "circumstances": in the Moor's angry demand to

have an answer to his "What ... How ... who ... ?" in the scene of the
night brawl (II.iii.169–78); in Iago's "I will make him tell the tale anew: /
Where, how, how oft, how long ago, and when / He hath, and is again to
cope your wife" (IV.i.84–6); and in Emilia's "Why should he call her
whore? Who keeps her company? / What place? what time? what form?
what likelihood?" (IV.ii.137–8). Iago, we remember, promises "If impu-
tation and strong *circumstances* / Which lead directly to the door of truth /
Will give you satisfaction, you might have't" (III.iii.406–8; my italics), in
the absence, precisely, of "ocular proof."

"Circumstances" both amplify and accuse, like the potentially crossed
senses of the "close dilations" of the Temptation Scene. But they also
contain a further link with the third sense evinced for the Folio's "dilations"
—"delay." Minsheu's famous *Dictionary* of 1617 gives under "circumstance" not only "a qualitie that accompanieth a thing, as time, place,
person, etc.," but also a "circuit of words, compasses, or going about the
bush," a sense which it carries in *The Merchant of Venice* ("You ... herein
spend but time / To wind about my love with circumstance"; I.i.153–4).
This sense too emerges in Iago's complaint, at the very beginning of
Othello, against the wordy evasion of Othello's "bumbast circumstance /
Horribly stuff'd with epithites of war" (I.i.13–14), and gives us elsewhere
the Moor's own curiously amplified and even inflated "purple passage" of
farewell to the "Pride, pomp, and circumstance of glorious war" (III.iii.
354). The other appearance of dilation in this text is precisely in this sense
of delay, in Iago's counsel to an impatient Roderigo that "wit depends on
dilatory time" (II.iii.372). And, as Rymer complained, the play itself is full
of delays occasioned by verbal amplitude. All three senses of "dilations"
from that vexed Folio text, then—amplification, accusation, delay—
combine with "circumstances" both verbal and judicial in ways that
suggest the resonant contours of this portmanteau phrase within the entire
play,[22] beyond those "close denotements" to which, as the more neutral
and less textually justifiable phrase, "no reasonable objection can be
made."

Rhetorical "circumstances," then, both dilate and indict, in that crossing of rhetorical and judicial which is so much at the heart of the whole
tradition inherited from Cicero and Quintilian, and in a way rich with
implications not just for the Folio text of those crucial lines from Act III but
for the crossing of dilation and accusation within *Othello* as a whole. But
the term also resonates elsewhere, in both comic and more tragic contexts.
Autolycus questions the frightened rustics in a scene from *The Winter's
Tale* whose detailing of the "circumstances" might have come straight out
of descriptions of the form most "commonly requisite in presentments
before Justices of peace":[23] "Your affairs there? what? with whom? the
condition of that farthel? the place of your dwelling? your names? your
ages? of what having? breeding? and any thing that is fitting to be known

—discover" (IV.iv.717–20). The fact that this judicial form for ferreting out the truth should be used by a figure whose very name from the *Odyssey* links him with fables and lies is suggestive in a play which not only turns on the questionable verisimilitude of the fabrications of jealousy but also claims verisimilitude, precisely by "circumstances," for its own fabulous events ("Most true, if ever truth were pregnant by circumstance. That which you hear you'll swear you see, there is such unity in the proofs"; V.ii.30–2).[24] Rhetorical and judicial "circumstances" are linked as well in the accusation of Hero in *Much Ado About Nothing*, a play whose comic outcome depends on the interposition of an interval of delay: "circumstances short'ned (for she has been too long a-talking of), the lady is disloyal" (III.ii.102–4). And interrogation and potential "delation" form the subject of the tedious verbal amplifications of Polonius ("If circumstances lead me, I will find / Where truth is hid"; *Hamlet* II.ii.157–8), in a play which has to do not just with delay, but with the whole wider problem of ferreting out a mystery, of trying to find what, in the absence of ocular proof, would prove or disprove an accusation made from the play's very beginning.

The General and the Particular

Where's our general? ... Here I am, thou particular fellow.
(*Henry VI, Part 2*)

One of the principal organizing structures of argument and discourse is the disposition of the "general" into its "particulars." This is the tradition which Bottom mangles, along with so much else in *A Midsummer Night's Dream*, when, anxious to improve the level of organization, he responds to Quince's "Is all our company here?" (I.ii.1) with advice to "call them generally [that is "individually" or "particularly," says the gloss] man by man, according to the scrip" (I.ii.2–3). Abraham Fraunce, in *The Lawiers Logike*, speaks of "Methode" in discourse as a disposition of "divers coherent axiomes" in which "the most generall," as the head or "principall," is placed "first" and where the order then "descends" from the "generall" to the "special" or the "particular": "Therefore this method descendeth alwayes from the generall to the specials, even to the most singular thing, which cannot be divided into any more parts."[25] He then goes on to treat of the "distribution" of the "general," making it clear that, in true Aristotelian fashion, discourse is to mirror the form of hierarchical descent from "general" to "particular."

Shakespeare plays constantly on this language of "general" and "particular," not just in more straightforward lines like the old Duchess of

York's complaint in *Richard III* ("Alas! I am the mother of these griefs: /
Their woes are parcell'd, mine is general"; II.ii.80–1), but also in paronomastic juxtaposition with the political "general" or head, as in *Henry VI, Part 2*,
where Jack Cade—whose rebellion threatens hierarchy or proper order
and descent in the body politic—answers his follower Michael's "Where's
our general?" with "Here I am, thou particular fellow" (IV.ii.111–112).

Two plays in the canon recall with particular resonance, however, this
discursive language of descent. In *Othello*, as we have seen, the tradition of
the amplification of discourse is evoked in that speech in Act I where
Othello reports on Desdemona's desire to hear the whole of what she had
heard only "in parcels," or in some particulars. One way of opening out or
parceling the "general" is by dividing it into its "circumstances," in the
form we have already seen at work. But when we come to this play from
the punning elsewhere in the canon on the "general" both as distinguished
from the "particular" and as the military "general" or head, we may hear
something more in its own multiple references to Othello as "our noble
general" (II.ii.11), and in what happens when the action descends into the
particular and even the minute particulars of the domestic tragedy it
becomes—in which Othello's "occupation" as general is "gone" (III.iii.
357) and in which the sign of descent into the particular becomes the
handkerchief, that "trifle" of which Rymer so famously complained.

This descent into the domestic also bears implications for the question
of gender in this play and the specifically domestic hierarchy of headship
which at least one sixteenth-century discussion of descent from "general"
to "particular" illustrated in combining a handbook of logic and rhetoric
with a treatise on "household government."[26] The conclusion of Act III
has puzzled commentators unsure of what Bianca means when she says
"'Tis very good; I must be circumstanc'd" after Cassio has impatiently
asked her to be gone because he waits upon more important things: "I do
attend here on the general, / And think it no addition, nor my wish, / To
have him see me woman'd" (III.iv.193–5). Cassio "woman'd" in the
homosocial world of war which dominates the male bondings of this
tragedy recalls an earlier locution which similarly makes Desdemona an
adjunct of the general ("But, good lieutenant, is your general wived?";
II.i.60), or hintings that the doting and fondly "prating" (II.i.224) general,
wived, has already abandoned his proper station as "head" ("Our general
cast us thus early for the love of his Desdemona"; II.iii.14–15). For the
"circumstancing" of Bianca not only involves the sense of her being put off
or delayed in her suit, one of the possible resonances of "circumstanc'd"
here, but makes her by implication an adjunct or "addition" to Cassio as
he attends upon the "general." This resonance both catches the movement
of the play from great things to small, general to particular, and,
as feminist critics of the play have seen, ultimately also attaches to
Desdemona, who, even as she is portrayed as having become the "general's

general"—in a reversal Iago clearly contemptuously intends should in-voke the familiar topos of woman on top—is in fact forced to become, as the play proceeds, simply and reductively an "adjunct," whose minute particulars increasingly preoccupy the "general" himself: "Our general's wife is now the general—I may say so in this respect, for that he hath devoted and given up himself to the contemplation, mark and denotement of her parts and graces" (II.iii.314–18). When this language appears, then, in Iago's advice in the same scene to Cassio on how to "recover the general again" (II.iii.272), the underlying resonances of the term pose the question of how—in the relentless linear logic in which the most minute particular, that "trifle," is pursued—this "general" might recover himself, and how far he will descend before the tragedy reaches its "bloody period."

It is in *Troilus and Cressida*, however, that this polarity of terms on which order and vertical hierarchy depend is most relentlessly, and most subversively, exploited. Paronomastic play on the "general" and the "particular" is pervasive here, as is the simultaneously grammatical and political sense of "decline" (II.iii.52).[27] Cressida mockingly remarks, of the few "three or four hairs" on Troilus' youthful chin, that "Indeed a tapster's arithmetic may soon bring his particulars therein to a total." Ulysses in the scene of the Greek council speaks of "Severals and generals of grace exact" (I.iii.180). But in one of the most striking and extended of these instances, the play that ensues when Cressida is kissed first by the Greek "general," Agamemnon, and then "in general" by a whole series of Greek particulars, makes clear the potential reversal which lurks within the apparently polar opposites:

> *Agamemnon.* Most dearly welcome to the Greeks, sweet lady.
> 　　　　　　　　　　　　　　　　　　　　　　　　　*[Kisses her.]*
> *Nestor.* Our general doth salute you with a kiss.
> *Ulysses.* Yet is the kindness but particular,
> 　　'Twere better she were kiss'd in general. ...
> 　　　　　　　　　　　　　　　　　　　　　　　　　(IV.v.19–21)

"General" and "particular" here join in the promiscuous exchange, the "general" or "head" being only one "particular" in relation to the particulars which compose the generality. What Bottom seems simply to mangle in his confusion of "general" for "particular" in *A Midsummer Night's Dream* turns out to be a subversion of hierarchy potential within the exchangeability of the very terms of order—if the "general" is both the head *and* the commonality, and the "general" or single head here too "particular." The scene which makes most explicit the fact that women, including Cressida, function in the world of the play as mere objects of exchange itself turns on this exchange and reversibility of terms. If there is "language in her eye" (IV.v.55), as Ulysses remarks after proposing the kissing "in general," it is a language whose speculative instrument is the exchange in which she is only one form of declining.

The larger context for this reversibility and exchange is the play's relentless undermining of the language of order both in discourse and in the body politic, the logic as well as the rhetoric of "degree." It is the challenge to the authority of Agamemnon as "head and general" (I.iii.222) which prompts Ulysses' famous set piece on "degree, priority and place" (I.iii.86), all "in line of order" (88) down the "ladder" (102) from general to particular, and on the decline into which this order and, with it, the power of the "general," have fallen:

> The general's disdain'd
> By him one step below, he by the next,
> The next by him beneath; so every step,
> Exampled by the first pace that is sick
> Of his superior, grows to an envious fever
> Of pale and bloodless emulation.
>
> (I.iii.129–34)

This language dominates the scene in Act II where, as part of the plot to restore "degree" to the Greek camp and authority to Agamemnon, this general is counseled by Ulysses to "pass strangely by" Achilles (III.iii.39–40), in a language of passing or "passage" which this bookish and wordy play elsewhere links subtly with discursive proceeding. This ploy causes the recalcitrant particular, Achilles, to seek the "general" in a reverse of the former suing of the "head and general" to him ("*Agamemnon.* What says Achilles? Would he aught with us? / *Nestor.* Would you, my lord, aught with the general?"; III.iii.57–8). Given the use of "general" and "particular" elsewhere in the play to connote alternatively the common and the individual good, the question might connote both Agamemnon and the collective Greek cause from which this particular is in retreat.

It is, however, the exploding of this system of ordering, in politics as in discourse, which the play relentlessly pursues. Though Agamemnon himself speaks of "all the Greekish heads, which with one voice / Call Agamemnon head and general" (I.iii.221–2), Aeneas, arrived from the Trojan camp in this very scene, finds it impossible to distinguish the "general" from the particulars, as he fails to recognize this "head" ("How may / A stranger to those most imperial looks / Know them from eyes of other mortals?"; I.iii.222–4). Thersites will comment later that Ajax actually takes him for the "general" ("What think you of this man that takes me for the general?"; III.iii.262). And Act II opens with Thersites' variations on the "general" as a "matter" for argument and discourse:

Thersites. Agamemnon, how if he had biles—full, all over, generally?
Ajax. Thersites!
Thersites. And those biles did run—say so—did not the general run then? Were not that a botchy core?

Ajax. Dog!

Thersites. Then would come some matter from him; I see none now.

(II.i.2–9)

The "head and general," supposed to be a source of ordered and reasoned argument, the generation of "matter" for discourse as well as the hierarchical embodiment of order itself, is in this play only a "botchy core," the source of "matter" in an infected body politic.

Antimetabole, or The Counterchange

God send the companion a better prince!

(*Henry IV, Part 2*)

We began with the form of reversal known as "the preposterous." We end this preliminary sketch of Shakespearean exploitation of the terms of rhetoric and discourse with another form of reversal, "antimetabole," in Latin *commutatio*, and Englished by Puttenham as "The Counterchange." This figure makes its appearance in the *Ad Herennium* (IV.39) as the effect produced "When two discrepant thoughts are so expressed by transposition that the latter follows from the former, although contradictory to it"; and in the Renaissance, in Susenbrotus, as that scheme in which a "sentence is inverted by becoming its contrary." Scaliger's treatment draws out the proximity of "antimetabole" (where "a sentence is changed to its contrary") to "antimetathesis," as "When we allow words to change places" and an "opposite meaning may be derived from the transposing of words."[28]

Quintilian gives the most frequently repeated example of the trope— *non ut edam vivo, sed ut vivam, edo* ("I do not live to eat, but eat to live") —as well as expressing the sense that such antithesis can add "a special elegance" to a speech. But further investigation of this antithesis, and a transposition effected such that "the latter follows from the former, although contradictory to it," reveals more at stake in Shakespeare's use of this scheme and trope than mere stylistic elegance or the pleasures of verbal antithesis.

Let us start with some of its Renaissance descriptions. Puttenham, in his discussion of "*Antimetabole*, or the Counterchange" in *The Arte of English Poesie* (1589), begins "Ye have a figure which takes a couple of words to play with in a verse, and by making them to chaunge and shift one into others place they do very prettily exchange and shift the sense, as thus:

> We dwell not here to build us boures,
> And halles for pleasure and good cheare:

> But halles we build for us and ours,
> To dwell in them whilest we are here.

Meaning that we dwell not here to build, but we build to dwel, as we live not to eate, but eate to live,"[29] in what had long become the familiar repetition of Quintilian's example. Antimetabole thus involves the question of what is the means and what the end, and of the subordination reflected in their proper ordering.

Descriptions of this scheme and trope, however, also raise the possibility within it of a reversed relation of ends and means, or even, as in the *Ad Herennium* definition, of a contradictory relation between what follows from, or follows what. John Hoskins, in the *Directions for Speech and Style* (1599), writes that "Antimetabole, or Commutatio, is a sentence inversed or turned back," and, in a way reminiscent of Quintilian's "elegant," remarks on its usefulness as "a sharp and witty figure."[30] But its affinity with reversal—or, even further, with what Scaliger glimpsed as its proximity to "antimetathesis," where not just a turn of phrase but an "opposite meaning" may be derived from "the transposing of words"— involves, at least potentially, something more.

Shakespeare's recourse to antimetabole is striking not just in its remarkable frequency but in its linking precisely with structures of reversal, in logical and in other senses. For antimetabole is never far from the question of logic and the linear ordering of ends and means it depends upon. It is, as Sister Miriam Joseph points out,[31] one of the figures used repeatedly by Shakespeare in relation to logical processes, since it turns a "sentence" around:

> Plainly as heaven sees earth and earth sees heaven.
>
> (*Winter's Tale*, I.ii.315)

> Grief joys, joy grieves, on slender accident.
>
> (*Hamlet*, III.ii.199)

> For 'tis a question left us yet to prove,
> Whether love lead fortune, or else fortune love.
>
> (*Hamlet*, III.ii.202–3)

> And give to dust, that is a little gilt
> More laud than gilt o'erdusted.
>
> (*Troilus and Cressida*, III.iii.178–9)

> The fool doth think he is wise, but the wise man knows himself to be a fool.
>
> (*As You Like It*, V.i.31–2)

Shakespeare's use of and variations on this figure do serve the stylistic purpose of the highly wrought rhetorical turn, the comic or witty riposte, the neatly turned reply: the Duke's "And you, good brother father" to

Elbow's "Bless you, good father friar" in *Measure for Measure* (III.ii.11–12), for instance; Richard III's "There let him sink, and be the seas on him" to Stanley's "Richmond is on the seas" (*Richard III*, IV.iv.462–3); or Apemantus' turning of Timon's "What dost thou think 'tis worth?" into "Not worth my thinking" (*Timon of Athens*, I.i.213–14), to take just a few examples. But, if such uses were to be followed up and into the larger questions of particular plays, they would begin to adumbrate other important relations of reversal—reversals of direction, of cause and effect, of logical and ideological sequence.

Two of the examples above come from *Hamlet*. Another is that moment when, having killed Polonius by mistake, Hamlet summarizes the situation with "I do repent; but heaven hath pleas'd it so / To punish me with this and this with me" (III.iv.173). All of Joseph's instances from this play—though cited merely as verbal or logical reversals without any larger interpretive reference—might take us into that *Hamlet*-in-reverse in which not just elements within the play but perhaps even more radically the play itself turn "tropically" (III.ii.232) into their opposites.[32] They also, however, raise the question of the relation of such verbal instances of reversal to the sense in this play of tragic reciprocity as well as potential reversibility: not just the reversed pairing of Claudius's "Thanks, Rosencrantz and gentle Guildenstern" with Gertrude's immediately inverted "Thanks, Guildenstern and gentle Rosencrantz" (II.ii.33–4), but also the "mighty opposites" ("To punish me with this and this with me") who compose the central pairing of the tragedy itself.

Such instances would also take us much farther afield, into the general question of "turning" involved in such tropic turns. After one scene of verbal sparring in *Twelfth Night*, in which the turn and reversal of antimetabole is exploited in a fashion that turns a meaning around, we have the following reply:

> *Viola / Cesario.* So thou mayst say the king lies by a beggar, if a beggar dwells near him; or the church stands by thy tabor, if thy tabor stand by the church.
> *Feste.* You have said, sir. To see this age! A sentence is but a chev'ril glove to a good wit. How quickly the wrong side may be turn'd outward! (III.i.8–13)

Feste's comment seems apt enough as a commentary upon the uses of rhetoric—and of the newfangledness in which anything may be turned into its reverse. But the sense that things might indeed be capable of reversal has elsewhere in Shakespeare more than the sense of mere verbal turn, something like that "opposite meaning" which might, in Scaliger's phrase, obtain in such a verbal transposition, an "exchange" (Puttenham) which would indeed "shift the sense," including the sense, in antimetabole, of a proper relation or subordination of ends and means.

We need to note in particular, then, that several of the examples Puttenham gives of "*Antimetavole*, or the Counterchange" are political. For instance:

> A wittie fellow in Rome wrate under the Image of Caesar the Dictator these two verses in Latine, which because they are spoken by this figure of Counterchaunge I have turned into a couple of English verses very well keeping the grace of the figure.

> > *Brutus for casting out of kings, was first of Consuls past,*
> > *Caesar for casting Consuls out, is of our kings the last.*

And then again:

> Cato of any Senatour not onely the gravest but also the promptest and wittiest in any civill scoffe, misliking greatly the engrossing of offices in Rome that one man should have many at once, and a great number goe without that were as able men, said thus by Counterchaunge

> > *It seemes your offices are very litle worth,*
> > *Or very few of you worthy of offices.*[33]

One of the specifically political potentialities within this scheme or trope is the possibility not just of that verbal reversal, and subordination, in which, as the *Ad Herennium* puts it, "two discrepant thoughts are so expressed by transposition that the latter follows from the former, although contradictory to it," but also of its social counterpart, a *mundus inversus* or upside-down world, the sense given to it *in potentia* when a somewhat later text such as John Smith's *Mystery of Rhetoric Unveiled* (1657) speaks of it as "*Commutatio, Inversio*, a changing of words by contraries, or a turning of the words in a sentence upside down; derived from [*anti*] against, and [*metaballo*] *inverto*, to invert, or turn upside down." He goes on to speak of it as a "sentence inverst, or turn'd back," and remarks that it is "a form of speech which inverts a sentence by the contrary, and is used frequently to confute by such Inversion," that is, in logical argument.[34]

This aspect of antimetabole provides a perspective on at least one instance of its embedding in a text which has very much to do with political order and its temporary inversion—once again, *Henry IV, Part 2*. The linear movement of this play as it proceeds away from Falstaff and an only temporary prodigality to Law, Kingship, and Father has left more than one reader uneasy. We might note, then, that, within it, the potential alternative of reversal—which the play itself in its linear movement to ending and kingship makes only temporary, glimpsed in order to be cast out—is enacted rhetorically in a particular instance of antimetabole when the Chief Justice, representative of the Law which Falstaff evades and of the authority and state Hal will finally abandon him for, accosts the prodigal "companion" himself:

Chief Justice. Well, God send the Prince a better companion!
Falstaff. God send the companion a better prince! I cannot rid my hands
   of him. (I.ii.199–201)

The same scene, just after this, gives us yet another reversal in Falstaff's "A
pox of this gout! or a gout of this pox!" (I.ii. 243–4).

The possibility of reversing the relation of "companion" and "prince"
—a reversal unenactable as political reality or rewritten history—plays
rhetorically, if only for a moment, with the sense of direction in which the
plot is moving, as with the subordination of means or middles to their
proper ends. Like revenge or succession in *Hamlet*, the teleological
movement of drama is close to ritual, including the ritual of mock rule and
its rerighting. Natalie Davis has argued that these moments of overturning
have in themselves a kind of limited power, in spite of the foreclosure of the
order which rehearses them.[35] What I am suggesting is that tropes of
reversal, of insubordination or inversion, may ironize, precisely by
performing, the very structure of a particular direction and process of
deciding what is means and what is end—and, at least in figure, its
alternative.

Preposterous Conclusions

Our natures would conduct us to most prepost'rous conclusions
                                                          (*Othello*)

There are many more Shakespearean instances of rhetorical play involving
a play on rhetoric and linked through the verbal economy of the pun to
larger questions of interpretation and structure. Robert Weimann, in an
essay on metaphor in Shakespeare, has characterized Elizabethan English
as a language "which combined both a vast range of reference—social and
natural—with a unique freedom of *epiphora*," a "liberty of transference"
or translation.[36] The very term "translation," when it appears in Shakespeare—in the "translation" of Bottom in *A Midsummer Night's Dream*
(III.i.119), the translating of "fortune" into "style" in *As You Like It*
(II.i.19–20), the alienation of property in *Merry Wives*, or the transformation of "rivals" into "servants" in *Timon of Athens* (I.i.71–2)—recalls the
trope of metaphor itself, Englished routinely as "Translation" or "The
Figure of Transport." Beyond the literal resonances of the term, its
transferences would take us, if pursued, into a network of sustained
Shakespearean play on modes of transport, from the space of the stage in
the French–English channel crossings of *Henry V* to the imaging of
Pandarus the go-between as a ferry man or means of transportation in
Troilus and Cressida (I.i.104; III.ii.11).

Many of the instances we have considered are examples where rhetori-cal structures operate as silent interpreters, straight-faced in their struc-tural or their subversive force. *Geminatio* or the Doublet with no space of difference—in a play which generates not just the name but the entire existence of a character called "old Double" out of its own verbal twinnings—subverts through its obsessive repetitions the more official proclamations of progress from father to son. Falstaff's antimetaboles leave the trace of a whole unenacted countermovement within the tele-ology of the history he is cast out by. "Cozen-german" lurks within or sidles alongside the more innocent "German," translating and alienating its more simple reference. So pervasive, indeed, is the subversion of singularity by figure that to focus exclusively on questions of social and political context—as one form of reaction to decades of formalism now proposes to do—or to foreground the "political Shakespeare" without also taking seriously the linguistic one, is, for all its recontextualizing value, not just to work to the detriment of the kind of formal analysis that still so much needs to be done but unnecessarily to short-circuit or foreclose the process of moving from literary text to social text.

In the structures of these tropes, and in the larger discourse and structures of rhetoric, is embedded, I would argue, not only a language we need to be able to recognize in order to be better formalist readers or editors of Shakespeare, but one that would enable us to pose, in different ways from those so far pursued, questions of politics and gender, of social biography and ideology. In the case of the "general" and the "particular," order in discourse is already directly linked with order in the body politic through the existence of a common lexicon. But, in more indirect and subtle ways, even the other rhetorical tropes we have examined in this preliminary fashion point beyond the kind of analysis we have come to associate with a simple formalism. Forms of reproduction at the level of the line bring to mind the prevailing Elizabethan anxiety, of political succession. The genealogical *hysteron proteron* within the Clown's "I was a gentleman born before my father," in *The Winter's Tale*, mirrors not only one of the details known about its creator's biography but a common social practice as well—a son's retroactive creation of his father as a "gentleman" in an act which retrospectively created a line of descent for himself, the way that Shakespeare, like so many others of his social origin, rose suddenly (and not organically or "naturally") to the status of "gentle-man born." At this level, the verbal reversal of *hysteron proteron* repeats a form and social practice of retroactively constructed lineages and pre-posterous descents which would make Slender's "ancestors (that come after him)" something more than a simple comic malapropism, just as Bottom's reversal of "general" and "particular" turns out to be not simply a mistake that reflects on his inability to get anything right. More inciden-tally, it would also reveal the preposterous genealogical reversals of fathers and sons in the critico-biographical musings of Joyce's *Ulysses* to be in this respect among our more perceptive rather than, disparagingly, our more eccentric Shakespeare criticism.[37]

Other rhetorical structures of reversal and exchange—crossings negotiated not just in *The Comedy of Errors* or the verbal turns of *Hamlet* or the *Henriad*—link the language of particular plays to the language of social ordering and political disposition, including constructions of gender.[38] In *Love's Labour's Lost*, play on the logical, discursive and legal language of "in manner and form following" produces a man "following" a woman, a "prepost'rous event" (I.i.205–65) reflected in the play's own preposterous conclusion, in which the gender stereotypes of wordy women and silent men are reversed, and Berowne's punishment is, for a year, to "Visit the speechless sick" (V.ii.851, 888). In the passage of those enigmatic "close dilations" of *Othello's* great temptation scene, the description of Iago's pausing to "contract and purse" his brow, as if he had "shut up" in his "brain / Some horrible conceit" (III.iii.114–15), "Some monster ... / Too hideous to be shown" (107–8), explicitly echoes the play's opening figure of a "purse" which can be opened and closed at will, in the context there too of something secret and concealed.[39] The "close dilations" of Iago's accusations of Desdemona—opening his verbal "show" (III.iii.116) just wide enough to torment the outsider unfamiliar with an inside Iago understands better than he—similarly involve the controlled opening of something secret and concealed, like the births in the "womb of time" he promises "will be deliver'd" (I.iii.383). That minute particular or "thing" he has to "show"—a term elsewhere linked to the opening of a woman's secret place (*Hamlet*, III.ii.144)—involves a hidden and offstage act, inaccessible to vision, which turns her from "A maiden never bold" (I.iii.94) into a whore, and her chaste "chamber" into the chamber of a "bawd" (IV.ii.20). When, then, we reflect that the closely guarded "chamber" of a woman's body was also something described as that "which may be dilated and shut together like a purse,"[40] we might begin to see how attention to the language of rhetorical opening in this play, in the context of the simultaneously fascinated and tormented jealous gaze of an outsider who is also, as husband, both owner and "general," would lead into the powerful gender politics as well as race politics of the tragedy.[41]

Antimetabole and its reversals, finally, are important not just to political contexts of undirectionality—including the line of succession and historical sequence in the *Henriad*—but to gendered questions of subordination and telos. Stephen Greenblatt cites the lines on the reversibility of the "chev'ril glove" from *Twelfth Night* ("How quickly the wrong side may be turn'd outward!") in order to underscore the relevance of this image of inversion to a contemporary anatomical as well as social construction of gender—in which the female was understood to be a reverse or inverted male, with the outside turned in ("Turn outward the woman's, turn

inward, so to speak, and fold double the man's, and you will find them the
same in both in every respect").[42] To note , however, that the rhetorical context of these Shakespearean lines on the "wrong side ... turn'd
outward" is the structure of exchange known as antimetabole would be to
perceive a structure not just of simple reversal but of a specifically
asymmetrical reversal. In the exchange, it remains paramount what stays
subordinate and what principal—just as in the anatomical construction of
gender in which male and female were understood as a reversible inside
and outside it was clear what constituted a "wanton" (III.i.20) turning of
the wrong side outward in the sexual inversion of a woman's acting like a
man.

The study of rhetoric in the plays, with some exceptions and with recent
signs of real change in this regard, has for too long been viewed as the
simple cataloging of tropes and devices or proof of Shakespeare's more
than "small Latine & lesse Greeke." Such proof is helpful as a counter to
what is still frequent resistance to a Shakespeare more versed, as a
schoolboy, in the discourses he exploits than are his modern interpreters.
Clearly the playwright who could use what the rhetoricians called *gradatio*
at the same time as punning on the figure of "degrees" or "stairs" within
it—as he does in *As You Like It*, say—as easily as could the learned Jonson
in the "pretty gradation" of *Bartholomew Fair*, has suffered from the
critical effacing of the linguistic by the simply psychological or by later
versions of the Bard warbling his native woodnotes wild. To propose that
we pay attention to the structural force of rhetorical figures is not in any
way to propose the naive notion of a "master" or single revelatory trope,
even when, as in the case of the "Doublet" in the *Henriad*, the figure
appears so insistently. It is, however, to suggest that the impasse of a now
apparently outworn formalism and a new competing emphasis on politics
and history might be breached by questions which fall in between and
hence remain unasked by both. It is also to propose, as Kenneth Burke
somewhat differently did, the strategic and political resources of a technique that has too often been dismissed as merely formalistic and decorative, displayed prominently in early plays like *Love's Labour's Lost* and
then outgrown. Rhetoric, too long the province of dusty scholarship, has
returned in the different emphases of a more modern, formalistic,
theory. What is needed, however, is not just a return to the old-fashioned
study of tropes, or a "rediscovery of rhetoric" by learning once again to
use the names, or even the substitution of a more historically relevant
lexicon for a predominant New Critical one in describing the movement of
a soliloquy. Rather, we need to pay attention to the exploitation of the
terms and structures of rhetoric, in ways which would lead into the
figurative logic shaping both lines and scenes, and from the plays themselves into the order of discourse and discourse of order they both echo and
turn on.itself.

6

Motivated Rhetorics: Gender, Order, Rule

There are manifold relations of power which permeate, characterise and constitute the social body, and these relations of power cannot themselves be established, consolidated nor implemented without the production, accumulation, circulation and functioning of a discourse.

> (Foucault, "Two Lectures," *Power/Knowledge*)

Let discretion be the greatest and general figure of figures.

> (John Hoskins, *Directions for Speech and Style*, 1599)

I

The return to rhetoric in contemporary criticism and theory has had an important effect on recent studies of the Renaissance, a field which is rapidly becoming the locus for much of current discussion of language and power, of literature and its filiations with other kinds of discourse. Studies like Frank Whigham's *Ambition and Privilege*, an examination of the "social tropes of Elizabethan courtesy theory," point not only to the new social mobility which fostered the tremendous popularity of such theory, and the dissemination of new guides for the ambitious young man, but also to rhetoric itself as an instrument of civil order, crucial to the repair of civilization after the Fall. This is the focus with which Thomas Wilson's influential *Arte of Rhetorique* (1553) begins:

> Therefore even nowe [after the Fall] when man was thus paste all hope of amendemente, God ... stirred up his faythfull and elect, to perswade with reason, all men to societye. And gave his appoynted ministers knowledge bothe to se the natures of men, and also graunted them the gift of utteraunce .... And therefore, where as Menn lyved Brutyshlye in open feldes, ... these appoynted of God called them together by utteraunce of speache.[1]

The Ciceronian idea of the orator as forming civil society informs this and countless other passages linking order with the "utteraunce of speache." Yet the "presumptive link between rhetoric and the current God-given

order of things," exemplified in such a passage, "snaps," Whigham writes,
"when the Wilsons of the age, with fully conservative self-consciousness,
convert the tools of rule, of domination and self-determination, into a
commodity packaged for the open market of the literate."

Whigham's interest is primarily in the material and social causes of this
change and its reflection in the new modes of regulating behavior. My own
reason for beginning with a passage like this one from the "Wilsons of the
age" would take a very different direction, not immediately toward the
contradictions within an order which had to be perceived as "natural" in
order to be efficacious—though we will return to this question of the
naturalization of the constructed—but rather, first, to the motivated
discourse of rhetoric itself and the ordering it both stages and reflects.
Hierarchies of gender, as my subtitle makes clear, are central to this
problematics of ordering. But, throughout, the category of gender—of
unruly women and unruly tropes, and of the gendering of construction in
discourse—will be set against the background of the larger problem of
Ordo and its constructions, one in which questions of rule, of social
distinction, and of hierarchy are integral to the regulation of language.

It is not necessary to read far in the handbooks of rhetoric or discussions
of language in the English Renaissance—or, though it is beyond the scope
of this study, in other periods—to perceive an intimate and ideologically
motivated link between the need to control the movement of tropes and
contemporary exigencies of social control, including, though not limited
to, the governance of the household or *oikos*. Dudley Fenner's treatise
on *The Artes of Logike and Rethorike* (1584), which repeatedly
emphasizes order or "methode" in discourse, is illustrated by a work on
"methode in the government of the familie," which begins with "The
order of an householde called *Oiconomia*."[2] The model of the economic in
a larger sense is a persistent motif of descriptions of tropes themselves,
from Puttenham's naming of "SILLEPISIS, or the Double supply," to Dr
Johnson's famous characterization of metaphor as giving two for the price
of one.

The figure of *oikonomia* and social control not only governs the
ordering of tropes at many points in these discussions of rhetoric, however; it also yields a set of terms which have a place in both the rhetorical
and the political lexicon. "Disposition," for example, with its sense
of administration and governance as well as the orderly placement of
words. "Partition," with its links both to partition walls in real property
and to the divisions of discourse. And "joining," a term which has as much
to do with the putting together of words in sentences as it has with the
bonds of society, including the joining of matrimony; so that when
Hamlet, for instance, complains of the time that is "out of joint," or rails
against the incestuous "joining" or "union" of his mother's marriage, he
invokes a whole rhetoric of the copula and of copulation in discourse

which becomes the counterpart of the disgust he evinces for that "union," or for "incestuous sheets." To these we will return.

Actual definitions of figures, schemes, and tropes, moreover—in contexts which appear to be governed by the simple motivation of the example or by the desire to explicate rhetorical matters to an audience in need of instruction—frequently begin instead to turn into illustrations of the social order the figure would rhetorically reflect. *Distributio*—the rhetorical scheme by which a statement "may be distributed into parts"—is illustrated by the hierarchical distribution of the body politic: king, nobles, bishops, subjects, with the last category further subdivided into husbands, wives, servants—the divisions, in other words, of gender and social distinction within the "order of household" as well.[3] *Gradatio* or *concatenatio*—the "stepping" figure whose names already link it both to a "ladder" and to a "chain"—is the rhetorical trope of "climbing" illustrated by a political progression of "degrees" ("You could not injoy your goodnes without government, nor government without a magistrate, nor a magistrate without obedience").[4] Passages like this last, in which rhetorical gradation also becomes, with the simple addition of an "ergo," a form of logical progression, demonstrate how easily a figure adapted to rhetorical sequence and marshaling could become part of a series of things which "follow" from one another in a "chain," including the "chain" of government, or of Being.

The counterpart of this mutually reflective relation between particular tropes and the orders they exemplify is the social and political anxiety which permeates the discussion of certain others. Amphibology, for instance, or, as Steven Mullaney has suggestively called it, the trope of treason, carries in its ambiguous doubleness a more than linguistic threat. Defined by Abraham Fraunce as "When the sentence may bee turned both the wayes, so that a man shall be uncertayne what waye to take," in its darker form it is something like the *peripeteia* of signification which meets Oedipus or Macbeth at crossroads they did not even suspect.[5] It threatens the possibility of control over the meaning of words; and its social import emerges in a passage from Puttenham's *Arte of English Poesie* which links its ambiguous doubleness to "insurrections" within the state:

> [Such ambiguity] carryeth generally such force in the heades of fonde people, that by the comfort of those blind prophecies many insurrections and rebellions have bene stirred up in this Realme, as that of *Iacke Straw*, and *Iacke Cade* in *Richard* the seconds time, and in our time by a seditious fellow in Norffolke calling himselfe Captaine Ket and others in other places of the Realme led altogether by certaine propheticall rymes, which might be construed two or three wayes as well as to that one whereunto the revelles applied it. (p.267)

In a way that might seem extreme from the standpoint of a modernist credo which posits the separation of politics from poetics, this social consequence of amphibology leads to Puttenham's caution to the poet or speechmaker to "therefore avoyde all such ambiguous speaches unlesse it be when he doth it for the nonce and for some purpose" (p. 267). The end of the discussion of this figure as one of the "vices" in speech is followed by the entire concluding discussion, in the *Arte of English Poesie*, of the concept of decorum, which links order in language to social orders and hierarchies of distinction.

Handbooks of rhetoric and poetry like Peacham's and Puttenham's are not the only textual locus in which the proper discipline or placement of words is intimately allied with questions of social regulation. Thomas Wilson's other text, *The Rule of Reason* (1551), the widely reprinted first manual of logic in English, is very much concerned with "what follows," with the chain of "consequence" in a societal as well as a logical sense, and with a particular sequence of reasoning well "grounded" in the traditional "places" of invention. It is this grounding in the "places," along with the avoidance of "doubtfulness" or the slippery doubleness of words, which provides the ground for "the rule of reason" itself and which—unlike the "transports," say, of a trope like metaphor—gives a firm foundation to argument, leading to proper logical conclusions and consequences.[6]

Wilson's particular concern in *The Rule of Reason* is to control the meanings of words, including the kind of paronomasia in which a word like "nobles," in ways unsettling in more than purely linguistic terms, could signify "not onely the peeres of a Realme" but also those "nobles in a mans purse" (p. 24), could verbally negotiate the distance, that is to say, between an aristocratic order and a new, more mobile monetary one. "Double meanyng," for Wilson, is inseparable from "errour" and "fraude" (p. 24), and the possibility that words may be "twoo waies taken" leads at one point in the text to the marginal lament that "The mistes of woordes have blinded all our blisse" (p. 163). Yet what might seem a purely theological or epistemological plangency—a doubleness in words which cuts against the optimism that a Ciceronian civility can indeed repair the ravages of the Fall—is also quite clearly a more socially motivated lament. (One of his examples is the double meaning which might be used to provide occasion for non-logical conclusions by "the unlearned, the wicked, or the sedicious Libertine.") The "doubtfulnesse" of words—their capability of being "twoo waies taken"—not only undermines reason's "rule" but may lead to specious and politically dangerous "consequentes" based on the transport of words outside an acceptable range of regulated meaning.

Such a link between order in the body politic and order in words is conveyed strikingly in the *Rule's* warning against "doubtful woordes" (p. 64) in certain kinds of syllogism, and specifically one where a word like "freedom" is metaphorically translated into a dangerous political conse-quence—the translation of the term in its New Testament sense ("Al that beleve the Gospel truely, are free") into the more subversive meaning the monitory marginal gloss calls "Anabaptistes reason," that "servauntes" or "apprentices" should be no more. A readily transported term, like "freedom," opens up the straitened progression of the syllogism to a multiplicity ("fower several termes") that would be politically radical in its consequence, and that must be denied by the very principles of logic on which this particular "rule of reason" depends. "Freedom" in the theological sense ("Whom the Sonne hath made free ...") must not be transported or metaphorically translated into "freedom" in the political sense. The errancy of a figure like metaphor is that it wanders, dangerously, from the fixed meanings that can be marshaled into the march of logical "consequence." As Wilson's example itself makes clear, one reason for the need to control such words is the tension between civil power (dependent on the harnessing of language to certain ends) and something —like theological "freedom"—potentially outside its control. Passages such as this one suggest what was at stake in the richly contradictory Pauline texts which both buttressed the order of the civil state and were, at least potentially, radically subversive of it.

Wilson's discussion of the threatening "doubtfulnesse" of words becomes explicitly one of amphibology, or Puttenham's figure of sedition, under the general heading of "Ambiguitie" (p.164), which again includes a political instance and which refers to the particular case of "partes diverslie poincted"—that is, the ambiguity resulting from diverse punctuation or "pointing," differently joining the words of a discourse and, like ambiguous syntax, treacherously subverting the order on which reason depends. His principal example of this subversion is Merrygreek's mispunctuated or "diverslie poincted" verse from Udall's *Ralph Roister Doister*, which turns a compliment into its opposite, an "example of soche doubtful writing, whiche by reason of poincting maie have double sense, and contrarie meaning" (p. 166). A different punctuation upsets the syntactical relations between words and leads to a different message: if "poinctes" give each word its meaning according to its syntactic place, then a discourse with its "partes diverslie poincted" radically disrupts the relations of those parts, improperly joining those which should not be joined.[7] Grammatical relations reflect social ones—in a tradition which reaches far back into the assimilation of cases themselves to the relations of order and rectitude.[8] Amphibology as ambiguous "pointing" offers a potentially subversive—and threatening—glimpse of what would happen if those divisions, and hence those relations, underwent a shift. It suggests the possibility of an unsettling lack of control over language, as if the very instrument of civil order—in Wilson's strategic formulation of Cicero— were open to radical inversion, in the sense of a treachery potential within language itself, or in the subversive uses to which it could be put.

In the light of the glimpses of social unrest, military disaster, and political sedition which greet the reader on page after page of *The Rule of*

Reason, it is not surprising to find strictures within it against the "doubtful-nesse" of words standing beside passages on the proper duties and obedience of a wife and the duties owed to political rulers. The choices of example, as well as of topics, are strikingly overdetermined. One of the words taken through all the "places" is the word "magistrate," in a section which makes repeated reference to the obedience due to a civil ruler or king. "A king declared by the places of Logique" (pp. 135 ff.) has for its "auctoritie" the familiar Pauline passages invoked to buttress civil power ("The xiii to the Romaines, let every soulle be subiecte to the powers. i.Peter ii. Be subiecte to the king"; p. 137). It goes on—in a demonstration in which we need to be reminded of Wilson's own religion and politics, his exile under Mary's Catholic reign, and his restoration under Burghley during Elizabeth's Protestant one—to draw two other terms, "priest" and "wife," similarly through all the "places" in order to prove "by Logique" that it is "lawfull for a Prieste to marie a wife."[9]

The way in which the discipline of logic, of following, and of similitude is described within this text raises right from the outset a similar question about the nature and motivation of its control.[10] Wilson prefaces the entire text on reason's "Rule" by explaining to English-speaking readers the meaning of "Logique" itself, beginning with a curious story whose point is by no means clear, though it starts from the explanation that "Logique" is simply the Greek term for the English "reason":

> And therefore, he that speaketh Logique, speaketh nothing els but reason, yea, there be many Greke woordes, made Englishe, whereof all men have not the meanyng. As for example, a young man of Cambridge, sittyng in his chaumbre, with ii or three of his felowes, and happenyng to fall in talke of a woman, then lately maried to a scholer, when every one had saied his phantasie as well of the man, as of the woman, comparyng the qualities of the one, with the propreties of the other, saiyng their pleasure every one of them, of her beautie and her bodie, *pro et contra*: this young manne chopping in with his reason, saied: I cannot tell my maisters, but surely I for my part, take her for a catholike woman, let other men thinke what thei list. When his felowes heard this drie report, thei laughed apace, as knowyng by their learnyng, what this woorde ment. For [Catholike] beeyng a Greek woorde, signifieth nothing in Englishe, but universal or commune. And we cal in Englishe a common woman, an evil woman of her bodie. Therefore, though termes be darke, and the meanyng unknowen to many, yet the trueth enclosed, is alwaies one, and geven us of God, use what termes we list: This then perceived, that Logique is the rule of reason, I thinke it as needlesse, to aske whether it be, or no, as to aske, whether any man can speake, or no.

What is being related in this anecdote is a variety of tendentious joke—most immediately at the expense of the ignorant "young man," unaware of the Greek behind the English "Catholike" and unwittingly opening it up to a meaning more obscene. But the example itself is principally of a woman—of talk of a woman, and at a woman's expense. And the story of young men of Cambridge, "saiyng their pleasure every one of them, of her beautie and her bodie, *pro et contra*," is given curiously as an *exemplum* or illustration ("As for example") of the Greek behind many English words, including the Greek "Logique" from *logos*. That it begins, however, to turn into the very digression or discursive "wandering" that Wilson will later inveigh against as contrary to the "Rule of Reason" is made clear by the abruptness and strange sense of non sequitur in the "Therefore" with which it moves back from the "common woman, an evil woman of her bodie" to a concluding "though termes be darke, and the meanyng unknowen to many, yet the trueth enclosed, is alwaies one." In a text preoccupied with proper linear "consequentes" and with proper progression and "joining," Wilson wanders into the anecdote of a "common woman" on the slim thread of the link between it and those ignorant of the Greek origin of "Reason" or "Logique" itself. We might ask, as would be asked of a trope like metaphor by someone approaching it from a more logical perspective as a shortened form of analogy or simile, what, precisely, is the point of resemblance here?

The Rule of Reason and texts like it link the control of reason, logic, *logos* itself, to the disciplining of the "errour" and potentially subversive "doubtfulnesse" of words, and both to the maintainance of order in language and in society. This control is reflected as well in—though, as these examples show, by no means restricted to—the question of the proper ordering of a "householde" (of the "Master of an householde" in relation to the "wife" as well as "servant" on the last rungs of the hierarchical ladder of "Similitudes"). It is to this, to the specific question of gender and of woman, that we now turn.

II

> Chuse a fixt eye, for wandering lookes display
> A wavering disposition. . . .
> Chuse thee no gadder, for a wife should bee
> In this respect (I'm sure) like to a Snaile,
> Who (hous-wifelike) still in her house we see.

(*The Description of a Good Wife; or, A Rare One Amongst Women* 1619)

> My exion is entered, and my case so openly known to the world.

(Mistress Quickly, *Henry IV, Part 2*)

What, we might ask, do women have to do with rhetoric? The answer—in countless Renaissance conduct books and treatises—is that they should have nothing whatsoever to do with it, that rhetoric is one thing that women should not be taught, even in the view of male authors who would leave other branches of study open to them. Leonardo Bruni, for example, in *De Studiis et Litteris*, a widely disseminated humanist text, though he recommends the opening of the study of the liberal arts to both sexes, adds a prohibition against the introduction of young girls specifically to rhetoric, which "lies absolutely outside the province of women."[11]

The reason behind this prohibition—and the sense that rhetoric was outside the sphere or proper place of women—had to do with the nature of rhetoric as specifically *public* speaking, the humanist training of young men to argue persuasively in public, including in the courts, a link of rhetoric with judicial cases (*causae*) which can, of course, be traced back to Cicero and Quintilian. It was the public nature of rhetoric—taking women outside their proper "province" or place—which disqualified them, in a long tradition dating from as ancient an authority as Aristotle's strictures that women were to be not only silent but identified with the property of the home and with the private sphere, with a private rather than a common place. (At least one Renaissance poet also linked this private place, in the *Politics*, with the Aristotelian distinction, in the *Rhetoric*, between *koinoi topoi* or "common places" and *idioi topoi* or "private places," and their sexual counterparts.)[12]

There were other strategic reasons too, including a sense of the weapon rhetoric would provide in the arsenal of scolding wives. Juvenal's Sixth Satire, that most influential of classical misogynist tracts, had already warned, "Let not the Wife of thy Bosom, that lies by thee, know any thing of the Art of Logick, how to come over you smartly with a brisk *Enthymeme*." And Puttenham, in his discussion of "the vices and deformities in speach and writing" which should generally be avoided, counsels that the niceties of rhetoric and the use of devices should not be pressed upon "the pretie Poesies and devises of Ladies, and Gentlewomen makers, whom we would not have too precise Poets least with their shrewd wits, when they were maried they might become a little too phantasticall wives" (p. 256).

But the clear link that would keep women from learning rhetoric as specifically public speech is the long association in which a "public woman," and especially one who spoke in public, could only be called a whore. The standard misogynist texts in the Renaissance have recourse to the figure of the roaming or "moovable" harlot of Proverbs 7, who is "full of babling and loude woordes, and ready to dally: whose feete can not abyde in her house, nowe shee is without, nowe in the streete, and lyeth in waite at every corner." Barnabe Rich's *My Ladies Looking Glasse* (1616), for instance, cites the fact that "Salomon thinketh that a good woman should be a home housewife ... shee must looke to her children, her servants and family: but the pathes of a harlot (he saith) are mooveable, for now shee is in the house, now in the streetes, now she lieth in waite in every corner, she is still gadding from place to place ... shee is ever more wandring: her feete are wandring, her eies are wandring, her wits are wandring"; and, in addition to her "errour" or "wandering," she is "full of words." The image of women as "shamefast," as "tortoises," who should be "wedded to their Houses" and not "gossippe it abroad" (*Asylum Veneris*, 1616) or be "public" in another sense, joins the Aristotelian tradition which, centuries later, would still be behind Rousseau's rejection of Plato's proposal for female guardians as "cette promiscuité civile." (Indeed, as recent a public woman as Luce Irigaray is still confronting it when in *This Sex Which is Not One* she evokes the familiar image, from "Solomon," of the woman in the street: "how can one be a 'woman' and be 'in the street'? That is, be out in public, be public—and still more tellingly, do so in the mode of speech. We come back to the question of family: why isn't the woman, who belongs to the private sphere, always locked up in the house? As soon as a woman leaves the house, someone starts to wonder, someone asks her: how can you be a woman and be out here at the same time?")[13]

Behind this concern for woman's "wandering," errancy, or "mooveable" ways lie anxieties about female sexuality,[14] but, even more specifically, about its relation to property, to the threat of the violation of this private place if it were to become a "common" place. A later text sums up a whole tradition of the link between property and a woman's private place, in its judgment against a man who commits adultery with his neighbor's wife, a sin

> very heinous in respect of our Neighbour, whose hedge we break down, and whose enclosure we lay wast; whilst we do not only purloyn and defile and dishonour that which is his most proper possession ... but we invade and incroach upon his Inheritance also by making our *Bastard* his *Heir*.[15]

Passages such as this one, or Barnabe Rich's remark in another text that "a womans honestie is pent up in a litle roome, it is still confined, but from her girdle downewards," make it clear that a woman must stay within a private place—the home—because her body contains a private place, a place or "enclosure" that adultery would break into, and make a "common" rather than a particular property. The very language translates the older logic of the *hortus conclusus*—and its mystical extensions in the body of the Virgin Mother who contains that by which she is contained—into the ideology and custom of *Oiconomia* or the emerging "householde," the privatization of the nascent bourgeois family which Lawrence Stone and others have described.[16] We might think, in reading such a passage, of

Desdemona's "chamber," kept by Emilia the "bawd" in *Othello*, a play in which a woman's private "thing" (or *res*, in a longstanding linguistic and sexual double entendre) is made public, shown forth to the view or revealed.

The wandering woman—out of her place, become a "harlot," and "full of words"—must be kept in her place, like her counterpart within the body, the wandering womb, that "mother" which is curiously "mooveable" and which in the language of contemporary gynecology causes problems and inversion when it strays from its proper place:

> The womb is frequently subject to suffocation. Suffocation is the name doctors give to a constriction of the vital breathing caused by a defect in the womb. This hinders the woman's breathing. It happens whenever the womb moves from its *proper place*.[17]

The "mother" or womb within the female body is subject to disorders to be avoided within the larger order of the household and the body politic, a disorder figured in *King Lear* as an inversion within a patriarchal body threateningly usurped and feminized ("O! how this mother swells up toward my heart! / Hysterica passio—down, thou climbing sorrow, / Thy element's below").[18]

The relation between a potentially uncontrollable female sexuality, a woman speaking in public, and a woman usurping her proper place is made even more explicit, finally, in the complex of misogynist double entendres surrounding the figure of the woman who takes upon herself the traditional male role of the public orator pleading a "cause" or "case" in court. Barnabe Rich's "a womans honestie is pent up in a litle room" evokes that female "case" or "casket" which, by a husband's property right, is to remain closed to those who might "break in and steal." But the loud and "babling" complaint of Shakespeare's Mistress Quickly that her legal "action" is "entered" and her "case so openly known to the world" (*Henry IV, Part 2*, II.i.30–1) not only opens what should be silent and closed but activates a long-standing link between legal case and female "case" which makes clear what was involved for a woman in pleading a "cause." So pervasive is the complex of connections between a privatized female sexuality as a sign and seal of property and the Latinate history of *casus* and *causa* that it lurks in a much darker context behind Othello's brooding "It is the *cause*, it is the *cause*, my soul" as he assumes the need for retribution against an adulterous making common of Desdemona's "chamber"—a resonance which would explain why, immediately following, he says it is a "cause" he cannot "name" to the "chaste stars" (*Othello*, V.ii.1–2). *Othello*, we recall, makes a good deal of women's garrulity or "blabbing," as it does of a harlotry which would violate a private enclosure. And the execution of a husband's judgment in Desdemona's death, in a striking departure from the play's source, is effected by stifling, or closing her "mouth."[19]

From at least Juvenal's Sixth Satire (which both describes a talkative wife who "litigates"—*litigat*—in bed and also complains that there is scarcely a trial at bar—*causa*—in which a woman is not in some way engaged) to the Renaissance, the link between the woman who is "full of words" and the woman openly pleading her "case" or "cause" persists. An antifeminist text such as *A Curtaine Lecture* in 1637 quotes liberally from Juvenal on the litigiousness of loud women proclaiming their "cause" in court, and cites his example of Manilia, the "bold-fac't Roman Matron" who "blusht not in open Court to bee her owne Advocate, and pleade her owne causes in publike assemblies." Between them, chronologically, Jean Lefevre's medieval French translation of the *Liber Lamentationum Matheoluli*—a virulently misogynist text—relates the story of "Carfania," a Roman matron who demonstrated her control of oratory by arguing cases in court, an example which combines both the antifeminist motif of uncontrolled female garrulity and the sexual one of the woman whose "case" is "so openly known to the world" because she not only pleaded in public but finally showed her own case or "cul" openly in court (II.183–6).[20]

*

They that dally nicely with words may quickly make them wanton.

(*Twelfth Night*)

The extravagantly "mooveable" and talkative harlot—with the extreme example of the woman publicly arguing her "case"—provide the influential monitory antitypes to the shamefast and silent woman, modestly observing her proper place and moving within a circumscribed sphere. What we need to consider, however, are not just the reasons behind the exclusion of women from rhetoric as the art of persuasion or public speech—and the anxieties about "wandering" women which inform its transformation into easy misogynist double entendre—but also the curious appearance of the female in discussions of tropes. For women, excluded from the study of rhetoric, figure curiously and prominently in Renaissance English discussions of rhetoric, and particularly in relation to questions of decorum and control.

We might begin with a translation of the famous description of metaphor from Cicero's *De oratore*. Cicero describes the trope of metaphor (*translatio verbi*, or the very trope of movement from place to place) as a figure whose movements must be carefully monitored: "the metaphor ought to have an apologetic air (*verecunda debet esse translatio*), so as to look as if it had entered a place that does not belong to it with a proper introduction ... not forced its way in" (*De oratore*, III.xli.165). Fenner's *Artes of Logike and Rethorike* opens by translating the famous Ciceronian passage with an addition which weights it more suggestively in the direction of an actual gendering:

The fine maner of wordes is a garnishing of speech, whereby one word is.
drawen from his first proper signification to another. . . . This changing
of words was first found out by necessitie, for the want of words, [and]
afterward confirmed by delight, because such wordes are pleasaunt and
gracious too the ear. // Therefore this change of signification must bee
shamefest, and as it were *maydenly*, that it may seeme rather to be led by
the hand to another signification, then to be driven by force unto the
same. Yet sometimes this fine manner of speech swerveth from this
perfection, and then it is . . .

the abuse of this fine speech, called KATACHRESIS.

Metaphor, here, is subject to a decorum of movement, "led by the hand"
to another place. "Katachresis," distinguished as *abusio* from the "shamefest" and "maydenly" way that metaphor should by contrast behave, is,
like Shakespeare's, another unruly and undomesticated "Kate."[21] One of
the many senses of "Katachresis" as "the figure of abuse" is that it is a
metaphor which is too "far-fetched," "phantasticall" or extreme.

We might take another instance in which the insertion of "women" into
what might be expected to be simply a neutral discussion of rhetorical
tropes evokes an already stereotypical association between women and
something "fetched from afar." This is the example of "METALEPIS, or the
FARREFET" from Puttenham:

as when we had rather fetch a word a great way off then to use one nerer
hand to express the matter aswel and plainer. And it seemeth the
deviser of this figure, had a desire to please women rather then men: for
we use to say by manner of Proverbe: things farrefet and deare bought
are good for Ladies: so in this manner of speach we use it, leaping over
the heads of a great many words, we take one that is furdest off, to utter
our matter by: as *Medea* cursing hir first acquaintaince with prince
Iason, who had very unkindly forsaken her, said:

> *Woe worth the mountaine that the maste bare*
> *Which was the first causer of all my care.*

Where she might aswell have said, woe worth our first meeting, or woe
worth the time that *Iason* arrived with his ship at my fathers cittie in
Colchos, when he tooke me away with him, and not so far off as to curse
the mountaine that bare the pinetree, that made the mast, that bare the
sailes, that the ship sailed with, which caried her away.

(*The Arte of English Poesie*, p. 193)

Why, we might ask here, does a description of a trope lead to a house-that-
Jack-built of female anger, to a woman who is "caried . . . away" in
another hardly buried sense, a woman who takes things as "far" as Medea
does, and whose curse is this extreme and "far-fetched"? What does

metalepis have to do with the extremes of female anger? Why is the example chosen the example of Medea's cursing of Jason? And why does it, in the midst of the discussion of a rhetorical trope, begin to sound like another contemporary text, devoted not to rhetoric or language but to other things, including women, whose complete title is *The haven of Pleasure . . . Profitable and delightfull to all, hurtfull and displeasing to none, except it bee to such peevish dames as do either foolishlie reject, or carelesly neglect the dutie of chast matrones* (1596) and whose last chapter is headed "Of the Nature, conditions, and manners of Women, and why that sex when they are angrie, are more fierce then Men, conceive anger sooner, chide more unmeasureablie, and are sooner overcome with any affection then men."

Puttenham illustrates another trope by invoking, first, a familiar *topos* of female speech in his description of *occupatio*—"PARALEPSIS or the PASSAGER" (p. 239):

> It is also very many times used for a good pollicie in pleading or perswasion to make wise as we set but light of the matter, and that therefore we do passe it over slightly when in deede we do then intend most effectually and despightfully if it be invective to remember it: it is also when we will not seeme to know a thing, and yet we know it well inough, and may be likened to the maner of women, who as the common saying is, will say nay and take it.

> > *I hold my peace and will not say for shame,*
> > *The much untruth of that uncivill dame,*
> > *For if I should her coullours kindly blaze,*
> > *It would so make the chast eares amaze. & c.*

Occupatio itself as a name of a trope already easily combined with the sexual double entendres surrounding "occupy" in Renaissance English—the sense of "occupant" as prostitute and, from Ovid's *Fasti*, of "occupy" as having to do sexually with a woman. Like "case," it also easily linked bawdy or misogynist with linguistic and rhetorical terms, as in Mercutio's description of his need to cut short his "tale large," "against the hair," and "occupy the argument no longer" (*Romeo and Juliet*, II.iv.95–9). Puttenham's verse example here of a trope or scheme in which (to cite Susenbrotus) "we say in passing what we deny we want to say at all" involves the other orifice, the gossiping "maner of women" who, whatever they protest, never refrain from speaking what they want heard. And its elliptical invocation of the misogynist topos of the garrulity of women reemerges in the text's concluding discussion of the central notion of "decorum" in speech, where a principal example of "undecencie" is an orator who spoke with so "small and shrill a voice" that his audience, the emperor Anthonine, made him "shorten his tale," saying that he was by his voice not a "man" but a "woman." A second is the example of a eunuch philosopher, "a little too talkative and full of words," who was therefore rebuked as being like "all women" (Book III, pp. 271–2).

A woman who talks too much, obscenely, or out of place, is also instanced in Puttenham in the "undecency of the word" not so much in itself as in the mouth of a particular speaker:

> Sometime the undecency ariseth by the indignitie of the word in respect of the speaker himselfe, as whan a daughter of Fraunce and next heyre generall to the crowne (if the law *Salique* had not barred her) being set in a great chaufe by some harde words giuen her by another prince of the bloud, said in her anger, thou durst not haue said thus much to me if God had given me a paire of, etc. and told all out, meaning if God had made her a man and not a woman she had bene king of Fraunce. The word became not the greatness of her person, and much lesse her sex, whose chiefe vertue is shamefastnesse, which the Latines call *Verecundia*, that is a naturall feare to be noted with any impudicitie: so as when they heare or see any thing tending that way they commonly blush, and is a part greatly praised in all women. (p. 274)

It is intriguing, to say the least, that the inappropriate speaker here is not only a female speaker but one who, but for the French Salic law that bars female heirs from the succession, might be monarch, and whose indecent word is one which names precisely what removes her right to rule. Puttenham's examples, like his descriptions of tropes, are so frequently overdetermined in this way that it would be tempting, in relation to the prohibition here against a particular speech in the mouth of a woman, exemplified by a story whose context is a specific legal prohibition against women, to turn back to that curious example given in his discussion "Of Proportion in Figure" in Book II. For there, the explicitly phallic or "pointed" graphic shape-poem or "proportion" called the "Pyramis" in Greek and the Obelisk or "*Obeliscus*" in Latin is illustrated by "two examples" which both praise Queen Elizabeth—female monarch of a realm with no such Salic law—and yet remind her graphically of what is "above" her, the second of the two explicitly placing "God" at its point and moving "downward" to that "madam" who derives her "maiestie" from "Him" (p. 109), placed under God in the most obvious of all graphic figures both of hierarchy and of its male emblem.

*

Women, then, are figured in discussions of rhetoric in ways which evoke links with the "far-fetched," with uncontrollable and even indecent garrulity or speaking out, and with the "mooveable" transportability of certain tropes. These associations join the more direct association of women with cosmetics, clothing, and decoration, and hence with tropes seen as secondary to the literal or "proper," and relating to it as "clothing," "cosmetic," or "ornament poeticall."[22] What is even more important, however, than the linking of women with the deceit, doubleness, or movable nature of tropes, and the social as well as sexual implications of such transportability—a link which after the Renaissance would appear in novelistic as well as political preoccupations with vagrant women, harlots, and other "wandering" vagabonds—is the question of the position of women in relation to the ordering of discourse itself. This relation is one we might approach first through tropes which involve reversal, the upsetting or exchange of proper sequential order, of grammatical and logical line.

The trope of "antimetabole" or Puttenham's "The Counterchange," for example, is described in the Renaissance by Susenbrotus as that scheme in which a "sentence is inverted by becoming its contrary."[23] Its later description in John Smith's *Mystery of Rhetoric Unveiled* (1657), under its other name of "*Inversio*"—"from [*anti*] against, and [*metaballo*] *inverto*, to invert, or turn upside down"—links its form of reversal to the possibility of a *mundus inversus* or social overturning as well. Besides Quintilian's "I do not live to eat, but eat to live," the other example of it is taken from Scripture, from the Pauline gloss on the sequence of Creation in Genesis: "For the man is not of the woman; but the woman of the man: neither was the man created for the woman; but the woman for the man" (1 Corinthians 11). The instance from 1 Corinthians, however, clearly goes beyond mere rhetorical turn or inversion to a question of subordination in which the reverse cannot and must not be true, and in which the ordering within the trope is determined by a vertical as well as a sequential hierarchy: "the head of the woman is the man" (1 Corinthians 11:3).

What motivates this particular example is the order and hierarchy elsewhere involved in the sense of change of place in *hyperbaton*, which always borders on a sense of "Trespass" (Puttenham), of a disorder and reversal which would be not just witty inversion but abuse. Antimetabole itself—the very possibility of a reversal in language which elsewhere in the culture would be interdicted—might be seen as introducing, or at least leaving open the possibility of, the interdicted reversal, of "the man for the woman," for instance. This may be one of the reasons why the question of control or of decorum as a category not just of style but of social, political, and familial ordering, looms so large in all such discussions of rhetoric and speech. Women out of their place—in tropes subject to decorum and to warnings against "Excesse" or abuse—are part of a potentially dangerous invasion of linguistic into social possibility, a fact we might keep in mind when, for example, we come to Book IV of Milton's *Paradise Lost*, complexly traversed as it is by this and other Pauline texts, and hear behind the famous figure of the subordination of female to male—"He for God only, she for God in him" (IV.299)—the authorizing text and familiar instance of antimetabole from 1 Corinthians.[24]

Such a relation between order in discourse and the proper sequential as well as hierarchical order of male and female also inhabits discussions of other tropes. Peacham writes that "Catacosmesis, in Latine ORDO," is "a meete placing of words among themselves, whereof there be two kinds, the one when the worthiest word is set first, which order is naturall, as when we say: God and man, men and women, Sun and Moone, life and death. And also when that is first told that was first done, which is necessary and seemly. The other kind of order is artificiall, and in forme contrarie to this, as when the worthiest or weightiest word is set last: for the cause of amplifying, which the Rhetoricians call Incrementum." Typically, he adds the "Caution" that "the grace and comelinesse of this order is often diminished, and much blemished through want of discretion, or by rashness of the speaker, putting the lesse worthie, before the more worthy, contrarie to civil observation and comelinesse as to say, it pleased the Counsell and the King to make this law: my Mistresse and my Master have them commended to your worship." Richard Sherry's *Treatise of Schemes and Tropes* similarly emphasizes the "naturall order" in discourse, "as to saye: men & women, daye and night, easte and weste, rather than backwards."[25] To put "Mistress" before "Master," or "women" before "men," like placing "Counsell" before "King," is here to trespass against an order not constructed but "naturall."

Peacham goes on to list what transgress this "naturall" order:

> To naturall and seemely order are repugnant Hyperbaton, and all his kindes, as Anastrope, Hysterologia, Hysteron Proteron, Tmesis, Hypallage, and Synchisis: all which are faultes of speech consisting of disorder and confusion.

One of these "Faults opposed to naturall & necessary order," as his marginal gloss puts it, is Hypallage, that "figure of Exchange" which Puttenham translates as "the Changeling"—"using a wrong construction for a right, and an absurd for a sensible, by manner of exchange"—a disorder "whereby the sense is quite perverted and made very absurd." Another is "Hysteron Proteron," or "the Preposterous," which Smith's *Mysteries* later noted involved putting the last first, [26] an unnatural placing or "disordered speech" which joins the unnatural placing that Wilson's *Art of Rhetorike* treats of in its abhorrence of putting "mother" before "father," like "Mistress" before "Master."

Not only does the placing of "male" before "female," then, have behind it the scriptural authority of the Pauline gloss on the secondary creation and hence secondary position of Eve ("Neither was the man created for the woman; but the woman for the man"). It is also prescribed in the order of discourse, in the strictures on the "naturall order" in which "the worthiest word is set first" and in which a "disorder" in speech would reflect another kind of disorder understood as "unnaturall." Thus when Lear makes his "daughters" his "mothers" in that reversal the Fool immediately assimilates to the familiar proverbial figure of *hysteron proteron*—putting the "cart" before the "horse" (I.iv.232–3)—he opens himself to an "unnaturall" order which in the ideology of rhetorical treatise, theological tract, and conduct book alike would involve a disordered and "preposterous" reversal, the placing of "woman," unnaturally, not only "on top," in Natalie Davis's phrase, but sequentially and discursively "first."[27] And the fact that the New Testament, which prescribed certain kinds of ordering ideologically useful to the state, also contained its own radical *hysteron proteron*, "the last shall be first," made it even more imperative to control the "transportability" of such notions between the divine order and the civil one, lest such contradiction, like scriptural "freedom" by the Anabaptists, be taken advantage of.

III

> What shall be done, sir, with the groaning Juliet?
> She's very near her hour.
> *Angelo.*   Dispose of her
> To some more fitter place; and that with speed.
>   *(Measure for Measure)*

> I beg the ancient privilege of Athens;
> As she is mine, I may dispose of her.
>   *(A Midsummer Night's Dream)*

We have had so far to do with questions of order both in language and in society, and with descriptions of the wandering and movability of tropes which resemble the familiar commonplaces of the "wandering" and endless discoursing of women; and hence with two kinds of texts— discussions of logic and rhetoric, on the one hand, and, on the other, conduct books and ideological tracts concerned with the imaging of *Ordo* in the cosmos, in society, and in "the order of an householde called *Oiconomia*." In order to obtain a larger perspective on the interpenetration of rhetorical and ideological, we need finally to follow out the implications of one particular organizing category in rhetoric, one which makes clearer the relation between discursive order and other kinds of "rule," including, though not restricted to, the subordination of women. This is the category of *dispositio*, or "disposition." For this central notion about the construction of sentences and propositions is fundamentally tied to the imperatives of *Ordo*; and its opposite—"ill disposition"—not only is classed among those "maner of speaches" which are "alwayes intollerable and . . . cannot be used with any decencie," but is a term that betokens unsettling social and political disruption.

Disposition has to do with orderly sequence leading to an end, the method "whereby is orderly, cunninglye, and perfectlye layde downe and

disposed, everye matter and cause in his due order, proportion & place."
As the traditional "second part of rhetoric," it is the counterpart to syntax
in grammar, and has to do with linear order, placement, and proper
joining.[28] It is important, however, to recognize what this "second part"
comes after. For it is directly in relation to the fertility of "invention" that
proper sequential placement or disposition assumes its importance, and
specifically as a form of bringing that abundance under some kind of
management. Sherry's *Treatise* (1550), for example, opens with a praise of
"fulnes" and "varietie" but soon moves to the necessity of taking "hede of
placinge" and of setting "apte and mete wordes" in proper "order" ("For
the myghte and power of eloquucion consisteth in wordes considered by
them selves, and when they be ioyned together. Apt wordes by searchyng
must be founde oute, and after by diligence conveniently coupled"). The
fertility of a plenteous "matter" must be submitted to proper sequential
ordering, so as to "make an Ende" or, in Bottom's phrase in *A Midsummer
Night's Dream* (in a context which as we shall see explicitly draws on and
phallicizes the language of rhetorical *dispositio*), to "come to a point."
"Making an end"—disposing a "matter" or *materia* in order to bring it to
a conclusion—is very much a concern of discursive "disposition,"[29] as it is
a source of the undercurrent of tension between copious invention and its
orderly arrangement.

   Dispositio as a form of governance, however, also connects the placement
of words in discourse—and prevention of endless wandering—to the very
institution of order in the civil state. Stephen Hawes begins his discussion
of Rhetoric in *The Pastime of Pleasure* with a praise of "invencion" but
also expresses a concern to introduce numbers and measure so as not to
allow the development of a "mater" to wander or "perambulate":

> And fourtely, by good estimacion
> He must nombre al the hole cyrcumstaunce
> Of thys mater wyth brevyacion
> That he walke not by longe continuaunce
> The perambulat waye full of all variaunce.
> By estimacion is made annunciate
> Whether the mater be long or brevyate.[30]

He then quickly proceeds to "Disposycyon," whose ordering and governance of the "matter" gives it nothing short of the title of the "*royal art*."
Before "disposycyon," writes Hawes, all was disordered, erring like the
"planettes"; then "By dysposicion the rethorician / To make lawes
ordinatly began" (X. 34–5). As he continues, once again the verse suggests
a tension between disordered discourse (here called "chatter," a term
which elliptically evokes the topos of undisciplined garrulity and endless
amplification) and that which brings it to an orderly end:

> Wythout dysposicion none ordre gan be
> For the dysposicion ordreth every matter,

And gyveth the place after the degre:
Wythout ordre, wythout reason we clatter,
Where is no reason it vayleth not to chatter.
Dysposycion ordreth a tale directly
In a perfit reason, to conclude truely.   (X.35)

Hawes's text, with its Ciceronian vision of the ordering power of
rhetoric, makes it clear that the disposition of discourse reflects the laws
that brought "ordre" and governance to society. Throughout treatises not
only on discourse but on other kinds of ordering, descriptions of *dispositio*
reflect the range of meanings the term itself conveyed—from placement
or arrangement, to the ability to manage something (including unruly
daughters) according to one's will, to the larger senses of administration
and government.[31] As a term encompassing both the "chain" of discourse
(what Spenser in *The Faerie Queene* termed "Words, well dispost,"
II.viii.26) and that cosmic order imaged in Homer's golden chain, it
appears centrally in those texts foregrounded in an earlier era of Renaissance criticism as the major *exempla* of Tillyard's static and conservative
"Elizabethan World Picture." The opening of Elyot's *The Governor*,
virtually Tillyard's proof text and the one whose praise of *Ordo* he
famously placed beside Ulysses' set speech on "degree," stresses "disposition and order" in the cosmos as in the body politic, and links the latter
to what Wilson called "the rule of reason." And Hooker's *Of the Laws of
Ecclesiastical Polity* also treats of hierarchical disposition, though he puts
divine disposal above the comprehension of that human reason which
orders and disposes in its own way, a contrast which once again, as with
the richly fissured Pauline texts, suggests the possibility of something
beyond both the comprehension and the rule of reason and the civil
power.[32]

The specific relation between social governance and the ordering of
discourse is made even clearer in Wilson's *Arte of Rhetorique* when, after
discussing amplification or copious dilation, he turns to speak "Of disposition and apte orderyng of thynges":

And the rather I am earnest in this behaulfe, because I knowe that al
thynges stande by order, and without order nothying can be. For by an
order wee are borne, by an order wee lyve, and by an order wee make
our end. . . . By an order Realmes stande, and lawes take force. Yea by an
order the whole worke of nature and the perfite state of all the elementes
have their appointed course. By an order we devise, we learne, and
frame our dooynges to good purpose. By an order the Carpenter hath his
Squyre, his Rule, and his Plummet. The Tailour his mette Yarde, &
his measure: the Mason his Former, and his Plaine, and every one
accordyng to his callyng frameth thynges thereafter. *For though matter
be had, and that in greate plentie: yet al is to no purpose, if an order be*

not used. As for example: What availeth Stoone, if Masons doe not worke it: What good dothe clothe, if Tailours take no measure, or do not cutte it out: Though Tymber be had for makying a Shippe, and al other thynges necessarie, yet the shippe shal never be perfite, till worke men begynne to set to their handes, and ioyne it together. In what a comenly order hath God made man, whose shape is not thought perfite, if any parte be altered: yea al folke would take hym for a monster, whose feete should occupie the place of his handes. An army never getteth victorie, that is not in araie and sette in good order of battail. So an Oration hath litle force with it, and doth smally profite, which is utterde without all order. And needes must he wander, that knowes not howe to goe, neither can he otherwyse chouse, but stumble: that gropyng in the darke, can not tel where he is.   (fols 83–4, my emphasis)

The image of "matter ... readie to be framed of the woorkeman" is repeated again and again in descriptions of proper disposition, including in Wilson's own *Rule of Reason*: "it shall no more profit a manne, to find out his argumente, excepte he first know, how to ... shape it accordyngly ... then stones or timber shal profit the Mason, or Carpenter, which knoweth not how to woorke upon the same." It is only this proper disciplining and "disposing" of a matter that gives form to its "plentie," avoiding the danger of erring or "wandering" rather than coming, in orderly fashion, to an "Ende." We have again, as with the "wandering" of tropes or of the loud "harlot" of Proverbs 7, to do with a discipline in discourse which would keep to the model, as in grammar, of the line.

There is, however, in this very language of the ordering of "matter," an even more specific relation between disposition and gender in particular. For Wilson's emphasis on disposition as shaping and bringing order and rule to a "matter" which, though "in great plentie," is "al ... to no purpose, if an order be not used," calls attention to affinities between this language of the control of matter in discourse and the reigning gynecological conception of the male as "disposing" the female in generation, together with the conception of a woman as a potentially wayward, "wandering," uncontrollable, and excessive *materia*. This is the legacy of Aristotle—who in his discussion of generation in the *De generatione* uses the image of the "carpenter" for the shaping male[33]—and of the predominantly Aristotelian theory in which the mother provides the passive, "material" cause, and the father the formal or "efficient" one:

The seede [of the male] is the efficient beginning of the childe, as the builder is the efficient cause of the house. ... The seede of the man doth *dispose* and prepare the seede of the woman to receive the forme, perfection, or soule.[34]

Woman here, as the "vessel" and even "weaker vessel" (1 Peter 3) in the production of issue, was to submit to the forming and shaping power of the male. And "disposition" in the area of generation had its counterpart in the "order of an housholde called *Oiconomia*," in descriptions, like Robert Greene's in *Penelope's Web* (1587), of the virtues of wifely obedience:

> And as the Mathematicall lines which Geometricians doe figure in their carrecters, have no motion of themselves, but in the bodyes wherein they are placed, so ought a wife to have no proper nor peculiar passion or affection, unlesse *framed after the special disposition of her husband*: For, to crosse him with contraries, as to frowne when he setleth him selfe to mirth, or amidst his melancholie to shewe her selfe passing merrie, discovereth either a fond or froward will, opposite to that honorable vertue of Obedience.[35]

There is one specific term in the lexicon of *dispositio* which links it further to gender and the "order of an housholde." This term is "joining," as when Richard Sherry speaks of the proper "placinge, and settinge . . . in order" of words as a joining together or "coupling" of them, in a passage reminiscent of the traditional language of verbal copulation or the "copula." The very notion of the "rule of reason" is in Wilson crucially concerned with proper "joining," with judging "the knittyng of woordes" and seeing "what thing maie truely be ioigned to other . . . accordyng to the commune ordre of Nature" (p. 20):

> Even the very ordre of nature requireth that first of all we should speake of severall woordes . . . and afterwarde ioigne sentences together, and frame Proposicions by knittyng several woordes in ordre. . . . For a man were litle better then a brute beaste, if he could but onely apprehende seuerall woordes, hauying no gifte, or aptenesse to ioigne them in ordre, and so iudge how thinges are iogned together.(pp. 45–6)

Wilson's *Rule* is thus also preoccupied with the disorder that can result from improper or unauthorized joining—"The ioignyng of woordes that should be parted" and "The partyng of woordes that should be ioigned" (p. 106). Both interfere with the statements and propositions on which logical discourse and rational comprehension are based. It is therefore no accident that its whole discussion of the "ioigning together of those thinges, whiche should be dissevered" comes immediately after the examples in the text of the "doubtful writing" and "contrarie meaning" produced by the subversive mispointing from Udall, where the shifting of "points" or punctuation marks involves precisely such misjoinings and severings—and hence a change in the message radical enough to turn a compliment into an insult.

Wilson's use of "joining" elsewhere in *The Rule of Reason*, like that of numerous other Renaissance handbooks, makes it clear that proper joining and dividing are crucial to order as well as reason—from the level of single words and the joining together of larger syntactical units which grow to a "point," to the larger ideological constructs which depend on a similar series of careful joins. Descriptions of "joining" in discourse, in Sherry, Wilson, and others, also uncannily echo the "joining" or "knitting" of the marriage ceremony—not just in descriptions of the "partes coupled together" (*The Rule of Reason*, p. 42) or the "knittyng of woordes" (p. 20) but also in the strictures concerning "what wordes maie be truely ioined together" (p. 22) in passages which distinctly recall the language of what may be "lawfully joyned together" in the Book of Common Prayer. When Wilson seeks to prove "by Logique" that it is "lawfull for a Prieste to marie a wife," he takes "both the partes of [the] proposicion"—priest and wife—through the "places" to see if they "agree" and can properly be joined as "parts"; the fact that the "manner" (one of the "places") of the wife is to be "obedient" and cured of shrewishness (p. 145) simply adds to the ideological language of the proposition. The entire discussion of "coupling" in Wilson's text and elsewhere makes proper severing and joining fundamental both to the construction of discourse and to order in marriage and the body politic.

The discipline of surveillance in a text such as *The Rule of Reason*, then, extends not just to the chastening of tropes such as metaphor, or anxiety about the ambiguous doubleness and wandering of words, but to the teleological project of making an "Ende," of moving through the ordered sequence and "consequence" upon which "reason" depends. Its concern with what is lawful in language involves the joining of that which should be joined, and the severing of that which cannot be lawfully joined together. But the terms of texts such as Wilson's also suggest more generally a contradiction within the conception of order itself: that it is both legitimated as a representation of something existing and "natural," and, in the anxious as well as the more confident passages of such texts, presented as a form of construction, one that institutes rather than simply reflects. Approaching the language of "degree" in the body politic—or of disposition and its golden chain within the touchstone texts of the "Elizabethan World Picture"—not from the point of view of a static order and its divine authorization but rather from the perspective of the terms they have in common with the lexicon of construction in logic and rhetoric, might enable us to see *Ordo*, in this sense, as precisely the constructed discourse its figures of "mason" and "carpenter" suggest, and thus to see more clearly what is at stake in the ordering of language. *Dispositio*—like the tropes of Elizabethan courtesy theory, which Whigham's project differently outlines—links something described as divinely sanctioned or "naturall" to something that can not only be learned and manipulated but disrupted, and hence is in need of being hedged about by careful distinctions, social enforcements, and laws. It may be for this reason that rhetoric and language were so much the locus of anxieties about the problem of

control, including the link between the ordered "chain" of discourse and
the disposition of a potentially wayward or unruly female *materia*.

IV

The unity and married calm of states.

(*Troilus and Cressida*)

One way of seeing the language of disposition, joining and the control of
tropic reversals as a motivated construct would be to turn, finally, to a
textual locus in which the terms we have traced have been so naturalized as
to have become almost invisible. The language of rhetorical disposition,
division, and joining is everywhere in Shakespeare—as is play upon and
play with the implications of rhetorical tropes and terms. Cleopatra puns
on *dispositio* in its discursive as well as its psychological sense in
her description of Antony's "well-divided disposition" (*Antony and
Cleopatra*, I.v.53). *Troilus and Cressida*—whose speech on "degree"
evokes the language of the copula in the "unity and married calm of states"
(I.iii.100)—treats of what it calls the "bitter disposition of the time"
(IV.i.49) and sets the whole lexicon of order in discourse loose in a context
in which rhetorical terms, like the "digest" of its Prologue, turn into their
appetitive counterparts, "consum'd / In hot digestion of this cormorant
war" (II.ii.6). A single scene in *As You Like It* combines all the kinds of
joining—joining in matrimony and the workman whose craft it is to join
together, in the unlawful coupling of Audrey and Touchstone ("this fellow
will but join you together as they join wainscot"). The link to joining or
misjoining in discourse emerges in the very name of this joiner—"Sir
Oliver Martext" (III.iii.41–89).

But there are two plays in particular which exploit the language of
"joining" and of "disposition" in more specifically political and ideological contexts. One is *Hamlet*. The crucial opening speech of Claudius in Act
I—the speech which establishes his right to the succession after Hamlet's
father's death and which is itself, as has often been remarked, a consum-
mate example of rhetorical joining and misjoining—is filled with the
language not only of joining but of sequence and consequence, of the
sequitur or what follows and succeeds in a logical as well as genealogical
line. "Our sometime sister, now our queen, / Th'imperial *jointress* to this
warlike state" (I.ii.8–9) links the joining of matrimony with the form of
inheritance through "jointure," which may indeed have been the very
means of this king's succession. Next, "Now *follows that* you know young
Fortinbras, / . . . thinking by our late dear brother's death / Our state to be
disjoint or out of frame," (I.ii.17–20) introduces the crisis which more

immediately motivates the strategic need for this political and this verbal joining. The rhetorical joinings here—that linear logic which allies Claudius, in James Calderwood's suggestive evocation of a modern linguistic lexicon, with the metonymic—serve both to consolidate a political succession or following which might otherwise be open to question (as in Horatio's "Indeed, my lord, it *follow'd hard upon*"; I.ii.179) and to counsel a recalcitrant heir who opposes these joinings and who by the end of this opening Act will proclaim that the "time is out of joint" (I.v.188).[36] Accepting and bending to this logic of succession and consequence is presented as bending to the counsel of "reason" (I.ii.103), as to a principle of economy and management which Hamlet mockingly reduces to its barest linear or metonymic form ("Thrift, thrift, Horatio, the funeral bak'd meats / Did coldly furnish forth the marriage tables"; I.ii.180–1).

The carefully oiled joinings of Claudius's speech resemble in this respect his narrative version of Old Hamlet's death—an account the Ghost terms a "forged process" (I.v.37), a phrase which conveys the sense of "forged" as construction but also as counterfeit, and of "process" as verbal sequence.[37] It is this narrative and oratorical joining which enables the new king's power through succession, and hence ultimately the "sovereign process" (IV.iii.63), or lawful command, of his authority. The language of "joining" and of following, of succession and of sequitur in Claudius's opening speech, combined with the "incestuous sheets" and joining of his marriage with Gertrude, introduce into the play a language of the copula which continues into the play's final scene, as Hamlet offers the poisoned cup and its pearl to Claudius: "Is thy *union* here / *Follow* my mother" (V.ii.326–7). It also pervades the language of the play in Hamlet's disgust at all the couplings and joinings—"we will have no moe marriage" (III.i.147)—he tries before that end to uncouple or disjoin. In contrast to the ostensibly "naturall & necessary order" of Claudius's *dispositio*, then—to the logic of succession and consequence parodically reiterated in Polonius's "It *must follow*, as the night the day" (I.iii.79)—we might begin to hear a new resonance in Hamlet's "*antic* disposition," with its mad language of puns, its licentious or "tropical" turns—"Marry, how? tropically" (III.ii.237)—its reversals and reversed directions—"for yourself, sir, shall grow old as I am—if like a crab you could go backward" (II.ii.203–4)—and its collapsing of a logical with a narrative "*that follows not*" (II.ii.412).

If *Hamlet* exploits the language of copula and sequitur in a context of political succession, the Shakespearean play that most suggestively reproduces the language of discursive *Ordo* in the context of the disposition of the genders and of the orders of society is *A Midsummer Night's Dream*. As a "marriage" play, it is centrally preoccupied with the question of joining in matrimony: its counterpart to the form of construction invoked in the coupling of Audrey and Touchstone is a workman actually bearing the name of "Snug the Joiner." And it opens with a father's claim to "dispose" of the troublesome matter of an unruly daughter. To link the question of order and rule in this Athenian play to the tradition of the order of "discourse" (a term it several times repeats) is something its own explicit allusions to the rhetorical tradition already encourage, and not just in the reminder of the "partition" of discourse in Act V (V.i.167). When Wilson in *The Arte of Rhetorique* turns from the fertility of "invention" to a discussion "Of disposition and apte orderyng of thynges," he invokes the figures of "Carpenter," "Tailour," and other "woorke-men." *A Midsummer Night's Dream* both presents and parodies the language of the proper construction of discourse in the mouths of those workmen (including a Carpenter, a Tailor and a Joiner) who struggle unsuccessfully to reproduce it and in their very failure reveal its joints and seams.

The first lines in which we see these "rude mechanicals" (I.ii) are those containing Bottom's attempted imitation of the handbooks in his advice to Quince on the proper disposition and ordering of his speech ("*First*, good Peter Quince, say what the play treats on; *then* read the names of the actors; and so *grow to a point*"). But each of the three scenes involving these workmen also involves disruption of an order that depends upon orderly sequential disposition and proper pointing. In the casting scene, Bottom wants to play all the parts himself—rather than having them spread out or distributed—and has to be called to order by a directorial Quince. In the rehearsal scene, Thisbe/Flute speaks all his "part at once, cues and all" (III.i.99), as if it were a single continuous line or sentence, with no intermediate "points," and is similarly called to order by Quince. And in the performance Quince, speaking as "Prologue," misses the proper punctuation marks (prompting Theseus' "This fellow doth not stand upon points"; V.i.118) and thereby turns an address to his aristo-cratic onstage audience into an insult.

Quince's not standing upon "points"—producing what Theseus, in an invocation of the privileged image of *Ordo*, calls "a tangled chain ... all disorder'd" (V.i.125–6) and what Hippolyta, the play's defeated Amazon, terms a sound not "in government" (V.i.123)—has, however, an even more particular resonance. For it may well have been inspired by exactly the example of mispointing from Udall so widely disseminated by Wilson's *Rule of Reason*, the text that expounds that "cool reason" which Theseus himself is the Athenian exponent of (V.i.6). The role of the workmen of this play—their botching of the very activity of construction—may be to put this language into play in a context not just of reason but of govern-ance, one which extends both to the question of order in the body politic and to the disposition and subordination of the female within it.

It has often been noted how frequently *A Midsummer Night's Dream* echoes the language of the marriage ceremony ("Therefore what God hath joined together, let no man break asunder"), but less often the ways that its "rude mechanicals" (including Snug the Joiner) become part of a pervasive network of discursive and rhetorical joining and misjoining. Wilson's description in *The Rule of Reason* of "the joining of words that should be parted" involves the kind of misplacing or improper joining which the language of these workmen so frequently commits ("I see a voice ... / To spy and I can hear my Thisby's face"; V.i.192–3). His second disorder— the "dividing of thinges, whiche should be ioigned together ... or elles a dissevering of twoo partes which should be but one"—has its counterpart in the dividing Wall of Pyramus and Thisbe and the whole series of severings and misjoinings in the period of disorder in the woods, before the return to Athens and Theseus' famous speech on "cool reason" and what it "comprehends" (V.i.6). This disordered and disorienting middle involves the joining of the wrong "Jack" to the wrong "Jill" (III.ii.461) as if the pairs of virtually indistinguishable lovers were transportable units or terms. Wilson's description of proper "disposition" and the controlling of a plenteous "matter" so as to "make an Ende" evokes the figure of the "worke men" needed to "ioyne ... together" a properly ordered discourse. But it also speaks of the "monster" produced by an improper joining, and of the "wandering" and "groping in the dark" which results when no such proper order is to be had, in ways uncannily echoed in the plot of *A Midsummer Night's Dream*, from Bottom whose body is monstrously joined to the head of an ass to the lovers parted and joined in the disorderly interlude in the woods, who finally do grope and stumble in the dark, wandering and unable to find their way.

This middle period of disorder echoes the disorderings of a number of figures and tropes associated with *hyperbaton* and listed by Peacham as repugnant to "naturall & necessary order." David Marshall has already allied "Hypallage, or the Changeling" (as Puttenham calls it) to the "changeling" boy who causes the disordering and revolt of Titania against the rule of her husband Oberon, as a figure for the verbal exchanges of a "wrong construction for a right" in the speeches of the "rude mechani- cals." [38] The link becomes even more evocative when we note that Puttenham actually compares this figure to the disorder represented by the "changeling" of "fayries" (p. 184). *Hysteron proteron*—or "The Preposterous"—is echoed in Puck's description of the disorder in the woods where things turn out "prepost'rously" (III.ii.121), where Titania temporarily rules Oberon, and where maids pursue men as if the proper roles of the sexes were reversed. The "translation" of Bottom ("Bless thee, Bottom ... / Thou art translated"; III.i.119), like the "translation" Helena desires (I.i.191), and then gets, into Hermia, echo the trope of translation, metaphor, before both in the end are returned to what would be, from one perspective, their proper place. The return to order after this interval of "tropical" disorder is a return both to Athens and to its ruler Theseus, about to wed his chastened Amazon. But it is to a Theseus who not only amends the ambiguous mispointing of the "rude mechanicals"—like that of his other subjects who make "periods in the midst of sentences" (V.i.96)—into the discourse of an intended praise, but delivers a speech on "cool reason" and what it "comprehends" only after the echoes, in Bottom's awakening from his dream (IV.i.204–14), of a potentially subversive Pauline passage on the limited comprehension of both Athenian "reason" and the "rulers of this world."[39]

We might, then, consider what happens to this interlude of disorder and to the female in this "marriage" play from the perspective of its repeated evocation of the language of joining and disposition and of its own final proceeding to this "Ende" or "point." Egeus' claim to "dispose" of his rebellious daughter, put forward in the play's opening Act, is not itself literally fulfilled: his daughter has the limited freedom to choose the man to whom she will be lawfully joined, a freedom obtained—as it so often is in Shakespeare—by the limited expansiveness of that intervening middle. But the end to which the play proceeds as it returns to Athens and to Theseus is reflected in another kind of disposition of an unruly feminine *materia*. The Titania whose name links her with that earthly matter is finally subordinated and returned to her proper role. Wilson's emphasis on "disposition" as shaping a "matter" which though "in great plentie . . . is to no purpose, if an order be not used" already, as we have seen, provides the counterpart in discourse to the conception of woman as potentially uncontrollable "matter," of the male as the controlling ruler and shaping form, and of the female as a "vessel" in the production of an "issue." The passage which most explicitly evokes the pleasures of Titania's preposterous female rule—the description of the votaress whose swelling belly is fertile with the "changeling" child (II.i.123–35)—images her as a "vessel" rich with "merchandise"; and her end might be seen to figure proleptically the end of this extended middle.[40] The tradition of *dispositio* as the "royal art" already foregrounds the aspect of "rule" and "governance" that this play will reproduce in its evocation of the "ordered chain" of discourse. But its pervasive Aristotelian and Neoplatonizing language extends to its participation in the disposition of the genders as well.

Discussions of decorum and *dispositio* were, as we have seen, anything but unmotivated rhetorics, hermetically removed from anxieties about other forms of rule. It is by no means irrelevant to our consideration of this motivated discourse that a play like *A Midsummer Night's Dream*— which ends with Oberon's remastery of Titania and Theseus' finally consummated marriage to his defeated Amazon—echoes the very language of "disposition," just as it contains a mispointed prologue like Merrygreek's in *The Rule of Reason*, the text which represented to an English audience the very Greek or Athenian "Logique" which Theseus' "rule" and "cool reason" reflect. The pervasive echoing of the marriage

ceremony in discussions of joining and coupling in discourse suggests why
this marriage play should both so ubiquitously evoke this rhetorical
tradition and move to its own conclusion through the series of joinings in
matrimony which allow it to "grow to a point." For this marriage play not
only concludes by bringing an Amazon and an unruly Titania to their
proper subjection to their husbands as "head" (a restoration to the proper
order of 1 Corinthians: "Neither was the man created for the woman; but
the woman for the man"), but, in its joining of right "Jack" to right "Jill,"
corrects an earlier potentially Amazonian and finally unlawful union of
woman to woman, the "union in partition" of Helena and Hermia
(III.ii.210–16) which improperly echoes the ceremony of matrimony in its
exclusion of "men."

Throughout this discussion of logic and rhetoric, we have moved
between the specific question of gender and the general one of social and
political order, as the handbooks themselves do. *A Midsummer Night's
Dream* in this sense as well provides a telling textual instance. For its final
scene folds gender distinctions back into distinctions of social position, as
the two lively younger women join an aristocratic audience in which their
men speak while they are silent, and where even Hippolyta's famous
rejoinders issue from the class voice of a defeated Amazon queen.

Yet this ending and disposition are not the whole, or even the final, story
in this marriage play; and this fact may give us a perspective on the
language of *Ordo* so extensively at work within it. Matrimonial joining as
the conventional way for plays to end had already been distanced as such
in *Love's Labour's Lost* ("Our wooing doth not end like an old play. Jack
hath not Gill"; V.ii.874–5). *A Midsummer Night's Dream* is a play in
which Theseus's reason is revealed in its limitations by, precisely, what it
cannot "comprehend," and in which characters contemptuously called
"rude mechanicals"—those "workmen" who figure as virtual embodiments of the familiar images of discursive joining and construction—
mangle by their failed and untutored imitations the very rules of that
construction. Their concern not to produce a convincing and naturalized
theatrical illusion in their play before the "gentles" in Act V is matched by
their very botching of the construction of discourse. And this inability has
the effect of laying bare the mechanics of that *Ordo*, of that "meete placing
of words" (Peacham) spoken of in the handbooks as a "naturall" order
which tropes such as hypallage and *hysteron proteron* transgress. They
serve, that is to say, to call attention to the process of construction itself,
just as any imperfectly learned language typically creates what we have
learned to call, after Althusser and Macherey, a "distanciation" effect. In
evoking the language and larger implications of proper joining both in
matrimony and in discourse, and of the controlling or disposing of a
potentially wayward *materia*, Shakespeare is not necessarily, as some
readers of this play's ending conclude, dramatically validating, for better

or for worse, the Elizabethan World Picture, but rather laying out and laying bare, demonstrating precisely as a "process," its own forms of construction, ones in which the "ordered chain" of discourse is related to other orders and chains as well.

To focus on a play like *A Midsummer Night's Dream* in this regard is not to privilege a literary text over what a fuller reading of the texts of rhetoric and logic might reveal as opening up within their own contradictions or classificatory impasses. What is striking the more one reads in the treatments of order in discourse or the regulation of tropes is that the very terms that are supposed to produce or reflect order lead to a querying of its construction. We cannot separate rhetoric from logic here, or *elocutio*—the management of tropes and figures—from the governance of *dispositio*.[41] To focus on the dislocations and instabilities within the tropes of rhetoric or the copulation of words—on those features which made it something more slippery than a straightforward civil instrument—would make a Derridean point about its leftovers and reserves. But it would locate this perception within the specific political and gender anxieties which suggest what was at stake in concerns about rhetorical amplification, reversal, or "excesse." To focus on the naturalization of the constructed would make a Machereyan point about the domestication of an ideology—about the relation between discourse and its external reference and the stakes of political power dependent on forging that link.

We have to guard, here, against falling into a language or logic of cause and effect—the language of sequitur and "effect defective" so mercilessly queried in *Hamlet*. In the juxtaposition of rhetorical handbook with conduct book or political manual, it is not clear whether rhetoric is the model of a certain social ordering and gendering or the reflection of it. But we can offer a reason for focusing on discussions of rhetoric, logic and language in particular. A term like "disposition," or orderly sequential placement making it possible to "make an Ende," appears equally in sixteenth-century discussions of the divine distribution of the sequence of history, the institution of order in the civil state, the placement of words in sentences and logical propositions, and the disposition of the female and the "order of an householde." But it is the handbooks—indices of the rise of rhetoric and its pedagogy in the early modern period—that reveal, deliberately or not, that what is presented in all these different contexts as ostensibly "naturall & necessary" is instead something both constructed and manipulable.

7

Rhetorics of Property: Exploration, Inventory, Blazon

> That love is merchandiz'd whose rich esteeming,
> The owner's tongue doth publish every where.
>
> (Shakespeare, Sonnet 102)

> Blaze not her beauty with thine own tongue.
>
> (Alexander Niccholes, *A Discourse of Marriage and Wiving*, 1615)

> Virtue seeks concealment as much as vice delights to show itself. ... A woman's glory is to be little spoken of; very different from men, who act, unmasked, on the world's wide theatre ... whereas women are to perform their parts only, as it were, behind the scenes.
>
> (*The Ladies Friend*, 1771)

The series of juxtapositions which follows has its origin in the intersection of recent studies of what might seem at first to be separate domains—Nancy Vickers's suggestive investigations of the tradition of the blazon, the taking control of a woman's body rhetorically through its division into parts, what Shakespeare called "the blazon of sweet beauty's best, / Of hand, of foot, of lip, of eye, of brow" (Sonnet 106); Wayne Franklin's important work on the role of discourse, of discursive strategies and structures, in the discovery and possession of America, with Annette Kolodny's foregrounding of the gendering and sexualization of that discourse; Carole Fabricant's brilliant analyses of aesthetic, economic, and sexual forms of possession in discussions of landscape in eighteenth-century England; and, finally, the intersection of these separate studies with my own interest in the link between rhetoric and property, and in the terms which cross the boundaries between what we have come to think of as distinct disciplinary realms.[1]

The link between property and rhetoric is one reinscribed in different modalities through different historical periods. The account that follows approaches this link in the early modern period by juxtaposing a literary text, Shakespeare's *Cymbeline*, in which a woman's body is "inventoried" as part of the discourse of a sexual theft, first with the "invention" of an America gendered as female and finally with the reflection of this New World discourse in the intersection of economic, visual, and representational in the eighteenth-century tradition of the "prospect," of property aestheticized and controlled through its display to a beholder's eye. In all three, the focus will be on the interestedness, in Habermas's sense, rather than the simple existence or neutrality of a descriptive tradition, both in its structures and in what motivates the structuring. I will begin with the bodily interest of the blazon.

I

> I will not praise that purpose not to sell.
>
> (Shakespeare, Sonnet 21)

The term "blazon," as Vickers's work reminds us, "derives both from the French *blasonner* and from the English 'to blaze' ('to proclaim as with a trumpet, to publish, and, by extension, to defame or celebrate')."[2] But it also named simultaneously a "conventional heraldic description of a shield, and ... a conventional poetic description of an object praised or blamed by a rhetorician-poet." The most prominent examples of the poetic blazon in French appear in the *Blasons anatomiques du corps femenin* (1543), a collection in which each contribution praised a separate part of the female body, speaking in turn "of hand, of foot, of lip, of eye," or "of brow." The blazon thus had both a static sense—the heraldic shield which stood as a sign of a particular family, name, and property, or the division of the woman's body into its parts—and a more active or kinetic one: the "proclamation" or "publishing" by such description to an audience. We need, however, immediately to notice that static and more active here interpenetrate right from the beginning, both in the idea of a narrative "description" of a still object and in the sense that the narrated object, treated as "picture" (as in the limit of *ut pictura poesis*), might be said to "publish" or "proclaim." Like Keats's Grecian urn, it is both stasis and movement, *pictura* and descriptive narrative at once.

It is also both of these in its involvement with "display," which comes from the Latin *displicare* ("to scatter" but also later, as Vickers remarks, "to unfold to view"). For "display" means, as the *OED* reminds us, "to unfold or spread out, to describe at large in representation or narrative, and to exhibit ostentatiously to the view." It involves simultaneously an act of unfolding, offering to the eye, and the more static sense of something to be gazed upon and seen. As Vickers puts it, the description involved in the blazon is "a gesture of display, a separating off and a signaling of particulars destined to *make visible* that which is described" (my emphasis). In this sense, its "object or matter is ... submitted to a double power-relation inherent in the gesture itself: on the one hand, the describer controls, possesses, and uses that matter to his own ends; and, on the other, his reader or listener is extended the privilege or pleasure of 'seeing'" (p. 96). Readers of a later literature than Vickers deals with might think of the jealous speaker of Browning's most anthologized monologue, whose displaying of his last duchess to another's view is inseparable from the rhetoric of possession and property: "none puts by / The curtain I have drawn for you, but I."

Vickers's powerful analysis of this rhetoric of display, in juxtaposition with a blazon which both details the particulars of a woman's body and "publishes" news of her abroad in Shakespeare's *The Rape of Lucrece*, rightly underlines its ever-present merchandising context, one so common that it can simply be elliptically summoned in a single Shakespearean line ("I will not praise that purpose not to sell"). But I would like to consider another context for the language of the blazon—one which triangulates its relation to the economic, or merchandising, through a particular form of rhetoric, itself described as a form of displaying merchandise or purposing to sell. This is the rhetorical language of which the blazon in one of its aspects—the link of its "display" with the "display of rhetoric"—is described as a part, a language which has repeated recourse to the figure of merchandising as an opening to the gaze, or view, the selling of a commodity as dependent first on the unfolding of it.

The rhetorical tradition I refer to here is the one involving the techniques of "division," "partition," and "distribution," of dividing a matter or *materia* into its parts in order to make it "increase and multiply," but also as a way of opening it up and opening it to the view. Erasmus, for example, explains in *De Copia*—a work whose title already institutes a relation between rhetorical abundance and economic wealth—that the best way to amplify a discourse is to divide it into its separate parts, and directly invokes for this rhetorical enterprise the analogue of purposing to sell. Even more specifically, however, his definition puts its emphasis on appealing to the eye or *oculus* through such opening: "This is just like displaying some object for sale first of all through a lattice or inside a wrapping, and then unwrapping it and opening it out and displaying it more fully to the gaze" ("deinde eadem evolvat aperiatque, ac totam oculis exponat"). The whole tradition of rhetorical unfolding reiterates this image of wealth, both in the register of display and in the register of counting, accounting, or summing up. Francis Bacon writes: "So when a great moneyed man hath divided his chests and coines and bags, hee seemeth to himselfe richer then hee was, and therefore a way to amplifie any thing, is to breake it, and to make an anatomie of it in severall partes." And John Hoskins, in the influential *Directions for Speech and Style*

(1599), repeats Bacon's dictum and offers yet another version of the commercial metaphor: dilation or amplification by division, he writes, is like "the show which peddlers make of their packs, when they display them."[3] Dilation, or "opening," in Erasmus's phrase—and specifically opening something which had been closed or hidden to the eye—involves an opening up to "show," a term which also carried an explicitly gendered sexual connotation, as Hamlet's play on "show" as the revealing of a woman's secret "parts" makes clear (*Hamlet*, III.ii.144).

Vickers's analysis of that "display of rhetoric" which constitutes the blazon points our attention to its structurally triangulated nature, in which the speaker describing the body of woman as what Cixous in another context has called "the uncanny stranger on display" speaks not directly to that woman, but rather of her, to others.[4] In its specifically lyric form— in countless "Petrarchan" poems, for example—"a lyric 'I' does not privately speak to a lyric 'you' but rather, by 'publishing' his love, interjects a third term: 'I' speaks 'you' to an audience that, it is hoped, will in turn purchase 'you.' The relationship so constructed involves an active buyer, an active seller, and a passive object for sale" (p. 97), the woman being described or opened up to view. The blazon itself, in its most frequent form, specifically genders the triangulation. It moves the terms of the "display of rhetoric" into the sexual politics of a form in which the simultaneously described and excluded other is most frequently female; and it reveals the "potential consequences of being female matter for male oratory," in a text like *The Rape of Lucrece*, where the description of a woman's parts becomes part of the "motivated discourse" of an act of possession and rape.

What is striking about the wider discussion of rhetorical display—the construction of discourse through the strategy of dividing into parts—is that its terms are themselves already subtly gendered in the texts in which they appear, and in ways which might make the blazon, presented within the texts of rhetoric as simply a subset of the larger category of rhetorical amplification by partition, ultimately a figure for the larger motivations of the whole of which it is supposedly simply one part. For the language of "opening" by division or partition—and specifically of opening up to the eye or gaze—is in these texts linked by its very language to the possibility of an eroticized, even potentially prurient and voyeuristic, looking. Here Peacham's *Garden of Eloquence* (1593)—but only as exemplary instance—might be cited in its description of "division" and "partition." Peacham links rhetorical amplification by division with an opening up of both the mysteries and the riches of a clearly and traditionally feminized "nature" by dividing it into its "several kinds, whereby the large and bountifull worke of nature is spread abroad" (p. 123). He then goes on to say, in an even more revealing passage, that the figure of *divisio* is "an apt and ready forme of speech to *open the bosom of nature* and to shew her branches, to that end they may be *viewed and looked upon, discerned and knowen.*"[5] Hamlet's sense of "show," and perhaps Iago's of that private female "thing" uncovered and offered to the gaze, hovers behind the very language of this "opening" and "showing," the language of the discovery of something brought into the light, in order that it may be "known." And a specifically economic metaphor lurks within Peacham's discussion elsewhere of the setting forth of matter for discourse by "distribution"—another term which readily suggests an analogy from nature or natural wealth ("Distributio is a generall word, comprehending diverse special kindes, by which we dilate and spread abroad the generall kinde"; p. 123).

The blazon itself, as we have seen, is understood as an instance of amplification or dilation by division in which a whole—here, the body of a woman—is "distributed" into parts. Puttenham, under "*Merismus,* or the Distributer" in *The Arte of English Poésie* (1589), defines it as "a figure very meete for Orators or eloquent perswaders," whereby "we may conveniently utter a matter in one entier speach or proposition and will rather do it peecemeale and by distribution of every part for amplification sake."[6] It involves, he writes, a division of a matter for discourse into its particulars or "circumstances" ("which this figure of distribution doth set forth every one apart"). One of the examples he gives is of a blazon in praise not just of any woman but of Elizabeth, "the maiden Queene," through a detailing of her attributes which "would not seeme to wrap up all her most excellent parts in a few words them entierly comprehending" but would rather, by an amplifying "distributor," provide a particularizing of her "honord parts."

One form taken by this economic figure of division or distribution of a female body into "parts" is the figure of the inventory, a figure already prepared for by the lexicon of merchandising—of praising with purpose for to sell. A whole scene of *Twelfth Night* turns on the "negotiation" of a wooing which is also a commercial transaction evocative of such an inventory, in the ever-present imagery of the *hortus conclusus,* or enclosed garden, of the Song of Songs:

> *Viola [disguised as Cesario].* 'Tis beauty truly blent, whose red and
> white
>   Nature's own sweet and cunning hand laid on.
>   Lady, you are the cruell'st she alive
>   If you will lead these graces to the grave,
>   And leave the world no copy.
> *Olivia.* O, sir, I will not be so hard-hearted; I will give out divers
>   schedules of my beauty. It shall be inventoried, and every particle
>   and utensil labell'd to my will: as, *item,* two lips, indifferent red;
>   *item,* two grey eyes, with lids to them; *item,* one neck, one chin, and
>   so forth. Were you sent hither to praise me? (I.v.239–49)[7]

The economic motive of itemizing—the detailing of a woman's parts as an inventory of goods—makes explicit an aspect of the rhetorical tradition's own relation to natural plenitude, copia, wealth, or increase. For, although the emphasis in the initial stages of the discussion of copia is on the faculty of "invention" as the finding out of fertile "matter" for discourse, these descriptions always move quickly to the motive of shaping, controlling, or limiting that fertility in a particular way.[8] If the rhetorical enterprise of the amplification or dilation of discourse has at its inaugural moment the figure of natural wealth or abundance—the discursive counterpart to the command to an Edenic Adam and Eve to "increase and multiply"—this discourse is also concerned, even anxiously, to control that "increase," to keep it from taking over or dominating the speaker who would make a particular "matter" his own. Peacham's descriptions of copious invention and fertility of amplification—of the "plenty and variety" made possible by the "multitude of branches" a matter might be opened up to (as in that "apt and ready forme of speech to open the bosome of nature and to shew her branches")—are anxiously accompanied by a series of "cautions" against proliferation or "excess."

The "matter" of discourse, then, is to be made plentiful, by a shaper outside it who "opens" it to the gaze, but also to be kept firmly under control. The inventory or itemizing impulse of the blazon (in a way which would connect with Vickers's central focus) would seem to be part of the motif of taking control of a woman's body by making it, precisely, the engaging "matter" of male discourse, a passive commodity in a homosocial discourse or male exchange in which the woman herself, traditionally absent, does not speak. The "inventory" of parts becomes a way of taking possession by the very act of naming or accounting. We might note, then, that the other context in which a blazon appears in Shakespeare is in the midst of an imperial language lesson, part of the taking possession of both conquered territory and a foreign bride, as Katherine of Valois is schooled in the language of that English Henry whose conquest of her will be the effective sign of his newly acquired dominion:

> Le foot et le count! O Seigneur Dieu! ils sont les mots de son mauvais, corruptible, gros, et impudique, et non pour les dames de honneur d'user. Je ne voudrais prononcer ces mots devant les seigneurs de France pour tout le monde. Foh! le foot et le count! Néanmoins je réciterai une autre fois ma leçon ensemble: d'hand, de fingre, d'nailès, d'arma, d'elbow, de nick, de sin, de foot, le count.
>
> (*Henry V*, III.iv.52–9)

The woman in question, gendered sign of the territory to be conquered and occupied, is made, in the seductive register of the quaint and charming, to name obscenely the parts of her own body, in a language she apparently does not understand. This rhetorical partitioning and display, in a context whose ghostlier demarcations include the sexual sense of "occupy" (as in Ralegh's "they occupied the Citie, Lands, Goods, and Wives of those whom they had murdered"),[9] provide symbolically an inventory of Henry's new possession and the language it will have to learn in order to name itself, to become the bride of that "Adam the namer" who in the final scene of voluntary submission proleptically proclaims his dominion over her and her country as well.

II

> Ah, but some natural notes about her body,
> Above ten thousand meaner moveables
> Would testify, t'enrich mine inventory.
>
> (Cymbeline)

So far we have charted the intersection of economic, sexual, and rhetorical which links the blazon as a mode of description to a particular discursive strategy it both illustrates and subtends. The argument is that a particular mode of control over a woman's body—through the "display of rhetoric" —is linked to merchandising and to dominion, to conquest of a territory traditionally figured as female and controlled by its partition or division into parts; but also that the influential tradition of rhetorical and discursive opening already, in the language of its own self-description, suggests a link with such gendering and control. What I propose to do now is to set into juxtaposition a series of texts—literary, rhetorical, and "economic" in the older sense which links the household or *oikos* with the management of other kinds of property—and to note the complex set of exchanges these terms negotiate between what might appear to be widely different spheres.

I will begin with a text which Vickers—in her analysis of the setting into motion of the rape in *The Rape of Lucrece*—elliptically mentions as coming out of the same tradition of the blazon, of the description of a woman in the context of a rivalry between men. This text is Shakespeare's *Cymbeline*, which contains within it, as the crucial pivot of its plot, a contest in which the husband or possessor of the "jewel" of his wife "blazes" her virtue and beauty so strongly as to incite the envy of another man. My interest will be both in the triangulation—of a situation of male rivalry in which a woman becomes, with disastrous consequences for her, the enabling matter of male discourse—and in the crossing the text suggests between "invention" and "inventory," between the finding of a copious and fertile matter and the itemizing of it; this link will also lead us into the uneasy tension within the term "invention" itself, between the sense of discovering or uncovering something already there and the sense of fictive narration, of something more open to manipulation and control.

The scene in *Cymbeline* is first one in which a new male arrives in already established company, and from the beginning it invokes the catalogue or inventory. Iachimo, the villainous rival-to-be, responds cynically to the praise of the newcomer Posthumus: "But I could then have look'd on him without the help of admiration, though the catalogue of his endowments had been tabled by his side and I to peruse him by items" (I.iv.4–7). Like Troilus, the "minced man" of Cressida's unimpressed response in another Shakespearean exploitation of the language of partition, Posthumus is here introduced through the possibility of a "catalogue of his endowments." But this kind of narrative or "story" is also contrasted with the better witness of sight: "How worthy he is," says the host Philario, "I will leave to *appear* hereafter, rather than *story* him in his own hearing" (I.iv.32–4).

The scene quickly moves to a recounting of two earlier male boasting contests, which lead in turn here to another, when the "Frenchman" of the scene relates his reason for being already acquainted with Posthumus:

> It was much like an argument that fell out last night, where each of us fell in praise of our country mistresses; this gentleman at that time vouching (and upon warrant of bloody affirmation) his to be more fair, virtuous, wise, chaste, constant, qualified and less attemptable than any the rarest of our ladies in France.

Iachimo immediately seeks to make this past "argument"—in the more modern sense as cause for contention and the older one of matter for discourse—into a present one ("You must not so far prefer her 'fore ours of Italy"), and as the contest heats up there is both an affirmation and a cynical denial of the difference between a woman as something for sale and as something which cannot be sold:

> *Iach.* Either your unparagon'd mistress is dead, or she's outpriz'd by a trifle.
> *Post.* You are mistaken: the one may be sold or given, or if there were wealth enough for the purchase, or merit for the gift. The other is not a thing for sale, and only the gift of the gods.

The distinction leads, however, only to Iachimo's sneering "you know strange fowl light upon neighboring ponds. Your ring may be stol'n too: so your brace of unprizable estimations, the one is but frail and the other casual. A cunning thief, or a (that way) accomplish'd courtier, would hazard the winning both of first and last." He boasts that he can possess this "prize" if he is allowed access to and conversation with her: "With five times so much conversation, I should get ground of your fair mistress; make her go back, even to the yielding, had I admittance, and opportunity to friend" (I.iv.100 ff.). The metaphor of "getting ground" is from fencing, but it suggests both the acquisition of territory and its sexual counterpart. There then follows the traditional male wager, in which Iachimo again speaks of women as something to be bought and sold ("If you buy ladies' flesh at a million a dram, you cannot preserve it from tainting"), and which is itself a form of trade, whose language intensifies the reification of Imogen into simply another "jewel":

> *Iach.* . . . If I bring you no *sufficient testimony* that I have enjoy'd the dearest bodily part of your mistress, my ten thousand ducats are yours, so is your diamond too: if I come off, and leave her in such honor as you have trust in, she your jewel, this your jewel, and my gold are yours.

"Articles" (156) are drawn up between the two wagering men, and Iachimo's testing of Imogen, in England, is spoken of as a "voyage," just as in *The Rape of Lucrece* Lucrece's breasts, before the avid gaze of her ravisher, are described as "A pair of maiden worlds unconquered" (408):

> *Post.* . . . if you make your *voyage upon her* and give me directly to understand you have prevail'd, I am no further your enemy; she is not worth our debate. If she remain unseduc'd, you not making it appear otherwise, for your ill opinion and th'assault you have made to her chastity, you shall answer me with your sword.

The image is that of the merchant adventurer, translated into the language of a sexual assault, or "gaining ground," which continues throughout. Posthumus sends Iachimo with a letter which both gains him entry and repeats the language of "value" ("He is one of the noblest note, to whose kindness I am most infinitely tied. Reflect upon him accordingly, as you value your trust"; I.vi.22–4). The scene of Iachimo's arrival to make this "voyage upon her" is filled with images linking women with mercantile venture. Iachimo, falsely telling Imogen that Posthumus has been unfaithful (with "tomboys" or harlots), puts the accusation in the following terms: "to be partner'd / With tomboys hir'd with that self exhibition / Which your own coffers yield; with *diseas'd ventures,* / That play with all infirmities for gold / Which rottenness can lend nature" (I.vi.121 ff.).

After he finds that this "false report" (I.vi.173) will not corrupt her, the voyager shifts instead to the "business" of a gift for her father, the stratagem of the trunk which will get him secretly into her bedchamber at night. Here in particular, the language bears the sign of the play's transposition of its bourgeois sources, whose characters are merchants, into the putatively aristocratic setting and ritual gift-giving of classical Rome. For Iachimo himself is a patently Italian Renaissance merchant disguised as

Roman nobility, as all his language of trade and "diseased adventures" (in both senses) suggests.

It is the scene in Imogen's bedchamber, however, that most clearly reifies Imogen's body as part of the contents of an inventory or catalogue of "items." Iachimo enters in the trunk, like the Trojans entering Troy through the stratagem of the horse, and is compared explicitly to Tarquin before he awakened and raped Lucrece. What he performs, however, is significantly not an actual act of rape, but something which will substitute for it—a careful inventory of the room, of its items or particulars, and of those of the body of Imogen. His expression of admiration before her sleeping form—"How bravely thou becom'st thy bed!" (II.ii.15)—will by the end of the scene carry a very different resonance; for, in this scene, Imogen "becomes" in a more purely material sense not only her bed but her entire "chamber," thus preparing for Iachimo's inventory of her and it ("the flame o' th'taper / Bows toward her, and would under-peep her lids, / To see th'enclosed lights, now canopied / Under these windows"). He proceeds not to rape her but rather to "write all down" the contents of this "chamber" in lines which link her body with its contents, and both with narrative or "story" in a double sense:

> But my design!
> To note the chamber I will write all down:
> > [*Takes out his tables.*]
> Such, and such pictures: there the window, such
> Th'adornment of her bed: the arras, figures,
> Why, such and such; and the *contents o' th' story.*
> Ah, but some natural notes about her body,
> Above ten thousand meaner *moveables*
> Would *testify*, t'enrich mine *inventory.*

"Story" here can be both the story or narrative represented on the arras— a narrative which would be only suggested by the static pictorial representation on the arras itself—and the room or "chamber" whose particulars Iachimo's inventory here remarks and will report back to Posthumus as a kind of proof, an inventory whose narrativization will take the place of an actual rape. "Moveables" (the word which still gives us the word *meubles* for "furniture" in French) provides yet another way in which Imogen "becomes her bed" along with the other parts of this "story," reduced to only the most prized object in its "contents"—another term which could apply both to the particulars of a property and to the details of a narrative account.

The particular "part" of her body—the strongest "voucher" of this inventory—is the mole on her left breast, the counterpart to the "pryvy token" which in the play's bourgeois source, *Frederyke of Jennen*, is recognized as decisive evidence:

> Here's a voucher,
> Stronger than ever law could make; this secret
> Will force him think I have pick'd the lock and ta'en
> The treasure of her honor. No more: to what end?
> Why should I write this down, that's riveted,
> Screw'd to my memory? She hath been reading late
> The tale of Tereus: here the leaf's turn'd down
> Where Philomele gave up.

She has been reading a "story" from Ovid which is itself a story of rape: the substitute for the rape of Philomel occurs at the point in the story where Philomel "gave up." The lines subtly link reading, or "story," with the parts of an inventory whose terms recall the topos of the "house of memory" and of "invention" itself as tied to place, to the "commonplaces" or topoi.[10] Imogen will, at the point of suspension, "Where Philomel gave up," be raped by an inventory which also depends on a careful noting of places and place, an inventory which will produce the narrative of an act Posthumus then assumes to have occurred, a narrative which is "invented" in the other sense of counterfeit. Significantly, Philomel in the archetypal Ovidian story of rape is locked up in a secret place, a metonomy for the secret place of her rape, and, her tongue cut out, is unable to speak. The inventory here—like the original male wager which led to it—will similarly deprive Imogen of speech; she will not be invited to reply, or to counter the charge made against her, when these particulars become the "voucher" of her guilt. The association of a female body with a "chamber" is finally inseparable from the violation of the chamber to which her sexuality is reduced—the case or casket containing that "treasure" which Iachimo, having "pick'd the lock," might then indeed have proceeded to steal. Assimilated to the rhetoric of property, but also to the language of place which permeates the discourse of rhetoric, this casket or "treasure" case is a place within a place, or, in the cynical pun which hovers behind other Shakespearean scenes, a private place which is about to become a common place. The "particular" here, in an inventory which substitutes for rape, would convert a private place into precisely this kind of opened one, a figure which pervades all of Shakespeare's treatments of the jealous husband or lover faced with a "voucher" that his own property, or private place, has become common and public, too open to the view.

In contrast to the movement from blazon to the actual violation of a woman's body in *The Rape of Lucrece*, Iachimo's inventory becomes a substitute, then, for an actual act of rape, in the scene where he reports back to those who await his narrative "account." When Iachimo returns to Rome and is greeted by Posthumus on his return from the "voyage" of his "vessel nimble" (II.iv.28 ff.), he intensifies this language—as in those New World promotional tracts concerned with the "return" to be gained by investors in such ventures—by reporting, first, that his venture was commercially worthwhile:

> *Post.* Sparkles this stone as it was wont, or is't not
>   Too dull for your good wearing?
> *Iach.*   If I have lost it,
>   I should have lost the worth of it in gold.
>   I'll make a journey twice as far, t'enjoy
>   A second night of such sweet shortness which
>   Was mine in Britain, for the ring is won.
>
> (II.iv.40–5)

Iachimo brings back a report of his "voyage" in both a sexual and a mercantile sense ("Had I not brought / The *knowledge* of your mistress *home*, I grant / We were to question farther"), and proceeds to substantiate her violation by detailing the particulars of this knowledge, those "circumstances" which are the more detailed "contents" of both a narrative report and a proof:

> *Iach.*   Sir, my circumstances,
>   Being so near the truth as I will make them,
>   Must first induce you to believe; whose strength
>   I will confirm with oath, which I doubt not
>   You'll give me leave to spare when you shall find
>   You need it not.
>
> (II.iv.61–6)

"Circumstances," here, are the particulars of narrative invention, which the final scene of the entire play will prominently invoke in Cymbeline's burning desire to hear in detail the whole "story" of what he himself could not directly witness ("When shall I hear all through? This fierce abridgment / Hath to it circumstantial branches, which / Distinction should be rich in"; V.v.382–4).[11] The whole last scene, in which Iachimo's confession of his "invention" takes place, indeed repeatedly emphasizes the retailing of narrative itself, in the larger context of a romance which is, as Jonson said of *Pericles*, only a "mouldy tale," with no corresponding "voucher" of its veracity.

As Iachimo details the particulars of Imogen's room or "story," Posthumus initially doubts its veracity, until the voyager Iachimo produces the bracelet taken from the sleeping Imogen's arm and, beyond that, the "voucher" of the mole under her breast. At that point, on Iachimo's "Will you hear more?", the tormented Posthumus's "Spare your arithmetic, never count the turns. / Once, and a million" (II.iv.142–3) explicitly translates Iachimo's inventory of the "contents o' th'story" into an accounting—another term which links narrative, or the *plaisir de conter*, with the impulse to count one's wealth. *Conter* in French—the term in the language lesson from *Henry V* which includes the more obscene sense of a female "count"—still links the relation of a narrative with the activity of counting or taking account. That network is present in this scene of inventory, narrative invention, and counting as a form of "arithmetic," with the buried sense of a recounting that the tormented Posthumus does not want to hear any more than Othello does, the recounting of "turns" in its sexualized and erotic sense.

When, however, Iachimo confesses his calumny of Imogen and its incitement—Posthumus's original "description" which gave his "mistress' picture" by his "tongue" (V.v.175), his verbal display of a mistress who was "For condition, / A *shop* of all the qualities that man / Loves woman for" (V.v.165–7)—he makes clear once again that the larger context both of the inventory of Imogen and of her counterfeited "theft" was the original "blazing" or publishing, in the traditional bragging contest between men. To chart the whole of this plot would be to uncover the perverse logic at the heart of such rhetorical "opening" and display: that the husband who wins this homosocial contest through the description of a possession presented as exclusively his thereby opens up the possibility of what the play calls "theft." *Cymbeline*, the later of the two, makes explicit what *The Rape of Lucrece* already suggests—that the verbal description or "blazoning" is already a substitute for a potential rape; that Collatine had already in his bragging "Unlock'd" the "treasure" (*Lucrece*, 16) of his exclusive possession; and that the two moments, rhetorical display and sexual theft, are already in a sense the same: "Why is Collatine the publisher / Of that rich jewel he should keep unknown / From thievish ears because it is his own" (*Lucrece*, 33–5). What would appear to be at work is a conflict within a male economy of possession: the "blazer" not only wants to open to the view, and display, what is privately his, but also wants to keep it within his exclusive control. This is joined by another and equally powerful aspect of its perverse logic—that a woman should not be talked about, should not be "in the mouths of men" at all, and if she is, she is in some sense to blame for such an opening and publicity. Lucrece, we remember, both in the classical version and in Shakespeare's, takes in her death the taint of her rape, and its violation of a property, upon herself.

Before turning to our second focus, descriptive narratives of actual mercantile voyages upon a feminized land, we need to consider one more link between the rhetorical tradition and the question of displaying something to the gaze. Iachimo's promise of descriptive "circumstances" invokes a form of description known as *enargeia* or *evidentia*, a display or unfolding in language so vivid that it provides a substitute for "ocular proof." Quintilian—eliciting the root of *evidentia* in *video* or seeing— writes that in "vivid description ... the facts are displayed in their living truth to the eyes of the mind." Richard Sherry, in *A Treatise of Schemes & Tropes* (1550), writes that "*Enargia*, evidence or perspicuitie called also descripcion rethoricall, is when a thynge is so described that it semeth to the reader or hearer that he beholdeth it as it were doyng"; and Puttenham traces its etymology to "*argos*, because it geveth a glorious lustre and light," thus connecting it with Argus, the mythological beast of many eyes.[12] This emphasis on the *oculus* or eye already pervades Erasmus's description of rhetorical division as "displaying some object for sale first of all through a lattice or inside a wrapping, and then unwrapping it and opening it out and displaying it more fully to the gaze" ("ac totam oculis exponat"). But *enargeia* or *evidentia* raises this visual aspect to what Erasmus himself describes as a "picture" set before the eyes: "Instead of setting out the subject in bare simplicity, we fill in the colours and set it up like a picture to look at, so that we seem to have painted the scene rather than described it," a description which calls on the combination of the visual "colors" of a painting with the famous figures or "colors" of rhetoric. This is exactly the term *The Rape of Lucrece* turns on as Tarquin moves from the static picture of Lucrece's face—the Petrarchan parts of the traditional blazon—to the motive for rape. The evocative "colors" of rhetoric transform words into a picture which powerfully presents a scene to the receiver's gaze or view, even in contexts like Iachimo's inventory or report, which pick up the more ominous overtones in Puttenham's Englishing of *enargeia* not just as vivid rhetorical display but as "Counterfeit Representation."

Evidentia, or "evidence," then, takes the already visual aspect of rhetorical display even further into the region of the gaze. It is therefore no accident that it appears not only in contexts which raise the issue of representation but in relation to the gaze of jealousy in particular (Erasmus's description of the "lattice" might even lead us to think of the other meaning of *la jalousie*). For the jealous gaze seems in this context to be the ultimate form of the rhetorical display of a picture to the eye, of a place which can be gazed upon and a private place laid open to others' eyes. In *Cymbeline* or *Othello*, verbal description is all that is needed as a "proof"; and what they evince, beyond the specific context of a violated property, is the visualizing and organizing power of *enargeia* to bring into being what it "invents," to present a scene convincingly to the hearer's eye—as "Noses, ears, and lips" become at a crucial point in *Othello* not just a static inventory of parts but the particulars of a narrative the jealous possessor both wants and does not want to hear.

Enargeia or *evidentia*, we need also to remark before passing to the vivid narratives of a feminized New World, is principally in drama the function of the messenger—the means of bringing back verbal reports from afar, a substitute for direct ocular experience for those who could not be present to see with their own eyes, a vivid "display in rhetoric" which carries with it the authority of the eyewitness account.[13] It is for this reason that it is shadowed by "counterfeit" or lying tales, especially the "fantasticall lies"

(as Iago ironically calls them) of travellers' tales—like the kind that
Othello recounts having told in wooing Desdemona in the first place.

III

Oh my America, my New Found Land.

(Donne, "To His Mistresse")

We have remarked that rhetorical *enargeia*, convincing description or
vivid report, contains within it the same visual root as the name of
"Argus," sent with his many eyes to spy. We turn now to another instance
of vivid description and of the dispatching of spies, this time not in the
context of a Iachimo sent to make his "voyage upon" the body of a woman
and bring back a report but in the context of an actual mercantile voyage,
concerned with the territory of Virginia named after Elizabeth, the Virgin
Queen.

In 1585 the elder Richard Hakluyt declared that, with respect to the
"soile and climate" of Virginia, the voyagers were "with *Argus eies* to see
what commoditie by industrie of man" the region might be made to
"yield."[14] Hakluyt's dispatching of voyagers with the commission that
they "see" with "Argus eies" both evokes the classical figure associated
with a spying motivated by sexual jealousy and asks the voyagers to
become messengers, to bring back a report. The figure is nicely overdetermined, evoking not only the classical story of jealousy and the
archetypal figure of eyes or seeing, but the biblical paradigm of the spies
dispatched to Canaan to spy out the Promised Land, that "land of milk
and honey" which the New World as New Canaan was so quickly
assimilated to. Hence *enargeia* or "evidence" in Iachimo's more exclusively commercial sense, the recounting and accounting in the report of
what "return" might be expected from the venture.

The elder Hakluyt's dispatching of spies and messengers who are to
report back, providing an inventory of what they have seen—the commodious landscape of Virginia translated into the vocabulary of use and
"commodity"—also participates, with its "yielding," in that traditional
sexualizing of this "New Found Land" which Annette Kolodny and others
have observed. What Columbus initially described as "a land to be
desired" became, in various reports back from this New World, Ralegh's
description of Guiana in 1595 as "a country that hath yet her maydenhead,
never sackt, turned, nor wrought"; John Smith's description of the New
England coast as a species of virginal garden, "her treasures having never
yet beene opened, nor her originalls wasted, consumed, nor abused";
Thomas Morton's complaint in 1632 that New England had been neglected

by colonists who had left her "Like a faire virgin, longing to be sped, / And meete her lover in a Nuptiall bed"; or Robert Mountgomry's later description of Carolina as a *"Paradise* with all her Virgin Beauties."[15]

Such genderings of America as female, and as waiting for her lover or conquerer, draw upon the same biblical texts—including the eroticized Song of Songs—which inform the "colors" of the traditional blazon, the ones echoed, for example, in the inventory of Olivia in *Twelfth Night* and in *The Rape of Lucrece*. The biblical image of the Promised Land or Paradise as a female body wedded by her Bridegroom informs not just the eulogies which filled the promotional tracts—including what Kolodny rightly terms the "big sell" of the Hakluyt collections, or something like John Hammond's 1656 treatise entitled "Leah and Rachel: or, The Two Fruitfull Sisters Virginia and Mary-land"—but also the later laments over the rape or despoliation of this land, which similarly invoke the great biblical tirades against Israel the Bride who has become a harlot or adulterous wife. Yet, while, as in the biblical context, the tirade is against the inhabitants who have strayed, the gendering of the land tends to shift the balance and the blame onto the personified female herself. Hammond complains of Maryland's having been raped and violated "by her own Inhabitants." But he also creates the sense that "she" has somehow invited her own rape, "that its extraordinary goodnes hath made it rather desired than envied, which hath been fatall to her (as beauty is often times to those that are endued with it)."[16] It is reminiscent of the logic of the blazon, where Lucrece takes upon herself the taint to a property in her own rape. More close to hand, it recalls the promotional tracts themselves, in which the land described is said, in a barely disguised gendering, to "invite" all comers, when it is the promoter who is doing both the displaying and the inviting.

What the reporter or spy was providing in these promotional narratives was a "blazing" or publishing of the glories of this feminized New World, of the possibilities of commercial abundance and "return." But an even more specific aspect of these vivid descriptions links them to the rhetorical tradition in which they often self-consciously participate as a form of rhetorical display. When John Smith writes of New England's "treasures" as "having never yet beene *opened*, nor her originalls wasted, consumed, nor abused," his language brings to mind that of Iachimo, sent not only to bring back a report but also self-sent to "open" the "lock" on Imogen's secret "treasure," a language shared by *The Rape of Lucrece*. When Robert Johnson's "Nova Britannia" (1609) not only describes Virginia as a female body (her "Valleyes and plaines streaming with sweete Springs, like veynes in a naturall bodie") but writes of her "hills and mountines making a sensible proffer of hidden treasure, never yet searched,"[17] his language performs the very "display" at work within the rhetorical tradition of such opening or unfolding of something hidden, bringing it forth to the light and to the view.

There is, then, a link in the discourse itself between the blazon and its form of rhetorical display, the tradition of opening the "bosom of nature" to view, and the language of the discovery of a feminized new land, opened to its developer. We might, indeed, approach this link through a figure who combines the notion of bringing to light something "hid" by means of an unfolding or displaying to the eye, and the narratives of the discovery (with its own strong sense of "uncovering") of a previously hidden New World. Francis Bacon, the principal theorist of the new epistemology which emerged from the discovery of the New World, used Columbus as an example of the "voyager" whose explorations could provide the emblem and impetus for uncovering "the remoter and more hidden parts of nature as well." His *Novum Organum* has recourse to the following analogy in its argument for this new knowledge: "Nor must it go for nothing that by the distant voyages and travels which have become frequent in our times many things in nature have been *laid open and discovered* which may let in new light upon philosophy. And surely it would be disgraceful if, while the regions of the material globe—that is, of the earth, of the sea, and of the stars—have been in our times *laid widely open and revealed*, the intellectual globe should remain shut up within the narrow limits of old discoveries." His *Advancement of Learning* strikingly combines "invention" with the language of the inventory of a property, and both with the "commodities" to be had from economic investment and New World "discovery." The impetus of discovery, of the new science, of uncovering and mining the hidden treasures of the earth, and of rhetorical "display" or opening to the view, all intersect in the gendered language of a showing forth to the eye, a bringing to light or uncovering of something hidden. "Invention" itself in all senses, including the rhetorical, participates in a sense of a transgressive uncovering or opening up of a secret place, of exposing what was hidden in the womb of a feminized Nature, a sense of transgression like that which surrounds the activity of mining and invention of gunpowder by the Satanic crew of *Paradise Lost* ("in a moment up they turned / Wide the celestial soil, and saw beneath / The originals of nature in their crude / Conception"; VI.509–12).[18]

We need also to remember, in citing Bacon as a crucial hinge figure in this respect, that the new Baconian inquiry was not only one in which "a method rightly ordered leads by an unbroken route through the woods of experience to the open ground of axioms" (p. 80)—a method whose very language suggests the link—but an epistemology in which words were to be signs of things, the rhetoric of *evidentia* effaced as rhetoric and taken to be a true report of the things themselves. In the "new continent" of knowledge, as in a New World which was not an ancient fable or "mouldy tale" (as the explorers never tired of reminding their audiences), words were to be the "vouchers" or evidence for things, and not the reports, as

Bacon puts it, of "talkers and dreamers who . . . have loaded mankind with promises" (p. 85). These travelers' accounts were intended to be "ocular proof," or "evidence" in a more modern sense.

Yet, precisely in the face of this occluding of the rhetorical in the new Baconian inquiry which would present nature "laid widely open and revealed," the salutary reminder of Wayne Franklin's study of the New World narratives is that they were indeed narratives, dependent like all discourse on the organizing structures the inquirers brought with them. Though Franklin does not explore the categories which link these narratives with rhetoric or with the discourse of property, the texts he foregrounds make clear that the "diligent writers" of his subtitle ("Send those on land that will show themselves diligent writers") brought with them the traditional commonplaces or rhetorical topoi, even though what they were encountering, as they themselves so frequently reiterate, was a very uncommon place. The intersecting terms of property and rhetoric, the language of "distribution," "partition," and "display," together inform what Edmundo O'Gorman has called "The *Invention* of America."[19]

We have already seen, in the context of *Cymbeline*, how easily the terms of accounting, counting, or recounting are transferred to the "story," in the material and narrative sense, which Iachimo brings back from his "voyage upon" Imogen. Discovery narratives of the New World were also a matter of accounts, both in the sense of purportedly eyewitness narratives which sought to distinguish themselves from the "many scandalous and false reports past upon the Country, even from the sulphurious breath of every base ballad-monger,"[20] and in the more specifically commercial sense of providing a detailed inventory of the riches to be gained as part of an accounting to actual or potential investors. Their narratives perform a twofold function, reporting or "blazing" the wonders of the New World to those who have not seen it with their own eyes, and inciting the desire of the hearer to "voyage upon" the new land, if only by proxy and as financial investment. Christopher Columbus, in an inaugural gesture that subsequent reports from the New World would frequently reiterate, plays on his own name ("Christo-ferens") as a conveyer or *translatio* figure, bringing the faith of Europe to the new land. But the reporting or "blazoning" of the beauties of this feminized territory also had merchandising and conquest as its motives, extending the logic of the blazon into a more direct form of pandering.

The same elder Hakluyt, who declared in 1585 that with respect to the "soile and climate" of Virginia the voyagers were "with Argus eies to see what commoditie by industrie of man" the region might be made to "yield," begins his "Inducements to the Liking of the Voyage Intended towards Virginia" with a list of thirty-one such "inducements," and then goes on to describe the overall purpose of the voyage itself:

The ends of $\left.\begin{array}{l}\text{1. To plant Christian religion}\\\text{2. To trafficke}\\\text{3. To conquer}\end{array}\right\}$ Or, to doe all three
this voyage
are these:

Stephen Greenblatt has described. the purposes of Thomas Harriot's *A Briefe and True Report of the New Found Land of Virginia* (1588)—to provide an inventory or descriptive catalogue of the "natural goods of the land" convertible into social goods or "merchantable commodities," and also to outline the strange customs of the Indians, in ways which might lead to efficient domination and control. To this relation, between discursive amplification (Harriot's description "at large"), bringing to light, and bringing under control, we will return.[21] The text I propose to juxtapose with *Cymbeline* and with the whole underground sense of the "display in rhetoric" and the blazon itself as ironically a form of pandering is, however, a later one—George Alsop's *A Character of the Province of Mary-Land* (1666).[22] For Alsop's *Character* not only combines exploratory narrative with the tradition of descriptive display but also sexualizes the language of its discovery more extensively than any other such New World document. It presents itself, in an extravagant and broad version of the literary language of the time, as a formal text, complete with dedicatory verses and references to Apollo and the Muse. It also dramatizes the bringing of the feminized "body" of Maryland into England through the medium of its own verbal representation ("I have had so large a Journey, and so heavy a Burden to bring *Mary-Land* into *England* that I am almost out of breath"); and, in one of the letters appended to it, it explicitly evokes the tradition of rhetorical "blazing," in verses on the death of the "great Rebel" Cromwell which speak of "such Lights" as "blaze forth the vertues dead" (p. 82). Even more specifically evocative of the rhetorical tradition of the display or opening up to view of the body of a woman, however, is the laudatory poem printed on the frontispiece beneath a portrait of Alsop himself, which praises him who "hath drawne exact the Province Mary Land / *Display'd* her Glory in such Scenes of Witt / That those that read must *fall in Love* with it," a direct evocation of the language of "blazoning" as the presentation of a picture to the eye.

In presenting "To all the Merchant Adventurers for Mary-Land" what he calls his "dish of Discourse," Alsop protests that his verbal description is not the pure invention or "imaginary supposition" of the lying traveler's tale but rather the "ocular" testimony of the true messenger: "What I present I know to be true, *Experientia docet*; it being an infallible Maxim, *That there is no Globe like the occular and experimental view of a Countrey.*" And another laudatory poem by William Bogherst alludes to his describing at large what Columbus had conveyed in sum:

> Who such odd nookes of Earths great mass describe
> Prove their descent from old Columbus tribe:

> Some Boding augur did his Name devise,
> Thy Genius too case in th'same mould and size;
> He made relation of that World in gross,
> Thou the particulars retail'st to us.

Both "retailing" and the evocation of "particulars" draw directly on the rhetorical tradition of opening which Alsop also repeatedly invokes for his own enterprise, beginning with the Table of Contents and its division of the Theophrastan "Character" of Mary-Land into "four distinct Parts," including its "plenty" and other matters *opened in view*," and continuing through the language of the affixed letters in which he has repeated recourse to the rhetorical tradition of demonstrating "both particularly and at large" (p. 95). His description also makes use of the traditional image of discourse itself as a series of places or a house of memory ("I am afraid I have kept you too long in the Entry, I shall desire you therefore to come in and sit down").

In a fashion reminiscent of the prejudices of his day, and the historical distance between 1666 and the age of Harriot, he disparages "Rhetoric" ("artificial Syllogisms drest up in gilded Orations"; "Tautologies of a long-winded Speech"). Yet the familiar topoi of the older rhetorical tradition of opening and display literally fill both his text and the published responses to it. The poem by Bogherst goes on to speak of Alsop's opening up "Some Mines at last which may enrich the World," making it clear that these are not just the literal mines of the New World but the promise of a greater wealth of discourse which this "short Abridgement" can only offer glimpses of. Again, the language reveals the gendered context of this whole tradition of description, display, or show: "Thou has describ'd its superficial Treasure, / Anatomiz'd its bowels at thy leasure; / That MARY-LAND to thee may duty owe, / Who to the World dost all her Glory shew." Another poem describes Alsop's report as having "opened" to view or "discover'd" what was hidden in lines which recall the typical situation of the male descriptive contest and blazon; his description, it writes, has

> Discover'd hidden Earth so plain, that we
> View more in this, then if we went to see.
> MARYLAND, I with some thousands more,
> Could not imagine where she stood before;
> And hadst thou still been silent with thy Pen,
> We had continu'd still the self-same men,
> Ne're to have known the glory of that Soyle,
> Whose plenteous dwellings is four thousand mile.

This is the testimony of the audience of men for whom "Mary-Land" is displayed and opened up, by means of a descriptive "blazing" whose purpose is precisely to incite voyages upon this feminized "hidden Earth." And this language continues in the description of a land who "within her own imbraces" is "extraordinary pleasant and fertile" and whose "natural womb (by her plenty) maintains and preserves the several diversities of Animals that rangingly inhabit her Woods."

There is, however, another important aspect of this description, one which lays emphasis not on her fertility but on the question of her ordering and governance. For, if this feminized "Mary-Land" is portrayed as sensuous and inviting in her "plenty," she is also portrayed as a dutiful and tractable woman. What another laudatory verse calls "This plain, yet pithy and concise Description / Of Mary-Lands plentious and *sedate* condition" (my emphasis) is underlined when Alsop goes on to describe her as sober and silent as a good wife should be (in chapter 2, "Of the Government and natural disposition of the People"): "such is her wisdom in a reserved silence, and not in pomp, to shew her well-conditioned Estate" that he "that desires to see the real Platform of a quiet and sober Government extant" should "look on *Mary-Land* with eyes admiring, and he'le then judge her, *The Miracle of this Age*." Native women, perhaps significantly in this context, are characterized as "much more talkative then men" (p. 24); and as follows, in a shocked description of the obscenity of their custom of openly performing a very private function: "the Women stand bolt upright with their armes a Kimbo ... in so confident and obscene a posture, as if they had taken their Degrees of Entrance at *Venice*, and commenced Bawds of Art at *Legorne*." Other cultural stereotypes of women—of Italian women, like this one, or of old England as "Margery the old Matron of the Celler"—balance Alsop's invitation to whoever "out of curiosity desires to see the Landskip of the Creation drawn to the life," to "view *Mary-Land* drest in her green and fragrant Mantle of the Spring." Mary-Land is to be both an innocent Eve and a sober and silent wife: and the "LAND-SKIP" or rudimentary map of its parts which accompanies the text has what appears to be a native woman, properly noble savage rather than obscenely open native woman, pointing in deference towards her male counterpart, who is pictured pointing his firearm and discharging it further into the wilderness. Alsop's text enacts the double impulse within the whole tradition of "opening" a female body up to view: to display it but also to preserve its chastity, to present a woman both inviting and under control, praised not just for her beauty but for her virtue.

IV

Yet higher than their tops
The verdurous wall of Paradise up sprung:
Which to our general sire gave prospect large
Into his nether empire neighbouring round.

(Milton, *Paradise Lost*, IV)

We come finally to the question of "prospect," which as a matter both of property and of the eye links the appropriation of a feminized New World to the emerging discourse of feminized landscape at the center of the empire, at the culmination of two centuries of imperial consolidation and of landed enclosure. Franklin distinguishes two "moments," the discovery and the exploration of the "New Found Land," as two types of figure and narrative—first that of the discoverer, rapt in wonder before this "uncommon place" and at a loss for words before its strangeness and plenitude; and that of the explorer, who brings into this suspension of "wonder" the exigencies of narrative and of time. Yet very often one gets the sense in reading accounts of the New World that the very act of taking in with the eye or gaze, as a visual or an economic "prospect," provides the initial moment of strangeness, stupefaction, and wonder with its saving countersublime, its gaining or regaining of "ground." It is difficult to separate admiring description—the detailing of the "particulars" of a potentially overwhelming abundance—from the catalogue of potential commodity and profit, even in the earliest narratives of the New World. The second voyage of Columbus is described by his accompanying physician in terms which readily juxtapose the "marvel" of the discovery ("era meravilla") with the discoverer's taking "possession" of it in the Old World "form of law," the economic motive inscribed in the project right from its inception. The "Memorandum of Christopher Columbus, sent to Ferdinand and Isabella, by Antonio de Torres" details by "item" the spices, gold, and other details of the discoveries, as later narratives of the New World would convert its commodious "plenty" into the language of commodity and use, into the potential for profit to those who came both to discover and to claim dominion over it.[23]

This separation but ultimate interrelation of moments provides a last link between the discourse of the blazon, of dominion over the body of a woman, and the opening of a "treasure" in the discovery of a feminized New World. Both *Cymbeline* and *The Rape of Lucrece* contain similar first moments of stasis and wonder, when the "voyager" is temporarily suspended before the beauty of the body he has come to "gain ground of." Encountering Lucrece, "Enchanted Tarquin" stands in "silent wonder of still-gazing eyes" (83–4); but a later stanza makes clear that this "wonder" or suspended beholding soon gives way to the kinesis of conquest ("What could he see but mightily he noted? / What did he note but strongly he desired? ... / With more than admiration he admired"; 414 ff.), until finally gazing leads to a rape that is described as the conquest of a "land":

> His drumming heart cheers up his burning eye,
> His eye commends the leading to his hand;
> His hand as proud of such a dignity,
> Smoking with pride, march'd on, to make his stand
> On her bare breast, the heart of all her land. (435–9)

Iachimo, similarly, pauses before the sleeping Imogen until he remembers his "design" (*Cymbeline*, II.ii.23), which turns out to be "merchandising" rather than Tarquin's lust, the inventory of her room that is "enough" (II.ii.46) for his real purpose. When Milton recalls both of these purely temporary moments of wonder in that moment when Satan gazes upon Eve before he remembers his real mission ("That space the evil one abstracted stood / From his own evil, and for the time remained / Stupidly good, of enmity disarmed"; *Paradise Lost*, IX.463–5), we encounter a text which mediates between the realm of the male gaze and the moment of "wonder" before a feminized New World; for Satan's whole voyage to Eden, and voyage upon Eve, brings with it all the associations of an Exodus to this Earthly Paradise or New Canaan, a voyage with a purpose not just to wonder at but also to colonize it.

The movement of Milton's voyager from wonder to an act which does indeed, as Franklin says of the "explorer" moment, bring time itself into this pictured stasis, makes explicit the gendered context, and contest, of the whole tradition it recapitulates. Satan's proceeding to his conquest comes only after the potentially disarming "rapine sweet" (IX.461) which the initial sight of Eve first performs on him. Something similar appears to happen to that initial moment of wonder and speechlessness that Franklin describes in the "ravished observer" of the New World scene, in which conquest by discourse as well as by actual exploration and colonization seems to involve precisely a form of countersublime, a regaining of speech as an integral part of its own gaining or regaining of "ground." The explorer or voyager is sent out to America as Iachimo sets out to "voyage upon" Imogen, and both send back a report. But it is not just the conquest but the discourse itself which possesses. Language and its Old World topoi—though temporarily at a loss—also function as a vehicle of appropriation and control.[24]

Examples such as the one Franklin cites, of Cortés' admission that the palace of Montezuma was "so marvelous" that it would be "impossible to describe its excellence and grandeur," and the breaking off of his inventory before its "unnameable excess," record this initial moment of wonder and speechlessness.[25] Yet inventories and categorizations abound right from the first moments of the discovery of the New World; and they become a principal instrument not only of promotion but of domination, just as Desdemona in *Othello* is ironically described as beyond the reach of "blazoning pens" (II.i) and yet is precisely caught within Iago's powerful *enargeia* or vivid verbal "evidence." In both cases, something initially portrayed as beyond the reach of language and description is set forth to the gaze in forms that also carefully control it by the topoi of invention itself.

Here too we might perceive the structural affinity between a rhetorical tradition concerned to find out or discover a plenteous "matter" and bring it under proper disposition or control, and the way in which the New World was processed, in texts which suggest that the abundance and "unnameable excess" of this feminized New Land also constituted a potential threat, something not just to be marveled at but to be mastered. Arthur Barlowe, who sailed the Carolina coast with Philip Amadas in 1584 on Ralegh's behalf, wrote of it as a realm of "wonderful plenty" where "the earth bringeth foorth all things in aboundance, as in the first creation, without toile or labour." But Harriot's *Briefe and True Report of the New Found Land of Virginia* in 1588 is much more taken up with economic concerns, with inventory rather than simple or "rapt" wonder. Christopher Carleill's *A Briefe and Summary Discourse upon the Intended Voyage to the Hithermost Parts of America* (1583) had already treated the "greate abundance" of "matter" to be found as the promise of turning it into "greater and more assured commoditie" and more "notable profite" than other competing markets for investment. And, though Alsop speaks of Maryland's "multiplicity, or rather Nature's extravagancy of a super-abounding plenty," of its "increase" and the "rich variety and diversities of all things," he also provides an ordered inventory of it, a translation of this plenty not only into the language of commodity but also into the discursive forms of order and dominion.[26]

We have already noted the intersection of "counting" and "recounting" in Iachimo's inventory of the body and "circumstances" of a woman; and the functioning of the rhetorical tradition of "increase and multiply" as an instrument both of plenty and of mastery, a way of keeping "increase" within some kind of boundary. Franklin suggests that in Carleill's discussion of "the matter especially looked for" in any commercial venture, the mathematical art of multiplication itself—displaying the plenty to be had but keeping any attendant specter of an undesirable multiplicity under control—allows its increase to be kept within a particular horizon.[27] The treatment and organization of the abundant *materia* of this New World indicates many such parallels with the motive of containment in the art of discourse. *Distributio* in rhetoric, for example, typically draws, for the analogue of its distribution of a "matter" into parts, on the division of the body politic into its distributed functions. Similarly, when the younger Hakluyt in his *Discourse of Western Planting* (1584) considers the new territory as a field for development and use, he gives a list of "Arrowhead-makers, Bowstave preparers, Glewmakers ... Grubbers and rooters upp of Cipres, Cedars, and of all other faire trees for to be employed in coffers deskes &c. for traffique ... Millwrightes ... Sawyers ... Carpinters ... Joyners ... Blacksmithes ... Brickmakers," and so forth, as part of the economic process of the distribution of the labor necessary to develop the abundance of this new land.[28] An integral aspect of this conflation is the subtle and important transformation of an older language of rhetorical and political control—of copious "plenty" both "distributed" and "disposed"—into an emergent bourgeois language of property and commodity, at work both in the colonies and at home in England, and linking the economic with the visual sense of "prospect." Hobbes, for example, in an extraordinary instance of just such a transformation in the passage from *Leviathan* devoted to the "Nutrition, and Procreation of a Common–wealth" (II.xxiv), reworks older rhetorical categories of increase and order in discourse—*Divisio, Distributio, Dispositio*—into this nascent bourgeois language, as he describes the need for the "Distribution" and "Division," according to the principle of "Propriety" or property, of the "Plenty of Matter" which comes "from (the two breasts of our common Mother) Land and Sea."[29]

If the inventory is both a rhetorical and an economic instrument, one way of controlling the territory in question and reducing its otherness is to "distribute" and divide up its plenty into precisely such a survey of economic prospects. Careful detailing of its abundance, displaying its riches to the view, provides the discursive counterpart to the visual prospect of dominion, those repeated moments when the explorer brings the strange land under his gaze from a commanding height.[30] The blazon itself, as we have seen, is a form of "distribution," the amplification of a discourse by a detailing of a woman's "parts." The displaying to view and "partition" of a woman's body and the surveying and partitioning of a geographical territory were already linked in passages like the one in Shakespeare's *Comedy of Errors* where an extended hyperbolic blazon of an ample female body depends upon her division into a map of the world.[31] "Partition" of a territory is a way of organizing its copious expanse, not just in the actual division of the land, but in the map-making impulse which accompanied the discovery and exploration of the New World, showing, as a much later eighteenth-century text like Jonathan Carver's *Travels* (1778) would, a large stretch of territory "partitioned ... into plantations or subordinate colonies."[32]

"Partition" in this sense becomes part of the institution of private property in a land of plenty thought originally to be without it. But its justification was also related to the economic imperative of "increase and multiply." Daniel Denton's *Brief Description of New York* in 1670 notes that the "plentiful increase" of this "terrestrial Canaan" is made possible only by labor; his warning might be placed beside the many complaints that early colonizers of these territories were succumbing to a life of paradisal *otium* and unproductive ease in nature's lap, or beside Milton's Adam, who is to labor and cultivate even in the midst of Eden. As in the rhetorical tradition, descriptions of the need to "increase and multiply" by the partition of the land into spaces for productive labor repeatedly recall the gendered tradition of the Platonic demiurge working that female *materia* to which he gives form. A much later writer like Nathaniel Ames, for instance, writes that English settlers will discover in America "a vast

Stock of proper Materials for the Art and Ingenuity of Man to work upon" or that "Nature thro'all her Works has stamp'd Authority on this Law, namely 'That all fit Matter shall be improved to its best Purposes'." The language of disposition and dominion still informs Emerson's essay on "Nature" and the epic catalogues of Whitman as he "dilates" his soul in America.[33]

One man concerned to control both a feminized Nature and the other strangenesses of the New Land suggests the complex mixture of imperial and horticultural motives involved. The *hortus conclusus* or figurative enclosed garden which the blazon tradition draws on as figure of a woman's body took literal form in the famous Philadelphia garden of the botanist John Bartram, arranged into framed and carefully disposed parts by the same man who provided an inventory of the "troublesome plants" which needed to be tended in his native state. Bartram, under the triangulated aspect of the rivalry between British and French imperialism for this feminized new land, also recorded the details of his journey to the Canadian frontier in 1743 in the company of a topographer and an Indian negotiator. On that journey, the threat of a wilder nature and of the "barbarous, inhuman, ungrateful natives" converge in an encounter with a proliferation of branches, an "abundance of old trees lying on the ground, or leaning against live ones," so thick, the record provocatively adds, "that we concluded it almost impossible to shoot a man at 100 yards distant, let him stand never so fair." The text of a later letter by this same botanist juxtaposes advice on how to keep the native element under control ("unless we bang [them] stoutly, and make them fear us, they will never love us, nor keep peace long with us") with praise of the "variety of plants and flowers" of "old Madam Flora," which though "beyond expression" (like Desdemona, beyond the reach of "blazoning pens") he nevertheless hopes to dispose and arrange in his collection of "curiosities."[34]

The links in Bartram between various kinds of control make explicit the Georgic impulse which runs through all such New World texts and which associates the organization and laying out of land with other forms of order, including discursive ones. But the impulse in such writings—as in the tradition of the blazon and of rhetorical display—to bring something under the control of the eye or gaze calls to mind not just Virgil's *Georgics* but also his *Aeneid*, the epic of empire self-consciously present for so many of the "diligent writers" of the New World. Both its cartographic impulse and its repeated topos of taking command from a high place might suggest why imperial gaze and male gaze come together so readily in these New World texts, where the impulse to master or dominate a feminized landscape is at the same time a matter for the eye.

It is this Virgilian topos of *imperium* and of imperial gaze or "prospect" which provides the background for Adam's "prospect large" into his "nether empire neighbouring round" (as in the epigraph to this section) and for the fallen Adam's survey of the world that lies before him at the end of *Paradise Lost*.[35] But it is also this topos of gaze and "prospect" which provides the link between narratives of the New World—with their repeated gendering—and the emerging discourse of property not in the outer reaches of the empire but in England itself, in a century (that of Bartram and Carver) which both consolidated its hold on this empire and intensified the massive enclosure and consolidation of land at home.

Carole Fabricant's provocative study of eighteenth-century landscape descriptions has already remarked their combination of "aesthetic, economic, and sexual forms of possession." Though omitted or unperceived in the virtual multitude of academic studies devoted to the literature of Augustan landscape, gender and the anxieties of property pervade the very language of these descriptions. What I would propose to do, finally—via the topos of the "prospect," the possessing of a landscape or territory with the eye—is to consider this discourse and its typical language in relation to the others we have remarked, the rhetoric of the blazon and domination of the New World.

To turn from a focus on empire to a focus on landscape might seem a somewhat abrupt turn. But the connection was by no means as difficult for eighteenth-century writers on landscape to envisage. Pope slides easily from empire to gardening, for instance, in his observation that Lord Peterborough "tames the Genius of the Stubborn Plain / Almost as quickly, as he conquer'd Spain" (*Satire II*, i.131–2). Fabricant's study of the gendering of such landscape descriptions, when encountered after the earlier texts and contexts we have considered, suggests not just the language but a logic of private property that is as double and contradictory as that of the blazon—the desire simultaneously to display a possession to others' eyes and to control it or protect it from "theft." Since her interest is in gender rather than rhetoric, Fabricant does not foreground the discursive lexicon of these descriptions. But they repeatedly treat of the "Disposition," "Distribution," and "circumstances" of a feminized Nature displayed in her plenty and seductiveness and yet also brought under the domination of the eye, in ways which link the discussion of landscape to the older language of rhetorical "opening" and display.[36] Stephen Switzer writes of Nature's secret parts "laid open to View"; Lord Shaftesbury of her "inmost recesses" as available to the eye and yet at the same time reserved for his private sight, for the spectator-owner whose property she is.[37] The materials of a traditionally feminized Nature here are described by the categories which also govern rhetorical organization and display, shifted to the mode of the English country gentleman displaying his property to the admiring gaze of those he invites and wishes to impress.

The familiar Christianized Platonism we have already seen at work both in the rhetorical tradition and in the texts of the New World—of a male god working a passive and tractable female *materia*, here the "careless and loose Tresses of Nature" herself—recalls in a new mode the terms of the rhetorical tradition which would seek both to open nature and a copious "matter" up to view and to establish its boundaries. Most strikingly, the notion of "prospect" everywhere in these texts invokes both the Miltonic sire's commanding height—like the "Mount" from which Pope at Twickenham could invite his guests to "overlook the various *Distribution* of the Thickets, Grass plots, Alleys, Banks, &c."—and the opening up of nature to the view of the selected few.[38] The emphasis throughout is on the eye, in ways which make it clear that both women and a feminized Nature are to be on display, opened up to the gaze of the possessor who displays her as part of a primary relation between men. To the passages cited by Fabricant we might add another which makes explicit this triangulation, not in a bragging contest, as in the blazon, but in its counterpart, the tendentious joke—in the observations of Thomson, author of *The Seasons*, on a tour of the country property of William Shenstone:

> "You have nothing to do (says he) but to dress Nature. Her robe is ready made; you have only to caress her; love her; kiss her; and then— descend into the valley." Coming out into the court before the house, he mentioned Clent and Waw-ton Hill as the two bubbies of Nature: then Mr. L. observed the nipple, and then Thomson the fringe of Uphmore wood; till the double entendre was work'd up to a point, and produced a laugh.[39]

In this discourse, as in the others considered, the emphasis is on a female figure at once external to the description and laid out, through it, to the view: Addison, in the appropriately named *Spectator* (no. 477), combines observations both on landscapes as "lying so conveniently under the Eye of the Beholder" and on women as passive and "lovely pieces of human nature," on display for "their Male-Beholders."[40] But it is also on property, possession and control, in ways which link this same "Mr Spectator's" remarks on the proper conduct of wives (to display themselves as part of the pride of male ownership but not to invite the counterpart of Tarquin's "theft") with the sense that Nature was to open up her beauties to the gaze of her owner and those to whom he chose to display his possession and yet conceal herself from vulgar, prying, or thieving eyes. This double impulse is again reminiscent of the blazon and is played out in the whole conflict between the desire to display one's garden and property without restricting the gaze and the need to establish definite boundaries around it, to make sure it was also "enclosed." Pope evokes the "spacious Garden" of Alcinous, opening up nature's plenitude, but also the "green Enclosure" all around it. And the author of the "Epistolary Description of Twickenham" observes, in language whose gendering we cannot miss after all the language of opening and exclusivity we have witnessed, that "Near the Bounds of the Garden, the Trees unite themselves more closely together, and cover the Hedges with a thick Shade, which prevents all prying from without, and preserves the Privacy of the interior Parts." As Fabricant shrewdly observes, nature is allowed to flaunt her superiority over the "rigid and confining forms of art," but she is also put in her place, subordinated to her possessor's eye and shaping hand, just as, in some of the earlier texts we have considered, a feminized "matter" is allowed to dilate or increase only so far before being shaped by an informing *dispositio*.[41]

The verbal display of a woman, opened up to view by her possessor; the narrative inventory of a feminized America, as in Alsop, "opened in view"; the Baconian description of the parts of nature "laid widely open and revealed"; and the expansive display of an English owner's property "laid open to View," but jealously guarded from intrusion—all participate in an imagery of opening and controlling something gendered as female before spectators and possessors gendered as male, in a process in which ostentatious display, *copia*, or "increase" is constrained within an economy of mastery and ownership. They suggest forms of economic, sexual, and epistemological possession, a gendering which goes beyond a simple matter of language minimized as such into the actual relations of power in a culture which displays and controls women and other strange things. The interrelations that enabled a wife to be spoken of as a "high-pric'd Commoditie" which might, through adultery or sexual theft, "light into some other merchants' hands," or as "our private Inclosure" which might prove "to be a Common for others," reveal in their very language the articulation of a discourse which, beyond the enclosures of the patriarchal family in the period we have considered, accompanied the increasing consolidation of the modern state and the increasingly enforced gentlemanly "enclosure" of land. (At a much later and more self-critical stage in this history, not of England but of one of its imperial rivals, it would yield a novel in a colonial setting entitled *La Jalousie*.) Categories of rhetoric and the construction of a "story" or "account"—even after the supposed demise of rhetoric—actively participate in this emerging discourse of private property, in a way that is causative and not just reflection or effect. They also participate in constituting a project in which what we have come to think of as "high" literature shares structures and agendas with products of that culture. As Edward Said has observed of Orientalism[42]—drawing on Foucault—we have here to do in a larger sense with a discourse, and one which includes science, politics, economics, and rhetoric within a more common discursive space, crossing in the process those disciplinary boundaries inherited as one of the effects of this history, the division of the textual instances we have considered into what in a revealing metaphor is commonly referred to as different "fields."

8

The (Self-)Identity of the Literary Text: Property, Proper Place, and Proper Name in *Wuthering Heights*

I

The end of linear writing is indeed the end of the book.

(Jacques Derrida, *Of Grammatology*)

In 1957, Ian Watt began *The Rise of the Novel* by tracing the parallels between the growing popularity of the novel form and a number of contemporary Enlightenment phenomena—the realist epistemology of Bacon, Descartes, Hobbes, and Locke; the growth of Protestantism with its fondness for personal inventory and for measuring time and progress in the sequential form of the journal or diary; economic individualism, with its division of labor and private property; and the "principle of individuation" enunciated by Locke:

> The "principle of individuation" accepted by Locke was that of existence at a particular locus in space and time: since, as he wrote, "ideas become general by separating them from the circumstances of time and place," so they become particular only when both these circumstances are specified. In the same way the characters of the novel can only be individualized if they are set in a background of particularized time and place.[1]

This principle is connected in Locke—who also wrote a defense of private property—with the differentiating function of proper names, the very indicators of individual identity, since, as Hobbes maintained, a "Proper Name" is "singular to one only thing."[2] Locke, whose work everywhere pervades the eighteenth century, established a principle in which individuality is linked to definitive placing—a place marked by the proper or "appropriated" name which designates an individual identity and prevents its being confused with another ("and therefore in their own species, which they have most to do with and wherein they have often to mention particular persons, they make use of proper names, and there distinct individuals have distinct denominations"; III.3.4). In literature, argues Watt, "this function of proper names was first fully established in the novel," with its attention to names as designating "completely individual-ized entities" so as to "suggest that they were to be regarded as particular individuals in the contemporary social environment." Names point a finger, or single out, as Foucault observes in his discussion of the primacy of naming or denomination in the Enlightenment; they say, as the preacher does to Lockwood in his first dream at Wuthering Heights, "*Thou art the man!*"[3]

More recently than Watt, Patricia Drechsel Tobin, in *Time and the Novel*, has extended this exploration of the relation between the novel and the phenomenon of linearity in all its Enlightenment forms—the line of time, of language, of narrative, and of thought, the model which informs the linear structure of Puritan diary and capitalist ledger-book, of genealogy and chronological history, of division into discrete serial entities or binary oppositions, the continuation of the Aristotelian Law of the Excluded Middle into the post-Cartesian logic of succession and sequence. With Barthes, Foucault, and Derrida, Tobin associates this linear logic with syntax itself, the sentence moving like a miniature narrative from beginning to ending and thereby linking logic with closure. Derrida, in his discussion of the line and the book in *De la grammatologie*, describes this linearity as "the repression of pluri-dimensional symbolic thought" and makes a connection between linear writing, logic, scientific and philo-sophical analysis, and history understood as a line or irreversible progress. Foucault characterizes it as a shift from a Renaissance fondness for resemblance to a preference for classification and sequential or causal reasoning, from metaphor's paradigmatic verticality to metonymy—the syntagmatic and sequential. Discourse, he observes, is understood in the classical *episteme* as "a sequence of verbal signs," a spacing out of the simultaneous into the successive, into a "linear order" whose parts "must be traversed *one after* the other." It is the linear model which produces what Foucault calls the "reciprocal kinship" between the "chain of discourse" (Hobbes), epistemology as "the chain of knowledge," the conception of time as chronology or irreversible sequence, and the En-lightenment preoccupation with progress. And it is this linear logic, combined with the conception of time as chronological sequence, which informs the novel as well, linked so closely with chronology as to be arguably "chronomorph," even when it appears to be transgressing that order.[4]

Hugh Blair and others in the eighteenth century were concerned with the establishment of rules for language itself, its mastery according to the dictates of "propriety"—a word still synonymous in this period with "property," in one of its senses—and with the decorum of proper place regulating the movement of tropes such as metaphor conceived of as "improper" (Quintilian, *improprium*) or "out of place." Foucault pro-vides a virtual paraphrase of the way in which what Blair calls language's "gradual progress towards refinement"—where "almost every object comes to have a proper name given to it"—is contrasted in the Enlightenment with the primitive mobility of words, before they could be assigned their proper places on the table or grid:

It is very probable that this mobility was even greater in the beginnings of language than it is now: today, the analysis is so detailed, the grid so fine, the relations of coordination and subordination are so firmly established, that words scarcely have any opportunity to move from their places. But at the beginning of human history, when words were few, when representations were still confused and not well analysed, when the passions both modified them and provided them with a basis, words had greater mobility. One might even say that words were figurative before being proper: in other words, that they had scarcely attained their status as particular names before they were being scattered over representations by the force of spontaneous rhetoric.[5]

We might keep in mind this connection between the primitive paucity of words and their mobility when we turn to Emily Brontë's *Wuthering Heights*, which involves a primitive setting seen through the eyes of a narrator whose name recalls Locke's, makes do with a curious paucity of proper names, and gives us Lockwood's own contrast between the story's more primitive setting and the civilized world from which he comes as that between "setting a hungry man down to a single dish on which he may concentrate his entire appetite" and "introducing him to a table laid out by French cooks" (VII, 102).

Foucault's concluding discussion of the Enlightenment suggests that it is possible to see in the very grid of linearity, analysis, and proper placing the "excluded" which was eventually to undo it:

if there is to be an articulated patterning of representations, there must be a murmur of analogies rising from things, perceptible even in the most immediate experience; there must be resemblances that posit themselves from the very start.... If language exists, it is because below the level of identities and differences there is the foundation provided by continuities, resemblances, repetitions, and natural criss-crossings. Resemblance, excluded from knowledge since the early seventeenth century, still constitutes the outer edge of language: the ring surrounding the domain of that which can be analysed, reduced to order, and known. Discourse dissipates the murmur, but without it it could not speak.

For Foucault, it is the repressed violence of both nature and tropes which undoes the linear "chain" of discourse and of knowledge: disorder in nature disrupts the "general ordering of nature," and the "ancient, enigmatic density" of words—the "reappearance of language as a multiple profusion"—disrupts the order of language as a "grid for the knowledge of things."[6] *Wuthering Heights* is crucially situated within this history, not only because of its own preoccupation with proper name and proper place, but because in so many ways it recapitulates both the linear Enlightenment grid and its exclusions, the "rise of the novel" and its potential unmaking. It may therefore be approached as one of those nineteenth-century texts which call into question—long before contemporary interest in this problem, which may be itself an after-effect of the disruption of the classical *episteme*—precisely the identity, or self-identity, of the text, by the simultaneous demonstration and undoing of the epistemological claims and ordering structures of the novel form.[7] In *Wuthering Heights* this undoing involves both nature, which is placed outside the orderly "house of fiction" in the binary opposition of nature and culture on which Lockwood's narrative partly depends, and the *unheimlich*, or uncanny, mobility of tropes such as metaphor traditionally described as "alien," part of the excluded which threatens the identity of that which seeks to control or master it.

II

We're dismal enough without conjuring up ghosts and visions to perplex us.

(Nelly Dean, *Wuthering Heights*)

the authoritarian demands put pressure on a narrative voice to turn into a narratorial voice and to bring about [*donner lieu à*] a narrative that would be identifiable.

(Derrida, "LIVING ON: Border Lines")

Wuthering Heights would seem to present us with a quintessential Enlightenment narrative in its preoccupation with the claims of superstition and reason, primitive and civilized, and in the ambivalent middle position occupied by its secondary narrator, Nelly Dean, between belief in the supernatural and her own housekeeper's sense of order and proper place. The novel opens with a date (1801) inaugurating the text of a narrator who identifies himself in the opening line ("I have just returned from a visit to my landlord—the solitary neighbour that I shall be troubled with"), very soon after records his own proper name ("Mr. Lockwood, your new tenant, sir"), and then provides a second date (1802) at the beginning of chapter XXXII. The generic identity of the text would appear to be that of the diary or journal—that sequential ordering of time and narrative that allies the novel with the linearity of chronology, genealogy, or history. Lockwood himself seems to belong on the side of enlightenment, as the master narrator whose distance from the superstitious and supernatural phenomena he encounters gives the novel, in the view of some of its readers, a reassuring sense both of progress and of closure. The question of the identity of the literary text, then, when raised with regard to *Wuthering Heights*, involves at least two related issues: its generic identity, the novel form, with its dependence on chronology, spacing, the principle of individuation, and the designating function of proper names; and the identity, or self-identity, of a text which appears from the beginning to be the unified production of a single hand—authorized by the conferring of his narrative signature or proper name.

In approaching the question of the identity or self-identity of *Wuthering Heights*, we might have recourse to a distinction from Maurice Blanchot, taken up again in a recent essay by Derrida which has precisely to do with the question of identity, and with the relationship between identity and placing. Blanchot distinguishes the "narrative voice" from the "narratorial voice," which in *Wuthering Heights* would be that of Lockwood himself, "the voice of a subject recounting something, remembering an event or a historical sequence, knowing who he is, where he is, and what he is talking about." The "narrative voice," by contrast, is, in Blanchot's phrase, "a neutral voice that utters the work from the placeless place where the work is silent." The narratorial voice can be located and identified—it has, says Derrida, and confers on the work, "une carte d'identité." But the narrative voice has no fixed place: it is both atopical and hypertopical, nowhere and everywhere at once. In Blanchot's terms, the neutral narrative voice is "ghostlike," a specter which haunts the narratorial text and, itself without center, placing, or closure, disrupts and dislocates the work, not permitting it to exist as finally completed or closed.[8]

This ghostlike atopicality and hypertopicality of something which resists definitive placing or closure may remind us in *Wuthering Heights* of its own principal ghost, that "Catherine" who haunts Heathcliff after her death, overrunning all boundaries by being at once everywhere ("I am surrounded with her image! . . . The entire world is a dreadful collection of memoranda that she did exist, and that I have lost her!") and in no single, definable place ("Where is she? Not *there*—not in heaven—not perished —where?"). The novel is full of ghosts, demons, and uncanny presences, from the "Catherine" Heathcliff begs to "haunt" him (XVI, 204) to the "ghostly Catherine" Linton (IV, 75) of Lockwood's second dream in the room at the Heights he describes as "swarming with ghosts and goblins" (III, 68); from Catherine's evocation of Gimmerton Kirk ("We've braved its ghosts often together, and dared each other to stand among the graves and ask them to come"; XII, 164) to Heathcliff's affirmation of his belief in ghosts (XXIX, 320), and his warning of the consequences of not burying him next to the open side of Catherine's coffin ("if you neglect it, you shall prove, practically, that the dead are not annihilated!"; XXXIV, 363). This repeated reference to ghosts in the novel is also countered, however, by their denial, from Isabella Linton's "It's well people don't *really* rise from their grave" (XVII, 216) to Lockwood's concluding assurance against the superstition that the dead Catherine and Heathcliff "walk," when he visits their graves in the closing lines of the text ("I lingered round them, under the benign sky; watched the moths fluttering among the heath and hare-bells; listened to the soft wind breathing through the grass; and wondered how anyone could ever imagine unquiet slumbers, for the sleepers in that quiet earth"). The exercise of closure itself, by the master narrator who confers on the text his own unifying identity and proper name, is linked with the laying, or denial, of ghosts, a forestalling of an uncanny return or "advent," a term the narrative several times repeats.

Wuthering Heights, then, offers the reader both the possibility of ghosts and the denial of them. But there is also in the novel a textual ghost, in Blanchot's terms, which inhabits and dislocates the identity conferred by Lockwood's narratorial order and its Enlightenment preoccupation with linearity, propriety, and proper place. All we have is Lockwood's text, but inscribed within it as its own uncanny other is an "alien" text inhabiting it and disrupting its ordering structures—Lockwood's diary, Nelly Dean's genealogical history, and the very sequential process of reading which the novel form invites. Derrida speaks, in his discussion of the "linear norm" and the "form of the book," of the undoing of the linear which takes place in the margins and "between the lines."[9] *Wuthering Heights*, with its own emphasis on marginal, competing, and heterogeneous texts—Catherine's manuscript writing, for example, inserted into the "margins" or "blanks" of "good books" (III)—itself provokes a double reading in which the text begins to lose the sense of coherent order or unified identity its organization under a single identifiable narratorial voice would confer upon the book. Not insignificantly, it is to books that Edgar Linton repairs in the midst of his wife's delirious ravings (XII), and books that Lockwood piles up in a "pyramid" to keep out a ghostly alien or "changeling" who seeks to reenter the house (III). Reading itself—in the proper left-to-right order in which Hareton Earnshaw learns to decipher the inscription which will restore him to his property and rightful place—is part of the process, in this novel, of civilization and enlightenment. But, in Derrida's terms, the "text"—like Heathcliff, both "orphan" and "alien"—works against the order and identity of the "book," and that which is in the margins or between the lines becomes part of the text's own "subversive dislocation of identity in general."[10]

Readers of *Wuthering Heights* have frequently commented on its apparent binary oppositions—nature and culture, good and evil, heaven and hell, primitive and civilized—and less frequently on the way in which it undermines this division in the very process of calling attention to it, as Shelley does in *The Witch of Atlas*, with its opening reference to the Enlightenment division into "those cruel Twins," Error and Truth. Both logic and the logic of identity are founded, for Derrida, on the opposition of inside and outside which inaugurates all binary opposition—where each of the terms is "simply external to the other." The expulsion of one involves a domination or mastery, like naming itself, which Nietzsche (speaking precisely of the opposition of "good " and "evil") links with a taking of possession or appropriation. But, once expelled, the "outside" functions as a ghost: the identical is haunted, as Foucault says of the Enlightenment table or grid, by what it excludes. The principal story in *Wuthering Heights* involves the usurpation of a house, or property, by a "houseless" (IV, 78) outsider or alien. Heathcliff, in a language the novel itself employs, is the "guest" who becomes the "master" of the house. What I will suggest is that Lockwood's own Enlightenment narrative— with the sense of unified identity it confers upon the book—is inhabited by a textual guest which threatens to become host, two terms used together in chapter III (68) at precisely the point where it is a question of Lockwood's having penetrated to the center of the house and encountered a "ghost."[11] To look for the identity of the literary text may in this, as in other nineteenth-century narratives, be finally to discover a Ghost Story.

III

Thrushcross Grange is my own, sir.

Heathcliff

For Derrida, the self-identity of the text is intimately linked to *propriété* in its widest sense. What must be emphasized, however, is that the complex of terms related to the "proper," a complex to which recent criticism has again called our attention, also engaged the Enlightenment, precisely in connection with the problem of identity. By considering the relation of property, proper place, and proper name in Lockwood's text to the question of its unified identity, we return to the context with which we began—the Lockean principle of individuation, its relation to discrete chronological sequence or line and to the boundary-marking of individual identity through what Locke termed the "appropriation"of the proper name. In the process, I shall suggest that the two sides of the debate over *Wuthering Heights*—between formalist critics who emphasize its narrative structures and Marxist or sociological critics who emphasize its involvement with the laws of private property—converge in this novel precisely on the question of "property" in its most radical or fundamental sense.[12]

Property and proper name are connected, first, in the figure of Lockwood himself: it is he who owns or masters his own text—as Hobbes says of the connection between Author and Owner (*Leviathan*, I.xvi)—and lends his name as the single unifying presence of a narrative which repeatedly calls attention to the importance of proper place, property, propriety, and proper name. The emphasis on place or position in Lockwood's text is everywhere: in the plot founded on the relation between the two houses, Wuthering Heights and Thrushcross Grange; in the sense of speech as placing characters by region or social class; and in Joseph's pharisaical insistence on the Sabbath as an inviolable place in time. This is joined by a more specific focus on ownership, possession, and property, from Heathcliff's opening "Thrushcross Grange is my own, sir" (I, 45), his reference to his own son as "property" (XX, 242), Lockwood's uncertainty about who is the "favoured possessor" of the female figure he encounters at the Heights (II, 55), and Earnshaw's finding the orphan Heathcliff without an "owner" (IV), to the principal exchange of the plot, in which Heathcliff acquires the very property from which he had been excluded. Private property and its dividing lines are reduced to an extreme in the scene in which the "divided" Linton children (VI, 89) almost rend a pet dog "in two" in their struggle for possession—a sacrifice of whole for part which recalls the judgment of Solomon and its revelation of the logic, and limits, of property. The careful guarding of the Linton property at Thrushcross Grange against all trespass is epitomized in the elder Linton's charge to the little "outlaws" Catherine and Heathcliff—"To beard a magistrate in his stronghold, and on the Sabbath, too!" (VI, 90). The biblical resonance of the charge recalls both Christ's trespass of the Sabbath and his breaking down of all barriers or partition walls (2 Corinthians 10:4: "For the weapons of our warfare are not carnal, but mighty through God to the pulling down of strong holds").

"Property" in the sense of the establishment of boundaries—and the prohibition of trespass fundamental to a society based on the laws of private possession—appears as well in the frequency in the novel of images such as windows, thresholds, and gates which mark the boundaries between places, or between inside and outside. From the opening chapter, the novel's establishment of boundaries or dividing walls is intimately linked with the language of its narrator, whose syntax raises barriers even as he pushes through the gate which keeps him from the Heights ("I do myself the honour of calling as soon as possible, after my arrival, to express the hope that I have not inconvenienced you by my perseverance in soliciting the occupation of Thrushcross Grange"), and whose convoluted speech contrasts pointedly with the abruptness of Heathcliff's replies and the Height's own unmediated entrance ("One step brought us into the family sitting-room, *without any introductory lobby, or passage*"). Lockwood, indeed, presents himself in a series of episodes involving the interposition of barriers: his rebuffing of the young girl whose attentions he had initially encouraged, his interposing of a "table" between himself and the dog whose fury he himself provoked (I), his piling up of books to keep out a ghostly "Catherine Linton" (III) and rubbing her wrist against the broken glass of a partition which no longer divides. These apotropaic gestures provide our first introduction to the narrator who will both request and relate the housekeeper's story from the framed and mediated distance of Thrushcross Grange. In the midst of the chaos he himself has caused by baiting the dogs, Lockwood assimilates them to the biblical "herd of possessed swine," and his hastening to interpose a table between himself and the fury he has raised proleptically enacts the function of the narrative which ensues, the casting out or distancing of demons too menacing to the enlightened mind, in a novel whose mediating perspectives and multiple narrations themselves both conjure and frame.

Lockwood's text, however, is remarkable for its emphasis not only on proper place, property, and boundary lines but also on trespass, transgression, or crossing, or on boundary lines which themselves become thresholds. Heathcliff, the figure through whom Earnshaw will pass into Linton and back again, is pictured frequently at doorways or other places of crossing. And the novel is filled with crossings or exchanges of place which are frequently also reversals of position. Edgar and Isabella Linton's arrival at the Heights reverses the direction of Catherine and Heathcliff's trespass. Catherine and Isabella exchange places through marriage, the former moving from Heights to Grange when she marries Edgar and the latter, in her elopement with Heathcliff, moving in the opposite direction. The subsequent longing of each to return would map another crossing: Catherine in her delirium in chapter XII imagines a return to the Heights; Isabella in the very next chapter writes "My heart returned to Thrushcross Grange in twenty-four hours after I left it"(XIII, 173). Heathcliff and Hindley change places as oppressor and oppressed; and the transformation of oppressed child into oppressive father which Kettle and others see as the central reversal of the novel is part of the general sense within it of things turning into their opposites or taking on the spirit of the place they exchange for another. Nelly remarks on the way in which Isabella and Heathcliff seem, after their marriage, to change positions ("So much had circumstances altered their positions, that he would certainly have struck a stranger as a born and bred gentleman, and his wife as a thorough little slattern!"; XIV, 184). "Crossing" is insisted on even at the purely verbal level—Nelly Dean's unsettling vision (XI) and Hindley's threatened burial (XVII, 221) at "crossroads"; characters repeatedly responding "crossly," not bearing "crossing," or described as "cross" (IX, 128; X, 134, 137); Nelly's warning Heathcliff, regarding Catherine, to "shun crossing her way again" (XIV,184); and even the name of Thrushcross Grange. The trope which is figured as a cross (*chi*, χ) is the figure of crossing known as chiasmus, the trope which Scaliger described as creating "a scissor formation in the sentence,"[13] and this kind of scissor formation frequently provides the closest diagrammatic form for the exchange or reversals of place in the plot itself.

We could go on listing the novel's various forms of crossing or transgression, from the undercurrent of incest which would undermine the sequential authority of the genealogical line, to the crossing of boundaries between animal and human, nature and culture, responsible for the heightened intensity of the novel's language.[14] When Catherine's brow is described as suddenly "clouded," a dead metaphor comes once again to life, loosed from the tomb of the banal or familiarly "proper," and she becomes for a moment a novelistic Lucy, wrapped up in rocks and stones and trees. Language which should be dead—if we think of the Enlightenment strictures against the improper crossings of tropes—becomes in this novel alive and even violent; and the air swarming with "Catherines" as Lockwood reads in chapter III may have its counterpart for the reader in the unsettling mobility of words which refuse to stay fixed in their single, or proper, meaning. "Bridle" in the scene in which Nelly sees Isabella's dog suspended where "a bridle hook is driven into the wall" (XII, 166) contaminates "bridal," as it stands as a menacing sign of Heathcliff and Isabella's elopement. Joseph's apparently peripheral and unreadable dialect is central to this kind of crossing, his "gooid-for-nowt madling" (XIII, 180) combining both "maid" and "mad," just as his earlier "marred" (180) crosses "married" and "marred." Readers of the novel soon learn to translate these dialect forms into standard English, as part of the accommodation of "primitive" speech to the civilized mind. But for a moment the words resist this standardization, and their very ambiguity, blurring the line between dialect and the lexicon of civilized speech, contributes to the novel's sense of menace, of something undermining the boundaries of the age both of Enlightenment and of the Dictionary.

IV

Die Namen individualisieren nur zum Schein.

(Stempel)

The narrative of *Wuthering Heights*, then, combines proper place and property on the one hand and transgression or crossing on the other, in a way which suggests that it is the very erection of boundary lines which creates the possibility of trespass. It also calls attention to the activity of proper names—those names which in Hobbes and Locke distinguish individual identities and in Watt's description are inseparable from the principle of individuation integral to the novel form itself. And it does so in a way which would enable us to suggest how this crossing of boundaries undermines the identity of the text, the very partitions which Lockwood needs in order to produce a satisfying Enlightenment narrative or "good book." An interest in names and their relation to identities already marks the dizzying series of aliases or multiple designations in the Gondal saga, whose profusion of names or initials capable of reference to several different characters suggests the accommodation involved for Brontë in moving to the more Lockean assumptions of the novel form—each name in its place and a proper place for every name. *Wuthering Heights* seems to be alerting the reader to the function but also to the potential autonomy of proper names by its insistence on their detachability, their application to more than one person, or the several names by which a single character may be called. If the function of proper names is to be the boundary markers of individual identity and thus to contribute to the coherence and readability of the narrative,[15] these very instruments of order and identity are in this text unreliable instruments. The confusion which makes Lockwood feel "unmistakably out of place" (II, 56) in the opening chapters results partly from the ambiguity of proper names as indicators of place or property—of who belongs to whom—or of position in the genealogical grid, since "Mrs Heathcliff" could be both Heathcliff's wife and his daughter-in-law (II), the "Catherine Linton" of Lockwood's second dream (III), either mother or daughter. Names in these opening chapters— including the "Hareton Earnshaw" whose appearance as inscription on the Heights prompts Lockwood to desire "a short history of the place" (I, 46)—are detached from clear or unambiguous reference and call out for histories, or explications.

Lockwood's confusion over names, identities, and proper placement reaches a climax in chapter III, which has itself strikingly to do with proper names and proper place, with both the establishment of boundary lines and their transgression. He finds on the window ledge of his room at the Heights writing which is "nothing but a name repeated in all kinds of characters, large and small—*Catherine Earnshaw*; here and there varied to *Catherine Heathcliff*, and then again to *Catherine Linton*":

> In vapid listlessness I leant my head against the window, and continued spelling over Catherine Earnshaw—Heathcliff—Linton, till my eyes closed; but they had not rested five minutes when a glare of white letters started from the dark, as vivid as spectres—the air swarmed with Catherines. (III, 61)

When he rouses himself "to dispel the obstrusive name" (p. 62), he finds yet another name ("Catherine Earnshaw, her book") introducing the marginal script—itself not in its proper place—which tells of the Sunday when Catherine and Heathcliff, compelled to "square" their "positions" for the appropriate Sabbath reading, throw the compulsory "good books" (p. 63) into the dog-kennel, are threatened by Joseph with being "laced . . .

properly" for it, and then "appropriate the dairy woman's cloak" for that crossing to the Grange which leaves a gap in the writing, taken up again only after the pair's crucial partition and Hindley's swearing to reduce Heathcliff to his "right place" (p. 64). This pivotal chapter is virtually obsessed with names: the proliferating and disturbingly mobile "Catherines"; the ghostly "Catherine Linton," called by Lockwood an *"appellation . . . which personified itself* when I had no longer my imagination under control" (p. 69, my emphasis); the name "Jabes," like "Zillah," taken from a biblical genealogy (1 Chronicles 4:9) or list of "Scripture names" like the one Catherine and Heathcliff are threatened with having to learn "if they don't answer properly" (VI, 88); the cudgel "denominated" a pilgrim's staff. But it is also preoccupied with the problems of proper place and with the erection, and crossing, of dividing lines or partitions: the blurring of the boundaries between real world and dream ("I began to dream, almost before I ceased to be sensible of my locality"); the pilgrim's staff as a sign of displacement, of not being in a proper place; the ironic echo of Christ's "breaking down the wall of partition," making the "two" into "one" (Ephesians 2:14) in the clergyman's "house with two rooms, threatening speedily to determine into one"; the multiplication of the sequential "partitions of discourse" in the *"four hundred and ninety parts"* of Branderham's sermon, each devoted to different "odd transgressions"; and the linear partition of time, since the partitions of the Puritan sermon traditionally correspond to the ages of history between Creation and Apocalypse (an association which may explain why, in the dream, reaching the final "head" or partition brings on eschatological echoes).

The sermon itself, on the "Seventy Times Seven, and the first of the Seventy-first," is a virtual *reductio ad absurdum* of sequential partition, in which something beyond accounting—the forgiveness of trespasses not "seven times, but until seventy times seven" (Matthew 18:22)—is reduced to sheer enumeration:

Oh, how weary I grew! How I writhed, and yawned, and nodded, and revived! How I pinched and pricked myself, and rubbed my eyes, and stood up, and sat down again, and nudged Joseph to inform me if he would *ever* have done. I was condemned to hear all out: finally, he reached the *"First of the Seventy-first."* At that crisis, a sudden inspiration descended on me; I was moved to rise and denounce Jabes Branderham as the sinner of the sin that no Christian need pardon.

"Sir," I exclaimed, "sitting here within these four walls, at one stretch, I have endured and forgiven the four hundred and ninety heads of your discourse. Seventy times seven times have I plucked up my hat and been about to depart—Seventy times seven times have you preposterously forced me to resume my seat. The four hundred and ninety-first is too much. Fellow-martyrs, have at him! Drag him down, and crush him to atoms, that the place which knows him may know him no more!

The rhetorically divided sermon picks up the image of the divided house through its own partition, what Blair, passing on the tradition in his *Lectures*, called the "method of dividing a Sermon into heads," the "formal partitions" the art of preaching shares with all "Discourse" (xxxi). But it also contravenes the traditional warning, echoed in Blair, against unnecessary "multiplication into heads," against dividing the subject into "minute parts" and so fatiguing the listener. There seems even to be an uncanny arithmetical logic at work in a dream in which a preacher with a name out of the genealogies of 1 Chronicles 4:9 preaches a sermon "divided into *four hundred and ninety parts*" on the topic of the "Seventy times seven." Division into parts "each discussing a separate sin," together with the text from Matthew on the forgiveness of trespasses, ironically links the very proliferation of partitions with the idea of "trespass." The "crisis" reached at the "*First of the Seventy-first*" involves a strangely literal reading of the partitioned text—the injunction in Matthew 18 to forgive "until seventy times seven"—since this is precisely the point where pardon here ends, and the "First of the Seventy-first" becomes the sin for which there is no forgiveness (Matthew 12:31), blasphemy against the Holy Ghost. The dream's dense and complex recall of a passage which invokes the image of a "house divided against itself" (Matthew 12:25), which has to do with a trespass against the law, and which demands distinguishing between a "holy" spirit and a daemonic "spirit" which returns to its "house" (12:44) elliptically raises the difficulty—even as it raises the necessity—of separating and distinguishing.

Arrival at the sermon's final partition leads in the dream to figures for biblical Endtime and for the upsetting of sequential order: Lockwood's "preposterously," with its sense both of "outrageously" and of the reversal of proper sequence; echoes of the eschatological penultimate Psalm ("execute upon him the judgment written") in the "concluding word" (III, 66) at which the assembly turns to violence; and a reminder of the Old Testament's penultimate book with its vision of coming judgment (Zechariah 14:13) in "every man's hand was against his neighbour," in the final "tumult," and, curiously, in the "branch" (Zechariah 3) which both breaks into this first dream and leads to the unsettling "return" of the next one. The boundary between dreamer and dreamed here, however, is also one of the partitions which threatens to break down. Branderham's accusation of Lockwood ("*Thou art the Man!*"; 66) recalls both a New Testament violation of a partition wall (Acts 21:28) and an Old Testament application of a parable to its hearer (2 Samuel 2:7). Lockwood and the preacher become increasingly hard to distinguish as the dream moves towards mutual violence and Jabes' accusatory "Thou"—echoing an address to a hearer unexpectedly inscribed within a story he had thought himself outside (2 Samuel)—turns the focus back on Lockwood himself, as nomination becomes virtually inseparable from accusation.[16] The Lockwood who objects to the multiplied partitions of Branderham's divided sermon himself scrambles to erect a partition or dividing wall of books in his second dream, when the ghostly child threatens to enter the house through a window which no longer keeps the outside out. And the multiplication of the partitions of discourse, which Lockwood objects to in that first dream, has its counterpart in Lockwood's own preference as narrator for the sequential narrative partitions which keep names, times, and events in their proper place after this unsettling night.

It is significant that it is after this night that Lockwood both loses his way in the snow when it removes the indicative function of signs ("the swells and falls not indicating corresponding rises and depressions in the ground"; p. 73) and blots out the "chart" in his mind with the "line of upright stones" that formerly served as "guides." But it is also after this night that he requests the housekeeper's explanatory "history," which begins with a sorting out of proper names and, as in Foucault's description of classical discourse, "sorts out" the simultaneous into the successive, into a "linear order" whose parts "must be traversed *one after* the other."[17] Mrs Dean begins by describing Heathcliff as "very near"—and then hastens to eliminate the ambiguity by adding that she means not "close" but "close-handed." But the parsimoniousness of Heathcliff and the parsimony which is one of the senses of "near" are joined by the extreme economy of names themselves ("Heathcliff" serving "parsimoniously," as Frank Kermode puts it, as both Christian name and surname),[18] a paucity emphasized by the novel's own striking juxtapositions. "Catherine, Mrs Linton Heathcliff now" (XXVIII, 316), for example, contains the names of both rivals for this *second* Catherine's mother. The swarming and disembodied names of chapter III, beyond Lockwood's control and endowed with an unsettling mobility, are themselves too compressed or "near"—sheer parataxis or juxtaposition, without explanatory syntax or reference, and with a power of combination neither logical nor chronological. It is only in the history provided by Mrs Dean, who presents herself as "a steady, reasonable kind of body," distinguished both by her housekeeping and by her familiarity with books (VII, 103), that the names are given their proper place within a genealogical line. Her history—which Lockwood insists should proceed "minutely," and which is accompanied by such emblems of *chronos* as the clock on the wall (VII, 102; X, 129)—moves in reassuring Enlightenment fashion in a single, irreversible direction from beginning to end, from the passionate Catherine and Heathcliff to the tamer, book-reading Cathy and Hareton, and imparts a sense of progress to the text as it moves to its ending. And yet, because Lockwood's request comes immediately after his disturbing night, the very linearity of the narrative, told from the Linton property at

Thrushcross Grange, links the mode of narration—the establishment of its boundaries or narratorial partitions, the assigning of a proper place to each proper name—with the boundary-marking of property, and creates thereby the specifically narrative possibility of trespass, of something which transgresses both the linearity and the identity of Lockwood's text, even as it calls attention to his narrative *as* narrative, as both demand and need, a spacing or *espacement* of the unbearably "near" into an order more accommodated to the civilized and enlightened—or novel-reading—mind. Logical and chronological are here inseparable; and what Barthes calls "the chronological illusion" is part of the function of logic itself, the overcoming of repetition through syntax or narrative.[19] Sequence struggles to master repetition in order, as we say, to get somewhere. And what in chapter III is called "nothing but a name repeated in all kinds of characters, large and small" is spread out over the characters of a housekeeper's history frequently read as a story both of progress and of enlightenment.

Nelly's tale performs its function, and the two characters who could embody the obtrusive "Catherines" are distanced by a generation. But there remains even in Ellen Dean's sequential narrative a sense of something which will not be accommodated to *chronos* or its logic—in the uncanny crossings, conflations, or reversals which transgress the categories of chronological time and sequence and, even more strikingly, within the activity of proper names themselves, the very markers of discrete identity. The novel's powerful, and disturbing, images of something that cannot be accommodated or contained—the "oak in the flowerpot" and "sea" in a "horse-trough" (XIV)—have their counterpart in the sense of something resisting Lockwood's ordered narratorial frame. Even after Nelly begins her story, proper names are not wholly reliable boundary lines. Northrop Frye observes that the word "identity" has a double aspect, identity *with* and identity *as*. The problem with proper names in this text is that they participate in this duplicity, disrupting by their repetition over several possible referents the very principle of individuation they exist to designate or mark.

The text's adherence to social conventions of naming—proper names in this society as indicators not only of identity but of proper social place— is as strict as its adherence to chronology or to property law: Heathcliff, for example, is degraded by a pointed distinction in the mode of naming ("You may come and wish Miss Catherine welcome, like the other servants"; VII, 94) and later ridicules his son for calling his own cousin "*Miss* Catherine" (XXI, 251). But, if this novel observes the carefully articulated system of naming in which the form of address reflects distinctions of position, it also calls attention, even after chapter III, to the multiple names a single character can be called and conversely to the potential for ambiguity when, as with the "Mrs Heathcliff" Lockwood erroneously places in chapter II, more than a single character can be identified by the same name. In chapter VI, for example, Hindley is called variously "Mr Hindley," "young Earnshaw," and simply "Hindley," depending on the socially appropriate form of address. But the first time he is called "Mr Earnshaw" ("I threw a shawl over my head and ran to prevent them from waking Mr Earnshaw by knocking"; p. 88), the reader may receive a shock, since the former "Mr Earnshaw," called in the previous chapter "by name" (V, 85) in order to wake him, before they realize that he is not sleeping but dead, is now dead and his name, as in all forms of genealogical succession, now transferred to his son. The identity of the name momentarily effaces the boundaries of individual identity which the proper name should properly preserve.

The ambiguity of proper names is joined by the possible detaching of name from person or proper place, as in the spectral rising of disembodied "Catherines" (III), the suggestion that the first Catherine's "name" might be a substitute for her presence or "voice" (XII, 158), or in the moment when that Catherine stares at her reflection ("'Is that Catherine Linton?'"; p. 159) and the name—hers in any case only by marriage—is, as it were, detached from her person even before it is transferred to a second "Catherine Linton" at her death. When Heathcliff says to Cathy, "I swear Linton is dying" (XXII, 266), the context, or narrative placing, indicates that he refers to his son. But that context's own references to a transferred name—"'Catherine Linton (the very name warms me)'"—and to exchange of place ("Just imagine your father in my place, and Linton in yours") make it possible to note that "Linton is dying" could, out of its proper place, also refer to Catherine's father or to the progressive effacement of the Linton name. Names in this text frequently appear as a place or space to be filled, as the alien Heathcliff takes the name left vacant by an earlier, legitimate son, as the second Catherine Linton gets her name on the death of the first and fills the place of "Miss Linton" after it has been vacated by Isabella's marriage, or as the initials "C." and "H." on the balls Catherine Linton and Linton Heathcliff find in a cupboard at the Heights (XXIV, 280) could as easily be filled by them as by "Catherine" and "Heathcliff," or later by "Catherine" and "Hareton," a possibility which would work against the narrative's carefully separated identities and times.

Names also participate in this text's transgressions or crossings. The curious mode of naming Hareton when he is first placed by Nelly on the genealogical grid—as "the late Mrs Linton's nephew" (IV, 75), rather than as the late Mr Earnshaw's son—subtly allies him with "the house on which his name is *not* carved,"[20] just as the inscription "Hareton Earnshaw" on the lintel or, in northern dialect, "linton" of Wuthering Heights may suggest a crossing of families which will in the narrative be achieved only after Hareton's marriage to Catherine Linton and their removal to the

Grange. The potential chaos of sheer naming or categorization is part of the oppressive weight of Lockwood's first dream; but a similar chaos may be conjured from the alliances and associations that names make independently of persons, almost as if they were engaged in a shadow play of combinations not permitted on the novel's more civilized surface, a mobility and transportability unsettling to the Enlightenment order or grid. Incest—the primal social trespass or crossing of boundaries —may be present not only in the uncertain relationship of Heathcliff and Catherine but in the promiscuous combination or confusion which remains open to names themselves, independent of genealogical or social placement.

Let us choose, for illustration, the most outrageous example. The female characters in the novel are variously called by their first and their family names, so that Isabella, for example, is also referred to simply as "Miss Linton." When she elopes with Heathcliff, Edgar Linton proclaims that she is to be thereafter "only [his] sister in name" (XII, 170). At the only level which makes any logical sense, this phrase "in name" is simply a formula for her disowning—a severing of a family tie in which the name will remain as the only trace of a former connection. But the other character who is, in the literal sense, his "sister in name" is his daughter, a "Miss Linton" who will also become, like Isabella, a "Mrs Heathcliff." This might hardly be noticed if it were not for the novel's insistent reference to names as virtually autonomous entities, a reference, however, wholly plausible in the marrying and giving in marriage which form the principal exchange of the plot. When Isabella says in chapter XIII, "My name *was* Isabella Linton" (p. 175), the phrase suggests what for a woman in a society where property relations extend to marriage is the repeated experience of detaching person from name, an exchanging of one name for another which Nelly reminds Heathcliff may involve a more radical change in identity ("'I'll inform you Catherine Linton is as different now, from your old friend Catherine Earnshaw, as that young lady is different from me'"; XIV, 185).

Frank Kermode points out that the three names Lockwood finds etched on the window ledge in chapter III—*Catherine Earnshaw, Catherine Heathcliff,* and *Catherine Linton*—map in their textual order the novel's principal crossing or exchange, from left to right the story of the first Catherine and in reverse that of the second, a reading of the text supported, I would add, by the housekeeper's own reference to "retracing the course of Catherine Linton" (XVI, 202) after her death, by Lockwood's striking textual metaphor of the daughter as a potential "second edition of the mother" (XIV, 191), and by Nelly's calling attention to the reverse order in which both Lockwood and the reader have been introduced to the two female figures who share the same name ("About twelve o'clock, that night, was born the Catherine you saw at Wuthering Heights"; XVI, 201). This plotting of the history through the names is possible only through a reversal, a reading first in one direction and then in the other. The reader aware of the way in which things in this novel change places or seem to turn into one another—human into animal, civilized into violent, ghost into person, and person into ghost—might even perceive a lurking palindrome or verbal reversal in the name of the housekeeper herself, variously called "Ellen" and "Nelly," a suggestion outrageous to readers of the naturalized *Wuthering Heights* preferred by Q. D. Leavis and others, but perhaps not entirely inappropriate for a character who, as go-between, meddler, and even "double-dealer" (XX, 266) in the plot, also mediates as a kind of boundary figure between superstition and enlightenment and moves as narrator in two directions, in towards the story in which she is involved, and out towards her civilized listener.

V

It is, indeed, in the literal sense of the word, preposterous.

(Coleridge, "The Friend")

Retracing or reversing the left-to-right order of reading involves an upsetting of the simple linear sequence of diary, chronology, or genealogy and calls into question the Lockwoodian text and its relation both to enlightenment and to the very idea of progress. The narrative itself is for the most part preposterous, in the still-current nineteenth-century sense of a reversal of proper order: it begins with the second Catherine and proceeds to the first. The dominating influence of mere sequence creates the illusion of proceeding away from the opening scene, when in fact, or in chronology, it proceeds *to* it: the shock of hearing at the beginning of chapter XXV, "These things happened last winter, sir" is the shock of the revelation that things which had seemed, in the familiar spatial metaphor, before us, are now just behind us, not distanced but close enough to overtake the present time. Even Nelly's carefully sequential "history" includes episodes which upset its own partitions between discrete identities and times, disrupting both the linear order of the text and the certainty of chronological placing. In chapter XI, for example, Nelly tells of the apparition or uncanny return ("all at once, a gush of child's sensations flowed into my heart") at a crossroads pillar—itself inscribed with the initials of three possible directions—of Hindley himself as a child; then of finding when she hastens to the Heights that the apparition has preceded her, that what she thought was behind her now stands before her very eyes ("looking through the gate"), before she reflects that this child must be not Hindley but his son Hareton; and finally of her panic when, after her request to Hareton to fetch his father, Heathcliff appears. Hindley (the grown man whose apparition as a child conflates the intervening twenty years), Hareton (the child whom Heathcliff later describes as "a personification of my youth, not a human being" and who has already appeared to the reader as a man), and Heathcliff (the figure who is, like Hareton, an oppressed child and, like Hindley, an oppressive father), are in this supernatural incident too "near," as the boundaries which should separate child from man, a child from his father, and individuals or discrete chronological times from each other here forsake even the housekeeper and send her back to the "guide-post" ("feeling as scared as if I had raised a goblin"; p. 149), before the apparition, "on further reflection," fades into the light of common day. The scene is virtually the narrativization of a preposterous Wordsworthian copula—"The Child is father of the Man"—a metaphor whose conflation of times and identities shocks, before the mind accommodates it logically and chronologically as a condensed analogy, and the conflation of times is spread out, or spaced, over what is called the "natural" life of a single individual.

Yet another conflation of times, or separate parts of the text itself, occurs in chapter XII, where a delirious Catherine Linton experiences a collapse of the distancing space of time ("the whole last seven years of my life grew a blank! ... I was a child"), in which the years between the crossing of the moors which first separated her from Heathcliff and her marriage at nineteen to Edgar Linton drop away ("supposing at twelve years old, I had been wrenched from the Heights, and ... converted, at a stroke, into Mrs Linton, the lady of Thrushcross Grange, and the wife of a stranger"; p. 163). These identifications of historically separated times may remind us of the aberrant "identity with" of metaphor—a transgression of the boundaries of both logic and chronology which would provide the temporal counterpart of Catherine's own radical copula "I *am* Heathcliff" (IX, 122).[21] But what is even more upsetting to both is this chapter's "preposterous" textual recalls, its repeated echoes of Lockwood's encounters in chapter III: the snowy down plucked by a "wandering" Catherine recalls Lockwood's "wandering" in the "snow"; the "blank" of the disappearing space of years recalls the "blank" filled by Catherine's marginal script; the "oak-panelled bed," "wind sounding in the firs," and opened "casement" of Catherine's delirium (XII, 162–3) recall Lockwood's enclosure in the same bed at the Heights, the "fir-tree" moved by the "gusty wind" and the terrifyingly open casement window (III, 66–7). These echoes create the uncanny sense that the "Catherine Linton" who in chapter XII is "no better than a wailing child" (p. 162), sees herself as the "exiled" and "outcast" twelve-year-old of the crossing Lockwood reads about in chapter III, and imagines a return to the Heights through the graveyard "ghosts" of Gimmerton Kirk, *is* the "wailing child" ("still it wailed"; III, 67) or ghostly "Catherine Linton" of Lockwood's second dream, who attempts to return to her "home" after wandering on the moors for "twenty years." The two chapters, on rereading, contaminate each other preposterously, upsetting the ordered linearity of the narratorial text. The recalling of chapter III in chapter XII—a phenomenon common enough in the sequential process of reading in which a later chapter may recall an earlier one—here involves an uncanny, or preposterous, reversal, since the earlier chapter which the later one recalls has its place, chronologically, almost twenty years after it.

The sense of fixed and inviolable place in time is also shaken by the uncanny sense of repetition in the return of the first Catherine in the second (whom Edgar Linton distinguishes from her mother by a difference in name) or by Joseph's calling Isabella (recently converted from a "Miss Linton" to a "Mrs Heathcliff") "Miss Cathy," and saying that "Hathecliff" will rebuke her for her tantrum (XIII, 180). The mind can accommodate the crossing by reference to Joseph's age or confusion; but the only character who is both "Miss Cathy" and one whose tantrums will be punished not by Hindley but by Heathcliff is the *second* Catherine, a Miss Linton who will also become a Mrs Heathcliff, a character who has already appeared to the reader and to Lockwood but who, in the story's chronology, is at this point not even born. Chronos in the myth devoured his children; the disruption of chronology in this novel allows children to come again.

Wuthering Heights refuses to let the reader forget that both the chronological sense of time and the linear habit of reading depend upon sequence, on events maintaining a syntax, or proper sense of place. But Lockwood's encounter with the swarming and spectral "letters," the undercutting of the rational explanation of his first dream (merely a "fir-tree") in the uncanny return of the second, Nelly's crossroads apparition, chapter XII's preposterous recalls, and Joseph's curious mistake are all episodes in which things refuse to keep their proper place. Tropes such as metaphor (Catherine's defiant "I *am* Heathcliff" or the sheer parataxis of the juxtaposed "Catherines") and *hysteron proteron* (the figure of reversal which Puttenham called "The Preposterous")[22] unsettle the careful boundaries and spaced linearity of Lockwood's text and reveal its own strategies of closure or enclosure as precisely that. The impulse to enclose is finally so intimately connected with the psychology of the narrator whose diary it is that all forms of closure, of shutting off or containing—including the narrative itself—become suspect or inadequate to their task, like the coffins of gothic fiction which refuse to stay shut. A neutral and "ghostlike" narrative voice inhabits and dislocates even Lockwood's final lines, which seem to promise a final forestalling of repetition, or uncanny return. What Foucault calls the return of both nature and tropes undermines the narrator's closing refusal to "imagine unquiet slumbers, for the sleepers in that quiet earth": nature, in the "soft wind breathing through the grass" and the "moths fluttering among the heath and hare-bells"; and writing, or tropes, in the appearance there of buried names, "Heathcliff" and "Hareton," the two oppressed children of the text itself. The curious absence of names in the description of the returning "ramblers" Lockwood hastens at this ending to "escape" creates, if only for a moment, the illogical possibility that these ramblers are not the solid, second-generation Cathy and Hareton but the ghostly Catherine and Heathcliff, whom the country folk insist still "walk."

The endless debate over whether the novel's second generation constitutes a progress or decline in relation to the first may be precisely endless because the two sides are simply the opposite faces of a single coin—two possibilities within the model of the line. The second generation only approximately repeats the first; and it is this difference within repetition which constitutes both "spacing" and the possibility of "progress." The novel proffers in familial and genealogical terms the twinned questions of progress and enlightenment which so preoccupied eighteenth-century discourse. "Reading" is part of the achievement of both enlightenment and progress in *Wuthering Heights*. But it is difficult to banish the suspicion that Cathy's civilizing of Hareton by teaching him to read is at least partly a project to forestall boredom, a way, as we say, of filling the time. The second-generation couple, who get together over the pages of an "accepted book" (XXXII, 345), and whose domesticating of the Heights Lockwood approves, are still shadowed by the "contrary" (XXXII, 338) activity of the first, if only in the margins which disrupt the "good book" provided in this ending by Lockwood himself. W. J. Harvey writes that it is precisely the "muting" of intratextual conflations or echoes "by the intervening mass of the novel" which makes the difference, in *Wuthering Heights*, between it and the "intolerable" or "gothic" reverberations which would have resulted if the echoes of one part of the text in another—the repetitions, for example, of that casement window from chapter III—had been "more closely juxtaposed."[23] But *Wuthering Heights* manages to reveal this very spacing as a strategy of the novel form itself, an accommodation to its "civilized" (Kermode) or "bourgeois" (Macherey) reading public.

We have, finally, to honor both the naturalized novel—or the sense of naturalizing or of "life" it produces by means of such spacing—and the uncanny conflations which disrupt both its unified identity and its linear structures. Lockwood is, as several readers suggest, a surrogate for the reader, and even Kermode's linear ordering is a form of Lockwoodian analysis—an ordering in sequence of the simple profusion of names in chapter III, which fill the air like the snowy feathers of chapter XII. The very binary oppositions by which readers traditionally structure meaning are in this text both generated and undermined. The difference between Earnshaw and Linton, salvation and damnation, nature and culture, primitive and civilized, or (paradoxically) graves that join and windows that divide, is finally a partition or dividing wall which does not really divide but is instead constantly crossed or transgressed by the novel's literal exchanges or by tropes such as metaphor which are "beyond good and evil," which appear amoral because as in any purely verbal exchange they proceed by a more, or less, than human logic. But, at the same time as it undermines these partitions, the text does not allow any satisfying or simple identity *with:* Catherine's copular "I *am* Heathcliff" suggests a unity beyond partition which in the novel nowhere appears. Metaphor itself involves a transgression of the boundaries of "property," but its radical union is, as Derrida would say, always already inhabited by difference. There is always "partition": the binary oppositions in this text both break down and are regenerated, as the revolt against the proliferating partitions of discourse in Lockwood's first dream moves to the reintroduction of a partition in the second. Even the text's uncanny conflations—or the potential identification of one part with another—cannot be conscripted to a conclusive identity. The distance between Catherine's delirium in chapter XII and Lockwood's second dream in chapter III is almost, but not quite, the twenty years of the ghost child's exile on the moors. The connection—neither logical nor chronological—remains and militates against logic, chronology, and the sense in both of progress, but cannot finally be forced to "make sense."

The identity of the literary text, both as unity and as a self-identity, guaranteed by the narratorial subject who offers the novel we read as his book, is in *Wuthering Heights* radically undermined: the text remains perpetually, and frustratingly, other to itself, forever inhabited by its own ghosts. The haunting of the narratorial text by something which escapes both identification and placing cannot simply be explained by recourse to the distinction between narrator and effaced author, to the substitution of one proper name—or one kind of mastery—for another. Indeed, we feel in reading Emily Brontë's novel the pertinence of at least one of her sister's prefatory remarks: "the writer who possesses the creative gift owns something of which he [sic] is not always master—something that at times strangely wills and works for itself."[24] Critics of *Wuthering Heights* as diverse as Fredric Jameson and Frank Kermode have remarked on its unsettling sense of automism, a staple feature of the gothic as a mode which foregrounds the unsettling mobility of *things*. Brontë's novel, whose "characters" are both the embodiments of a genealogical history and the unsettling graphic letters of chapter III, suggests that something as apparently modern as the notion of a text writing itself may have a peculiarly gothic pedigree. And the recurrence of the figure of the "specter" or "ghost" in contemporary narrative theory may return us to the ghost narratives of the period we call post-Enlightenment—if we understand that "post," as we now do that of "post"-structuralist, as still caught within the very structures it dismantles or undermines. *Wuthering Heights* calls into question not only private property but the very idea of the "proper"; its violation is not only of moral proprieties but of novelistic ones. In the terms of one of its own most persistent figures, it demands a reading which seeks to raise more demons than it casts out.

9

Coming Second: Woman's Place

I

In the beginning...

There are, as Mary Nyquist has brilliantly reminded us, not one but two creation stories in the Book of Genesis.[1] The first, now thought to be the product of the Priestly or "P" author and first in the received order of the sacred text, though it may actually have been produced second, is found in verses 26–8 of Genesis 1:

26. And God said, Let us make man in our image, after our likeness; and let them have dominion over the fish of the sea, and over the fowl of the air, and over the cattle, and over all the earth, and over every creeping thing that creepeth upon the earth.
27. So God created man [*hā-'ādām*] in his own image, in the image of God created he him: male and female created he them.
28. And God blessed them, and God said unto them, Be fruitful, and multiply, and replenish the earth, and subdue it: and have dominion over the fish of the sea, and over the fowl of the air, and over every living thing that moveth upon the earth.

The creation of male and female here comes at the end and climax of the six days of creation, as the culminating or crowning moment of a sequential, narrative hexameron. Verse 27 in particular—"So God created man in his own image, in the image of God created he him: male and female created he them"—deserves singling out. For it has long been the signal text of defenses of the equality of women, of the simultaneous creation of both sexes "in the image of God." One offshoot of this first creation story is the legend of Lilith, the first feminist, created in one version out of the dust of the earth simultaneously with Adam. As Louis Ginzberg, in *The Legends of the Jews*, recounts it, "she remained with him only a short time, because she insisted upon enjoying full equality with her husband," deriving her rights "from their identical origin."[2]

Whatever is made of the Priestly account—and there is very much more to be made, as we shall see later—it is not the only account of the creation of the sexes in Genesis. For, though it is narratively placed first, it is followed by a second, the account in Genesis 2 in which the creation of Eve also comes second, after the creation of an Adam whom traditional readings of this second story have read as designating the exclusively male. Because of its long history of justifying the subordination of woman to man, this is the one which to most in our culture will be the most familiar:

18. And the Lord God said, It is not good that the man should be alone; I will make him an help meet for him.

19. And out of the ground the Lord God formed every beast of the field, and every fowl of the air; and brought them unto Adam to see what he would call them: and whatsoever Adam called every living creature, that was the name thereof.

20. And Adam gave names to all cattle, and to the fowl of the air, and to every beast of the field; but for Adam ['ādām] there was not found an help meet for him.

21. And the Lord God caused a deep sleep to fall upon Adam, and he slept; and he took one of his ribs, and closed up the flesh instead thereof;

22. And the rib, which the Lord God had taken from the man [hā-'ādām], made he a woman ['iššâ], and brought her unto the man [hā-'ādām].

23. And Adam [hā-'ādām] said, This is now bone of my bones, and flesh of my flesh; she shall be called Woman ['iššâ], because she was taken out of Man ['îš].

24. Therefore shall a man ['îš] leave his father and his mother, and shall cleave unto his wife ['iššâ]: and they shall be one flesh.

This account, culminating not just in the creation of Woman, later called Eve (Genesis 3:20), but in the formula of the first marriage—pattern of the rest—follows sequentially from the description of the creation of "Adam" himself out of the "dust of the ground" (Genesis 2:7).

It is this second creation story in Genesis, in which woman has been seen as coming both out of and after man, which has for centuries authorized woman's place as second place, a coming after, in which priority in the temporal sequence has hierarchical superiority as its con-sequence or result.[3] Woman here is not just *after* man but *of* and *for* man; her genesis is a following from or sequel to the pronouncement that "It is not good that the man should be alone." In the rest of the Genesis text—in a reversal given its theological statement in Exodus 4:22—the second-born in the order of nature (Jacob, famously, in relation to the first-born Esau) has spiritual priority over the first. But in the misogynist tradition which grew out of this second Genesis account, the sequence which has woman similarly born second in the order of time, and after man, only makes her secondary to man. This is certainly the view articulated in 1 Timothy 2:11–14 ("Let the woman learn in silence with all subjection. But I suffer not a woman to teach, nor to usurp authority over the man, but to be in silence. For Adam was first formed, then Eve. And Adam was not deceived, but the woman being deceived was in the transgression"),[4] a passage whose last part, however, contains within it, as we shall see, the seeds of a reversed sequence of "following."

This second Genesis creation story has been wide-reaching in its influence, starting from the later texts of the Bible itself, most notoriously in the so-called Pauline Epistles. 1 Corinthians 11, the famous New Testament counterpart to the Genesis texts for later commentators, is only one among the many which create a logical "it follows that" out of the placing of male as first and female as second in the traditional reading of Genesis 2:22–3:

> 3. But I would have you know, that the head of every man is Christ; and the head of the woman is the man; and the head of Christ is God. . . .
> 7. For a man indeed ought not to cover his head, forasmuch as he is the image and glory of God: but the woman is the glory of the man.
> 8. For the man is not of the woman; but the woman of the man.
> 9. Neither was the man created for the woman; but the woman for the man.

The text of Ephesians 5 repeats the Genesis 2 marriage formula in a passage which begins with "Wives, submit yourselves unto your own husbands, as unto the Lord. For the husband is the head of the wife, even as Christ is the head of the church" and ends with the formula itself: "For this cause shall a man leave his father and mother, and shall be joined unto his wife, and they two shall be one flesh" (Ephesians 5:22–31). The resonant, and often echoed passage from 1 Peter 3, which begins "Likewise, ye wives, be in subjection to your own husbands," counsels husbands to "give honour unto the wife, as unto the *weaker vessel*" (1 Peter 3:1–7), a phrase in Tyndale's and later the King James Bible which became a catchphrase for the sex itself.[5]

This sense of woman as a deficient or "weaker vessel" persists in attempts to combine into some kind of congruence or unified single reading the two separate creation stories in Genesis 1 and 2. Both Augustine and Aquinas attempt to reconcile the first creation story in Genesis 1 with the passage from 1 Corinthians 11:7, where man is "the image and glory of God" while woman is "the glory of the man," followed by the gloss from the second creation story in Genesis 2: "For the man is not of the woman; but the woman of the man." What they emerge with is the explanation that "Woman is made in the image of God insofar as image is understood to mean 'an intelligent nature'; but insofar as man and not woman is, like God, the beginning and end (of woman), woman is not in God's image, but in man's image," having been created *ex viro propter virum*, out of man and for man.[6]

The second Genesis creation story, however, is not the only account of woman which places her in second, and hence inferior, place. The influential account of male and female in Aristotle, which retained its hold up to the seventeenth century and, in more disguised forms, still continues into the twentieth, provides a systematic exploration of the binary opposition male/female, in which the former of the two is the standard or universal equivalent. In the *Metaphysics*, Aristotle records a table of opposites attributed to the Pythagoreans:

male	female
limit	unlimited
odd	even
one	plurality
right	left
resting	moving
straight	curved
light	darkness
good	evil
square	oblong

Binary opposition—including the opposition of male and female—is, as this table from the sixth century BC makes clear,[7] by no means the invention of some recent structuralism, and its reiteration within Aristotle's text gave to such theories of sexual difference an extraordinarily tenacious influence. Book X of the *Metaphysics*, under the notion of "contraries," in which one must always be the privation of the other, presents the female as the privation and hence inferior of the male. The male in this duality is associated with form, activity, perfection, while the female is associated with matter, passivity, and deprivation, desiring the male in order to be complete. The opposition male/female is therefore paralleled by the oppositions active/passive, perfection/imperfection, form/matter, completion/incompletion as well as possession/deprivation. In Aristotelian terms, woman is less fully developed than man. Because of lack of heat in generation, her sexual organs have remained internal, as a sign of her deficiency—a corollary which makes Freud on penis envy or female lack such suggestive reading beside Aristotle on woman as an imperfect or botched male.

In the discussion of generation in *The Generation of Animals* (*De generatione animalium*), Aristotle takes over the Hippocratic idea of males as warm and dry and females as moist and cold, in order to make the lack of heat in the female the reason why she is unable to concoct seed—contrary to earlier theories of generation, which this knowingly replaces

See
Jacquart
& Thomasset
?

and suppresses—whereas semen, so to speak, is hot stuff (*De partibus animalium*, 736b, 35–737a, 8). In this text, still being echoed in a misogynist context in Milton, as we shall see, woman's active contribution to conception was thus rejected in the face of previous theories of generation that had maintained the presence of female seed. The mother provided only the passive "material" to the process of generation and was associated with the "body" to the father's "soul"; the father was the child's final, formal, and efficient cause, the mother only its material one. The production of female children—a deformation caused by a lack of heat in the generative process, which also led to their having weight lower down, in the belly and hips, rather than higher up, like men—was seen as a "deviation" (*Generation of Animals*, 767b, 10–15), if a necessary one for the history of the species. Woman is described in an influential passage of this text as ἐστὶ πεπηρωμένον; for which the usual Latin counterparts are "[Quasi]mas laesus" or "animal occasionatum," a phrase which also resonates in Milton. But, even more significantly, this series of weighted polarities in the sphere of biology and metaphysics had its corollaries in other areas—in the identification of male with rationality and female with irrationality (*Politics*, 1259b, 20–3; 1260a, 1–5) and hence the virtue of obedience for women and of ruling for men (*Politics*, 1260a, 4–12; 1254b, 16–25), and also in the area of speech, the association of the male with public speech and the adjoining of women not just to privacy and the home but to silence (*Politics*, 1260b, 28–31).[8]

Often simply reproduced in the Middle Ages and Renaissance, Aristotle's description set up a structure of thought which dominated the notion of woman for centuries, along with the account of the secondary female from Genesis 2.[9] These two traditions for the placing of woman, however, were by no means hermetically separated—even before Milton combined echoes of both the second creation story and Aristotle's "defective male" in *Paradise Lost*. Aquinas, for example, synthesized the account of male and female from Aristotle with the creation of woman in Genesis 1:26–7 and 2:22–3:

> It seems that woman ought not to have been produced in the original production of things. For Aristotle says that the female is an incomplete version of the male. But nothing incomplete or defective should have been produced in the first establishment of things; so woman ought not to have been produced then. ... Only as regards nature in the individual is woman something defective and *manqué*. For the active power of the seed of the male tends to produce something like itself, perfect in masculinity; but the procreation of a female is the result either of the debility of the active power, or of some unsuitability of the material, or of some change effected by external influences, like the south wind, for example, which is damp, as we are told in *De generatione animalium*.

But with reference to nature in the species as a whole, the female is not something *manqué*, but is according to the plan of nature [*intentio naturae*] and is directed to the work of procreation. Now the tendency of the nature of a species as a whole derives from God, who is the general author of nature. And therefore when he established nature, he brought into being not only the male but the female too.[10]

In this synthesis of Aristotle and Genesis, the obvious difficulty posed by Aristotelian theory for a Christian theologian is solved by a recourse to both Genesis creation accounts, the first in which both male and female are created at the same time, and the second in which woman is created after, and out of, the man. The combination of the biblical with the Aristotelian text from Aquinas onward also easily incorporated the "weaker vessel" of 1 Peter 3, from which scholastics in true Aristotelian fashion deduced the diminished mental powers of the female of the species. This Thomist synthesis was still going strong as late as the sixteenth century, in a commentary on the "imperfect male" of Genesis 2:

What the philosophers have said about the production of woman [that she is a botched male or *vir laesus*] is recounted metaphorically by Moses. There is a great difference between the point of view of philosophers and that of Moses; for the former considered the production of woman only in relation to sex, whereas Moses considered the production of woman not only as it concerns sex but also with regard to moral behaviour as a whole. Therefore he used a complex metaphor ... as the sleep of Adam should be understood metaphorically, Adam is described asleep, not being woken up or keeping vigil. A deep sleep is sent by God into the man from whom woman is to be produced, and this defect of male power bears a likeness from which woman is naturally produced. For a sleeping man is only half a man [*semihomo*]; similarly, the principle creating woman is only semi-virile. It is for this reason that woman is called an imperfect version of the male [*mas laesus*] by philosophers.[11]

The synthesis of Aristotle and Genesis was by no means uncontested, even before the seventeenth century, when some theologians, aware of the rejection in medical circles of the Aristotelian concepts of generation, were able to reject the assimilation of Aristotle in other areas.[12] But even where Aquinas's assimilation of Aristotle is met with hostility, as in Martin Luther's Reformation commentary on Genesis 1:27, which attacks the view of woman as botched male, opposition still preserves the inferiority of woman to man:

Lest woman should seem to be excluded from all glory of future life, Moses mentions both sexes [in Genesis 1:26–7]; it is evident therefore that woman is a different animal to man, not only having different members, but also being far weaker in intellect [*ingenium*]. But although Eve was a most noble creation, like Adam, as regards the image of God, that is, in justice, wisdom and salvation, she was none the less a woman. For as the sun is more splendid than the moon (although the moon is also a most splendid body), so also woman, although the most beautiful handiwork of God, does not equal the dignity and glory of the male.

Woman is not defective, writes Luther, but different; and that difference is her relative weakness of intellect and her inferiority to man, as the moon, splendid in itself, is yet not—in the most traditional of gendered oppositions—as splendid as the sun. Luther also, as Ian Maclean reminds us, "refers playfully in his *Tischreden* to the scholastic belief that the different shape of men and women is accountable to the latter's imperfect formation," remarking "that it is not because of insufficient generative heat and body temperature that women have wide hips and narrow shoulders, but rather a sign that they have little wisdom and should stay in the home."[13]

Even the most positive counters to the older versions of women's inferiority—such as Cornelius a Lapide's commentary on the assertion in 1 Corinthians 11:7 that man is "image and glory of God" while "woman is the glory of the man"—remain caught in this logic of first and second:

> Woman, insofar as she is a wife, is the glory of man, that is his glorious image, as I said above: because God formed woman, that is Eve, from man, and in man's likeness [*ex viro, ad viri similitudinem*], so that she might represent man as a copy [*exemplar*] of him, and be as it were his image. But woman is not in the full sense of the word the image of man, if we talk of image in the sense of mind and intellect, by which woman like man is endowed with a rational soul, intellect, will, memory and freedom, and can acquire, just as man, all wisdom, grace and glory. For woman is equal to man in possessing a rational soul, and both, that is woman and man, are made in the image of God [*tam mulier quam vir, factus est ad imaginem Dei*]. But she is the image of man in a restrictive and analogical sense; because woman was made from man, after man, inferior to him and in his likeness [*mulier tanquam posterior et inferior facta est ex viro, illique similis creata est*]. It is for this reason that St Paul does not say explicitly "woman is the image of man," but rather "woman is the glory of man"; because without doubt ... woman is an excellent ornament of man since she is granted to man not only to help him to procreate children, and administer the family, but also in possession and, as it were, in dominion, over which man may exercise his jurisdiction and authority. For the authority of man extends not only to inanimate things and brute beasts, but also to reasonable creatures, that is, women and wives.[14]

Posterior et inferior ... illique similis. The logic of coming after, of coming second, of following from and out of, of being in some sense in man's image, still governs even this apparent defense of women: *posterior et inferior*, after and inferior, also contains, as in the whole tradition of Genesis 2, the implicit "after and *therefore* inferior" that governs all such discussions of woman's place.

II

Tomer verkehrt!

(Theodor Reik, *The Creation of Woman*)

I began with this prologue from Aristotle and Genesis in order to set the context for a number of later texts which still may be seen as operating within their sphere of influence. But in order to move to those texts—of Milton, Rousseau, and finally of Freud—we need to consider both the logic of this tradition and glimpses of its reversal, including the reversal it may itself already have performed. The sequential or linear logic so far traced—of coming second and all that follows from it—is at play in the rich confusing of a temporal or narrative "it follows that" with a logical one, and in the consequences for women which ensue, but also in a whole narrative history of following or coming after, of repeating or imitating an original. In Bunyan's *Pilgrim's Progress*, for example, the story of Christiana follows or comes second after that of her husband Christian, just as *'iššâ* in the wordplay of Genesis 2 is so named because she is taken from *'îš*. But it is by no means alone in presenting both a woman who follows after her man, and the story of this *animal occasionatum* as a second or sequel, an occasional addition or apparent afterthought to the original conception, as Mary Wollstonecraft said of the narrative of "Woman" in Genesis 2.[15] Just as female difference follows after and out of the more universal case of generic "man," the story of Everyman in Christian is followed by the supplementary story of his wife (or more properly, in its Puritan bourgeois context, by the story of his wife and family) as a second story, both modeled on and different from the first. Christiana's following after, or coming second, is part of a larger logological structure and sequence[16] in which Christian's own journey is an imitation (or following in the footsteps) of Christ; the sequence as a whole enacts, by narrativizing, the verse already cited from 1 Corinthians 11 before it glosses the second creation story from Genesis 2 with "a man ... is the image and glory of God: but the woman is the glory of the man. For the man is not of the woman; but the woman of the man": "I would have you know, that the head of every man is Christ; and the head of the woman is the man; and the head of Christ is God" (1 Corinthians 3). Christiana's narrative sequel, like her following after, thus repeats at one further remove (as in accounts of the "Woman" of Genesis 2 as created at a further remove from the "image of God") the logic of the *imitatio Christi* itself.

We need, then, to stay a bit longer within this logic—of first and second, original and imitation or sequel—for its implications are not necessarily those derived from the Aristotelian synthesis with Genesis 2, or indeed of any of the commentaries on Genesis which proceed according to the logic of the priority of the temporally first. Since much of this weightier theological and philosophical discussion found its way not just into misogynist tracts but also into defenses of women, which for obvious reasons placed their major emphasis on the first creation story rather than the second, and since so many of the more popular discussions of male and female based on Genesis were forced, if only in watered-down form, to deal with the question of progression or sequence, we might consider just such a piece of this more occasional and popular literature, and the use it makes of the question of first and second from Genesis 2. The writer of a piece dated 1705 which takes up the argument "That women are of a more excellent nature than men," provides just one of many possible examples of a different construing of the sequence from Genesis 2, of the creation of man first and woman second, a construing already present in Cornelius Agrippa and others:

> Adam signifies no more than earth, but Eve signifies life, as if man lived only by woman, and was but a dead and insipid lump without her. And it is the testimony of God himself, that it was not good for man to be alone, I will (therefore) saith he, make him a help meet for him: the Hebrew has it, a help *before* him, that is, more excellent than him. If therefore the name given by God himself signifies the thing to be more excellent, who can dispute but that the nature of the thing is so too, except any should be so prophanely wicked as to affirm that Adam knew how to give more suitable names to the creatures, according to their natures, than God himself. ... In the next place, the method that God observed in the creation, plainly shews woman to be the most excellent of created beings. Which method of proceeding was *from the less to the more noble beings*, namely, from the mineral to the vegetable; from thence to the animal kingdoms; all of which being finished, he made men *and last of all women*, in whom all the creation was *perfected*, and all its beauty *compleat*. God having made woman, *ended* his work, *having nothing more excellent to create*, she containing so noble an epitome of the creator's wisdom and power, and *without whom the world ... had been imperfect*. And it is an absurd and ridiculous opinion to think, that God would conclude so great a world in any thing, but that which was the most perfect of all the rest.[17]

The sense of sequence from the account in Genesis 1—in which the creation of "male and female" comes as the culmination of the whole account—is here read into the creation of Eve after Adam in Genesis 2. The passage goes on to twist the primary argument for woman's secondariness, the creation of woman *ex viro*, out of and also for the man, in arguing that this coming after involves a progression beyond or surpassing of an original. Here, then, last is best, the climax or end without which all before it is imperfect or incomplete; it would be "an absurd and ridiculous opinion" to think that God would conclude the act of creation itself on an anticlimax, or (to shift the image to prosody) on a weak or "feminine" ending.

This is hardly an exceptional, though by no means a majority argument from Genesis. The view of the creation of woman as a completion of the imperfection of solitary man also shows up in earlier feminist defenses such as the reply to a highly popular piece of seventeenth-century misogyny—Joseph Swetnam's *Arraignment of ... Women* (1617)—by Rachel Speght, who draws the follow conclusion from the sequential second placing of woman in Genesis 2:

> Almighty God ... having made all things of nothing, and created man in his owne image ... to avoide that solitarie condition that hee was then in, having none to commerce or converse withall but dumb creatures, it seemed good unto the Lord, that as of every creature hee had made male and female, and man onely being alone without mate, so likewise to forme an helpe meete for him. Adam for this cause being cast into a heavy sleepe, God extracting a rib from his side, thereof made, or built, woman; shewing thereby, that *man was an unperfect building afore woman was made*.[18]

This particular defense of woman, then, reverses the argument from linear sequence; but it still relies, as Speght's own marginal gloss makes clear, on the second creation story from Genesis, in which woman is made from, and after, man.

*

There is, however, a wholly other tradition of the sequential placing of male and female—one in which the female comes first, and then is replaced by the rule of the male. Genesis itself—narratively before its second creation story and the version of creation in which woman comes second—retains some traces of such a reversed order, within the "In the beginning" of its own opening lines. Modern commentators have compared the Priestly account of creation in the opening chapter of Genesis with the Babylonian creation epic *Enuma Elish*, where the male god Marduk triumphs over the primeval mother Tiamat, from whose slaughtered body the universe itself is then formed. *Peake's Commentary on the Bible* notes, for example, the echo of Marduk's defeat of the chaos-dragon Tiamat in the Hebrew word for "the deep" (*těhōm*) in Genesis 1:2, before God pronounces his creative "Let there be light"; and comments on *těhōm* as the equivalent of the vanquished Tiamat, just as the subsequent Genesis creation in an ordered sequential fashion closely resembles Marduk's sequential ordering in the Babylonian creation story. Though signs of a prior struggle with a sea-monster surface at other places within the Hebrew Bible itself (Job 26: 13; 38:8–11; Psalm 74: 13–14; Isaiah 27: 1; 51:9–10), the Priestly account of God's *Fiat lux* effaces any trace of something before it.[19] But *Peake's Commentary* argues that "it is a mistake to suggest, as some commentators do, that there is no note of conflict in the Hebrew description of the divine activity in creation, or that the Hebrew word *bara* ('made') implies creation *ex nihilo*. Chaos, tempest, and darkness are all symbols of what is opposed to the divine purpose and must be overcome." Hence, "behind the apparently effortless display of creativity in the Priestly account there lies the symbolism of divine victory over chaos and darkness. The conquered deep becomes his servant."[20]

If, then, God's "In the beginning" at the opening of Genesis retains traces even as it effaces the story of the victory of another god over an antagonistic female figure, this *In principio* evokes at least the possibility of a reversal, in which a female must at first be overcome before her male antagonist can establish his priority, and so to speak "begin." Even clearer indications, however, of this progression from female to male—rather than the other way around, as in the account of the creation of Eve in Genesis 2—are provided in the ubiquitous myths of moving from matriarchy to patriarchy, studied in Bachofen's influential *Das Mutterrecht* (1861) and since.

The very ubiquity of such myths—of an original female rule and unruliness which male takeover then corrects—is truly astounding, whatever their ambiguous provenance. Since the unruliness of women is so often, across widely different historical periods, used to justify their subordination to men, this progression appears to be yet another constructed narrative of origins, another creation story rather than the historical document it presents itself as. For Bachofen and those he influenced, the progression from female to male dominance, from matriarchy or "mother right" to patriarchal rule, represented a real historical sequence, one parallel to the ritual of initiation in which a boy moves from the world of the mother to that of the father. But the sequence itself is not verifiable as a historical development, and has more recently been challenged by critiques such as Joan Bamberger's theory of the myth of matriarchy as functioning instead as justification of a felt reality—the subjection of women—by providing a purportedly historical account of how this reality came about.[21]

Bachofen himself, significantly, used chiefly poetic and mythological sources—including Hesiod's *Theogony*, a creation narrative which leads from an original female Earth Goddess to the male rule of the Olympian

Zeus—and focuses his argument for the defeat of *Mutterrecht* in Athens on a play, the *Oresteia*, which both narrativizes this progression from female to male and draws on the new theories of generation (the mere passivity of the mother and the primacy of the father) in order to authorize the transition. The progression from female to male also in this play involves a diminution of the powers of the female, and the eventual subordination of women within the institution of patriarchal marriage by the end. Clytemnestra is at first triumphant over Agamemnon, as Omphale was over Hercules—the very image of woman's misrule.[22] But, in the progression to the trilogy's second play, she is presented not just as an adulterous, murderous wife but as a bad and hostile mother, and the Furies or Erinyes, embodiments of all that is terrifying in the female, are tamed into the Eumenides or "kindly ones" in the institution of Athenian law as the play proceeds to its close. Bachofen, focusing on the confrontation between the Erinyes as champions of *Mutterrecht* and Apollo as advocate of father right in the trilogy's finale, notes the argument of Apollo, ultimately ratified by Athena as judge, that "The mother is no parent of that which is called / her child, but only nurse of the new-planted seed / that grows. The parent is he who mounts" (*The Eumenides*, 657–66). He also notes the appeal to the figure of Athena herself—born from her father Zeus "without any mother" (663)—and the fact that the very place of the judgment against "mother right" is a recall of the Amazons, those unruly females finally defeated by the Athenian Theseus, with even their own rulers ultimately subordinated as wives.[23]

We might for our own purposes, however, stay for a moment within what Froma Zeitlin, in putting forward a reading of the trilogy in these terms, so suggestively calls the *Oresteia*'s "linear logic."[24] If part of what is dramatized in Aeschylus' trilogy is the establishment of Athenian law after the cycles of violence and revenge enacted within the history of the House of Atreus, this transition also involves the establishment of a new "in the beginning." This is the one performed not just in the progression from a powerful Clytemnestra to a diminishment of female power by the final play but through a reversal of second and first in which the Hesiodic myth of birth from the male—Athena's springing from the head of Zeus—establishes a new beginning or genesis. The alternative to the terrifying power of the mother, earlier evoked by both Clytemnestra and the Erinyes, is nothing less than a second birth or rebirth from the father presented finally as the only genesis, with the mother now cast in a secondary and merely passive role. The new theories of generation here both join with and reverse the order of the drama of transition from mother to father—or of Theseus' actual defeat of the Amazons—by denying the mother alto-gether, in the figure of Athena, female born from male, not threatening mother but subordinate daughter. Hesiod's myth of Athena born from Zeus' head—the act through which Zeus consolidates his sovereignty even

as he appropriates the female reproductive principle itself—joins the
theory of the all-important semen originating in the brain and endowing
the child with the capacity for reason or *logos*. Out of the violence of
the trilogy which begins with Clytemnestra, then, comes a specifically
Athenian "Let there be light," associated with the rational and with
enlightenment. Theogony, or a narrative of creation and genesis, and
embryology, the *logos* of beginnings, combine in an ending which is
decisive because it both subordinates female to male within marriage and
wipes out all trace of the prior female in an "In the beginning" which starts
with the father alone.

Theodor Reik, in *The Creation of Woman*, calls to our attention the
similarities between the story of Athena's birth from the forehead of Zeus
and the account in Genesis 2 of the birth of Eve, from and for man.[25]
Perhaps even more to the point, however, would be to note the fact that the
very same year that Bachofen's *Das Mutterrecht* appeared (arguing the
historical and moral primacy of "mother right" and the rule of women),
Henry Sumner Maine's *Ancient Law* was published to bolster the opposing opinion—that in the beginning was the father, that patriarchy was
"the primeval condition of the human race"—an argument founded not
just on Roman law but on the opening chapters of Genesis.[26] Whatever the
debate that ensued between matriarchists and patriarchists in the intellectual circles of Europe after the simultaneous publication of these apparently opposed views (and these were to be important for Freud, as we shall
see), the linear narrative which has the transition to patriarchy as its
crowning telos or end is simply, as a superimposition of Genesis on the
Oresteia or Hesiod's *Theogony* would suggest, the counterpart of a theory
which, arguing from the creation of Eve after Adam in Genesis 2, would
posit the male as the definitive *arche* or beginning.

I have rehearsed these texts, and influential mythemes, not just because
they remain tenaciously influential, if only in unacknowledged and subterranean ways, but because the logic of first and second, and hence of
sequence, is still a logic which continues to inhabit the discussion of female
difference, in Milton, Rousseau, and Freud—to whose own developmental narratives we now turn.[27] To move from this background to more
detailed analysis of the text of Milton's presentation of the sexes in
Paradise Lost, to the echo of Genesis 2 in the final book of Rousseau's
Emile, or to the genesis and psychogenesis of the female in Freud is not to
deny the importance of a more specific historical nuancing and embedded-
ness: such study would, indeed, indicate how the very repetition of such
topoi and mythemes itself depends upon particular historical dynamics
of reinscription, and on the sense of the transhistorical such textual
reembedding produces as one of its effects. But since our final focus
in particular—the narrative of gender difference in Freud—is so fre-

quently seen as the starting point of certain modern developments, rather
than as the inheritor of traditions it subtly rewrites, the three studies to
which we now turn are placed both against this prologue and against each
other, in a specifically textual history that their own internal references
invite.

III

He for God only, she for God in him.

(Milton, *Paradise Lost*)

Milton's *Paradise Lost* is generally, as it was for both Rousseau and Freud,
a signal text in the complex history of female difference which proceeds
from the combined sources of Genesis and the Aristotelian legacy of
woman as subordinate to man. We begin with the picture of Adam and Eve
in the Garden before the Fall, as seen through Satan's eyes in Book IV:

> Two of far nobler shape erect and tall,
> Godlike erect, with native honour clad
> In naked majesty seemed *lords of all*,
> And worthy seemed, for in their looks divine
> The *image of their glorious maker* shone,
> Truth, wisdom, sanctitude severe and pure,
> Severe but in true filial freedom placed;
> Whence true authority *in men*; though both
> *Not equal, as their sex not equal seemed*;
> For contemplation he and valour formed,
> For softness she and sweet attractive grace,
> *He for God only, she for God in him*:
> His fair large front and eye sublime declared
> *Absolute rule*; and hyacinthine locks
> Round from his parted forelock manly hung
> Clustering, but not beneath his shoulders broad:
> She as a veil down to the slender waist
> Her unadorned golden tresses wore
> Dishevelled, but in wanton ringlets waved
> As the *vine* curls her tendrils, which implied
> *Subjection*, but required with gentle sway,
> And by her yielded, by him best received,
> Yielded with *coy submission, modest pride*,
> And *sweet reluctant amorous delay*.[28]

The passage is a subtle combination of the two creation stories in Genesis 1
and 2, or, perhaps more accurately, a progression without sharp break

from the first to the second. The first, with its "And God said, Let us make man in our image, after our likeness: and let *them* have dominion ... over all the earth" and "So God created man in his own image, in the image of God created he him; male and female created he *them*" (Genesis 1:26–7), is echoed first in the "Two" who "seemed lords of all," in whose "looks divine / The *image* of *their* glorious maker shone." The second, through the pivotal phrase "Whence true authority in men"—which could, for a moment, suggest generic "man" rather than the gender-specific one— begins to be echoed in the differentiation of the "he" and "she" through their "sex" ("though both / Not equal, as their sex not equal seemed"), in a progression which brings us to a "manly" ("*manly* hung") which is unmistakably gendered in a context of distinction and difference. The difference, almost imperceptibly established in this shading away from the language of Genesis 1, now proceeds according to the logic of the second creation story in Genesis 2:22–3: "And the rib, which the Lord God had taken from man, made he a woman, and brought her unto the man. And Adam said, This is now bone of my bones, and flesh of my flesh; she shall be called Woman, because she was taken out of Man." "He for God only, she for God in him" recalls, as editorial commentaries point out, the New Testament gloss on the second creation story of woman from, for, and after man: "the head of every man is Christ; and the head of the woman is the man; and the head of Christ is God. ... For the man is not of the woman; but the woman of the man" (1 Corinthians 11: 3–8). And it can be read not just vertically, as hierarchy, but sequentially according to the logic of first and second from Genesis 2: Adam made first, and in the image of God, Eve, as the later Miltonic dramatization of the text from Genesis 2 puts it, brought to the man "Whose image" (*Paradise Lost*, IV.472) she is—a relation which Milton explicates theologically in the *Tetrachordon*'s dictum that "the woman is not primarily and immediately the image of God, but in reference to the man."[29] The image of the "veil" from Pauline passages on the proper behavior of women, and the traditional image of the female as the dependent "vine" on the masculine elm, provide, then, the appropriate image of difference in the lines which move from Adam's "Absolute rule" to Eve's feminine "Subjection."

The final lines in this quoted passage ("Yielded with coy submission, modest pride, / And sweet reluctant amorous delay") take us forward proleptically to a moment in the narrative of the very first moments of the creation of Eve, the dramatization of the second creation story from Genesis 2 later in this same book. But already, in their oxymorons, they suggest the vestiges of a resistance overcome, one which projects a slightly different relation between male and female than the polarity of "Absolute rule ... subjection" might by itself convey. Eve's own narrative of these moments starts, once again, from an echo of Genesis 2:23, and its

gloss in the passage from 1 Corinthians 11 on the headship of the man, as
she addresses the man from whom she was made: .

> O thou for whom
> And from whom I was formed flesh of thy flesh,
> And without whom am to no end, my guide
> And head ...
> That day I oft remember, when from sleep
> I first awaked. ...
>
> (IV.440 ff.)

"End," in "without whom am to no end," combines both telos and
purpose, just as this beginning already forecasts, retrospectively, the
narrative end of the story Eve is about to tell. Like all autobiographical
narrative, its perspective even in the beginning is from an end; and
beginning in this way gives Eve's narrative the formal aspect of a confession, a recounting of the error she has come through. The story she tells,
familiar to readers of Milton, is of her first unknowing attachment to her
own "image" in the pool—a moment which explicitly recalls the story of
Narcissus—and of her conversion by that warning "voice" which takes
her beyond this "vain desire" to Adam, who, as her original in priority and
time, is to be both the end of her narrative and her own "end."[30] The
"voice" warns against her delight with her own image, in a passage which
ends with an Eve now explicitly converted to a "following" more consist-
ent with the fact (of which she is still ignorant) that she was created out of,
and for, man (*ex viro propter virum*), as in Genesis 2:

> What thou seest,
> What there thou seest fair creature is thyself,
> With thee it came and goes: but *follow* me,
> And I will bring thee where no shadow stays
> Thy coming, and thy soft embraces, he
> Whose image thou art, him thou shall enjoy
> Inseparably thine, to him shalt bear
> Multitudes like thyself, and thence be called
> Mother of human race: what could I do,
> But *follow* straight, invisibly thus led?
>
> (IV.467–76)

Eve here recounts both her movement beyond the moment of Narcissism and the "end" to which she, as follower, is now "led," brought
back to him "Whose image" she, unknowingly, is. But it also takes
her from this initial Narcissism—a pining with "vain desire" in lines
which suggest its ultimate sterility—to the vocation the name of
Hevah in Hebrew suggests, as "mother of all living." The conversion of
Eve here is into both a follower and a mother—the end of this amplified

Miltonic narrative of creation from man, and what in Genesis immediately
follows it.

In Milton's version, however, the actual progression to this end encounters some resistance from Eve herself, a resistance she here recounts to
Adam as the penultimate stage of the fuller narrative of conversion and
following:

> I espied thee, fair indeed and tall,
> Under a platan, yet methought less fair,
> Less winning soft, less amiably mild,
> Than that smooth watery image; back I turned,
> Thou *following* cried'st aloud, Return fair Eve,
> Whom fly'st thou? Whom thou fly'st, *of him thou art,*
> *His flesh, his bone;* to give thee being I lent
> Out of my side to thee, nearest my heart
> Substantial *life*, to have thee by my side
> Henceforth an individual solace dear;
> Part of my soul I seek thee, and thee claim
> My other half: with that thy gentle hand
> *Seized* mine, *I yielded*, and from that time see
> How beauty is excelled by manly grace
> And wisdom, which alone is truly fair.
>
>   (IV.477–91)

The actual end of this progression, the final turning point in her conversion
from a narcissistic self-attachment to "our general mother" (IV.492), is
veiled in rhetorical *reticentia*: we are not told what Eve saw or what Adam
finally showed her that made all the difference, that convinced her of the
superiority of his "manly grace." But the progression itself is towards a
destination whose actual arrival is not immediate but delayed, in contrast
to the more straightforward progression of the passage's biblical subtext
from Genesis 2, which passes from "the Lord God ... brought her unto the
man" to the formula of marriage in a mere two lines. Eve's end is to be
schooled not just by the warning "voice" of God but by that man whose
prior creation gives him prior and hence superior knowledge of her own
beginnings ("Whom thou fly'st, of *him* thou art," as Adam puts it); and the
education provided to this figure who is subsequently to be "Mother of
human race" (IV. 475) is that she owes her own "Substantial life" to him
whose "bone" and "flesh" and "image" she is.

It should, however, be said that this passage is not the only version
Milton's poem gives us of these same events, or of the moment of potential
female resistance to this "following." Adam gives his own account to
Raphael in Book VIII, just before the Fall, and it begins, not like Eve's with
a rehearsal of her telos or end, the headship of him "for whom / And from
whom" she was formed, but rather on the note of his own incompletion or

lack from Genesis 2:20 ("And Adam gave names to all cattle, and to the fowl of the air, and to every beast of the field; but for Adam there was not found an help meet for him," before God culminates his acts of creation in the final act of the creation of "Woman"). Adam's account in Book VIII amplifies, once again, this problematic space between, in Adam's own suing for a "help meet" in his solitude:

> Thou hast provided all things: but with me
> I see not who partakes. In solitude
> What happiness, who can enjoy alone,
> Or all enjoying, what contentment find?
>
> (VIII. 363–6)

When God answers that He himself is, after all, "alone" and has no "second" (405–7), Adam's reply is to contrast God's perfection ("Thou in thy self art perfect"; 415) with his own "deficience" (416) in such solitude, his oneness as not the self-sufficiency of divinity but rather a sign of his "single imperfection" (423) or incompleteness. As Leon Howard demonstrates, in a line of argument the Carey/Fowler gloss commends, Adam's awareness of this *deficience* "makes him the proegumenic or impulsive helping cause of the Fall," since "his need for companionship leads to the creation of Eve, who in turn will provide the procatarctic cause, or occasion," for it.[31]

Adam's account of the creation of Eve, then, occurs in the context of his own "imperfection" or "deficience," in a tradition which (as with the argument from the sequential order of Genesis 2 used by Rachel Speght and other defenders of women) construes the order of the second creation account (first Adam, second Eve) not in the first instance as authorizing the priority of the Man from whom she comes but rather in reverse, as the end or culmination of the entire progress of creation up to that final point:

> The rib he formed and fashioned with his hands;
> Under his forming hands a creature grew,
> Manlike, but different sex, so lovely fair,
> That what seemed fair in all the world, seemed now
> Mean, or in her *summed up, in her contained*
> And in her looks ...
>
> (VIII.469–74)

This "creature," however, as soon as she appears to him as that culmination without which he is incomplete, disappears ("She disappeared, and left me dark"; 478). Adam's account goes on to suggest a different perspective on the moments of female self-sufficiency and reluctance reported by Eve, which intrude into his telling both at the point immediately after her creation and, as with Eve's account, between the time she is first "brought unto" him and when she finally yields to his "rule." The moment narrated by Eve as that of her Narcissus-like self-reflection in the pool—the delay and difficulty of her conversion—is what appears in Adam's account as the threat of her absence or loss to him:

> She disappeared, and left me dark, I waked
> To find her, or for ever to deplore
> Her loss, and other pleasures all abjure:
> When out of hope, behold her, not far off,
> Such as I saw her in my dream . . .
> . . . on she came,
> Led by her heavenly maker, though unseen,
> And guided by his voice, nor uninformed
> Of nuptial sanctity and marriage rites.
>
> (VIII.478–87)

It is this first "turn" or return of Eve (491) from a self-sufficiency and Narcissism, represented from his perspective now as loss to *him*, which in Adam's account leads to his quotation of the concluding lines of the second creation narrative from Genesis 2. His "Bone of my bone, flesh of my flesh" and "woman is her name, of man / Extracted" (495–7) lead, as in the conclusion of Genesis 2, to the formula of marriage: "for this cause he shall forego / Father and mother, and to his wife adhere; / And they shall be one flesh" (497–9). Curiously, it is only at this point—with this "turn"—that Adam thanks God for the fulfillment of his promise to repair his "single imperfection" ("This turn hath made amends; thou hast fulfilled / Thy words, creator bounteous and benign"; 491–2). But it also turns out to be not the end of his account, which continues with yet another turning, potential absence, and return:

> She heard me thus, and though divinely brought,
> Yet innocence and virgin modesty,
> Her virtue and the conscience of her worth,
> That would be wooed, and not unsought be won,
> Not obvious, not obtrusive, but *retired*,
> *The more desirable*, or to say all,
> Nature her self, though pure of sinful thought,
> Wrought in her so, *that seeing me, she turned*;
> I *followed* her, she what was honour knew,
> And with *obsequious majesty* approved
> My pleaded reason. To the nuptial bower
> I *led* her blushing like the morn.
>
> (VIII.500–11)

The moment of turning away here, which Adam's account explains as a "virgin modesty" or "honour" which "would be wooed, and not unsought be won," is what in Eve's account is instead described as her preference for her own image over the one "Whose image" she is ("Till I espied thee, fair indeed and tall, / Under a platan, yet methought less fair, / Less winning soft, less amiably mild, / Than that smooth watery image; back I turned"; IV.477–80), before she literally converts, or returns, to the figure who is, as in Genesis 2, both her origin and her "end" (IV.442). Adam's account, with its "retired, / The more desirable," echoes the language of Book IV's "coy submission, modest pride, / And sweet reluctant amorous delay" (IV.310–11), a paraphrase of that venerable masculinist tradition of female delay in which reluctance makes the object of desire more desirable still.[32] If Eve is the end, in the sense of the final act, of creation itself, she is, in her turning away, an end which for Adam may also recede from him, turning him into not just a follower but an anxious follower of the figure without whom he was originally incomplete. His account here involves a reversal of the earlier account in Book IV where Eve, created second and out of Adam, is commanded by the warning "voice" to "follow me" (IV.469) to that first and head "without whom" she is "to no end" (IV.442), a command to "follow" echoed in Eve's own response ("what could I do, / But follow straight . . . ?; IV.475–6). For here, in Eve's turning, it is now Adam who "follows" ("she turned; / I *followed* her"; VIII. 507–8).

The Miltonic amplification on the text of coming second from Genesis 2 creates in these turns and counterturns a potential instability within the logic of "following" itself. In Eve's account of her creation in Book IV, the moment of narcissistic self-sufficiency at the pool is already foreclosed by a sense of an "end" narratively present from the beginning—like those Miltonic "loops in time" which present a whole trajectory initially from the perspective of the end. Eve, there, is commanded by the warning "voice" to "follow" to her own great original. But in Adam's account we now read "she turned; / I followed *her*" (VIII.507–8). The logic of sequence—of who is the proper "end" and who "follows" whom—is thus put into play by two passages in which "following" is itself verbally emphasized and, with it, the possibility of a reversal. But here, at the end of Adam's account, before the Fall, there is a restoration of the proper order and sequence, as Eve, returning to him and approving his "pleaded reason," yields to him with an "obsequious majesty" which both repeats the oxymorons of the earlier "coy submission, modest pride, / And sweet reluctant amorous delay" and combines in "obse*qui*ous" the properly ordered combination of hierarchy and sequence, of compliance to a superior as well as a following after him.

The whole context of Adam's account, however, beginning with his own "deficience," that lack which the creation of Eve is to supply, and leading up through his sense of everything before her as "in her summed up" (VIII.473) to the moment when she turns from him and he follows her, is ominously continued in what precisely *follows from* this account to

Raphael of her creation in Book VIII. For Adam's concluding statement is both the end of his narrative and a praise of Eve herself as end or "sum" ("Thus I have told thee all my state, and brought / My story to the sum of earthly bliss, / Which I enjoy"; VIII.521–3):

> here
> Far otherwise, *transported* I behold,
> Transported touch; here passion first I felt,
> Commotion strange, in all enjoyments else
> *Superior and unmoved*, here only *weak*
> Against the charm of beauty's powerful glance.
> Or nature failed in me, and left some part
> Not proof enough such object to sustain,
> Or from my side *subducting*, took perhaps
> More than enough; at least on her bestowed
> Too much of ornament, in outward show
> Elaborate, of inward less exact.
> For well I understand in the *prime end*
> Of nature her the *inferior*, in the mind
> And inward faculties, which most excel,
> In outward also her *resembling less*
> *His image who made both*, and less expressing
> The character of that dominion given
> O'er other creatures; yet when I *approach*
> Her loveliness, so *absolute* she seems
> And *in her self complete*, so well to know
> Her own, that what she wills to do or say,
> Seems wisest, virtuousest, discreetest, best.

                                        (VIII.528–50)

The passage—with its own parenthetically incorporated acknowledgment ("For well I understand"; 540) of that female secondariness which should follow from the creation narrative of Genesis 2—leads instead in a different direction, implicitly from Adam's own lack or imperfection before the creation of Eve to the reverse sequential logic of Eve as a superlative "end" beyond the rest. The sense of Eve here as "heaven's last best gift" (V.19),[33] of her creation as the end or culmination of a narrative progression, is translated into the conclusion of her self-sufficiency and completeness as well. Adam goes on from here to say, in an ironically reversed echo of the Aristotelian *animal occasionatum*, "Authority and reason on her wait, / As one intended first, not after made / Occasionally" (VIII. 554–6). The Miltonic Eve may correctly acknowledge Adam her origin as also her "end" (IV. 442); but Adam's Eve here appears as the end of Adam's own story as she is of the sequential narrative of creation itself —the "sum" of both. This sense of possible reversal persists in the midst of the reminders here of her inferiority, her greater distance from the ultimate Original. And the Narcissism of the moment of self-reflection in the pool, which causes Eve to turn away from Adam in a gesture then interpreted by him as "virgin modesty," as a desire to "be wooed, and not unsought be won," here returns in his version of a self-sufficiency or completeness in herself ("so absolute she seems / And in her self complete") which contrasts pointedly with the "deficience" and incompleteness of Adam which led to her creation in the first place. She, created last, is to find her "end" in that figure who was created first, a beginning and end echoed subtly here in nature's "prime end." But this passage creates the possibility of a reversal of this proper order, which Raphael ("To whom the angel with contracted brow"; 560) will then counter in lines which ominously foreshadow the reversal or *peripeteia* involved in the Fall, in which Adam will follow Eve—into sin, and history.

Raphael quickly moves to correct Adam's words on the primacy of Eve, warning him against "attributing overmuch to things / Less excellent" (VIII.565–6) and advising him that Eve is "worthy well / Thy cherishing, thy honouring, and thy love, / Not thy subjection" (VIII.568–70)—words that echo 1 Peter 3:7 on the honoring of the "weaker vessel." But this danger within the Miltonic text is borne out when in Book IX Adam, responding to the already fallen Eve (as 1 Timothy reminds us, the first to sin), addresses her: "O fairest of creation, *last and best* / Of all God's works, creature in whom excelled / Whatever can to sight or thought be formed" (IX.896 ff.), a repetition of the familiar figure of Eve's secondariness from Genesis 2, but this time turned around, as Adam at this point is in fact about to follow Eve. It is precisely of this properly ordered sequence from Genesis 2 and its New Testament gloss in 1 Corinthians ("For the man is not of the woman; but the woman of the man") that God reminds Adam, when the latter offers his excuses after the Fall:

> This woman whom thou madest to be my help,
> And gavest me as thy perfect gift, so good ...
> She gave me of the tree, and I did eat.
>   To whom the sovereign presence thus replied.
> Was she thy God, that her thou didst obey
> Before his voice, or was she made thy guide,
> Superior, or but equal, that to her
> Thou didst resign thy manhood, and the place
> Wherein God set *thee above her made of thee*,
> *And for thee*, whose *perfection far excelled*
> *Hers* in all real dignity: adorned
> She was indeed, and lovely to attract
> Thy love, *not thy subjection*, and her gifts

> Were such as under government well seemed,
> *Unseemly to bear rule.*

(X.137–55)

Adam, in his misogynist speech to Eve in Book X, recoils to the reverse of his former complaint of his own "imperfection" or incompleteness before her creation, in lines which explicitly echo not just centuries of speculation on Genesis 2:22 but also the Aristotelian tradition of woman as a lacking or defective man:

> a rib
> Crooked by nature, bent, as now appears,
> More to the part sinister from me drawn,
> Well if thrown out, as *supernumerary*
> To my just number found. O why did God,
> Creator wise, that peopled highest heaven
> With spirits masculine, create at last
> This novelty on earth, this *fair defect*
> Of nature, and not fill the world at once
> With men as angels without feminine,
> Or find some other way to generate
> Mankind?

(X.884–95)

Adam's words not only echo Aristotle's *De generatione* on the female as a botched or defective male, along with the famous passage from Euripides' *Hippolytus* (161 ff.) which expresses the desire for male parthenogenesis,[34] but characterize Eve now as a "supernumerary" rib, left over from something already in itself complete.

Very little of the centuries of commentary on the creation stories in Genesis or on the nature and proper place of woman, from Plato and Aristotle through Philo and Aquinas to the Renaissance *querelle des femmes*, ultimately escapes incorporation into Milton's epic on the first male and female. But it is the logic of sequence and hence of consequence —a logic which in another dimension of this epic inhabits the problem of narrative, of syntax, and ultimately of language itself—which here bears pursuing.[35] For it sets up a generative instability, not just within *Paradise Lost* or, as we shall go on to see, in the text of Rousseau, but perhaps even within the Genesis story which stands as their common original. Is there something, we might ask, within the second creation story in Genesis 2 which already creates the possibility that Adam will fall in following that figure whose creation followed his—into, precisely, *history*? Or does it arise from the very logic of the sequential in which a first seen as incomplete without what follows it will end up following in turn? "Flesh of flesh / Bone of my bone thou art" from Genesis 2:23 is echoed several times in Milton's epic before its appearance in Book IX—and in the context of its New Testament gloss, that woman was made after and from the man and should therefore be subordinate to him. But when it is quoted by Adam as he is about to follow Eve in the Fall, it is he who is now turned round and ready to follow her. All the turns and counterturns of the separate narratives of Eve's creation and Adam's in Books IV and VIII— overlaying the text from Genesis with more secular (particularly Ovidian) stories of flight and pursuit—might be seen in this perspective as preparing for the possibility of this crucial *peripeteia* or reversal and all that follows from it. Indeed, once on the sequential axis at all, all kinds of reversals are possible—an instability that haunted Rousseau as well, and one which will take us in his texts into the logic of the female as a dangerous supplement.

IV

In everything not connected with sex, woman is man.

(Rousseau, *Emile*)

In a famous passage from *Some Psychical Consequences of the Anatomical Distinction between the Sexes* (1925), Freud writes of little boys and little girls: "In examining the earliest mental shapes assumed by the sexual life of children we have been in the habit of taking as the subject of our investigations the male child, the little boy. With little girls, so we have supposed, things must be similar, though in some way or other they must nevertheless be different."[36] Pursuing this motif in Freud will, as we shall see, take us back once again both to Aristotle and to the second creation story in Genesis 2. But we begin with this master preceptor—observer of the development of boys and girls—in order to keep the Viennese master in the background while we follow an earlier, Genevan one, the author of the narrative of male and female in Book V of *Emile*, that text which, even more than Milton's, animated Mary Wollstonecraft's *Vindication of the Rights of Woman*.

In approaching Book V of *Emile*—dedicated to "Sophie, ou la femme" —we are led, however, not forward to Freud but, once again, backward to the text of the creation of woman in Genesis 2. *Pace* its recent translator, Allan Bloom, who claims that Rousseau "begins from thoroughly modern premises—not deriving from Biblical or Greek thought," Book V opens with an explicit echo of the second creation story in Genesis: "Il n'est pas bon que l'homme soit seul. Emile est homme; nous lui avons promis une compagne, il faut la lui donner" ("It is not good for man to be alone. Emile is a man. We have promised him a companion. She has to be given to him").[37] Book V comes at the very end of *Emile*, in what its opening lines

call "the last act of the drama of youth, but ... not yet ... the denoue-
ment." Sophie or "Woman," that is to say, comes only after and at the end
of the story of Emile, created by that Rousseau who will more than once
implicitly compare himself to the God of Genesis who brings the woman to
the man as a companion in his solitude. This preceptor's "last best gift"
also involves, as in Genesis 2, the final act of marriage with which *Emile*
will conclude.

The account of "Sophie, ou la femme," then, begins with an echo of that
creation story in which the woman comes after and out of the man, and is
created as a helpmeet for him; and, as in Genesis 2 or in Bunyan, the
woman's story is narrated in second place. In ways which recall the figure
Rousseau later in this text will praise as "the divine Milton," as well as
their common original in Genesis, Sophie is first described in terms of
the male original, the model on which the whole of the text up to the
creation of this second figure and last act has been based: "In everything
not connected with sex, woman is man" ("En tout ce qui ne tient pas au
séxe, la femme est homme").

All at the beginning of Rousseau's discussion is based on the prior model
of the male: except for her sex, Sophie is a man. The fact that the reverse
does not present itself—"but for his sex, a man is a woman"—indicates
clearly that the man is not only first in the narrative order here but the
standard in what will ensue, "our own sex," as Rousseau later describes it
to his readers.[38] It is the degree to which woman deviates from this
standard of the species by reason of her sex that will be the focus of the
Book which is to unfold. For, if Sophie comes, as in Genesis 2, after Emile,
in Rousseau's text she is also very quickly defined by her difference.

The discussion of that difference begins in what seems an evenhanded
way, without bowing to the traditional Aristotelian figure of woman as a
defective man:

> The only thing we know with certainty is that everything man and
> woman have in common belongs to the species, and that everything
> which distinguishes them belongs to the sex. ... These relations and
> these differences must have a moral influence. This conclusion is evident
> to the senses ... and it shows how vain are the disputes as to whether one
> of the two sexes is superior or whether they are equal—as though each,
> in fulfilling nature's ends according to its own particular purpose, were
> thereby less perfect than if it resembled the other more! In what they
> have in common, they are equal. Where they differ, they are not
> comparable. A perfect woman and a perfect man ought not to resemble
> each other in mind any more than in looks, and perfection is not
> susceptible of more or less. (p. 358)[39]

It is amazing, however, given this initial premise, how quickly the text
moves to a specification of this difference, and all of the consequences

which ensue, in terms which might well remind us of the legacy of both Genesis and Aristotle. The "first assignable difference" ("la prémiére différence assignable") is the moral relation of the two sexes: "One ought to be active and strong, the other passive and weak" ("L'un doit être actif et fort, l'autre passif et foible"). Rousseau then moves quickly to "what follows" from this initial difference: "Ce principe établi, il *s'ensuit que* la femme est faite spécialement pour plaire à l'homme"—"This principle established, *it follows that* woman is made specially to please man" (p. 358; my italics). (Something akin to this movement is recapitulated in the passage where we move from "each obeys, and both are masters" to "Since women are not in a position to be judges themselves, they ought to receive the decision of fathers and husbands like that of the Church"; p. 377). The main issue at the opening of Book V rapidly becomes the social and other distinctions imposed by the differences between the two genders, and the consequences that emerge from those differences. It is perhaps no surprise, then, that, after this opening echo of Genesis, we soon encounter a reminiscence of Eve in her final biblical and Miltonic incarnation as "mother of mankind," the further corollary of motherhood as "the proper purpose" or "destination" (p. 362) of women ("leur destination propre"). If the work of Rousseau is the first major attempt to justify equality among men—one of the reasons it excited the admiration as well as the anger of Mary Wollstonecraft—this text also does much to elaborate, as a consequence of a premise of difference, a justification of the inequality of men and women. We move here from an initial statement of the perfection of each sex to a description of the weakness of the second sex, just as in the *Discours sur l'origine et les fondements de l'inégalité parmi les hommes* the narrative progresses from a basic sameness in the condition and manner of living of men and women to the establishment of the hut, in which women become more sedentary as well as the mothers of children. We begin to understand Michelet's comment that "L'Emile est un livre très mâle."

This secondary position, of "Sophie, ou la femme," following from the binary opposition of strength and passivity, is, however, not all that this text presents, even in its own beginning. And this fact introduces into it a crucial instability, in spite of its own more programmatic statements on woman's proper place. In a way which recalls Eve's "sweet reluctant amorous delay" in Milton—Adam's finding Eve "retired, / The more desirable"—as well as anticipating a motif in Freud that is curiously similar to both, Rousseau goes on from this opening to speak of how this second and weaker sex may enslave the stronger and first:

> If woman is made to please and to be subjugated, she ought to make herself agreeable to man instead of arousing him. Her own violence is in her charms. It is by these that she ought to constrain him to find his strength and make use of it. The surest art for animating that strength is

to make it necessary by *resistance*. Then amour-propre unites with desire, and the one triumphs in the victory that the other has made him win. From this there arises *attack and defense*, the audacity of one sex and the timidity of the other, and finally the modesty and the shame with which nature armed the weak in order to enslave the strong. (p. 358)[40]

The rapidity with which the opening of Rousseau's text moves from the statement of women's passivity and secondariness to this somewhat different relation is striking. And very quickly, once again, we move from this imbalance to the stock examples of female domination of men, Omphale's effeminating of Hercules and Delilah's power over Samson ("ce même Hercule qui crut faire violence aux cinquante filles de Thespitius fut pourtant contraint de filer près d'Omphale, et le fort Samson n'étoit pas si fort que Dalila"; *OC*, IV, 697; *Emile*, p. 361).

There is more than a hint of mother Eve—and her female descendants— in "Sophie, ou la femme." The transition from this initial counsel to "resistance," "timidity," and "modesty," in order to animate male desire, to a vision of the submission of this aroused strength to Omphale and Delilah comes through an intervening passage on the threatening, voracious sexuality of women, introduced by lines which bear a faint recollection of the Amazons: "given the ease with which women arouse men's senses and reawaken in the depths of their hearts the remains of ardors which are almost extinguished, men would finally be their victims and would see themselves dragged to death without ever being able to defend themselves" (p. 359). The fear of female sexuality and its consequences emerges in the very language with which (like Aristotle) Rousseau dismisses Plato's proposal for female guardians—"cette *promiscüité civile* qui confond par tout les deux séxes dans les mêmes emplois" (*OC*, IV, 700)—as earlier, in Book IV, it had emerged in the presentation of "une fille publique" (*OC*, IV, 518) in the sense of "whore."[41] The text goes on to discuss the danger not just to the family but to property represented by the adulterous wife—something, we might add, which Sophie herself is to become in what would be the supplementary addition or "sequel" to *Emile*.

The vision of female dominance near the beginning of Book V is, however, only temporary and is folded back into the more stable mode of an all too familiar opposition. The logic of female secondariness and inferiority, and not just of difference, goes on to govern much of the rest of the text, giving us statements such as "it is part of the order of nature that the woman obey the man" (p. 407); or "Woman, honor the head of your house. It is he who works for you, who wins your bread, who feeds you. This is man" (p. 437); or "dependence is a condition natural to women, and thus girls feel themselves made to obey" (p. 370). The difference between the two sexes also means that if the whole concern of the text, as its title indicates, is *Emile, ou de l'éducation*, the education of Sophie must also be different ("Woman is made to yield to man and to endure even his injustice. You will never reduce young boys to the same point"; p. 396). Emile is educated to resist the dictates of society; Sophie is brought up to conform to them.

It also means that, in contrast to Emile who has been raised with a healthy disregard for the mere opinions of others, Sophie must be vigilant of the opinion she holds in other minds. In one particular passage which would be of interest to those familiar with the prominent "O"s in Monique Wittig's *Les Guérillères* or with the relation of the "O" itself to the sexuality of woman, a young girl is described later in Book V of *Emile* as having learned to write before she could read, and as having a passion for making nothing but "O"s—"She incessantly made big and little O's, O's of all sizes, O's inside one another, and always drawn backward" (p. 369)—until she caught a glimpse of herself one day in a mirror and, "finding that this constrained attitude was not graceful for her," abandoned writing altogether; her brother, on the other hand, disliked it only for the discomfort and not for the appearance it gave him. But it becomes clear in other passages that this specular gaze is also the male gaze; for, in a passage directed in part against Ninon de l'Enclos, an older female caught in the act of writing is similarly described in an aside to "Readers" who can only be in this instance male: "Readers, I leave it to you. Answer in good faith. What gives you a better opinion of a woman on entering her room, what makes you approach her with more respect—to see her occupied with the labors of her sex and the cares of her household, encompassed by her children's things, or to find her at her dressing table writing verses, surrounded by all sorts of pamphlets and letters. ... Every literary maiden would remain a maiden for her whole life if there were only sensible men in this world" ["Toute fille lettrée restera fille toute sa vie, quand il n'y aura que des hommes sensés sur la terre"; *OC*, IV, 768] (p. 409). This kind of self-reflection, whose other context is the remark against learned and brilliant women—that "A brilliant wife is a plague to her husband, her children, her friends, her valets, everyone" (p. 409)—also stands behind the conclusion that if, to paraphrase Pope, the proper study of mankind is man, the proper study of woman is specific men:

> Woman, who is weak and who sees nothing outside the house, estimates and judges the forces she can put to work to make up for her weakness, and those forces are men's passions. ... She must have the art to make us want to do everything which her sex cannot do by itself and which is necessary or agreeable to it. She must, therefore, make a profound study of the mind of man—not an abstraction of the mind of man in general, but the minds of the men around her, the minds of the men to which she is subjected by either law or opinion ["non par abstraction l'esprit de l'homme en général, mais l'esprit des hommes qui l'entourent, l'esprit des hommes auxquels elle est assujetie"; *OC*, IV, 737]. (p. 387)

Part of the logic of coming second, of being a sex created not just after but for man—"faite pour plaire et pour être subjuguée" (*OC*, IV, 693)—is the logic of this specular reference. It is clear, within *Emile* as a whole, however, that this subordination of woman—her coming in the text after the man for whom her Author has created her, but also her self-definition in terms of him—has its threatening other side, that this "heaven's last best gift" may also dominate man in ways which would take us back, once again, to the "divine Milton." I mentioned that the very opening of the text leads, through the device of a logical "Il s'ensuit que," from the initial premise of difference—activity in man, passivity in woman—to its consequence for women, and that this subordinate or second place very quickly yields to a hyperbolic vision of its polar opposite, men tyrannized by women and become their victims ("tirannisés par elles ... enfin leurs victimes"), and ultimately to the figures of Hercules' enslavement by Omphale, and Samson's by Delilah. This includes the following:

> Here, then, is a third conclusion drawn from the constitution of the sexes—that the stronger appears to be master but actually depends on the weaker. This is due not to a frivolous practice of gallantry or to the proud generosity of a protector, but to an invariable law of nature which gives woman more facility to excite the desires than man to satisfy them. This causes the latter, whether he likes it or not, to depend on the former's wish and constrains him to seek to please her in turn, so that she will consent to let him be the stronger. Then what is sweetest for man in his victory is the doubt whether it is weakness which yields to strength or the will which surrenders. And the woman's usual ruse is always to leave this doubt between her and him. (p. 360)[42]

This strength in weakness, however, must be controlled. Woman's rule, in Rousseau's description, is indistinguishable from woman's role. The earlier-quoted passage which states that "it is part of the order of nature that the woman obey the man" (p. 407) then goes on to declaim against a marriage in which "the woman, pretending to authority, acts as a tyrant toward the head of the house, and the master becomes a slave and finds himself the most ridiculous and most miserable of creatures" (p. 408). This is followed by a carefully hedged description of the nature of this "empire" of woman:

> I expect that many readers, remembering that I ascribe to woman a natural talent for governing man, will accuse me of a contradiction here. They will, however, be mistaken. There is quite a difference between arrogating to oneself the right to command and governing him who commands. Woman's empire is an empire of gentleness, skill, and obligingness; her orders are caresses, her threats are tears. She ought to reign in the home as a minister does in a state—by getting herself

commanded to do what she wants to do. In this sense, the best households are invariably those where the woman has the most authority. But when she fails to recognize the voice of the head of the house, when she wants to usurp his rights and be in command herself, the result of this disorder is never anything but misery, scandal, and dishonor. (p. 408)[43]

In a passage not long before this, which describes a similar contrast between an imperious command and the proper authority of woman over man, Rousseau comments, in a revealing phrase, "This seems to me to be a noble empire, and *one well worth the price of its purchase*" (p. 393—"cet empire ... vaut bien la peine d'être acheté"; OC, IV, 745).

The logic of this "empire," then, is the transposed logic of the "sweet reluctant amorous delay," a resistance which is not only to stimulate male desire but to make the conquest all the sweeter in the end. This narrative dynamic of overcoming does not, therefore, end with the dominion of "heaven's last best gift" or the male lover's enslavement to her, but rather in the completed narrative in which such delay is only a stage on the way to the "proper destination" of marriage and motherhood, an "empire" of woman gently wielded within the bounds of patriarchal marriage and the ultimate headship of men. It is no accident, then, that the reigning iconography of this relationship of male and female, of dominance and submission, is—though it may at first seem curious—the figure of Circe who, though the symbol *par excellence* of a threatening female domination over men, nevertheless yields herself to Odysseus, the one man she cannot control.

In Homer's *Odyssey*, which, along with Fénelon's *Télémaque*, is evoked expressly as a parallel to the story of Emile and Sophie, Circe tyrannizes over men whom she transforms, but is subdued by Odysseus' sword. Sophie is explicitly compared to her, as to the virginal Nausicaa waiting for a husband: "She did not want a lover who knew no law other than hers. She wants to reign over a man whom she has not disfigured. It is thus that Circe, having debased Ulysses' companions, disdains them and gives herself only to him whom she was unable to change" (p. 439 — "Elle n'a point voulu d'amant qui ne connut de loi que la sienne; elle veut régner sur un homme qu'elle n'ait point défiguré. C'est ainsi qu'ayant avili les compagnons d'Ulysse, Circé les dédaigne, et se donne à lui seul qu'elle n'a pu changer"; OC, IV, 810). The whole of Book V is represented by the engraving on its frontispiece of Circe's surrender to Odysseus (figure 3) which Rousseau selected himself and explained as follows: "The illustration at the beginning of the fifth book ... represents Circe giving herself to Ulysses, whom she was not able to transform." This passage likening Sophie to a conquered Circe follows quickly after the previously cited "Woman, honor the head of your house. It is he who works for you, who wins your bread, who feeds you. This is man" (p. 437) and the reverse

Figure 3   Ulysses and Circe: from the frontispiece to Book V of Rousseau's
Emile *(Paris, 1762), from the collection and with the permission of the*
Thomas Fisher Rare Book Library, University of Toronto.

of the Hercules–Omphale figure in an italicized *"Hercule est vangé"*
(OC, IV, 808), "Hercules is avenged" (p. 438). The frontispiece representation of Circe's capitulation to Ulysses—the classical emblem of the
overcoming of a powerful and threatening female—stands "in the beginning," at the head of a text which introduces "Sophie, ou la femme" only
after Emile and in explicit imitation of Genesis 2.

There is, however, another way in which, in *Emile* as a whole, and not
just in this last book, Hercules is avenged, and the Circe story of initial
female domination reversed is narrativized within the text. This illustration, kept until the last, as the frontispiece of the final book in which
"woman" is made to appear and is brought unto the man, might be seen
from its endpoint to govern the whole of the text, not just in its end but in
its beginning. For not only does *Emile* end with Sophie, created second and
given to Emile by the Author of them both, as the last act in the drama of
the exemplary "abstract man," but it also begins with woman, and
specifically with women whom Rousseau is to replace. The entire text of
Emile, long before Sophie makes her appearance in its final book as this
author's "last best gift," includes in its beginning an address to the mother

("C'est à toi que je m'address, tendre et prévoyante mére"), to which he adds the following note: "The first education is the most important, and this first education belongs incontestably to women; if the Author of nature had wanted it to belong to men, He would have given them milk with which to nurse the children. Always speak, then, preferably to women in your treatises on education" (p. 37—"La prémiére éducation est celle qui importe le plus, et cette prémiére éducation appartient incontestablement aux femmes; si l'auteur de la nature eut voulu qu'elle appartint aux hommes, il leur eut donné du lait pour nourrir les enfans. Parlez donc toujours aux femmes par préférence dans vos traités d'éducation"; *OC*, IV, 246).

But if women here come first—if the "first education" belongs "incontestably" to them, because of mother's milk—they are also the first enslavers encountered in civil society: "Civil man is born, lives, and dies in slavery. At his birth he is sewed in swaddling clothes; at his death he is nailed in a coffin. So long as he keeps his human shape, he is enchained by our institutions" (p. 43—"L'homme civil nait, vit et meurt dans l'esclavage: à sa naissance on le coud dans un maillot; à sa mort on le cloüe dans une biére; tant qu'il garde la figure humaine il est enchaîné par nos institutions"; *OC*, IV, 253). The beginning of *Emile, ou de l'éducation*, then, moves to that bad beginning and to those responsible for it, those "sage-femmes" or midwives who knead the heads of newborns out of their natural shape. The "you" he here addresses are also women: "You thwart them from their birth. The first gifts they receive from you are chains" (p. 44—"vous les contrariez dès leur naissance: les prémiers dons qu'ils reçoivent de vous sont des chaînes"). The terms recall the famous opening lines of *Du contrat social* ("l'homme est né libre, et par-tout il est dans les fers" (*OC*, III, 351)—"man is born free, and everywhere he is in chains"), with a crossing of contexts which would suggest another almost imperceptible shift from generic to specific "man."

Lest we think, however, that there is a clear distinction here between the "mothers" of the praised "first education" of children and the bad "sage-femmes" of this first enslavement of "civil man," we are told that children are delivered into the hands of such women by those very mothers who, "despising their first duty" and no longer wanting to nurse their own children, give them over to mercenary nurses who swaddle them in order to keep them under control, so that the mother herself is free to abandon both child and home and roam free: "Do they know, these gentle mothers [*douces méres*, a term equivalent in the tone of the passage to *sage-femmes*] who, delivered from their children [*débarrassées de leurs enfans*], devote themselves gaily [*se livrent gaiment*] to the entertainments of the city, what kind of treatment the swaddled child is getting in the meantime in the village?" (p. 44). This description of irresponsible mothers at the beginning is then joined by an apocalyptic vision of the end that will ensue, of "the impending fate of Europe" which will result from the even worse fact that women, "Not satisfied with having given up nursing their children ... give up wanting to have them": "The sciences, the arts, the philosophy, and the morals that this practice engenders will not be long in making a desert of it. It will be peopled with ferocious beasts" (p. 44—"Les sciences, les arts, la philosophie et les mœurs qu'elle engendre, ne tarderont pas d'en faire un desert. Elle sera peuplée de bétes feroces; elle n'aura pas beaucoup changé d'habitans"; OC, IV, 256).

Not only are mothers the first beginning of the education of "civil man," but maternal neglect is the first depravity, from which everything else follows. This picture of the bad mother and the disasters that ensue from such mothering is what enables Rousseau—by a progression reminiscent of the linear logic of myths of an irresponsible matriarchy giving way to the more ordered rule of men—to take over from the mother, to do, in fact, nothing less than begin again: "Do you wish to bring everyone back to his *first* duties [*ses prémiérs devoirs*]. *Begin* [*Commencez*] with mothers. You will be surprised by the changes you will produce. Everything follows *successively* from this *first* depravity "("Tout vient *successivement* de cette *prémiére* dépravation"). "This *first point*, this point alone, will bring everything back together. ... Let women once again become mothers, men will soon become fathers and husbands again."

What appears, however, to be a simple contrast between bad mother and good mother, and a new beginning with the mother who will deign to nurse her own child, turns out to be a different kind of beginning again. If Sophie at the end of *Emile* is transformed from the potentially dangerous female to the obedient one, from the Circe who rules over and ruins men to the daughter Nausicaa under the tutelage not only of her own parents but of the *"maître"* who is both her preceptor and creator, then this return to the beginning or origin from which everything else is said to "follow *successively*" will also involve a kind of second birth, not from the mother but from the substitute father, Rousseau himself. Something like this logic, not of sequential second-coming or following, but of reversal, appears in a signal passage within Book V itself, when Rousseau remarks: "The good constitution of children initially depends on that of their mothers. The first education of men depends on the care of women. Men's morals, their passions, their tastes, their pleasures, their very happiness also depend on women. Thus [*Ainsi*] the whole education of women ought to relate to men. To please men, to be useful to them, to make herself loved and honored by them, to raise them when young, to care for them when grown, to counsel them, to console them, to make their lives agreeable and sweet—these are the duties of women at all times, and they ought to be taught from childhood" (p. 365). Though the education of women focused on men seems to follow from the importance of the training that male children under their control receive, it is not difficult to see in this remarkable passage the reversal performed within its logical "Ainsi" in which the subordination of women to men is in some sense an overturning or "avenging" of man's initial dependence on them. This suspicion is borne out by a passage not too long after, where once again the sin of Eve seems to figure between the lines: "Amidst our senseless arrangements a decent woman's life is a perpetual combat against herself. It is just that this sex share the pain of the evils it has caused *us*" (p. 365—"la peine des maux qu'il *nous* a causés"; OC, IV, 709).

The argument in Book I, in fact, proceeds by the familiar linear logic of movement from mother to father, but one which prepares for beginning again with "le maître." Rousseau assumes, first of all, that mothers will not want to embrace that "first point" which will "bring everything back together"—nursing their children themselves: "Les femmes ont cessé d'être mères; elles ne le seront plus; elles ne veulent plus l'être"; OC, IV, 258). And his own takeover from the presumed bad mother is prepared for by this. "A child spends six or seven years in the hands of women, victim of their caprice and of his own" (p. 48) before this "factitious being" ("être *factice*"—Rousseau's key term for the depravations of civil society) is handed over to a false preceptor who completes the process of artificial development. The true developmental movement, he writes, should be from mother to father: "As the true nurse is the mother, the true preceptor is the father ... let the child pass from the hands of the one into those of the other" (p. 48—"Comme la véritable nourrice est la mère, le véritable précepteur est le père... que des mains de l'un l'enfant passe dans celles de l'autre"; OC, IV, 261). But—in the all too familiar sequential chain of cause and effect employed here by the very writer who would cast off other kinds of chains—since the mother is a bad mother, it follows that the father, in turn, will refuse to be the child's preceptor ("Let us not be surprised that a man whose wife did not deign to nurse the fruit of their union does not deign to raise him"; p. 49). Within the education of the fictive Emile which ensues, the function of the father will thus have to be taken over by Rousseau, that author who even in the very praise of mothers in that long opening note had commented that, when the mother "is mistaken" ("se trompe"), she "will have to be enlightened" ("il faut l'éclairer"), a *fiat lux* or language of enlightenment which is the creative word of *Emile* itself. Rousseau, who would refuse his fitness as an actual preceptor, turns to writing as one, in this developmental progression from the mother who had been "first," and creates *ex nihilo*, Zeus-like from his own brain, that imaginary pupil ("élève imaginaire") he will call "Emile," and ultimately "Sophie, ou la femme."

Emile, then, from its first beginning with the mother and with bad mothers from whom all the ills of the world successively ensue, now begins again with the creation of Emile, with a new beginning in order to move forward to a better end: "I have hence chosen to give myself an imaginary pupil, to hypothesize that I have the age, health, kinds of knowledge, and all the talent suitable for working at his education, for conducting him *from the moment of his birth up to the one when, become a grown man*, he will no longer have need of any guide other than himself" (p. 50), or, as we shall see by that end, no other guide than the *Deus absconditus* who will continue to be Rousseau. We have thus moved back from the six- or seven-year-old who, having spent the first years of his life as the "victim" of women, is passed on to the preceptor contemptuously termed an "être factice," to a new birth and a different developmental progress which will henceforth be charted as the work not of a preceptor but of the "governor" of the *Emile* proper. Indeed, Emile is to be chosen even before his birth from the female, in a passage which depends on a sorting out of beginnings and ends: "If the governor must be chosen with so much care, it is certainly permissible for him to choose his pupil as well, especially when what we are about is propounding a model" (p. 52—"il s'agit d'*un modéle* à proposer"). Emile is a "model" to be *followed*, just as he will be at the beginning of Book V, a recall of the first man, that Adam who has no mother but only an Author who conceives of him before his creation and who is the creator of both "male" and "female" in this text.

It is not surprising, then, that the "governeur" who is Rousseau himself is to come not at the end of a process but before its beginning: "This choice cannot be made on the basis of the child's genius or character, which can be known only at the *end* of the work [*qu'on ne connoit qu' à la* fin *de l'ouvrage*], whereas I am adopting the child *before his birth* [*que j'adopte* avant *qu'il soit né*]." The text continues, in lines which offer a pastiche of passages from a displaced version of that Decalogue which enjoins the child to "honour ... father and mother" but has as its first commandment "Thou shalt have no other gods *before* me": "Emile is an orphan. It makes no difference whether he has his father and mother. Charged with their duties, I inherit all their rights. He ought to honor his parents, but he ought to obey only me. That is my *first* or, rather, my sole condition" (p. 52— "Emile est orphelin. Il n'importe qu'il ait son pére et sa mére. Chargé de leurs devoirs, je succéde à tous leurs droits. Il doit honorer ses parens, mail il ne doit obéir qu'à moi. C'est ma prémiére ou plustôt ma seule condition"; *OC*, IV, 267). The logic of priority, here, is built upon a reversal of the order of nature, as the very formulation *succéde à* verbally suggests: this is a takeover which presents itself as first, and establishes its priority in its "first" condition. He reverses the order of nature in another way as well: a real father, he goes on to write, "cannot choose his child, but has to take the one he has been given" (p. 53). But "whoever imposes on himself a duty that *nature has in no way imposed* on *him* ought to be sure *beforehand* that he has the means of fulfilling it" (p. 53— "Mais quiconque *s'impose* un devoir que *la nature ne lui a point imposé*, doit s'assurer *auparavant* des moyens de le remplir"; *OC*, IV, 268). The contrast between the reflexive *s'impose* and the sense of what "nature" might "impose on him" nicely underlines the difference between a creation in which he, from the beginning, can mold a being of his choice and one which a father inherits from "nature," who here too, and not only in the gender of the language itself, is also a potentially prior female this self-reflexivity escapes.

The beginning we then move back to, and forward from, as *Emile* proper now begins, is one in which the mother defers to the wishes of the "governor," just as Sophie in Book V is first created by Rousseau and only later provided with a mother, whom he frequently has to overrule. We move back to the beginning, to infancy, but to a different beginning, with the master Rousseau himself now in control: "With life there begin needs. For the newly born a nurse is required. If the mother consents to perform her duty, very well. She will be given *written instructions*, for this advantage has its counterpoise and keeps the governor at something more of a distance from his pupil. But it is to be believed that the child's interest and esteem for the one to whom she is willing to confide so dear a deposit will make the mother attentive to the master's opinion [*attentive aux avis du maitre*]" (p. 56).

The "advantage" of maternal nursing—presented earlier as the true beginning and *premier point* from which everything follows and which "will bring everything back together"—here has its "counterpoise" in a disadvantage: it will keep the pupil and his master more distant or apart, in contravention of his earlier condition that they be inseparable. Rousseau returns to his figure of the bad or unwilling mother, in proceeding to assume the need for a nurse, but one now of whom the *maitre* will be in control, preventing swaddling (pp. 60–1) over the strong opposition of nurses who "are less bothered by a well-garroted child than by one who has to be constantly watched" and who, since it is impossible to "reason" with them ("Ne raisonez point avec les nourrices"), must simply be issued with orders the master must see will be followed ("Ordonnez, voyez faire").

In both the beginnning and the end, the first and last book, of *Emile*, then, we have a beginning or a first premise and all that follows from it: in "Sophie, ou la femme," the activity of the male and the passivity of the female; in Book I, which begins with mothers and has as its frontispiece and governing illustration the picture of the mother Thetis plunging her son Achilles in the Styx, the description of bad mothers and the apocalyptic end that will "follow successively" from them. Even before the first Book has come to an end, the figure of Thetis has already been detached from such mothers (p. 44), as in Book V it will be transferred to the substitute father, Rousseau (pp. 443–4).

In examining this relation of beginnings and ends, firsts and seconds, we might return once more to the echoes in *Emile* both of Genesis and of "le

divin Milton." In Book VIII of *Paradise Lost* Adam, in suing his author for
a companion before the creation of "the woman" Eve, argues his own
"deficience" in contrast to God's perfection and his numerical "oneness"
—not the oneness of God, the divine monad which contains all other
numbers and is therefore complete and perfect in itself, but rather a
creaturely singleness which is a "single imperfection" or incompletion, the
lack of a second member of the species through which to "propagate" as
well as of the "dearest amity" of "Collateral love" (VIII.415–26). Near the
beginning of *Emile* we read:

> Natural man is entirely for himself. He is numerical unity, the absolute
> whole which is relative only to itself or its kind. Civil man is only a
> fractional unity dependent on the denominator; his value is determined
> by his relation to the whole, which is the social body. Good social
> institutions are those that best know how to denature man, to take his
> absolute existence from him in order to give him a relative one and
> transport the *I* into the common unity, with the result that each
> individual believes himself no longer one but a part of the unity and no
> longer feels except within the whole. (pp. 39–40)[45]

This passage precedes the darker one on "civil man" which introduces the
"sage-femmes" who are his first enslavers: "Civil man is born, lives and
dies in slavery. At birth he is sewed in swaddling clothes; at his death he is
nailed in a coffin. So long as he keeps his human shape, he is enchained by
[*enchaîné par*] our institutions" (p. 42). "Enchaîné" here, in a context
which speaks so frequently of what "follows successively" ("s'ensuit
successivement") from the origins of civil man's life in the hands of
"douces méres" and "sage-femmes," is inseparable from the logic of the
sequential chain as well—the linearity which leads out of the absolute
wholeness of "natural man" into the subsequent history of "dependency."
Like Adam's image of the chain—"the *link* of nature draws me"—as he is
about to set in motion the history entailed in following Eve, the chain
which enslaves is also a chain of events, the very introduction of succession
and its dependencies. With regard to the sequence of reversals within
Emile itself, we might juxtapose this difference between natural and civil
man—"numerical unity, the absolute whole which is relative only to itself or its kind" as contrasted with "a fractional unity dependent on
the denominator"—with that passage in the *Discours sur l'origine de
l'inégalité* in which it is precisely women who take man out of the state of
nature, through falling in love, an artificial sentiment ("un sentiment
factice") cultivated by women in order to reverse the natural order of male
domination and to assert an unnatural form of power over men:

> Let us begin by distinguishing the moral from the physical in the
> sentiment of love. The physical is this general desire which moves one
> sex to unite with the other; the moral is that which determines this desire

and fixes it on one object exclusively or which at least gives to this desire for the preferred object a higher degree of energy. Now it is easy to see that the moral in relation to love is an artificial sentiment; born from the custom of the society, and *celebrated by women* with a great deal of skill and care, in order to *establish their empire* and make *dominant the sex which ought to obey*.[46]

In this passage—beside whose final words Voltaire wrote his famous "Pourquoy?"[47]—women and their "empire" are associated with the passage out of the state of nature, just as the creation of Eve leads to the fall from Paradise. And, indeed, in a passage from *Du contrat social*, at the end of the second chapter of its first book (*OC*, III, 354), we read: "on ne peut disconvenir qu'Adam n'ait été Souverain du monde comme Robinson de son isle, tant qu'il en fut le seul habitant."

We have already noted the echoes of Genesis 2 at the beginning of Book V of *Emile*, the Book which introduces "Sophie, ou la femme" because "it is not good for man to be alone" and ends with marriage and the family, and with Emile's embracing of the duties of civil man. We might note now, then, that the reference to the "divine Milton" and his picture of the unfallen Adam and Eve (p. 424) within this fifth book comes just after Emile has, in falling in love, become Sophie's slave: "whatever she commands, he does not reply, and often, when leaving to obey her, he looks at me with eyes full of joy telling me: 'You see that she has taken possession of me.' Meanwhile, the proud girl observes him stealthily and smiles secretly at her slave's pride" (p. 424). Or again: "O Emile ... how far you seem to have fallen! Where is the young man brought up with such hardness ... who yielded only to reason, and depended on nothing except himself? Now, softened by an idle life, he lets himself be governed by women" (p. 431).[48] Very soon after this, the text informs us that Emile's own earlier self-sufficiency and wholeness are now gone, as his teacher addresses him:

When you entered the age of reason, I protected you from men's opinions. When your heart became sensitive, I preserved you from the empire of the passions. If I had been able to prolong this inner calm to the end of your life, I would have secured my work, and you would always be as happy as man can be. But, dear Emile, it is in vain that I have *dipped your soul in the Styx*, I was not able to make it everywhere *invulnerable*. A new enemy is arising which you have not learned to conquer and from which I can no longer save you. This enemy is yourself. ... You were bound to nothing other than the human condition, and now you are bound to all the attachments you have given to yourself. In learning to desire, you have made yourself the slave of your desires. ... How pitiable you are going to be, thus subjected to your unruly passions! There will always be privations, losses, and alarms. ...

As a result of having wanted to *follow* only your passions [*pour n'avoir voulu* suivre *que tes passions*], you will never be able to satisfy them. You will always seek repose, but it will always flee you [*il fuira toujours devant toi*]. (pp. 443–4)

What had previously been described (p. 437) as fleeing before Emile, precisely in order to be caught, was Sophie herself ("Les femmes ne sont pas faites pour courir; quand elles fuyent, c'est pour être atteintes"; OC, IV, 807): here, the very image of Emile's loss of wholeness—the "fractional unity" dependent on a "denominator"—is to follow something which will always "flee" before him. The very figure which Rousseau appropriates from the mother in Book I—Thetis, whose dipping of her son Achilles in the Styx stands as the frontispiece to the Book which begins by addressing itself to mothers—is, at its very moment of appropriation here, a figure, instead, of vulnerability and loss of control. And Rousseau's presentation of this dangerous supplement, of that Sophie whom Mary Wollstonecraft, borrowing from Genesis, contemptuously termed this "after-thought of creation," as what takes man out of the numerical self-sufficiency of the state of nature and its absolute wholeness, also tries vainly to contain this receding figure. As Allan Bloom puts it (in a reading of *Emile* in the sense in which, perhaps, this aspect of the *livre mâle* might like to be read) the "relation between man and woman is the crucial point, the place where the demands of Emile's wholeness and those of civil society meet," and Sophie is chosen because she "will complete him without alienating him."[49] Adam, at a similar moment of absence in *Paradise Lost*, had ominously complained: "She disappeared, and left me dark, I waked / To find her, or for ever to deplore / Her loss" (VIII.478–80). Unlike Adam, who follows Eve ("Flesh of flesh / Bone of my bone") into sin and, henceforth, self-alienation, Emile must learn to do without her if she should sin, when his author and hers, he that gives and can therefore also take away, commands him to leave her.

One difference between the story of Sophie and Emile and the "divine Milton's" story of the unfallen Adam and Eve, or, behind it, the story of "la femme" in Genesis, is that the fallen Eve's example already lurks behind the portrait of Sophie in Book V, and the constraints on her—as representative of "Woman"—which seek to reverse the story of this first female:

Always justify the cares that you impose on young girls, but always impose cares on them. *Idleness* and *disobedience* are the two most dangerous defects for them and the ones least easily cured once contracted. Girls ought to be vigilant and industrious. ... They ought to be constrained very early. This misfortune, if it is one for them, is *inseparable from their sex*, and they are never delivered from it without suffering far more cruel misfortunes. All their lives they will be enslaved to the most continual and most severe of constraints—that of the proprieties. They must first be exercised in constraint, so that it never costs them anything to *tame all their caprices in order to submit to the wills of others.* ... Dissipation, frivolity, and inconstancy are defects that easily arise from the corruption and continued indulgence of their first tastes. To prevent this abuse, teach them above all to conquer themselves. Amidst our senseless arrangements a decent woman's life is a perpetual combat against herself. *It is just that this sex share the pain of the evils it has caused us.* (p. 369)[50]

Behind this passage stand both the role of woman in taking man out of the state of nature in the second *Discours*, and the whole tradition stemming from the story of the Fall in Genesis, in which the serpent is represented with the face of Eve. The only way of righting the evils women have helped to bring about is for women to give themselves totally to their roles of wife and mother, for Sophie to "govern" Emile by a marital version of the unfallen Miltonic Eve's "sweet reluctant amorous delay," but within a hierarchy in which she must obey him as her head. Within the complexly triangulated relationships in which Jean-Jacques, as the "maitre" of his text, plays both God and disapproving Raphael to Emile's Adam and Sophie's Eve, and Mentor to Emile's Telemachus, the master hands his pupil over at the end to Sophie herself, just as Virgil, Dante's "maestro," hands his ephebe over at the end of the part of the journey he can control: "Here my long task ends, and another's begins. Today I abdicate the authority you confided to me, and Sophie is your governor from now on" (p. 479—"ici finit ma longue tâche et commence celle d'un autre. J'abdique aujourd'hui l'autorité que vous m'avez confiée, et voici desormais vôtre gouverneur"; *OC*, IV, 867). But he also returns as "le maitre des jeunes maitres" when at the very end of the narrative Sophie is about to become a mother, to continue as the removed but still present Author of the text.

Yet a remark which we find right at the beginning of *Emile* on the impossibility of complete "mastery" even of the education over which it is possible to have the maximum control (p. 38) might apply as well to the end of the text. For what literally follows from Book V, which introduces, second in creation and as its "last act," the figure of "woman," is not this carefully stabilized ending—with the marriage and impending mother-hood with which, in all too traditional fashion, it formally concludes. It is, rather, the adulterous Sophie of the text which goes on to supplement it, as its "sequel," and in which the second sex not only takes the lead in sin but, having abandoned the private sphere which is her proper place and violated both property and family in bearing another man's child, turns "sweet reluctant amorous delay" into absolute refusal and passes, as Emile's first letter complains, out of all control, including that of "le maitre."

V

In the beginning, the little girl is a little boy.

(Freud)

The logic of coming out of and coming second, which first took us back to
Aristotle and Genesis, brings us finally to that other master of the development of little girls and little boys, Freud. To place the text of Freud
against and within this complex scene and its influential mythemes is not
as arbitrary as it may at first appear. Recent psychoanalytic work has
already, in more and strikingly less nuanced forms, emphasized the link
with Aristotle. But what needs to be added to this is the pervasive influence
of Genesis 2, and the centuries of commentary on it, and even of *Paradise
Lost*, listed by Freud as one of his own "favorite books."[51] Theodor Reik
notes Freud's remark in a letter to Jung that the biblical narrative of the
creation of Eve has "something about it that is quite peculiar and singular," as well as, at a more anecdotal level, the Hasidic lore behind
that part of *The Interpretation of Dreams* where Freud himself recounts a
memory of his mother's reenactment of a rabbinical "proof" from the
creation narrative of Genesis 2.[52] And a crucial section of *Moses and
Monotheism*, as we shall see, invokes Bachofen's very example—*The
Oresteia*—in its own description of the passage from matriarchy to
patriarchy, from motherhood to the more "intellectual" concept of
paternity.

   Let us then begin again with Freud by returning to that passage from
*Some Psychical Consequences of the Anatomical Distinction between the
Sexes* (1925) originally set beside the opening of Book V of *Emile*:

> In examining the earliest mental shapes assumed by the sexual life of
> children we have been in the habit of taking as the subject of our
> investigations the male child, the little boy. With little girls, so we have
> supposed, things must be similar, though in some way or other they
> must be different. (*SE*, 19, 249)

The little boy, as commentators have increasingly pointed out, is here as in
other texts of Freud the starting point or model from which emerges
female difference, both in the practical sense of an instance added later, or
as an afterthought, to the principal subject of investigation, and in the
sense of a development out of a chronological beginning in the narrative of
sexuality. The latter, in particular, might well be placed at the end of a
history beginning with Aristotle and Genesis. For various passages scattered throughout the work suggest that, for all the changes of language
from embryology and theology to the psychoanalytic, the model of coming
second, of priority and secondariness, from Genesis in particular still
inhabits the plotting of female difference in Freud; and, even more

importantly perhaps, the crucial intervention of a narrative of genesis or psychogenesis within some of the most fissured and problematic of Freudian texts.

The model of male priority and the priority of the male model is, indeed, repeatedly invoked by Freud.[53] We read in *On the Sexual Theories of Children* (1908): "In consequence of unfavourable circumstances, both of an external and an internal nature, the following observations apply chiefly to the sexual development of one sex only—that is, of males" (*SE*, 9, 211). In *The Economic Problem of Masochism* (1924), after stating that feminine masochism is easier to observe than the masculine form, Freud nevertheless takes the male, for pragmatic reasons, as the model to be discussed: "We have sufficient acquaintance with this kind of masochism in men (to whom, owing to the material at my command, I shall restrict my remarks)" (*SE*, 19, 161). In *On Narcissism* (1914), after a lengthy discussion of a potentially threatening female difference from the model of the male, the text moves to a summary of its findings which, as in the familiar absorption of the female into a supposed universalizing generic "man," speaks only of a "person" implicitly gendered as male. When in *The Infantile Genital Organization* (1923) Freud makes a general law of the primacy of the phallus, he remarks that he can describe only the little boy ("Unfortunately ... the corresponding processes in the little girl are not known to us"; *SE*, 19, 142); the primacy and singularity of the male model presents itself, once again, as the limitation of the merely empirical.

What Freud puts forward, however, is not just the primacy of the male model for discussions of sexuality but, as with *Emile*, a whole developmental narrative which follows from and out of it. Here we might take the last of these cited texts, *The Infantile Genital Organization* of 1923, as one of several such sequential narratives or Freudian creation stories:

> At the height of the course of development of infantile sexuality, interest in the genitals and in their activity acquires a dominating significance which falls little short of that reached in maturity. At the same time, the main characteristic of this "infantile genital organization" is its difference from the final genital organization of the adult. This consists in the fact that, for both sexes, only one genital, namely the male one, comes into account. What is present, therefore, is not a primacy of the genitals, but the primacy of the phallus.
>
> Unfortunately we can describe this state of things only as it affects the male child; the corresponding processes in the little girl are not known to us. (*SE*, 19, 142)

In the narrative of this little boy, we read that he first assumes that all living beings have an organ like his own; then (through accidental sight of the body of a little girl) that some women have been deprived of a penis as punishment—that they have had one but now lack it—before guessing

that all women, including his own mother, lack one as well: "And, along
with this, quite complicated theories are built up to explain the exchange
of the penis for a baby. In all this, the female genitals never seem to be
discovered" (p. 145).

The stages which then ensue in this fascinating text might well be placed
not only beside Rousseau's *Emile* but beside the relationship, and sequential interpretation, of the two distinct creation stories in Genesis, in which
the later or second, both in traditional and less orthodox elaborations on
it, tells of the separating out of female from male, the further creational
stage of female difference:

> It is not unimportant to bear in mind what transformations are under-
> gone, during the sexual development of childhood, by the polarity of sex
> with which we are familiar. A first antithesis is introduced and the
> choice of object, which, of course, presupposes a subject and an object.
> At the stage of the pre-genital sadistic-anal organization, there is as yet
> no question of male and female; the antithesis between active and
> passive is the dominant one. At the following stage of infantile genital
> organization, which we now know about, maleness exists, but not
> femaleness. The antithesis here is between having a male genital and
> being castrated. It is not until development has reached its completion at
> puberty that the sexual polarity coincides with male and female. Male-
> ness combines [the factors of] subject, activity and possession of the
> penis; femaleness takes over [those of] object and passivity. The vagina
> is now valued as a place of shelter for the penis; it enters into the heritage
> of the womb. (*SE*, 19, 145)

The passage proceeds on the very assumption of sequential stages, by that
narrativizing of the psyche long since naturalized as "developmental"
psychology; and to a final stage in which female is separated from male at
the very point where it becomes possible to distribute the initial polarity of
"active" and "passive" into the different sexes now distinct as two. Female
passivity—identified in Rousseau with the institution of the "hut" or place
of shelter, where woman embraces motherhood—is here also linked with
such a place, not as initial fact but as part of a narrative of development. As
in the story in Genesis of the creation of "Woman" out of "Man," the
differentiated female comes only at the end of a temporal as well as
narrative sequence. And here, with the true emergence of the second, and
secondary, sex, we have a Freudian version of the institution of marriage
and the *Hevah* of Genesis 2. She (and he) have now found her "place"; the
vagina, now valued as a "place of shelter" for the penis "enters into the
heritage of the womb." Be it ever so humble, there's no place like home.

This originally masculine character—before the differentiation of the
specifically female—also emerges in the sequential narrative order of
Three Essays on the Theory of Sexuality (1905). Before puberty, the

"auto-erotic activity of the erotogenic zones is ... the same in both sexes, and owing to this uniformity there is no possibility of a distinction between the two sexes such as it arises after puberty. So far as the auto-erotic and masturbatory manifestations of sexuality are concerned, we might lay it down that the sexuality of little girls is of a wholly masculine character. Indeed, if we were able to give a more definite connotation to the concepts of "masculine" and "feminine," it would even be possible to maintain that libido is invariably and necessarily of a masculine nature, whether it occurs in men or in women and irrespectively of whether its object is a man or a woman" (SE, 7, 219). Here too we encounter a developmental narrative of the transition to maturity of the little girl defined first in terms of this masculine libidinal economy.[54]

Even as complex and initially tentative a text as the late lecture on "Femininity" which Sarah Kofman takes up in the whole second half of L'Enigme de la femme[55] has strategic recourse to a narrative of genesis as psychogenesis, a recourse Freud there describes as crucial to the program of psychoanalysis itself: "In conformity with its peculiar nature, psycho-analysis does not try to describe what a woman is [was das Weib ist]—that would be a task it could scarcely perform—but sets about enquiring how she comes into being, how a woman develops out of a child with a bisexual disposition" (SE, 22, 116). In Genesis, the text moves from the first creation story to the second, the one in which woman emerges only out of and after man. In "Femininity," Freud moves from the affirmation of an original bisexuality which turns out to be more clearly the domination of the male model to the narrative of how the "little girl" who is in the phallic stage a "little boy" moves towards that differentiated feminine in which passivity becomes the defining characteristic of women. It is this genesis narrative of the production of "woman" that leads to the final assimilation of masculinity to activity and femininity to passivity, though the subtle multivocality, the implied erlebte Rede of the text's more complex beginning places the conventional associations of active male and passive female in a more ambiguous and unstable position. This new "In the beginning," in its very descriptive simplicity, is produced only by an effacing of what both the tone and the context of the text's actual beginning more problematically raise. For what is unsettled at the opening of this text, at the level of traditional descriptions of "what woman is"—including her passivity in contrast to the activity of the male—is then reintroduced by the agency of the subsequent genesis account, the text's sequential narrative of the proper development and destination of the little girl. What commentators point to as Freud's dependence elsewhere on sequential narrative and logical sequence, in the straightening out of the hysteric's discourse,[56] here assumes another form. What matters ultimately is theogony as much as theology. It is the narrative of development itself that literally makes the difference.

Once again, however, a developmental progress, in which the little girl develops a second and secondary sexual difference out of a masculine model conceived of as prior and first, is founded on a reversal not unlike those we have already considered. The famous discussion in the late work entitled *Female Sexuality* (1931) describes the discovery in girls of a pre-Oedipal phase of strong attachment to the mother as analogous to "the discovery, in another field, of the Minoan–Mycenean civilization behind the civilization of Greece," an historico-cultural reference which strengthens the text's echoes of the familiar narrative of the progress not just individually from mother to father but culturally and politically from matriarchy to patriarchy. At the very point where Freud acknowledges in woman a difference apart from any parallelism or symmetrical repetition of an exclusively masculine model, it is to describe the turning away from mother to father as a movement in which a powerful original female is found to be defective in relation to what emerges not just as telos or end of this process of conversion but as the model or prototype from which that defectiveness or lack or, by perverse reversal, that secondariness is judged:

> When the little girl discovers her own deficiency, from seeing a male genital, it is only with hesitation and reluctance that she accepts the unwelcome knowledge. As we have seen, she clings obstinately to the expectation of one day having a genital of the same kind too, and her wish for it survives long after her hope has expired. The child invariably regards castration in the first instance as a misfortune peculiar to herself. ... When she comes to understand the general nature of this characteristic, it follows that femaleness—and with it, of course, her mother—suffers a great depreciation in her eyes. (*SE*, 21, 233)

For the little girl, this turning away from the mother also involves a concomitant turning away from the active or clitoral side of her own sexual impulses and a substitution of the passive ones (*SE*, 21, 237–9). The transition to "the final normal female attitude, in which she takes her father as her object and so finds her way to the feminine form of the Oedipus complex" (*SE*, 21, 230), is accomplished "with the help of the passive trends," and, with them, "the path to the development of femininity now lies open to the girl" (*SE*, 21, 239). Superimposed, the developmental movement from mother to father and from masculine to feminine sexuality in this text is one in which the exchange is not just the symmetrical crossing essential to the focus on the mother as the initial love object of both little girl and little boy, but a crossing and chiasmic structure like the one, say, in the debate between "matriarchists" and "patriarchists" which Bachofen's *Das Mutterrecht* provoked, an essential affinity at the heart of an only superficial opposition.

Once again, as with the various narratives of the rejection of a prior female dominance or rule, this overturning of the little girl's initial attachment to the mother involves a transvaluation in which the second is now better than the rejected, and defective, first:

> When we survey the whole range of motives for turning away from the mother which analysis brings to light—that she failed to provide the little girl with the only proper genital, that she did not feed her sufficiently, that she compelled her to share her mother's love with others, that she never fulfilled all the girl's expectations of love, and, finally, that she first aroused her sexual activity and then forbade it— all these motives seem nevertheless insufficient to justify the girl's final hostility.... Perhaps the real fact is that the attachment to the mother is bound to perish, precisely because it was the first and was so intense; just as one can often see happen in first marriages of young women which they have entered into when they were most passionately in love. In both situations the attitude of love probably comes to grief from the disappointments that are unavoidable and from the accumulation of occasions for aggression. As a rule, second marriages turn out much better. (*SE*, 21, 234)

Kofman's nuancing of Irigaray notwithstanding,[57] Freud's presentation of the female as a mutilated or defective male—even in this text on the "primacy" of the mother—is traversed by the long-dominant Aristotelian view of woman as deformity or lack, even as it is reminiscent of the progression of the child from the "bad" mother in a text like *Emile* not just to the father but to a father-subsitute, the "maitre." And the sense in the late text on *Female Sexuality* of a generalized debt to the whole discussion sparked by the publication of Bachofen's *Das Mutterrecht* is strengthened by the paragraph in the even later *Moses and Monotheism* (1939), which comes out of a discussion of the opening up of a "new realm of intellectuality" beyond the senses, and which has recourse to the *Oresteia* as its primary textual instance:

> Under the influence of external factors into which we need not enter here and which are also in part insufficiently known, it came about that the matriarchal social order was succeeded by the patriarchal one—which, of course, involved a revolution in the juridical conditions that had so far prevailed. An echo of this revolution seems still to be audible in the *Oresteia* of Aeschylus. But this turning from the mother to the father points in addition to a victory of intellectuality over sensuality—that is, an advance in civilization, since maternity is proved by the evidence of the senses while paternity is a hypothesis, based on an inference and a premiss. Taking sides in this way with a thought-process in preference to a sense perception has proved to be a momentous step. (*SE*, 23, 113–14)

The turning away from the mother described in *Female Sexuality* (1931), accompanied by the itinerary traced in *The Infantile Genital Organization*

(1923) in which the transition is from clitoris to vagina as "a place of
shelter for the penis" (*SE*, 19, 145), is also an itinerary in which, as Irigaray
has put it, a woman is to leave and "hate" her own mother so as to "satisfy
man's lasting desire to make love with his mother, or an appropriate
substitute."[58] Or, in the terms of the logic we have traced, it is a narrative
of sequence but also of reversal, so that the first may return as second, in a
displaced and now no longer threatening form. The little girl as second to
the primacy of the phallus, developing her own passive and vagina-
centered sexuality as a secondary offshoot of an initial "masculine" phase,
is thus to be second so that she can substitute, in acceptable and now
distanced fashion, for a female first. As in *Emile*, we begin with a mother
and end with a wife, in that Oedipal economy in which the primary story
becomes the institution of the male.

We need, however, to look more closely not just at the reversal in which
a threatening prior female returns in second place but at the narrative of
that sequential development. I have already pointed out the statement, in
Three Essays on the Theory of Sexuality, that "the sexuality of little girls is
of a wholly masculine character" as one of the ways in which the little girl
is "in the beginning" a little boy. But we might follow more closely the
little narrative of the creation, so to speak, of this differentiated female
from an initial "masculine" sexuality — one which invokes once again the
whole masculinist tradition of what *Paradise Lost* had termed this secondary female's "sweet reluctant amorous delay":

> If we are to understand how a little girl turns into a woman, we must
> follow the further vicissitudes of this excitability of the clitoris. Puberty,
> which brings about so great an accession of libido in boys, is marked in
> girls by a fresh wave of repression, in which it is precisely clitoridal
> sexuality that is affected. What is thus overtaken by repression is a piece
> of masculine sexuality. The intensification of the brake upon sexuality
> brought about by pubertal repression in women serves as a stimulus to
> the libido in men and causes an increase of its activity. Along with this
> heightening of libido there is also an increase of sexual over-valuation
> which only emerges in full force in relation to a woman who *holds
> herself back* and who denies her sexuality. When at last the sexual act is
> permitted and the clitoris itself becomes excited, it still retains a func-
> tion: the task, namely, of transmitting the excitation to the adjacent
> female sexual parts, just as—to use a simile—pine shavings can be
> kindled in order to set a log of harder wood on fire. Before this
> transference can be effected, a certain interval of time must often elapse,
> during which the young woman is anaesthetic. This anaesthesia may
> become permanent if the clitoridal zone refuses to abandon its excit-
> ability, an event for which the way is prepared precisely by an extensive
> activity of that zone in childhood. ...

When erotogenic susceptibility to stimulation has been successfully transferred by a woman from the clitoris to the vaginal orifice, it implies that she has adopted a new leading zone for the purposes of her later sexual activity. A man, on the other hand, retains his leading zone unchanged from childhood. The fact that women change their leading erotogenic zone in this way, together with the wave of repression at puberty, which, as it were, puts aside their childish masculinity, are the chief determinants of the greater proneness of woman to neurosis and especially hysteria. These determinants, therefore, are intimately related to the essence of femininity. (*SE*, 7, 221 ff.)

The transference from masculine clitoris to more passive and female vagina—as from auto-eroticism to the "heritage of the womb"—is clearly not without its problems, including the possibility of a genuine developmental impasse in "putting aside such childish things" ("der gleichsam die infantile Mannlichkeit beiseite schafft"). The vague and distant echo of 1 Corinthians 13—with its potentially narcissistic speculum or mirror—manages to suggest something of what the little girl, like Milton's newborn Eve, must renounce before she can progress to her true telos or "end." But it is even more remarkable to note that the "sweet reluctant amorous delay" of Milton's Eve—which is Adam's interpretation of her more genuine reluctance before she is finally converted away from such "childish things" to him—or the holding off of "Woman" in order to further stimulate male desire and conquest in Rousseau's *Emile* emerges in Freud as well, as a specific stage on the path towards this final destination or end.

If Milton's interval of resistance and delay is a more amplified version of the text from Genesis 2—and of the space between the separation of the female from the male and the formula of the first marriage, prototype of the rest—Freud's narrative of the genesis of female difference is also one in which the girl's transition to that ultimate goal, and, with it, motherhood, is more problematic and protracted. Because a man has only one leading sexual zone, one sexual organ, whereas a woman has two—the vagina, or the female organ proper, and the clitoris, inferior version of the male—the path of female development is correspondingly more complex. The "development of a little girl into a normal woman is more difficult and more complicated, since it includes two extra tasks, to which there is nothing corresponding in the development of a man" ("Femininity," *SE*, 22, 117). The girl has to change not only her major sexual zone, from masculine clitoris to female vagina, but also her love object, from the rejected mother to the father. Psyche's path is more strewn with obstacles than Cupid's. The female's connection with twoness, then, further distinguishes her from male singularity; and Freud speaks, before Irigaray, of "this sex which is not one." But a sense of twoness is never finally separated from a masculinist tradition in which this female duality is also part of an enigmatic and threatening difference and division.

The recent work of Sarah Kofman and others has argued that this second or secondary place of the female in Freud—her transition to passivity and the "solution" to the problem of woman in motherhood—involves an overturning and reversal of a threatening and self-sufficient female "Narcissism" into a dependency and even sickness in which the male she turns to is not just husband but doctor as well, that relation of subordination so famously upset in the cases of Dora and Anna O.[59] Here again, we might set this narrative of female Narcissism overcome beside the account in Milton of Eve's original narcissistic moment of self-reflection in the pool and her conversion by an admonitory preceptor's "voice" to the primary figure whose "image," in the tradition from Genesis 2, she secondarily is.

We have already seen that the second story in Genesis, of woman created out of and after a primary male, comes after the Priestly opening of Genesis 1 in which the primal but ultimately subordinated female Tiamat is recalled and then effaced within the Hebrew text—a not unfamiliar transumption in other cultural contexts in which a second is presented as surpassing a first as part of a larger narrative of creation and development. Freud's *On Narcissism* includes in its own beginnings an actual invocation of a poetic version of Genesis, Heine's "picture of the psychogenesis of the Creation" (*SE*, 14, 85) as a movement beyond the "sickness" of Narcissism. The description within it of a specifically female Narcissism and its overcoming strongly suggests other narratives of such a process, both the defeat of the Amazons which figures in *Das Mutterrecht* and Milton's incorporation of a primary Narcissism into the Genesis narrative of the creation of Eve.

Kofman argues that Freud's entire theory of woman as a male *manqué*, defined according to a male model as defect or lack, is a reversal of his glimpse of the threatening self-sufficiency of women in this text, written while he was particularly attached to Lou Andreas-Salome.[60] This particular movement in Freud—whereby women are assigned a second place but only as the consequence of an overturning or reversal—recalls not just the familiar linear logic of Amazonomachy, of the fear of domination by women which justifies their subordination, but also the narrative of that other preceptor of the development of male and female, Rousseau.

In *On Narcissism*, the self-sufficiency (*Selbstgenügsamkeit*) of women possesses a fascination for men because it reminds them of their own renounced Narcissism. But it also has a reverse side: such women are fascinating but also threatening because of their terrifying inaccessibility, their independence, and indifference. In Kofman's description, the text reaches its own *peripeteia* or turning point when Freud steps back from this threat, and leads women along the path to their proper destination—to fully realized object-love and the heritage of the womb, or, as with the second Genesis creation story and the Miltonic Eve after her moment of narcissistic self-reflection, to marriage and motherhood.

Freud's narrative of male and female in this text reads almost like an unwitting replay of the different creation stories and early development of the Miltonic Adam and Eve, where Adam's perfected object-love is reflected in his desire for an other, and where Eve's conversion—her recognition and final voluntary subordination to him "whose image" she is, as well as her role as "mother of mankind"—comes only after a longer and more drawn-out process of delay:

Complete object-love of the attachment type is, properly speaking, characteristic of the male. It displays the marked sexual overvaluation which is doubtless derived from the child's original narcissism and thus corresponds to a transference of that narcissism to the sexual object. This sexual overvaluation is the origin of the peculiar state of being in love, a state suggestive of a neurotic compulsion, which is thus traceable to an impoverishment of the ego as regards libido in favour of the love-object. A different course is followed in the type of female most frequently met with, which is probably the purest and truest one. With the onset of puberty the maturing of the female sexual organs, which up till then have been in a condition of latency, seems to bring about an intensification of the original narcissism, and this is unfavourable to the development of a true object-choice with its accompanying sexual overvaluation. Women, especially if they grow up with good looks, develop a certain self-contentment [*eine Selbstgenügsamkeit*] which compensates them for the social restrictions that are imposed upon them in their choice of object. Strictly speaking, it is only themselves that such women love with an intensity comparable to that of the man's love for them. Nor does their need lie in the direction of loving, but of being loved; and the man who fulfils this condition is the one who finds favour with them. The importance of this type of woman for the erotic life of mankind is to be rated very high. Such women have the greatest fascination for men, not only for aesthetic reasons, since as a rule they are the most beautiful, but also because of a combination of interesting psychological factors. For it seems very evident that another person's narcissism has a great attraction for those who have renounced part of their own narcissism and are in search of object-love. ... The great charm [*Reiz*] of narcissistic women has, however, its reverse side; a large part of the lover's dissatisfaction, of his doubts of the woman's love, of his complaints of her enigmatic nature, has its root in this incongruity between the types of object-choice. (*SE*, 14, 89)

The potential danger of this "woman"—so lucidly reminiscent of the traditionally aloof and self-sufficient cruel mistress of the male imagination—involves a dynamic we have already encountered in Milton and Rousseau. Adam, who similarly feels himself attracted by Eve's "charm" (*Paradise Lost*, VIII. 533) and struck by her self-sufficiency ("so absolute she seems / And in her self complete"; VIII.547–8), is in danger of an "overvaluation" not unlike the one Freud describes here and is reproved for it by Raphael, the preceptor who warns him against "attributing overmuch to things / Less excellent" (VIII.565–6). In Rousseau, Emile's dangerous overvaluation of Sophie, as part of what is described as "the peculiar state of being in love," and in language which equally evokes the whole tradition of the self-involved and enslaving cruel mistress, presents a similar threat before Sophie is taught by this text's preceptor her proper relation to Emile as "head" and the path to marriage and motherhood.

It is important in relation to the Miltonic counterpart here to notice that the very stage in female development which in *On Narcissism* is described as the intensification, at puberty, of "the original narcissism," a stage "unfavourable to the development of a true object-choice" and hence, in a double and potentially threatening sense, fascinating to men, would coincide, if the two were superimposed, with the stage described in *Three Essays on the Theory of Sexuality* in which, at puberty, the initial clitoridal sexuality of little girls—part of their masculine sexuality—is repressed and the female holds herself back in a way which further stimulates male desire: "Along with this heightening of libido [in the male] there is also an increase of sexual over-valuation which only emerges in full force in relation to a woman who *holds herself back and who denies her sexuality*" (*SE*, 7, 221; my italics). For in Milton's two creation stories, the moment of primary Narcissism in the development of Eve—her turning to her own image in the pool—is interpreted by Adam, from his own perspective, as precisely such traditional female reluctance ("Not obvious, not obtrusive, but retired, / The more desirable"; VIII.504–5), an obstacle or stage to be overcome. What is crucial in both is the fact that this phenomenon is only a moment or stage in a fuller developmental narrative of progression to true femininity. Eve reluctant and delaying, or Eve narcissistically preferring herself—both are finally converted to recognize in the male and in voluntary submission in marriage her true "end" (*Paradise Lost*, IV. 442). What matters in both is a specifically narrative telos.

In the Freud texts which treat of female sexuality and its development, the narrative progress treats both the holding back and the primary Narcissism as only a stage on the itinerary or "road" of proper female development. In Milton's *Paradise Lost*, when Eve "sees" and is converted to Adam's evident superiority ("I yielded, and from that time see / How beauty is excelled by manly grace"; IV.489–90), the verse nowhere indicates what it is she specifically "sees." In Freud's "Femininity," the young girl's "self-love is mortified by the comparison with the boy's far superior equipment" (*SE*, 22, 126), a decisive sight which performs another kind of decisive conversion. In *Three Essays on the Theory of Sexuality* the initial stage of "holding back" is ultimately superseded, just as in *On Narcissism* the initial or primary Narcissism of the female is overcome in the narrative of an ultimate destination, that "road which leads to complete object-love" and the end of motherhood, the production of a substitute for the sign of lack in "*His* Majesty the Baby" (*SE*, 14, 89–91).

This logic of reversal, whereby a threatening primacy is converted into second place, appears not just in *On Narcissism* but in an important moment of *The Taboo of Virginity* as well, a text to which Lou Andreas-Salome herself responded by citing the movement from matriarchy to patriarchy,[61] and its legacy of *pavor feminae*:

> Wherever primitive man has set up a taboo he fears some danger and it cannot be disputed that a generalized dread of women is expressed in all these rules of avoidance. Perhaps this dread is based on the fact that woman is different from man, for ever incomprehensible and mysterious, strange and therefore apparently hostile [*Das Weib anders ist als der Mann, ewig unverstandlich und geheimnisvol, fremdartig und darum feindselig erscheint*]. The man is afraid of being weakened by the woman, infected with her femininity and of then showing himself incapable. The effect which coitus has of discharging tensions and causing flaccidity may be the prototype of what the man fears; and the realization of the influence which the woman gains over him through sexual intercourse, the consideration she thereby forces from him, may justify the extension of this fear. In all this there is nothing obsolete, *nothing which is not still alive among ourselves*. (*The Taboo of Virginity*, *SE*, 11, 198–9)

Delilah, if not Omphale, lurks in the wings of this description of that "influence" which woman gains over man through sexual intercourse, "the consideration she thereby forces from him." And, as Kofman suggests, Freud's procedure in this highly structured text once again involves a reversal of this primacy into the first cause of a female lack, the prior function of *Penisneid* towards which the text proceeds as it moves towards its own revelatory telos, the *peripeteia* which uncovers the answer to the "riddle" it sets out to explore.

In the complex layering of "explanations" for the primitive taboo against marital virginity through which this text proceeds, Freud rejects this explanation—the general dread of woman—as not accounting for the particular taboo against the husband's responsibility for the loss of his wife's virginity (*SE*, 11, 200). What is substituted for any such narrative of origins as Bachofen's model of a primitive matriarchy, or a genesis narrative of the "origin" of taboo observances, is again a *psychogenesis*. This genesis is not tied to historical origins, or to the differences the text elsewhere elicits between "primitive" and "civilized," but to a decisive stage in the separation and development of the female which will then be defined as "prior" to the later, active hostility the taboo itself would defend the husband against: the original penis-envy of woman, her recognition of female difference as diminishment, "envy ... because of the lack of it (actually because of its diminished size)" (SE, 11, 204).

Freud's own transhistorical genesis narrative—of female difference as the difference caused by lack—thus replaces the explanation of a more generalized male dread, as the text moves from this point toward the "explanation" of one particular "riddle," that situation in which "sweet reluctant amorous delay," whether psychically or socially produced, has deepened into female frigidity (SE, 11, 201). The only "explanation" which would be sufficiently transhistorical, which would explain the continuities between the reason behind the primitive taboo and the hostility that husbands still experience from wives they have been first to "deflower," has to do with that narrative of female secondariness which is independent of any historical distance between "primitive" and "civilized." It is this which provides the most satisfying explanation of the "riddle" of frigidity and of the primitive taboo of virginity as well: "Behind this envy for the penis, there comes to light [kommt ... zum Vorschein] the woman's hostile bitterness against the man, which never completely disappears in the relations between the sexes, and which is clearly indicated in the strivings and in the literary productions of 'emancipated' women" (SE, 11, 205). Immediately after this sentence, and curiously embedded within Freud's own final illumination of the riddle of such female "hostility"—though apparently only parenthetically and only to be rejected as one of those "speculations" safe enough to be employed "so long as one avoids setting too much value on them"—is another little genesis narrative. This genesis story, from Ferenczi, is reminiscent not just of the long and fertile crossing of the story of the creation of Eve with Plato's Symposium (a text Freud himself recalls in Beyond the Pleasure Principle) but also, distantly, of early commentaries on the "help meet" of Genesis 2:18 as a figure who could be "meet for him" (kenegdô) but also just as easily "against him" (lenegdô),[62] and hence of the whole history of that troublesome helpmeet, Lilith:

> In a palaeo-biological speculation, Ferenczi has traced back this hostility of women—I do not know if he is the first to do so—to the period in time when the sexes became differentiated. At first, in his opinion, copulation took place between two similar individuals, one of which, however, developed into the stronger and forced the weaker one to submit to sexual union. The feelings of bitterness arising from this subjection still persist in the present-day disposition of women. I do not think there is any harm in employing such speculations, so long as one avoids setting too much value on them. (SE, 11, 205–6).

The Taboo of Virginity is complexly traversed by the logic of first and second—as by its own strikingly intrusive repetitions of erst and zweite ("Es is erstens zu bedauern," "in diesem zweiten Punkte," "der erste

Erklarungsversuch"). This, indeed, might well be expected for a subject as obsessively associated with priority and firstness as "virginity" and a primitive taboo concerned precisely with the displacement of a dangerous priority, with ensuring that the first act of marital intercourse ("Die *erste* Sexualverkehr in der Ehe") be in actuality a second time. The firstness of both "virginity" and "primitive" is joined within this text by a dizzying series of firsts and seconds, from the text's self-reflexive reminder of its own structuring ("unserer *eingangs* gemachten Bemerkung") at the same time as it speaks of "the first sexual act" (*SE*, 11, 200), to the "fear of *first* occurrences" ("Erstlingsangst") and of "the beginning of every new undertaking, the start of every new period of time, the first-fruits of human, animal, and plant life"("mit dem Beginne jeder neuen Verrichtung, dem Anfange jedes Zeitabschnittes, dem Erstlingsertrag von Mensch, Tier und Frucht"), to the phenomenon of a woman's sexual bondage to the "first" man, the one who provides her introduction ("Eingang") to sexual experience ("Wer *zuerst* die durch lange Zeit mühselig zurückgehaltene Liebessehnsucht der Jungfrau befriedigt"). As the text proceeds, its initial opposition between "primitive" and "civilized" is joined by a whole structure of emphases not just on first and second but also on early and late, on earlier occurrences or times ("in früheren Zeiten") and on later developments or results.

Even before the revelation of something "earlier" than the "first time" of defloration which will reveal the mystery of woman's "hostile bitter-ness" against the man who provides this introduction, we find the notion of something prior to or earlier than what might otherwise have been assumed to be first—in the reminder, say, that the husband is only a substitute, coming second to the father ("it is another man—in typical cases the father—who has first claim to a woman's love, the husband at most takes second place"), or in the "primitive" notion of something which must occur *earlier* in time to the "first" of marital intercourse, something which must be carried out "beforehand" ("Wenn aber die Defloration nicht durch den *ersten* ehelichen Verkehr erfolgen soll, so muß sie *vorher* ... vorgenommen worden sein"). The text's repeated emphasis on two temporally separate events—its anthropological apparatus of the difference between "primitive" and "civilized"; the focus on the careful separation of ritual defloration into two parts, perforation and intercourse ("Der ganze Vorgang hat sozusagen *zwei Akte*"); the reflection of the primitive taboo in the reason why "second marriages" are much happier than the first—sets up a structuring of first and second, earlier and later, even before the crucial discovery of the text, Freud's own revelation of the profounder reason for the primitive taboo. But the polarity itself breaks down in the case of the initially constructed contrast of primitive and civilized, in precisely that passage on a primitive *pavor feminae* which had followed as a "third" to the first and second attempts at explaining the primitive taboo itself: "In all this there is nothing obsolete, nothing which is not still alive among ourselves." This is the explanation rejected by Freud at precisely that moment of reversal in the text when it moves from the description of this male dread of female power ("realization of the influence which a woman gains over him through sexual intercourse, the consideration she thereby forces from him") to the motif of castration and its influence on "the opinion in which women are held" (*SE*, 11, 199). This turn is a crucial pivot for the story the text then proceeds to uncover — the revelation of female lack and the origin of female hostility in the "early" effect of penis-envy. What is revealed as *before* the first act of intercourse is a prior deficiency. Whatever the order of subsequent events, the "masculine phase in the girl in which she envies the boy for his penis is in any case *developmentally the earlier*" (p. 205, my emphasis). What immediately follows the interpolation of Ferenczi's genesis narrative at this point in the text is the conclusion of the origin of the taboo in the original envy: "we may sum up by saying that a woman's *immature sexuality* is discharged on to the man who first makes her acquainted with the sexual act" ("das sie *zuerst* den Sexualakt kennen lernt").

The fear, and reality, of women's hostility, however, keeps breaking into this text, in spite of its linear movement away from the paragraph on the primitive's "generalized dread of women," rejected as an explanation of the taboo, and towards the light of its own revelation of the riddle and mystery. And it still dominates when the text ends with the most traditional of figures of female threat and castration, the biblical Judith who (as Milton reminds us in *Samson Agonistes*) is the Hebrew counterpart of Delilah—in the proof through "literature," and specifically through Hebbel's *Judith and Holofernes*, of the explanation Freud himself provides. "Archaic," in the text's concluding statements on the continuing hostility of women to the first man to deflower them ("defloration ... unleashes an archaic reaction [*eine archäische Reaktion*] of hostility towards him"), conveys the *arche* not just of a more primitive time but of what the text has now uncovered as the prior and "original" situation of the woman's own perception of a lack and hence of her secondariness and inferiority to a male original.

*

Kofman's analysis of Freud in *The Enigma of Woman* ends with two texts which might provide the context for the end of our discussion. One is Freud's own early letter to his fiancée, adjuring her to hold to the "old ways," of woman not as liberated by legislation or the right to vote but as "elevated" by that man for whom she is "an adored sweetheart in youth, and a beloved wife in maturity"—a version of feminine priority virtually identical to the kind of proper feminine "rule" described in *Emile*. The other is the anecdote from Nerval's *Un Voyage en Orient* of the monkey who runs away with Adam's rib and the woman created out of the monkey's tail, a story which if traced back beyond Nerval would take us into the whole web of traditions surrounding the creation of Eve in Genesis 2, including that passage in the Talmud where the word used in Genesis for "rib" is interpreted as "tail," with all the sexual and other double entendres that tradition engendered.

Perhaps this archaic anecdote is the place to reach our end as well. Or perhaps we cannot quite end here. If Freud's description of the proper or normal path or road follows the familiar logic of the "post," in which this differentiated female, like Milton's Eve, must be led by a warning voice to recognize in man not just her original but her true end, the problem for feminist analysis of women's traditionally secondary position—of that difference which is defined as difference from the same—is that it may itself be caught within the logic of that "post," or coming after. If this seems too abstract, or if recourse to a "logic" seems unnecessarily theoretical or even "French" in an era of empiricism comfortably recovering from a decade of theory, we might consider such much more pragmatic, legal, and political questions as contemporary arguments outside the academy over the legislation of the implications of female difference, or the fact that a text like the *Oresteia* cannot be isolated as a purely literary text, independent from the legal and cultural forms it both newly reflected and helped to produce, or that when Donne, say, repeats the familiar theologizing of Genesis 2 ("Man to Gods image, Eve, to mans was made") it is in the anything but purely literary context of its contemporary consequence, the barring of women from office in church or state.

The pragmatic or empirical, as Simone de Beauvoir long ago insisted in *The Second Sex*, is in more dissimulated and hence more pervasive and elusive ways inhabited by logics and hence by theory; and not the least by the logological logic of priority and beginnings. We need still to pursue this logic—both its genesis and what follows from it—not just in the pervasively influential texts of our culture, like Genesis, Freud, Rousseau, or Milton, but in all of its secondary manifestations, and in the priorities they generate.

Notes

2 Literary Fat Ladies and the Generation of the Text

This essay, first presented at Stanford University in 1983, has in subsequent versions benefited from comments from audiences at Cornell and Princeton Universities, the University of Chicago, the University of Wisconsin at Milwaukee, the Academy of Literary Studies, and the Association of Canadian University Teachers of English. It has also had the good fortune of comments and suggestions from Walter Swayze, Eve Kosofsky Sedgwick, Terry Castle, Mary Nyquist, David Quint, Diana de Armas Wilson, Maria di Battista, Patricia Meyer Spacks, Jennifer Brady, and, in its final version, David Riggs.

1 On Rahab in the Hebrew Bible, see Judith Baskin, "The Rabbinic Transformations of Rahab the Harlot," *Notre Dame English Journal*, 11, 2 (April 1979), pp. 141–57.

2 For Rahab as *dilatio*, see Jean Daniélou, *From Shadows to Reality: Studies in the Biblical Typology of the Fathers*, trans. Dom Wulstan Hibberd (London, 1960), pp. 250 ff. For the "dilation of Christendome," see St Thomas More, *Comfort against Tribulation* (1529), III, weeks 1213/2. And, for "différance," see Jacques Derrida, *Marges de la philosphie* (Paris, 1972), pp. 1–29; trans. Alan Bass as *Margins of Philosophy* (Chicago, 1982), pp. 1–27. The Donne sonnet cited is Holy Sonnet 179. On women's spreading of the word, see Lee W. Patterson, "'For the Wyves love of Bathe': Feminine Rhetoric and Poetic Resolution in the *Roman de la Rose* and the *Canterbury Tales*," *Speculum*, 58, 3 (1983), p. 664, citing the *Liber Lamentationum Matheoluli*. Unless otherwise noted, all italicization in the text is mine.

3 In *Inescapable Romance: Studies in the Poetics of a Mode* (Princeton, NJ, 1979), esp. pp. 54 ff. For Hamlet's "mother" and "matter," below, see Margaret W. Ferguson, "*Hamlet*: letters and spirits," in Patricia Parker and Geoffrey Hartman (eds), *Shakespeare and the Question of Theory* (New York and London, 1985), p. 295.

4 St Jerome, who repented of his own attraction towards rhetoric, interpreted the swine's food in the Parable of the Prodigal Son as "the song of the poets, prophane philosophy, and the verbal pomp of the rhetoricians." On Jerome and other patristic commentary on the Prodigal Son parable, see Bernard

Blumenkranz, "Siliquae Porcorum: L'exégèse médiévale et les sciences pro-
fanes," *Mélanges d'histoire du Moyen Age dédiés à la mémoire de Louis
Halphen* (Paris, 1951), pp. 11–17, and Richard Helgerson, *The Elizabethan
Prodigals* (Berkeley and Los Angeles, 1976), p. 55, together with Helgerson's
overall discussion of the importance of the parable for Renaissance English
literary men.

5 On Sidney and the attack on poetry as not fit for men, see Walter J. Ong, SJ,
"Latin Language Study as a Renaissance Puberty Rite," in his *Rhetoric,
Romance, and Technology* (Ithaca, NY, 1971), pp. 130 ff. The text used in all
subsequent citations from Ascham is *The Schoolmaster* (1570), ed. Laurence
V. Ryan (Ithaca, 1967).

6 See Sir John Harington (trans.), *Orlando furioso* (1591), sig. Mm iii and sig. ¶
viii–viii^v (UMEES, Reel 194), with Helgerson, *Elizabethan Prodigals*, pp.
38–9.

7 See Mary Jacobus, "Is There a Woman in This Text?," *New Literary History*,
14, 1 (Autumn 1982), pp. 117–41. I use "subtext" here in the sense of an
informing predecessor text. See Thomas M. Greene, *The Light in Troy:
Imitation and Discovery in Renaissance Poetry* (New Haven and London,
1982), pp. 18–31.

8 I am, of course, aware that Calypso comes chronologically later than Circe in
the homecoming journey of Odysseus. But the *narrative* order moves from
Calypso, and an initial latency, to the victory over Circe. The *Odyssey* is
traditionally characterized as a romance or *romanzo* in Renaissance discussions of the form.

9 See Ariosto, *Orlando furioso*, VII.74.1–4; Parker, *Inescapable Romance*, pp.
30–1; and Roland Barthes, *S/Z: Essai* (Paris, 1970). There is clearly an
important difference between closural forms in the Bible, even with its open-
ended ending, and the *Odyssey*, where we are told within the text that
Odysseus, after reaching home and Penelope, will one day set out again. But
the conflation within later literary, and specifically romance, tradition of
temptress figures from both texts suggests the perceived links between the
trajectory of "homecoming" in both.

10 See Desiderius Erasmus, *De Copia*, in *Collected Works of Erasmus*, vol. 24, ed.
Craig R. Thompson (Toronto, 1978); the warnings against "Excesse" in, for
example, Henry Peacham's *The Garden of Eloquence* (1593 edn), ed.
William G. Crane (Gainesville, Florida, 1954). For the "wall" or *paries* and
Cicero's *Topics*, see T. W. Baldwin, *William Shakspere's Small Latine and
Lesse Greeke*, 2 vols (Urbana, 1944), vol. II, p. 110. The link between weaving
and the dilation of discourse, as of the play, in *A Midsummer Night's Dream*,
might be most succinctly conveyed through the fact that the name of "Bottom"
the "Weaver" comes from that "bottom" of thread which Francis Bacon, in
The Advancement of Learning (II.xviii.8), has recourse to as a figure for
"rhetoric" as having to do with discoursing "at large," and the attendant need
to avoid "proxility" ("as skeins or bottoms of thread, to be unwinded at large
when they come to be used"). Though the relation between Bottom's name and
the play's constant playing on the dilation and partition of discourse has not
been discussed, the link with "bottom of thread" both in relation to weaving
and in relation to phallic "point" has. See Wolfgang Franke, "The Logic of

Double Entendre in *A Midsummer-Night's Dream*," *Philological Quarterly*, 58 (1979), pp. 284, 287 ff. For further discussion of *A Midsummer Night's Dream* in relation to its incorporation of the language of rhetoric, see chapter 6, "Motivated Rhetorics," below.

11　See *The Sermons of John Donne*, ed. George R. Potter and Evelyn M. Simpson, 10 vols, vol. V (Berkeley and Los Angeles, 1959), p. 56; and the discussion of the *ars praedicandi* tradition in John S. Chamberlin, *Increase and Multiply* (Chapel Hill, NC, 1976), and Patterson, "'For the Wyves love of Bathe'," p. 675.

12　See Ascham, *The Schoolmaster*, pp. 106–14; Erasmus, Epistle 899, quoted in Izora Scott, *Controversies over the Imitation of Cicero* (New York, 1910), vol. II, p. 84, and, for the reference to "bignesse," Cornwallis's essay "Of Vanity" (1601), both cited in George Williamson, *The Senecan Amble* (Chicago, 1951), pp. 19 and 106. For Lipsius, see Morris W. Croll, "'Attic Prose' in the Seventeenth Century," *Studies in Philology*, 18 (April 1921), p. 98.

13　See, respectively, Ficino's use of *dilatio* in his translation of Plotinus' Fifth *Ennead*, with his translation of *Enneads*, 6:7.2,3; *De immortalitate animorum*, I.iii;v.x; and *De vita coelitus comparanda*, ch. 1; John Erskine Hankins, *Source and Meaning in Spenser's Allegory* (Oxford, 1971), p. 291; Parker, *Inescapable Romance*, pp. 54–6; Hugh Latimer's sermon of 1552 on the Lord's Prayer, where he remarks that heaven, unlike earth, is a place where God's will is done "without dilation"; Richard Taverner's 1539 English translation of the *Adages* of Erasmus; and Milton, *Paradise Lost*, IV.986.

14　See Herbert of Cherbury's "Ode upon a Question Mov'd" ("So when one wing can make no way / Two joyned can themselves dilate, / So can two persons propagate"). For the obstetrical tradition, as well as the use of the term "dilation" for the sexual opening of a woman, see *The Works of Aristotle, the Famous Philosopher*, in the reprint edition by Arno Press (New York, 1974), pp. 10, 81. For "dilating or enlarging of a matter by interpretation," see John Smith's *Mysterie of Rhetorique Unvail'd* (1657), under "Paradiastole or distinctio." Audrey Eccles' *Obstetrics and Gynaecology in Tudor and Stuart England* (Kent, Ohio, 1982), pp. 28 and 40, also cites passages on the "opening of the cervix in Copulation ... and in childbirth."

15　The language of legal "dilation" still continues in Hobbes's *Leviathan* (I.xiv: "the not decreeing Execution, is a decree of Dilation," its "deferring till another time"). I am indebted here to the reading of the ordering of the *Canterbury Tales*, of the Wife of Bath as putting off the Parson's Tale, and of the link with literature in Lee Patterson's "'For the Wyves love of Bath'," pp. 676 ff.

16　For the tradition of erotic dilation or putting off, see Andreas Capellanus, *De Arte Honeste Amandi*; and Addison, *Spectator*, 89 (1711), with Patterson, "'For the Wyves love of Bath'," p. 671n. on Andreas's substitution of *dilatio* for the *mora* of Ovid's *Ars amatoria*. The "Wall" between the lovers which must be "down" in the play of Pyramus and Thisbe in *A Midsummer Night's Dream* is linked by a series of obscene double entendres to the hymeneal wall, and the imagery there draws on the traditional typological assimilation of Ephesians' "wall of partition" to the "wall" of Canticles 2:9. For this assimilation see, for example, *The Sermons of John Donne*, ed. Potter and Simpson, vol. II (Berkeley and Los Angeles, 1955), pp. 108, 110–11. In *A Midsummer Night's Dream*, Hippolyta is identified with the erotic delay: C. L. Barber, in *Shakespeare's Festive Comedy* (Princeton, NJ, 1959), p. 125, provides a formulation indicative of the continuance of this gendered tradition: "Theseus looks towards the hour with masculine impatience, Hippolyta with a woman's happy willingness to dream away the time." The edition used for all citations from Shakespeare is *The Riverside Shakespeare*, ed. G. Blakemore Evans (Boston, Mass., 1974).

17 See St Bonaventure's Sermon no. 6 (*De verbo incarnato*) in *Opera theologica selecta*, ed. Quaracchi (Florence, 1964), vol.V, esp. pp. 309 ff.

18 See Lisa Jardine, *Still Harping on Daughters* (Brighton, 1983), p. 131.

19 See Barber, *Shakespeare's Festive Comedy*, p. 137; and Quintilian, *Institutio oratoria*, XII.x.37, in the Loeb translation.

20 For discussion of *A Midsummer Night's Dream* in relation to the Aristotelian tradition of the female as "a vessel" and rhetorical *dispositio*, see chapter 6, "Motivated Rhetorics," p. 123 below.

21 See Ephesians 5:16 and Hal's "Redeeming time when men think least I will" (*1 Henry IV*, I.ii.217). One particularly suggestive scene for the association of fat Falstaff with the copious dilation of discourse and lean Hal with its corrective is Act II, scene iv of *Henry IV, Part 1*, where Falstaff's expanding tall story of proliferating thieves yields to comic invective on Hal's thinness ("you starveling, you eel-skin") when the amplified tale is in danger of being exposed (and finally is by Hal's contrastingly brief "plain tale").

22 For a fascinating reading of this mastery of languages in the *Henriad* in these terms, see Steven Mullaney, "Strange Things, Gross Terms, Curious Customs: The Rehearsal of Cultures in the Late Renaissance," *Representations*, 3 (Summer 1983), pp. 53–62. On the feminization of Falstaff within the *Henriad* itself, see Gayle Whittier, "Falstaff as a Welshwoman: Uncomic Androgyny," *Ball State University Forum*, 20, 3 (Summer 1979), pp. 25–35.

23 The text of "Women are words, men deeds" is from Thomas Howell's *Devises* (1581). For Robert Greene on "babling Poets," see *Penelope's Web*, in Robert Greene, *The Life and Complete Works in Prose and Verse*, ed. Alexander B. Grosart, 15 vols (New York, n.d.), vol. V, p. 158. All subsequent references are to this edition. For stimulating discussions of the inhabiting of male or misogynist discourse with the female loquacity that is its subject, see Patterson, "'For the Wyves love of Bathe,'" pp. 660 ff.; R. Howard Bloch, "Medieval Misogyny," *Representations*, 20 (Fall 1987), pp. 1–24; and, for the later case of Milton, Jim Swan, "Difference and Silence: John Milton and the Question of Gender," in Shirley Nelson Garner *et al.* (eds), *The (M)other Tongue* (Ithaca, NY, 1985), pp. 142–68.

24 See Maurice Charney, *Style in Hamlet* (Princeton, NJ, 1969), pp. 88, 94, 100, 104; and for a contemporary assimilation of wordiness and idleness, Francis Bacon, *Advancement of Learning*, II.xxiii.6 ("words and discourse abound most where there is idleness"). For *dilatio* as *tarditas* or *accidia/melancholia*, see Reinhard Kuhn, *The Demon of Noontide* (Princeton, NJ, 1976), p. 40 n.2. For links between Falstaff and Hamlet, see G. R. Hibbard, "*Henry IV* and *Hamlet*," in *Shakespeare Survey*, 30, ed. Kenneth Muir (Cambridge, 1977), pp. 1 ff.

25 Hamlet's "interlarding" in the revised commission makes use of the amplifications and embellishments he has learned ("many such-like as's of great charge," V.ii.43), and does so in order to substitute for Claudius' commission an equally pointed message—of death. The assimilation of Hamlet at this point to a "king" is underscored both by Horatio's double reference in "Why, what a king is this!" (V.ii.62) and by the fact that Hamlet uses his father's seal for the kingly commission. It is at this point in the play, after his return from England, that critics of *Hamlet* traditionally see the former delay replaced by a new sense of purpose and end. The effeminating associations of mere railing are conveyed elsewhere in Shakespeare by the appellation of Thersites as "Mistress Thersites" in *Troilus and Cressida* (II.i.36). I have departed from the Riverside text for the "dilated articles," above, because the Q2 "delated" chosen by the Riverside editor is, as the gloss notes, a variant of "dilated."

26 The line is from Jonson's Pindaric Ode "To the Immortall Memorie, and Friendship of that Noble Paire, Sir Lucius Cary and Sir H. Morison." I have treated this pun and its evocativeness within the Ode in greater detail in "Deferral, Dilation, Différance: Shakespeare, Cervantes, Jonson," in Patricia Parker and David Quint (eds), *Literary Theory / Renaissance Texts* (Baltimore, 1986), pp. 198–203.

27 The edition used in all references to *Bartholomew Fair* is that of *The Complete Plays of Ben Jonson*, ed. G. A. Wilkes, based on the edition of C. H. Herford and Percy and Evelyn Simpson (Oxford, 1982), vol. IV. For Donne, see his sermon no. 3 (on Psalm 38:4, "For mine iniquities are gone over my head, as a heavy burden, they are too heavy for mee"), in *The Sermons of John Donne*, ed. Potter and Simpson, vol. II, pp. 95–118. In a way directly significant for the complex we have been tracing, this sermon also contains reference to the "wall of partition" of Ephesians 2, and the multiplication or "increase" of sin made possible by the proliferation of "partitions," in the midst of a sermon which, in self-conscious fashion, is itself constructed according to the *ars praedicandi* principles of dilation by partition.

28 See, respectively, Jackson I. Cope, "*Bartholomew Fair* as Blasphemy," *Renaissance Drama*, 8 (1965), p. 129, on the echoes of Judgment Day; R. B. Parker, "The Themes and Staging of *Bartholomew Fair*," *University of Toronto Quarterly*, 39 (1969–70), p. 294, on Ursula's booth and "Hell"; Peter Stallybrass and Allon White, *The Politics and Poetics of Transgression* (Ithaca, NY, 1986), pp. 44 ff., on the symbolics of the pig and on Ursula as "the celebrant of the open orifice" (p. 64). I am grateful to David Riggs for his comments and suggestions here.

29 For the extraordinary exploitation in this play of all the resources of rhetorical *copia* and *amplificatio*, see Jonas Barish, *Ben Jonson and the Language of Prose Comedy* (Cambridge, Mass., 1960), pp. 188–219; and Eugene M. Waith's introduction to the Yale Ben Jonson edition of *Bartholomew Fair* (New Haven and London, 1963), pp. 3 ff.

30 For these identifications, see, respectively, Cope, "*Bartholomew Fair* as Blasphemy," p. 144, and R. B. Parker, "Themes and Staging," p. 297.

31 *As You Like It*, III.ii.249–50.

32 See *Fifty-Five Enigmatical Characters, All Very Exactly Drawn to the Life* (London, 1665), p. 33.

33 Robert Greene, *Penelope's Web*, in *The Life and Complete Works*, vol. V, the edition to which all parenthetical page references in the text refer.

34 See *A Curtaine Lecture* (London, 1637), attributed to Thomas Heywood, p. 17; Alciati, *Emblemata* (London, 1551), p. 78; and Geoffrey Whitney, *A Choice of Emblemes* (Leyden, 1586), p. 50. For further discussion of the misogynist topos of the garrulity of women, see "Motivated Rhetorics," pp. 104–10 below.

35 On this male pedagogical economy, dominant in spite of more minor humanist encouragements of the education of women, see Ong, "Latin Language Study as a Renaissance Puberty Rite," pp. 113–41.

36 Play on "case" is ubiquitous in the Renaissance, as in Ben Jonson's *The Case is Altered*. For the bawdy and bodily associations of grammatical "case," see Roland Barthes, "L'Ancienne Rhétorique: Aide-mémoire," *Communications*, 16 (1970), p. 174. The nominative case was understood as the *casus rectus* or "erect" case from which others deviated or declined. See J. B. Greenough *et al.* (eds), *Allen and Greenough's New Latin Grammar* (New Rochelle, NY, 1983), p. 209. On Mistress Quickly's "case" as "so openly known to the world" and the legal/sexual "case," see chapter 6 below, pp. 106–7.

37 Helgerson, *Elizabethan Prodigals*, p. 42, quoting John Lyly, *Euphues*, ed. Morris W. Croll and Harry Clemons (1916; repr. New York, 1964), p. 200.

38 For this economy of translation, from father tongue, through English, and back to father tongue, see, for example, Roger Ascham, *The Schoolmaster*, pp. 15, 83. John Brinsley's later text, *A Consolation for Our Grammar Schooles* (1622), makes it clear as well how intimately tied this translative economy would become to the marginalizing and even eliminating of competing tongues as part of an imperial project to enforce the study of English ("that all may speake one and the same language"), since it was directed especially to "all those of the inferiour sort, and all ruder countries and places; namely Ireland, Wales, Virginia, with the Sommer Islands." The model here is of a translation from and back to the *sermo patrius* in which there is to be no difference between the paternal original and the dutiful copy ("and to turne or reade the same, out of the Translation into good Latine . . . so as in most, you shall hardly discerne, whether it be the Authors Latine or the Scholars"; p. 52).

39 *The Womens Sharpe Revenge* (London, 1640), a reply to the misogynist author of the Juniper and Crabtree lectures, puns on "gender" and "genera-tion" (pp. 16–17) and, in remarking that its opponent is "quite out in all the Cases" in his attack on women, observes of his mistake in the genitive: "In the Genetive, by making us to be loose, lascivious, wanton, wilfull, inconstant, incontinent, and the Mothers of misbegotten Children" (p. 19).

40 Thomas M. Greene, "Erasmus' 'Festina lente': Vulnerabilities of the Humanist Text," in *The Vulnerable Text* (New York, 1986), pp. 1–17. For one Renaissance passage which explicitly engages the problem of having "no certain end," see Richard Hooker, *Of the Laws of Ecclesiastical Polity* (London, 1907), Book I, p. 200.

41 See Jonathan Culler, "Apostrophe," in *The Pursuit of Signs* (Ithaca, NY, 1981), pp. 135–54.

42 The emphasis on "page," "letter," "post," and printed text is insistent throughout *Merry Wives*. See for example the exchange on the identical "letters" sent to Mistress Page and Mistress Ford (II.i.70–9); the various go-betweens who act as bearers of messages; the "postmaster's boy" (V.v.199) who substitutes for Ann Page at the end; and the Page ("Robin") who "will carry a letter twenty mile as easy as a cannon will shoot point-blank twelve score" (III.ii.32–4). Play on "Page" and "page" is not exclusive to Shakespeare. See Nashe's preface to the "Pages" in *The Unfortunate Traveller* and Margaret W. Ferguson, "Nashe's *The Unfortunate Traveller*; The 'Newes of the Maker' Game," *ELR* (Spring 1981), pp. 166 ff.

43 See Mullaney, "Strange Things, Gross Terms, Curious Customs," pp. 40–67; and Stephen Greenblatt, "Invisible Bullets: Renaissance Authority and its Subversion," *Glyph*, 8 (1981), pp. 40–61.

44 On the figure of the female and outrageously pregnant Pope Joan, see C. A. Patrides, *Premises and Motifs in Renaissance Thought and Literature* (Princeton, NJ, 1982), pp. 152–81.

45 See "Bantams in Pine-Woods" and, for "fluent mundo," the end of *Notes Toward a Supreme Fiction* (x). On Stevens as a "eucalyptic" (another term involving covering) rather than "apocalyptic" poet, see the marvelous study by Eleanor Cook, "Directions in Reading Wallace Stevens: Up, Down, Across," in Chaviva Hošek and Patricia Parker (eds), *Lyric Poetry: Beyond New Criticism* (Ithaca, NY, 1985), pp. 298–309. For "Revelation," see Flannery O'Connor, *The Complete Stories* (New York, 1979), pp. 48–50.

46 See Elaine Showalter, "Feminist Criticism in the Wilderness," *Critical Inquiry*, 8 (1981), pp. 179–206; and Luce Irigaray, *This Sex Which is Not One*, trans. Catherine Porter (Ithaca, NY, 1985), p. 111. Annie Leclerc speaks in *Parole de femme* of the need to "invent a language that is not oppressive, a language that does not leave speechless but that loosens the tongue"; Hélène Cixous's *Vivre l'orange* (Paris, 1979) is written in French and English, but includes Portuguese, German, and Italian in a proliferation of mother tongues. See Dianne Hunter, "Hysteria, Psychoanalysis, and Feminism: The Case of Anna O.," in Shirley Nelson Garner *et al.* (eds), *The (M)other Tongue* (Ithaca, NY, 1985), p. 114.

47 See Roland Barthes, *S/Z* and "L'Ancienne Rhétorique: Aide-mémoire." The passage on the "Closets of Womens thoughts" is from the description of "Aspertions laid upon Women" (pp. 44–5) in the response of Ester Sowernam (pseud.), in *Ester hath hang'd Haman* (London, 1617), to the famous misogynist tract by Joseph Swetnam. The continuation into the eighteenth century of the masculinist tradition of feminine erotic dilation or holding off is suggested by such instances as Jeremy Collier's remark in "Of Whoredom," that "difficulty and danger heighten the success, and make the conquest more entertaining," in *Essays upon Several Subjects*, 3rd edn (London, 1720), vol. III, pp. 114–15.

48 See, respectively, Pope's *Peri Bathous or The Art of Sinking in Poetry* (1727), ch. 8, on amplifiers "but for which, the tale of many a vast romance, and the

substance of many a fair volume might be reduced to the size of a primmer";
Henry Fielding, *Joseph Andrews*, Book II, ch. 1; Mary Shelley's Introduction
to *Frankenstein*; and Charles Maturin, *Melmoth the Wanderer* (1820; Lincoln,
Neb., 1961), p. 18. I am grateful to Susan Wolfson and Terry Castle for these
last two references. For Milton, see my "Dilation and Delay: Renaissance
Matrices," *Poetics Today*, 5, 3 (1984), pp. 526–7.

49 The two cited texts are Mordecai Moxon, *The Character, Praise and Commendation of a Chaste and Virtuous Woman, in a Learned and Pious Discourse
Against Adultery* (London, 1708), p. 7; and *News from the New-Exchange:
or, the Common-wealth of Ladies: Drawn to the Life, in their several Characters and Concernments*, 2nd edn (London, 1731), pp. 7–12.

50 See, most recently, the essays in *Representations*, 14, special issue, *Sexuality
and the Social Body in the Nineteenth Century* (Spring 1986), in particular the
essay by Catherine Gallagher entitled "The Body Versus the Social Body in the
Works of Thomas Malthus and Henry Mayhew."

51 I am indebted in what follows to various readers and hearers of the oral version
of this essay; on Radcliffe and Austen, to Eve Kosofsky Sedgwick; on Henrietta
Stackpole, to Deborah Esch; on Beckett and Joyce, to Maria di Battista and
Jennifer Levine. The reference to David Miller below is to the highly suggestive
discussion of Austen in his *Narrative and its Discontents* (Princeton, NJ,
1981). On Freud, Breuer, and the multilingual Bertha Pappenheim, see Dianne
Hunter, "Hysteria, Psychoanalysis, and Feminism: The Case of Anna O.," pp.
89 ff.

52 See Ernst Bloch, as cited by Georg Lukács, "Realism in the Balance" (1938),
reprinted in *Aesthetics and Politics* (London, 1977), p. 38.

3 The Metaphorical Plot

This is a shortened version of the essay of the same title which first appeared in
David S. Miall (ed.), *Metaphor: Problems and Perspectives* (Brighton, 1982).

1 Aristotle, *Poetics*, 1457b, 6–9.
2 Paul Ricœur, *La Métaphore vive* (Paris, 1975), trans. R. Czerny, *The Rule of
Metaphor* (Toronto, 1977), p. 17.
3 Aristotle, *Poetics*, 1457b, 7 and 3; Ricœur, *The Rule of Metaphor*, p. 19.
4 Cicero, *De oratore*, Loeb translation, xli.165. For the earlier citations from
Cicero see, respectively, III.xxxix.157, xxviii.155, xxxix.158, xl.161.
5 Quintilian, *Institutio oratoria*, Loeb translation, in particular VIII.vi, VIII.vi.6.
All subsequent parenthetical references are to this text.
6 A. J. Greimas, *Sémantique structurale* (Paris, 1966).
7 C. C. Dumarsais, *Les tropes* (1757 edn), X, pp. 133, 134.
8 George Puttenham, *The Arte of English Poesie* (1589), III.xviii.
9 See, for example, Isidore of Seville, *Etymologies*, I.xxxvii.2: "metaphora est
verbi alicuius usurpata translatio."
10 Puttenham, *The Arte of English Poesie*, III.xvii.
11 John Locke, *Essay Concerning Human Understanding* (1690–1700), III.10.

12 Jacques Derrida, "The *Retrait* of Metaphor," *Enclitic*, 2, 2 (Fall 1978), p. 7.

13 Paul de Man, "The Epistemology of Metaphor," in S. Sacks (ed.), *On Metaphor* (Chicago and London, 1979), p. 21.

14 All parenthetical references are to chapter and page in the Penguin edition of *Wuthering Heights*, ed. David Daiches (Harmondsworth, 1965).

15 Northrop Frye, *Anatomy of Criticism* (1957; New York, 1966), p. 124.

16 Ibid., p. 123.

17 See Frank Kermode, *The Classic* (New York, 1975), pp. 122–3.

18 Cicero, *De oratore*, XXX.xl.160.

19 St Augustine, *Confessions*, VII.x, XII.xiii; 1 Corinthians 12.

20 Jacques Derrida, *De la grammatologie* (Paris, 1967), pp. 156–7.

21 See also the assimilation of metaphor to the figure of the "heliotrope" in Jacques Derrida, "La Mythologie blanche," *Poétique*, 5 (1971), trans. F. C. T. Moore, "White Mythology," *New Literary History*, 6, 1 (Autumn 1974), pp. 5–74.

22 See Owen Barfield, *Romanticism Comes of Age*, rev. edn (Middletown, Conn., 1966), p. 156, and Terence Hawkes (ed.), *Coleridge on Shakespeare* (Harmondsworth, 1959).

23 I. A. Richards, *The Philosophy of Rhetoric* (London, 1965); P. Wheelwright, *The Burning Fountain*, rev. edn (Bloomington, Ind., 1968), p. 102; W. Empson, *Seven Types of Ambiguity* (New York, 1955), p. 3; Owen Barfield, "Poetic Diction and Legal Fiction," in *Essays Presented to Charles Williams* (London, 1947).

24 Paul Valéry, *Œuvres*, ed. J. Hytier (Paris, 1957), vol. I, pp. 1449–50 ("Calepin d'un poète"), p. 1372 ("Propos sur la poésie"); vol. II, p. 1264 ("Les Droits du poète sur la langue").

25 See Gérard Genette, *Figures* (Paris, 1966), p. 209; C. S. Peirce, *Collected Papers* (Cambridge, Mass., 1931–58), vol. 5, para. 484; Kenneth Burke, "Rhetoric—Old and New," repr. in M. Steinmann, Jr, *New Rhetorics* (New York, 1967), p. 75; Geoffrey Hartman, *Beyond Formalism* (New Haven and London, 1970), pp. 340–1; M. Bakhtin, *Problems of Dostoevsky's Poetics*, trans. R. W. Rotsel (n.p., 1973), pp. 90, 151; M. Bakhtin, *Rabelais and his World*, trans. H. Iswolsky (Cambridge, Mass., 1968).

26 Ricœur, *La Métaphore vive*, study 5, s. 2 ("L'espace de la figure"), with reference to Jean Cohen's *Structure du langage poétique* (Paris, 1966), and Ricœur's condensation of his argument, and critique of Barthes, in "The Metaphorical Process as Cognition, Imagination, and Feeling," in Sacks (ed.), *On Metaphor*, pp. 141–57, the text to which parenthetical page numbers refer.

27 Michael Riffaterre, *The Semiotics of Poetry* (Bloomington, Ind., 1978). Page numbers in parentheses refer to this text.

28 Ricœur, "The Metaphorical Process as Cognition, Imagination, and Feeling," p. 144.

29 For the debate over Heidegger's association of metaphor and metaphysics, see Derrida, "La Mythologie blanche," Ricœur's critique of it in study 8 of *La Métaphore vive*, and Derrida's reply in "The *Retrait* of Metaphor."

30 Barfield, "Poetic Diction and Legal Fiction," p. 110.

31 Northrop Frye, *The Educated Imagination* (Toronto, 1963), p. 21.

32 Roman Jakobson, "Two Aspects of Language and Two Types of Aphasic Disturbances" (1953), in R. Jakobson and M. Halle, *The Fundamentals of Language* (The Hague, 1956).

33 Christine Brooke-Rose, *A Grammar of Metaphor* (London, 1965), p. 144.

34 Frye, *The Educated Imagination*, p. 11.

35 See T. Cohen, "Metaphor and the Cultivation of Intimacy," in Sacks (ed.), *On Metaphor*, pp. 1–10; Geoffrey Hartman, "Psychoanalysis: The French Connection," in G.H. Hartman (ed.), *Psychoanalysis and the Question of the Text* (Baltimore, 1978), p. 94; P. Wheelwright, *Metaphor and Reality* (Bloomington, Ind., 1962), p. 16; Kenneth Burke, *Permanence and Change*, rev. edn (Los Altos, 1954), pp. 89–96, and Harold Bloom's adaptation of Burke's notion of the "perspectivism" of metaphor in *A Map of Misreading* (New York, 1975), pp. 94 ff.; M. Black, *Models and Metaphors* (Ithaca, NY, 1962), pp. 39 ff.

36 See Paul de Man, "Semiology and Rhetoric," *Diacritics*, 3 (Fall 1973), and his analysis of metaphor in Rousseau in his *Allegories of Reading* (New Haven and London, 1979); Richard Klein's conception of metaphor as creating "the fiction of its repose," in "Straight Lines and Arabesques: Metaphors of Metaphor," *Yale French Studies*, 45 (1970); Riffaterre on the "retroactively fantasized" non-literary "norm" in *The Semiotics of Poetry*, p. 164; Peirce, *Collected Papers*, vol. 1, p. 171, on the succession of signifiers.

4 Suspended Instruments: Lyric and Power in the Bower of Bliss

This essay is a revised version of the English Institute essay of the same title, published in Marjorie Garber (ed.), *Cannibals, Witches, and Divorce: Estranging the Renaissance* (Baltimore, 1987). I am grateful for the readings given it by Mary Nyquist, in preparation for its original presentation at the English Institute in 1984, and by Maureen Quilligan and Richard Strier.

1 The edition used for this and all subsequent quotations from Spenser is *Poetical Works*, ed. J. C. Smith and E. de Selincourt (London, 1912).

2 Geneva Bible (1560) version. I am indebted to John Hollander's valuable discussion of the different versions and pervasive poetic influence of this psalm in *The Oxford Anthology of English Literature*, ed. Frank Kermode *et al.* (New York, 1973), vol. I. pp. 534–42. For the influence of the psalms themselves on Renaissance lyric and lyric theory, see, *inter alia*, O. B. Hardison, Jr, *The Enduring Monument: A Study of the Idea of Praise in Renaissance Literary Theory and Practice* (Chapel Hill, NC, 1962), pp. 95–102, and Barbara Kiefer Lewalski, *Donne's Anniversaries and the Poetry of Praise* (Princeton, NJ, 1973), pp. 11–41.

3 See Calvin, *Commentaries on the Book of Psalms*, trans. James Anderson, 5 vols (Grand Rapids, Mich., 1949), pp. 189–90, and Augustine, *Expositions on the Book of Psalms*, trans. J. Tweed *et al.*, 6 vols (Oxford, 1847–57), p. 163.

Armida's garden appears in Tasso's *Gerusalemme liberata*, 16. Calvin's commentary doubles "hanged our harpes" with singers themselves held "in suspense," and this paralleling of the suspended instruments with a more properly psychological or spiritual "suspension" in the singer is continued in the versions of Thomas Campion, Thomas Carew, and Sir John Denham cited by Hollander in *The Oxford Anthology*.

4 See, for example, the analyses in Paul Alpers, *The Singer of the "Eclogues": A Study of Virgilian Pastoral* (Berkeley and Los Angeles, 1979), pp. 97 ff., 102, 134.

5 Jacopo Sannazaro, *Arcadia*, ch. 10, prose.

6 See, for example, the discussion in Richard Helgerson, *Self-Crowned Laureates* (Berkeley and Los Angeles, 1983), pp. 65–82; and Louis Adrian Montrose, "'The perfecte paterne of a Poete': The Poetics of Courtship in *The Shepheardes Calender*," *Texas Studies in Language and Literature*, 21 (1979), pp. 34–67.

7 The Bower of Bliss episode twice uses "toyes" for "trifles" or "trifling." Thomas Watson, *Hekatompathia or Passionate Centurie of Love*, ed. S. K. Heninger, Jr (Gainesville, Fla., 1964), p. 5, speaks of poems themselves as "idle toyes proceeding from a youngling [i.e. prodigal, errant] frenzy." Sir John Harington, Elizabeth's godson and translator of Ariosto, feared that, in becoming "a translator of Italian toys," he was wasting his education and later bade farewell to his "sweet wanton Muse." See Ludovico Ariosto, *Orlando furioso*, ed. Robert McNulty, trans. Sir John Harington (Oxford, 1972), pp. 14–15; Sir John Harington, *Nugae Antiquae*, ed. Henry Harington (London, 1804), vol. I, p. 333; and Helgerson's seminal discussion of these and other texts in relation to the profession of poetry in *Self-Crowned Laureates*.

8 The crossing of phallic with lyric instruments is of course not an exclusively Spenserian one, "instruments" being itself a fertile source of sexual double entendre. Cloten in *Cymbeline* (II.iii.13–14), setting up with his musicians to woo Imogen, arranges his lyric entertainment in the hope that it will "penetrate" ("Come on, tune: if you can penetrate her with your fingering, so: we'll try with tongue too").

9 See Madlyn Millner Kahr, "Delilah," in Norma Broude and Mary D. Garrard (eds), *Feminism and Art History* (New York, 1982), p. 137, an essay first brought to my attention by Mary Nyquist. That the evocation of Samson and Delilah would not be inappropriate within a Renaissance *locus amoenus* such as the Bower of Bliss is suggested as well by Kahr's citation of the reclining Samson in the *Small Garden of Love*. Kahr's entire discussion of the oral and maternal aspects of this iconography is useful in juxtaposition with Spenser's scene. In one representation (*c.* 1508) by the great Dutch graphic artist Lucas van Leyden, Samson has laid his shield and halberd on the ground beside him, stressing his defenselessness as he sleeps in Delilah's lap; in another by the same artist (*c.* 1517–18), the abandoned weapon is a spiked club, perhaps a reference to the club of Hercules.

10 See Neil Hertz, "Medusa's Head: Male Hysteria under Political Pressure," *Representations* 1, 4 (1983), pp. 40–50.

11 See Peter Hawkins, "From Mythography to Myth-Making: Spenser and the

Magna Mater Cybele," *Sixteenth Century Journal*, 12, 3 (1981), pp. 51–64. Hawkins reminds us that Isabel Rathborne long ago conjectured that Cybele was one of the literary ancestors of Gloriana: see her *Meaning of Spenser's Fairyland* (New York, 1937), p. 35. I am indebted to Hawkins's discussion of Cybele for the more general sense here of a link with *The Faerie Queene*, II.xii.

12 The episode in Book V also makes clearer the role of Britomart in this regard. She is the "martial maid" who defeats Radigund, but who, after the battle, softens from the counterpart of a warlike Amazon (V.v.29) into a waiting "Penelope" (39) who then, as reigning "Princess," the "liberty of women did repeale, / Which they had long usurpt; and them restoring / To Mens subiection, did true Iustice deale" (42.3–7). More detailed examination of the Britomart–Radigund pairing in relation to the Aćrasia canto would suggest the tissue of contradictions at work in the reign of a Queen so clearly an exception to the patriarchal norm and under whom the situation of other women remained unchanged. The monstrosity of the rule of women is attested to, among other documents, by John Knox's attack on female rulers in his *First Blast of the Trumpet against the Monstrous regiment of women* (1558) and, after Elizabeth's accession as a female ruler sympathetic to Protestantism, his condition conveyed in a letter to her minister William Cecil that he would do "reverence" to the "miraculouse worke of God's comforting his afflicted by an infirme vessell," but only if the Queen would acknowledge "that the extraordinary dispensation of Godes great mercy maketh that lawfull unto her, which both nature and Godes law denye" to other women. See James E. Phillips, "The Background of Spenser's Attitude Toward Women Rulers," *Huntington Library Quarterly*, 5 (October 1941–July 1942), pp. 19–20.

13 See Maureen Quilligan, *Milton's Spenser: The Politics of Reading* (Ithaca, NY, 1983), pp. 67 ff.; and Louis Adrian Montrose, "'Shaping Fantasies': Figurations of Gender and Power in Elizabethan Culture," *Representations*, 1, 2 (1983), pp. 61–94.

14 The Muses' lament indicts the English nobility in phrases that directly recall the Bower of Bliss from the first installment of *The Faerie Queene* ("loathly idlenesse" (p. 335); "base slothfulnesse" (p. 99); "men depriv'd of sense and minde" (p. 156); together with an image of navigation that parallels that of the journey of Guyon and his Palmer guide: "But he that is of reasons skill bereft, / And wants the staffe of wisdome him to say, / Is like a ship in the midst of tempest left / Withouten helme or Pilot her to sway" (pp. 139 ff.)).

15 See the influential discussion of the Bower of Bliss in Stephen Greenblatt, *Renaissance Self-Fashioning* (Chicago, 1980), pp. 165 ff.

16 See Francis Bacon, "On the Fortunate Memory of Elizabeth Queen of England," trans. James Spedding, in *The Works of Francis Bacon*, ed. James Spedding and Robert Ellis (London, 1857–74), vol. VI, p. 317; and Greenblatt, *Renaissance Self-Fashioning*, pp. 166–7. Elizabeth was also both a forbidding Virgin and, in the words of Thomas Wenden, a yeoman subject, an "arrant whore." See Peter Stallybrass, "Patriarchal Territories: The Body Enclosed," in Margaret W. Ferguson *et al.* (eds), *Rewriting the Renaissance* (Chicago, 1986), p. 132.

17 See Sir John Harington's "Remembrauncer," *Nugae Antiquae* (1779; repr. Hildesheim, 1968), vol. II, p. 211, cited in Louis Adrian Montrose, "The

Elizabethan Subject and the Spenserian Text," in Patricia Parker and David Quint (eds), *Literary Theory/Renaissance Texts* (Baltimore, 1986), p. 326, and Montrose's larger discussion there of the dynamic of subjection and remastery, esp. pp. 317–26.

18 Nancy Vickers, "Diana Described: Scattered Woman and Scattered Rhyme," in Elizabeth Abel (ed.), *Writing and Sexual Difference* (Chicago, 1982), pp. 265–79. I am indebted to Vickers's suggestive discussion of the "scattering" of Laura and of the Orpheus-like respite between seeing and dismemberment. See below.

19 Leonard Barkan, "Diana and Actaeon: The Myth as Synthesis," *English Literary Renaissance*, 10, 3 (1980), p. 328, notes the Latin pun and George Sandys's explication of the myth as illustrating "how dangerous a curiosity it is to search into the secrets of Princes." See Sandys, *Ovid's "Metamorphosis" Englished, Mythologiz'd and Represented in Figures* (Oxford, 1632), pp. 151–2.

20 See Mariann Sanders Regan, *Love Words: The Self and the Text in Medieval and Renaissance Poetry* (Ithaca, NY, 1982), pp. 50–82.

21 See Montrose, "'Shaping Fantasies,'" p. 77. For a different discussion of the link between Elizabeth and Dido or Elissa, see Stephen Orgel, "Shakespeare and the Cannibals," in Marjorie Garber (ed.), *Cannibals, Witches, and Divorce: Estranging the Renaissance* (Baltimore, 1987), pp. 60 ff.

22 See, for example, Greenblatt, *Renaissance Self-Fashioning*, p. 177.

23 Laura Mulvey, "Visual Pleasure and Narrative Cinema," *Screen*, 16, 3 (1978), pp. 6–18.

24 Helgerson, in *Self-Crowned Laureates*, pp. 86–7, suggests as well a link between Verdant, "the green youth," and Spenser.

25 See Mulvey, "Visual Pleasure," pp. 12 ff.; and A. Bartlett Giamatti, "Spenser: From Magic to Miracle," in Herschel Baker (ed.), *Four Essays on Romance* (Cambridge, Mass., 1971).

26 Greenblatt, *Renaissance Self-Fashioning*, p. 177, also notes this sense of implicit repetition or reenactment, remarking on "why Acrasia cannot be destroyed, why she and what she is made to represent must continue to exist, forever the object of the destructive quest. For were she not to exist as a constant threat, the power Guyon embodies would also cease to exist." My analysis would also invoke this sense of reencounter, but it would shift the emphasis more clearly to the specifically sexual politics of this episode.

5 Transfigurations: Shakespeare and Rhetoric

The first three sections of this essay were originally delivered at the MLA Convention in 1984. I am grateful to audiences at Berkeley, Bryn Mawr College, and the Folger Institute for comments helpful in its revision.

1 The edition of Shakespeare's plays used throughout is *The Riverside Shakespeare*, ed. G. Blakemore Evans (Boston, Mass., 1974).

2 See respectively George Puttenham, *The Art of English Poesie* (1589), p. 181; Angell Day, *A Declaration of . . . Tropes, Figures or Schemes* (1599), p. 83; and

Henry Peacham, *The Garden of Eloquence* (1593 edn), pp. 118–19. Descriptions of the placing of "men" before "women" invoke an implicit gender politics, described in chapter 6, "Motivated Rhetorics," p. 112 below.

3 See Jacques Derrida, "Coming into One's Own," in Geoffrey Hartman (ed.), *Psychoanalysis and the Question of the Text* (Baltimore, 1978), p. 144.

4 See, for example, *The Winter's Tale*, IV.iv.721 ff., and its play on "plain fellows" as opposed to "rough and hairy"; *The Merchant of Venice*, I.iii.66 ff., and the exchange between Launcelot Gobbo and his father in II.ii; and the echoes of the Jacob and Esau figures in *The Comedy of Errors*, in the mother's preference for the younger and the father's for the elder twin in its opening scene, and in the comic play on "hairy men" and "plain dealers without wit" in the exchange on "bald" Time in II.ii. The implication of this last is discussed below.

5 For specific discussion of this reversal in *Lear* in relation to the preposterous placing of "women on top," see chapter 6, "Motivated Rhetorics," p. 113 below.

6 See Thomas Wilson, *The Arte of Rhetorique*, fol. 107; Angell Day, *Declaration*, p. 15; Quintilian, *Institutio oratoria*, IX.iii.28.

7 Bacon, "Of the Coulers of good and evill, a fragment" (1597), printed in his *Essays* (London, 1597; repr. New York and Amsterdam, 1968), p. 27.

8 On rhetorical "increase" or copiousness in relation to Falstaff in particular, see chapter 2, "Literary Fat Ladies and the Generation of the Text," pp. 20–2 above.

9 On *copia* and "copy," see Terence Cave, *The Cornucopian Text: Problems of Writing in the French Renaissance* (Oxford, 1979), p. 4, and the translation of "to COPIE" as "Doubler, *duplicare*" in John Minsheu, *Ductor in Linguas* (*Guide into the Tongues*) (1617). The difference between a fruitful development, or difference, and mere imitation or copy might, in a larger reading of the Shakespearean canon, be seen to be raised frequently in generational form, specifically in the relation of fathers and sons.

10 See C. T. Lewis and C. Short, *A Latin Dictionary*, 1st edn (1879; repr. Oxford, 1962), under "germanus."

11 For a fuller discussion of this Erasmian term, see Cave, *Cornucopian Text*, pp. 88–91. Cave cites Erasmus's own play on the sense of the *sensus germanus* as the "German sense" in a letter of 1523.

12 Cave, *Cornucopian Text*, p. 90.

13 On the speculation surrounding these mysterious Germans, see H. I. Oliver's introduction to the Arden edition of *The Merry Wives of Windsor* (London, 1971), pp. xlvi–xlix.

14 M. M. Mahood, *Shakespeare's Wordplay* (London and New York, 1957).

15 See Thomas Blundeville, *The Arte of Logike* (1599; London, 1619), pp. 102–3. M. R. Ridley, editor of the Arden edition of *Othello* (London, 1958), p. 4, cites both some of the speculation about a possible wife and the kind of proverb form ("l'hai tolta bella? tuo danno") which would suggest a jumping to conclusion.

16 Julius Caesar Scaliger, *Poetices Libri Septem* (Lyon, 1561), IV, xxxviii.

17 For Cuningham's assumption of an "oversight" and Foakes's of a "conflict of details," see respectively *The Comedy of Errors*, 2nd edn, ed. Henry Cuningham (London, 1926), and *The Comedy of Errors*, ed. R. A. Foakes (London, 1962),

on these lines. I have discussed this matter in greater detail in "Elder and Younger: The Opening Scene of *The Comedy of Errors*," *Shakespeare Quarterly*, 34, 3 (Autumn 1983), pp. 325–7.

18 I would argue, for example, that these biblical echoes and the typological nexus they form (which extends in this play well beyond the restricted verbal quibbles that Arden editor Foakes usefully points out) join the Plautine and other subtexts which make this comedy the densely allusive play it is, but not necessarily in the service of a conjunction rather than a disjunction of its various discourses.

19 As Kenneth Muir, in "The Uncomic Pun," *The Cambridge Journal*, 3, 8 (May 1950), pp. 472–85, proposes we take Shakespeare's puns more seriously, for instance.

20 See Ridley's extended gloss on *Othello* (London, 1958), III.iii.127. *The Plays of William Shakespeare* (London, 1813), vol. 19, is a useful source of editorial glosses on the Folio's "close dilations," including Warburton's and Malone's and that of Samuel Johnson, below. I have dealt in more detail with the implications of this textual crux for a reading of the play as a whole in "Shakespeare and Rhetoric: 'Dilation' and 'Delation' in *Othello*," in Patricia Parker and Geoffrey Hartman (eds), *Shakespeare and the Question of Theory* (New York and London, 1985), pp. 54–74.

21 See Bishop Joseph Hall, *Christian Moderation* (1640), ed. Ward, 38/1. The *OED* cites under "delate" three Renaissance uses of the term as "to accuse, bring a charge against, impeach, to inform against," including "dilatit of adultry," a phrase suggestive for *Othello* in particular; under the meaning of "to report, inform of (an offence, crime, fault)," Ben Jonson's *Volpone*, II.vi ("They may delate / My slackness to my patron"); and under "delation," "delatory," and "delator" ("an informer, a secret or professional accuser") a good number of Renaissance examples. For the variant spelling "delate" for "dilate," as "to speak at large" or amplify, see, for example, the 1581 edition of Thomas Howell's *Devises* ("Some . . . with delayes the matter will delate") in the Clarendon Press edition (Oxford, 1906), p. 53, or Nashe's *Piers Penilesse* (London, 1592 edn), p. 11, "Experience reproves me for a foole, for delating on so manifest a case." Norman Sanders, editor of the New Cambridge *Othello*, adopts the "close dilations" of the Folio text but in his supplementary note on it refers to adoption elsewhere of Johnson's "delations," "despite the facts that the evidence for such a usage in Shakespeare's time is non-existent, and that Iago's pauses could hardly be described accurately as accusations."

22 For the relation of one branch of the rhetorical tradition of the dilation of discourse to the misogynist topos of women's *copia verborum*, and its importance for the stopping of women's mouths in *Othello*, see chapter 6, "Motivated Rhetorics," p. 106 below. Rymer repeats the topos in his remark on Desdemona's continuing to talk even after she has been smothered: "We may learn here, that a Woman never loses her Tongue, even tho' after she is stifl'd." See *The Critical Works of Thomas Rymer*, ed. C. A. Zimansky (New Haven, 1956), p. 161.

23 Abraham Fraunce, *The Lawiers Logike* (1588; repr. Menston, 1969), p. 44.

24 In this sense as in so many others, *The Winter's Tale* seems a late romance version of *Othello*, particularly with regard to the potentially dangerous

verisimilitude of this discourse of jealousy and its relation to the *enargeia* or "Counterfeit Representation" (Puttenham) essential to dramatic representation itself.

25 Abraham Fraunce, *The Lawiers Logike*, Book II, ch. 17, p. 113.

26 See Dudley Fenner, *The Artes of Logike and Rhetorike* (1584), Book II, ch. 6.

27 A fuller exploration of the language of rhetoric in this play would include Cressida's description of Troilus as a "minced man" (I.ii.256) when he is rhetorically divided into his "parts"; Achilles' perusal of the body of Hector "joint by joint" (IV.v.233); and its pervasive evocation of the tradition of *divisio, digestio,* and so forth. "Passage" and "passing by" in the combined sense of an extended discourse and an actual procession informs some of the more subterranean links within the scene in Act I (I.ii) which is taken up with the passing by, one by one, of the Trojan soldiers, and in the meantime involves an extended anecdote retailed by Pandarus, which Cressida describes as having been "a great while going by" (I.ii.170).

28 See Joannes Susenbrotus, *Epitome Troporum ac Schematum et Grammaticorum et Rhetorum* (Zurich, 1541), pp. 82 ff.; Scaliger, *Poetices Libri Septem*, III, xxxvii; Quintilian, *Institutio oratoria*, IX.iii.85.

29 Puttenham, *The Arte of English Poesie*, p. 217.

30 See John Hoskins, *Directions for Speech and Style* (1599), ed. Hoyt H. Hudson (Princeton, NJ, 1935), pp. 14–15.

31 For a description of antimetabole and the following instances from Shakespeare, see Sister Miriam Joseph, *Shakespeare's Use cf the Arts of Language* (New York and London, 1966), p. 81.

32 For a reading of *Hamlet* in these terms, see Terence Hawkes's "*Telmah*," published in an earlier version of *Encounter*, 60, 4 (April 1983), pp. 50–60, and included in Parker and Hartman (eds), *Shakespeare and the Question of Theory*, pp. 310–32. Sequence in *Hamlet* is discussed in relation to its play on "following" and "joining" in chapter 6, "Motivated Rhetorics," pp. 119–20 below.

33 Puttenham, *The Arte of English Poesie*, p. 218.

34 See John Smith, *The Mystery of Rhetoric Unveiled* (1657; repr. Menston, 1969), p. 116. For antimetabole in relation to questions of gender in particular, see also chapter 6, "Motivated Rhetorics," pp. 111 below.

35 Natalie Davis, "Women on Top," *Society and Culture in Early Modern France* (Stanford, 1975), p. 130.

36 See·Robert Weimann, "Shakespeare and the Study of Metaphor," *New Literary History*, 6 (1974), p. 166.

37 I refer, of course, to the Scylla and Charybdis episode in the library in *Ulysses*, which also contains much reference to Jacob and Esau.

38 For more extended treatment of this relation, see "Motivated Rhetorics," chapter 6 below, pp. 111–125.

39 For Shakespeare's association of the opening of a "matter" with the opening of a "purse," see *The Two Gentlemen of Verona*, I.i.129–30 ("Open your purse, that the money and the matter may be both at once deliver'd"), a line which also links both with the opening of a womb. On "matter," *mater*, and matrix see also "Literary Fat Ladies," chapter 2 above, pp. 10, 15, and on "opening" a secret female place, "Rhetorics of Property," chapter 7 below, pp. 128–9.

40 For the gynecological/obstetrical image of woman as a "purse" which can be "dilated and shut," see *The Works of Aristotle, the Famous Philosopher* (New York, 1974), pp. 81–2.

41 For a brilliant analysis of Othello's anomalous position as both outsider/Moor and insider/possessor of his wife, see Peter Stallybrass, "Patriarchal Territories: The Body Enclosed," in Margaret W. Ferguson *et al.* (eds), *Rewriting the Renaissance: The Discourse of Sexual Difference in Early Modern Europe* (Chicago, 1986), pp. 135–42.

42 See both this passage from Galen and the analysis of the lines from *Twelfth Night* in relation to the reversibility of male and female in Stephen Greenblatt's "Fiction and Friction," in Thomas C. Heller *et al.* (eds), *Reconstructing Individualism* (Stanford, 1986), pp. 39, 49.

6 Motivated Rhetorics: Gender, Order, Rule

This essay has benefited from comments on earlier versions by Joel Fineman, Maureen Quilligan, Peter Stallybrass and David Riggs, and discussion of sections of it delivered at Berkeley and Johns Hopkins.

1 See Frank Whigham, *Ambition and Privilege: The Social Tropes of Elizabethan Courtesy Theory* (Berkeley and Los Angeles, 1984), p.2. Thomas Wilson's *Arte of Rhetorique* (London, 1553) is cited in the 1969 reprint published by the Theatrum Orbis Terrarum (Amsterdam and New York).

2 Dudley Fenner's *Artes of Logike and Rhetorike*, in the Middleburg (1584) edition cited throughout, translates the logic of Peter Ramus and Talaeus's Ramistic rhetoric. George Puttenham's *The Arte of English Poesie* (1589), cited in what follows in the Kent English Reprints reproduction of the 1906 reprint, introduced by Baxter Hathaway (Kent State University Press, 1970), moves readily and revealingly between linguistic and social terms, while Henry Peacham's *The Garden of Eloquence*, cited in the facsimile of the 1593 edition, ed. William G. Crane (Gainesville, Fla., 1954), similarly sees the need to control the potential waywardness of figures as an analogue to social order. All parenthetical page references in the text are to these editions.

3 See Cicero, *De oratore*, III.liii. 203. Thomas Wilson's *The Arte of Rhetorique* (1553; repr. Amsterdam and New York, 1969), fol. 99, begins its description of "Distribucion" with: "It is the duetie of a Kyng, to have an especiall care over his whole realme. It is the office of his nobles, to cause the kynges will to be fulfilled. . . . It is the part of a subiect, faithfully to do his princes commaundement, & with a willyng hart to serve him at al nedes." "Distribution" was also used to describe the sequential spacing out of all of creation. See, for example, Francis Bacon, *The Advancement of Learning*, I.vi.2, and Arthur Golding's praise of Ovid's rhetorical and narrative "distributions" of creation in the Dedicatory Epistle to his translation of the *Metamorphoses* (London, 1567), ll.403–9. All English translations from Cicero are from the Loeb editions.

4 For *gradatio* as a "ladder form," see Julius Caesar Scaliger, *Poetices Libri Septem* (Lyons, 1561), IV, xxxi. For the exemplifying of this trope by the steps which proceed from "government" to "magistrate" to "obedience," see John

Hoskins, *Directions for Speech and Style* (1599), ed. Hoyt H. Hudson (Princeton, NJ, 1935), p. 12. All subsequent page references to Hoskins are to this edition.

5 See Abraham Fraunce, *The Lawiers Logike* (1588; repr. Menston, 1969), p. 27, for the ambiguous "thou, king Pyrrhus, once shalt see, the Romaines overthrowne," where "overthrowne" may "either bee the nominative case and appliable to king Pyrrhus; or the accusative and attributed to the Romaynes." For this and Puttenham's description in the context of a fuller study of amphibology, see Steven Mullaney's brilliantly suggestive "Lying Like Truth: Riddle, Representation and Treason in Renaissance England," *ELH*, 47, 1 (Spring 1980), pp. 32–47.

6 See Thomas Wilson, *The Rule of Reason Conteinying the Arte of Logique*, ed. Richard S. Sprague (Northridge, Cal., 1972). All subsequent parenthetical references are to this edition. Shakespeare plays on the link between rhetorical topos and "ground" in *Love's Labour's Lost*, I.i.239 ("the ground Which? which, I mean, I walk'd upon"). For Puttenham's definition of metaphor as "The Figure of Transport," see *The Arte of English Poesie*, III.xvii. The edition used in all quotations from Shakespeare is *The Riverside Shakespeare*, ed. G. Blakemore Evans (Boston, Mass., 1974).

7 See Jane Donawerth, *Shakespeare and the Sixteenth-Century Study of Language* (Urbana and Chicago, 1984), pp. 19–20.

8 The nominative in Latin is called the *casus erectus* (a bias reflected in Greek as well). See J. B. Greenough *et al.* (eds), *Allen and Greenough's New Latin Grammar* (New Rochelle, NY, 1983), p. 209; Howard Bloch, *Etymologies and Genealogies: A Literary Anthropology of the French Middle Ages* (Chicago, 1983), pp. 41 ff., on the contexts for concepts of grammatical "rectitude," and, on "case" generally, chapter 2, "Literary Fat Ladies," pp. 27–30 above.

9 It is interesting in relation to other essays in this volume to note that under the "partes" of the "priest" is given a summary of the art of preaching, one branch of the rhetorical tradition of the ordering of discourse, while the corresponding section under "wife" consists in a blazon of her "partes" ("The head, the breast, the armes, the backe, the thighe, the harte, the vaines, bloude, and fleshe"). See chapter 2, "Literary Fat Ladies," p. 14 above, and chapter 7, "Rhetorics of Property," pp. 127–40 below.

10 I am grateful here to questions and comments on earlier oral versions of this paper given as lectures at Berkeley and Johns Hopkins.

11 Leonardo Bruni, *De Studiis et Litteris*, trans. W. H. Woodward, in *Vittorino da Feltre and Other Humanist Educators: Essays and Versions* (Cambridge, 1879; rpt ed. E. Rice, New York, 1963), p. 126, cited in Margaret W. Ferguson *et al.* (eds), *Rewriting the Renaissance* (Chicago, 1986), p. xvi.

12 This is one of the subtle resonances, I would submit, behind "the grave's a fine and private place" in Marvell's "To His Coy Mistress." For Aristotle's strictures on women's silence and place in the home, see the *Poetics*, 1260b, 28–31, and 1160b, 33–1161a, 2; and, on the Aristotelian tradition and influence more generally, chapter 9, "Coming Second," pp. 181–5 below.

13 See Barnabe Rich, *My Ladies Looking Glasse* (London, 1616), pp. 43–4; Jean-Jacques Rousseau, *Emile*, in *Œuvres complètes*, ed. Bernard Gagnebin

and Marcel Raymond (Paris, 1959), IV, 700; and Luce Irigaray, *This Sex Which Is Not One*, trans. Catherine Porter (Ithaca, NY, 1985), p. 144.

14 See Lisa Jardine, *Still Harping on Daughters* (Brighton, 1983), pp. 103–40.

15 Mordecai Moxon, *The Character, Praise and Commendation of a Chaste and Virtuous Woman in a Learned and Pious Discourse Against Adultery* (London, 1708), p. 4.

16 See Barnabe Rich, *The Honestie of this Age* (London, 1614); Lawrence Stone, *The Family, Sex and Marriage in England 1500–1800* (London, 1977). On the collocation of "mouth" and chastity see "Literary Fat Ladies," chapter 2, pp. 26–31 and, in their link with the "house," see Peter Stallybrass, "Patriarchal Territories: The Body Enclosed," in Margaret W. Ferguson *et al.* (eds), *Rewriting the Renaissance: The Discourse of Sexual Difference in Early Modern Europe* (Chicago, 1986), pp. 126–7.

17 Nicholas Fontanus, *The Womans Doctour; or, an exact and distinct Explanation of all such Diseases as are peculiar to the Sex* (London, 1652), p. 1.

18 For earlier discussion of Lear and the inversion of "daughters" and "mothers," see chapter 5, "Transfigurations: Shakespeare and Rhetoric," p. 69 above.

19 *Othello* abounds in glances at the proverbial talkativeness of women: in the exchange between Desdemona and Iago on the "tongue" of Emilia (II.i.101 ff.); in the echoes of the "Boulster-Lecture" tradition of incessant female talking both in this scene and in Desdemona's pledge to Cassio that her "lord shall never rest" and that she will "talk him out of patience" (III.iii.22–8); in Cassio's concern that Bianca will "rail in the streets" (IV.i.162); in Iago's injunction to Emilia to "Speak within door" (IV.ii.144), to "charm" her "tongue" (V.ii.183), and hold her "peace" (V.ii.219); and in Emilia's final declaration of the right to be "liberal" in her speech (V.ii.219–22). Desdemona's continuing to talk even after she has been smothered is itself attributed to the proverbial loquacity of women by Thomas Rymer, a ready source of this as of other prejudices ("We may learn here, that a Woman never loses her Tongue, even tho' after she is stifl'd"). See *The Critical Works of Thomas Rymer*, ed. C. A. Zimansky (New Haven, 1956), p. 161.

20 See *A Curtaine Lecture*, attributed to Thomas Heywood (London, 1637), p. 4, and Jean Lefevre's fourteenth-century French translation of the *Liber Lamentationum Matheoluli*, with Lee W. Patterson, "'For the Wyves love of Bathe': Feminine Rhetoric and Poetic Resolution in the *Roman de la Rose* and the *Canterbury Tales*," *Speculum*, 58, 3 (1983), pp. 661–2. For Carfania, Patterson refers the reader to Claudine Herrmann, *Le Role judiciare et politique des femmes sous la republique romaine*, Collection Latomus, 67 (Brussels, 1964), pp. 107–8. This story of a woman obviously threatening in her power, but put down within a misogynist narrative which sees her exposing of her "cul" as revealing at last her true nature, might, however, also be placed beside Machiavelli's anecdote in the *Discourses* about Caterina Sforza showing her "genital members" (*le membra genitali*) to her enemies as a defiant, phallicized, and Medusa-like sign of her generative capacity and hence of her power to escape their control. See *The Discourses of Niccolò Machiavelli*, trans. L. J. Walker, SJ, 2 vols (London and Boston, Mass., 1975), vol. I, p. 487, discussed by John Freccero, and by Neil Hertz, who cites him in response to discussions of his "Medusa's Head: Male Hysteria under Political Pressure," *Representa-*

tions, 4 (Fall 1983), p. 64, reprinted in his collection of essays entitled *The End of the Line*.

21 In a discussion of a version of this essay at Johns Hopkins, Jonathan Goldberg objected that "shamefast," like "maydenly," could also be applied to male subjects. This, of course, is true, and there are many Renaissance English instances of such an application. The point that needs to be made, however, is that while a man might choose to do without "shamefastness," for example, a woman did so at her peril. We might also cite the quotation from Puttenham below: "the chiefe vertue [of the female sex] is shamefastnesse, which the Latines call *Verecundia*."

22 See, for example, Puttenham's introduction to Book III of his *Arte*, devoted to figures, in an initial chapter ("Of Ornament Poeticall") taken up with the image of female adornment and cosmetics. The set of associations between women and the movability of tropes is not original with the Renaissance. R. Howard Bloch, in "Medieval Misogyny," *Representations* 20 (1987), pp. 1–24, points to the link between women and *les meubles* (now "furniture," but literally "movable property") and to the presumed opposition of woman to "grammar" and "logic" in a text such as Lefevre's translation of the *Lamentations de Matheolus*, in which "woman" is the figure of an unsettling amphibology ("figure d'amphibolie," I.v.1144).

23 For antimetabole, see the *Ad Herennium* (IV.39); Quintilian, *Institutio oratoria* (IX.iii.85), and Susenbrotus, *Epitome*, pp. 82 ff.; Julius Caesar Scaliger, *Poetices Libri Septem* (Lyons, 1561), III, xxxvii; Puttenham, *The Arte of English Poesie*, pp. 217–18; and John Smith, *The Mystery of Rhetoric Unveiled* (1657; repr. Menston, 1969), p. 116, the edition used in all subsequent references.

24 For this glossing of Milton's hierarchical version of male and female by the passage from 1 Corinthians 11, see *The Poems of John Milton*, ed. John Carey and Alastair Fowler (New York, 1972), p. 631. For a wider discussion of the implications of sequence in Milton, see chapter 9, "Coming Second," pp. 191–201 below. The text of the antimetabole from 1 Corinthians 11, used in Smith, and alluded to later in this essay, is from the King James version. The Geneva Bible version, more historically appropriate to earlier, Shakespearean texts, reads: "For the man is not of the woman, but the woman of the man. For the man was not created for the woman's sake, but the woman for the man's sake."

25 See Richard Sherry, *A Treatise of Schemes and Tropes . . . Gathered out of the Best Grammarians and Oratours* (London, 1550), p. 22.

26 See John Smith, *Mysteries*, p. 201.

27 Natalie Davis, "Women on Top," *Society and Culture in Early Modern France* (Stanford, 1975), pp. 124–51. For earlier discussion of *hysteron proteron* in Lear, see chapter 5, "Transfigurations," p. 69, above.

28 See Angell Day, *The English Secretorie* (1586; repr. Menston, 1967), p. 20. Abraham Fraunce's *Lawiers Logike*, in its second book "Of Disposition, or Taxis," explicitly compares the place of "disposition" as the "second part of logic"—after invention—to that of *syntaxis* as the second part of grammar, which "ordereth & disposeth simple words handled in the first," just as Roger Ascham in *The Schoolmaster*, as part of realizing his intention to "put in some order of writing" the "right order of teaching . . . for the good bringing-up of

children and young men," starts with the "right joining" of syntax or the "proper arrangement of words in sentences." See *The Schoolmaster*, ed. Ryan, pp. 8, 13.

29 See Thomas Wilson, *The Arte of Rhetorique*, fol. 84.

30 Stephen Hawes, *The Pastime of Pleasure* (1555 edn), chapter VIII, in *Early English Poetry, Ballads, and Popular Literature of the Middle Ages* (London, 1846), vol. XVIII, p. 30. All subsequent references are to chapter and page number in this edition.

31 The *OED* cites Palsgrave (1530), "I wyll dispose this matter as I shall thynke best," as well as his listing of synonyms for the term ("Disposyng," ADMINISTRATION; "Disposytion," GOUVERNEMENT, ORDRE; "I dispose goodes to dyvers folkes," JE DISTRIBUE).

32 See Sir Thomas Elyot, *The Book Named The Governor*, ed. S. E. Lehmberg (London, 1962), p. 5: "A public weal is a body living, compact or made of sundry estates and degrees of men, which is disposed by the order of equity and governed by the rule and moderation of reason"; Richard Hooker, *Of the Laws of Ecclesiastical Polity*, 2 vols (London, 1907), vol. I, pp. 159–63: "Consider the angels of God associated, and their law ... that which disposeth them as an army, one in order and degree above another," with its discussion of "what manner we dispose and order the course of our affairs"; and E. M. W. Tillyard, *The Elizabethan World Picture* (New York, n.d.). The association of rhetorical *dispositio* with governance involves both earthly rulers and the rule of God, as the "divine disposal" of Milton's *Samson Agonistes* (p. 210) or Satan's complaint against the "great Disposer" of *Paradise Lost* ("hee who now is Sovran can dispose and bid / What shall be right"; I.246) makes clear. The "disposition" of words in order to produce the orderly "chain" of discourse links the ordering of discourse not only to the ordering of society but also to cosmic order, including Homer's famous image of the golden chain: Abraham Fraunce, in *The Lawiers Logike* (part II, ch. 17), in a discussion of "Methode" which includes both "disposition" and "distribution," writes that "Methode is like to Homer's golden chayne, wherby thinges are sweetly united and knit so together, that if one Lynk fall of, the whole chayne is broken and dissolved" (p. 115).

33 For Aristotle's use of the image of the "carpenter," see *De generatione*, 730b, 18–24; for the Aristotelian tradition, see Ian Maclean, *The Renaissance Notion of Woman* (Cambridge, 1980); and Prudence Allen, RSM, *The Concept of Woman: The Aristotelian Revolution 750 BC–AD 1250* (Montreal, 1985), ch. 2. The later extensions of this tradition are discussed in chapter 9 "Coming Second," pp. 181–5 below.

34 *The Problems of Aristotle* (London, 1597). On the crossing of this tradition with the "weaker vessel" of 1 Peter 3, see chapter 9, "Coming Second: Woman's Place," p. 183 below.

35 Robert Greene, *Penelope's Web* (1587), in *The Life and Complete Works*, ed. Alexander B. Grosart, 15 vols (New York, n.d.), V, pp. 163–4.

36 James Calderwood, *To Be or Not to Be: Negation and Metadrama in "Hamlet"* (New York, 1983), pp. 134–5.

37 For "process" in this sense of "narrative account," see, for example, *Richard III*, IV.iii.32 and IV.iv.254; *Measure for Measure*, V.i.92; and *The Merchant of*

Venice, IV.i.274. For "process" in relation to law, see *Love's Labours Lost*, V.ii.743 and *Coriolanus*, III.i.312.

38 David Marshall, "Exchanging Visions: Reading *A Midsummer Night's Dream*," *ELH*, 49 (1982), pp. 568–71.

39 Bottom's "The eye of man hath not heard, the ear of man hath not seen ... what my dream was" (IV.i.211–14) echoes in a scrambled version the text of 1 Corinthians 2: 6–10, one of those passages thought to be Pauline which subvert the order of the civil and its "reason."

40 See chapter 2, "Literary Fat Ladies," pp. 18–19 above.

41 Rosamund Tuve, in *Elizabethan and Metaphysical Imagery* (Chicago, 1947), pp. 282 ff., long ago argued the interdependence of rhetoric and logic in the Renaissance. Many of the same writers wrote treatises on both.

7 Rhetorics of Property: Exploration, Inventory, Blazon

I am grateful to Margaret W. Ferguson, Mary Jacobus, Jonathan Arac, Wayne Franklin, and Ian Parker for their comments on earlier versions of this essay.

1 See respectively Nancy Vickers, "Diana Described: Scattered Woman and Scattered Rhyme," *Critical Inquiry*, 8(1981), pp. 265–79; Wayne Franklin, *Discoverers, Explorers, Settlers: The Diligent Writers of Early America* (Chicago and London, 1979); Annette Kolodny, *The Lay of the Land* (Chapel Hill, NC, 1975); and Carole Fabricant, "Binding and Dressing Nature's Loose Tresses: The Ideology of Augustan Landscape Design," *Studies in Eighteenth-Century Culture*, 8 (1979), pp. 109–35. For "distribution," "partition," "disposition" and "property" in different contexts in this volume, see chapter 6, "Motivated Rhetorics," pp. 98–9, 113-25 above; chapter 2, "Literary Fat Ladies," p. 14 above; and chapter 8 "The (Self-)Identity of the Literary Text," pp. 155–74 below.

2 See Nancy Vickers, "'The blazon of sweet beauty's best': Shakespeare's *Lucrece*," in Patricia Parker and Geoffrey Hartman (eds), *Shakespeare and the Question of Theory* (New York and London, 1985), p. 95, the essay to which subsequent parenthetical page references refer. Vickers draws here as well on feminist extensions and critiques of the triangulated model of mimetic desire developed in the work of René Girard, specifically Mary Jacobus, "Is There a Woman in this Text?," *New Literary History*, 14 (1982), pp. 117–141, and Eve Kosofsky Sedgwick, whose work appears more recently in *Between Men: English Literature and Male Homosocial Desire* (New York, 1985).

3 See respectively the opening of Book II ("Abundance of Subject-Matter") of Erasmus's *De Duplici Copia Verborum ac Rerum Commentarii Duo*, trans. Betty I. Knott in the *Collected Works of Erasmus*, ed. Craig R. Thompson (Toronto, Buffalo, London, 1978), vol. 24, p. 572; Bacon, "Of the Coulers of good and evill, a fragment," *Essays* (1597), F4r, under "colour 5"; and John Hoskins, *Directions for Speech and Style* (1599), ed. Hoyt H. Hudson (Princeton, NJ, 1935), p.22. For the Augustinian tradition of the link between hermeneutic richness and fertility or generation, see John S. Chamberlin, *Increase and Multiply* (Chapel Hill, NC, 1976).

4 See Vickers, "Shakespeare's *Lucrece*," pp. 96–7, with Hélène Cixous, "The Laugh of the Medusa," trans. Keith Cohen and Paula Cohen, in Elaine Marks and Isabelle de Courtivroń (eds), *New French Feminisms* (Amherst, 1980), pp. 249–50.

5 See Henry Peacham, *The Garden of Eloquence* (1593), ed. William G. Crane (Gainesville, Fla., 1954), pp. 123–4; Francis Bacon, *The Advancement of Learning*, Book II.

6 George Puttenham, *The Arte of English Poesie* (1589), introduced by Baxter Hathaway (repr. 1906), facsimile reproduction (Kent State University Press, 1970), pp. 230–3.

7 The edition of Shakespeare used throughout is *The Riverside Shakespeare*, ed. G. Blakemore Evans *et al.* (Boston, Mass., 1974). Except for this quotation from *Twelfth Night*, all italicization is mine, unless otherwise indicated. "Red and white" here elliptically evoke the bodily imagery of the Song of Songs, which easily combines with the traditional "colors" of rhetoric, discussed by Vickers ("Shakespeare's *Lucrece*," p. 107).

8 For this concern with controlling the rhetorical "increase" which was the counterpart of the command to "increase and multiply," see also chapter 2, "Literary Fat Ladies," pp. 15–16 above.

9 "Le count" here, meant for "gown," conveys simultaneously by sound both "cunt" and "account." For "occupy," see chapter 6, "Motivated Rhetorics," p. 109 above, and Sir Walter Ralegh's *History of the World*, V.i (1634 edn), p. 268. The relation between the "occupying" of property and of women as possession is also made clear in Marlowe's *The Massacre at Paris*, where an adulterous possession of a wife is described as tilling the "ground" which the husband and landlord should lawfully "occupy." See *Christopher Marlowe: The Complete Plays*, ed. J. B. Steane (Harmondsworth, 1969), and Peter Stallybrass's citation of this text in his "Patriarchal Territories: The Body Enclosed," in Margaret W. Ferguson *et al.* (eds), *Rewriting the Renaissance: The Discourse of Sexual Difference in Early Modern Europe* (Chicago, 1986), p. 128.

10 The intersection of rhetorical and sexual is also made possible by a history of sexual double entendres involving the commonplaces or *koinoi topoi* from Aristotle's *Rhetoric* as distinct from the *idioi topoi* or "private places." On this private place and "case," see chapter 6, "Motivated Rhetorics," pp. 104–7 above, and chapter 2, "Literary Fat Ladies," pp. 27–31 above. The identification is also of the female with the house, and the inventory of her body as part of the "house of memory" studied by Frances Yates.

11 "Circumstances" are, as Hoskins summarizes this tradition in *Directions for Speech and Style*, "the persons who and to whom, the matter, the intent, the time, the place, the manner, the consequences, and many more" (p. 22). They both particularize the items of a story or narrative, and add to the impression of its veracity. See also Abraham Fraunce, *The Lawiers Logike* (1588; Menston, 1969), p. 44; Thomas Wilson's *Arte of Rhetorique* (1553; repr. Amsterdam and New York, 1969), fols 72–3; and Henry Peacham's *Garden of Eloquence* (1593 edn), pp. 164–7. For "circumstances" in the parallel situation of a proof before a jealous husband, in *Othello*, see chapter 5, "Transfigurations," pp. 82–4 above.

12 See variously Quintilian, *Institutio oratoria*, VIII.iii.61 ff; Richard Sherry, *A Treatise of Schemes & Tropes* (London, 1550), p. 50; Puttenham, *The Arte of English Poesie*, pp. 155 and 245; Erasmus, *De Copia*, Book II, method 5, p. 577. For a highly suggestive discussion of *enargeia*, see Terence Cave, *The Cornucopian Text* (Oxford, 1979), pp. 27–32; and, for a more detailed account of these "colors," Nancy Vickers, "Shakespeare's *Lucrece*," pp. 106–7.

13 *The Winter's Tale* provides a suggestive evocation of this complex: the crucial scene of the reconciliation of father and daughter is offstage, hidden, and conveyed only through those narrative "circumstances" which turn the "ear" into an "eye" ("This news, which is call'd true, is so like an old tale, that the verity of it is in strong suspicion. ... Most true, if ever truth were pregnant by circumstance. That which you *hear* you'll swear you *see*, there is such unity in the proofs"; V.ii.27–32, my emphasis). This instance of a potentially suspect *evidentia* thus occurs in the same play as the "peddlar" Autolycus, who unfolds stories just as he unfolds his pack to display his wares, who is a ballad-mongerer (i.e. liar), and who is linked through his name from the *Odyssey* with a notorious descendant of Hermes, the hermeneut or message-bearer connected with lying and theft.

14 See *The Original Writings and Correspondence of the Two Richard Hakluyts*, ed. E. G. R. Taylor, Hakluyt Society, 2nd series, nos 76–7 (London, 1935), vol. II, p. 333. The intersection of sexual jealousy and anxious possession of a colony—as well as an anxious spying—bring to mind the much later text of Alain Robbe-Grillet's *La Jalousie*, whose political implications as a text in a colonialist setting have so often been eclipsed by purely formalist or psychologizing readings. See Fredric Jameson, "Modernism and its Repressed: Robbe Grillet as Anti-Colonialist," *Diacritics*, 6 (1976), pp. 7–14.

15 See respectively Christopher Columbus, *Select Documents Illustrating the Four Voyages of Columbus*, trans. and ed. Cecil Jane, Hakluyt Society (London, 1930), vol. I, p. 12; Sir Walter Ralegh's "Discovery of Guiana" (1595), in Richard Hakluyt, *Principal Navigations* (London, 1598), vol. X, p. 430; John Smith, "A Description of New England," in Peter Force (comp.), *Tracts and Other Papers, Relating Principally to the Origin, Settlement and Progress of the Colonies in North America, From the Discovery of the Country to the Year 1776*, 3 vols (Washington, DC, 1836–8), vol. II, p. 9; Thomas Morton, "New English Canaan" (London, 1632), in Force, *Tracts*, vol. II, p. 10; and Robert Mountgomry, "A Discourse Concerning the design'd Establishment of a New Colony" (1717), in Force, *Tracts*, vol. I, p. 6; with Kolodny's discussion of these texts and motifs of gendering in *The Lay of the Land*, pp. 10 ff.

16 See John Hammond, "Leah and Rachel; or, The Two Fruitfull Sisters Virginia and Mary-land" (1656), in *Narratives of Early Maryland 1633–1684*, ed. Clayton Colman Hall (New York, 1910), pp. 281–304.

17 See Robert Johnson, "Nova Britannia" (1609), in Force, *Tracts*, vol. I, p. 11.

18 See Francis Bacon, *The New Organon and Related Writings*, ed. Fulton H. Anderson (Indianapolis, 1960), pp. 13, 91, 81 (the text to which all subsequent parenthetical page references refer); and his discussion of "Invention" in *The Advancement of Learning*, ed. G.W. Kitchin (London, 1915), p. 122: "*Invention* is of two kinds, much differing: the one of *Arts* and *Sciences*, and

the other of *Speech* and *Arguments*. The former of these I do report deficient; which seemeth to me to be such a deficience as if in the making of an inventory touching the estate of a defunct it should be set down *that there is no ready money*. For as money will fetch all other commodities, so this knowledge is that which should purchase all the rest. And like as the West Indies had never been discovered if the use of the mariner's needle had not been first discovered, though the one be vast regions, and the other a small motion; so it cannot be found strange if sciences be no farther discovered, if the art itself of invention and discovery hath been passed over." For the sense of invention as transgressive uncovering, see Ullrich Langer, "Gunpowder as Transgressive Invention in Ronsard," in Patricia Parker and David Quint (eds), *Literary Theory/Renaissance Texts* (Baltimore, 1986), pp. 96–114. The epigraph and Second Preface to Kant's *Critique of Pure Reason* might be the most economical way of conveying the implicit gendering at work in the empiricism of Bacon and his followers, which professed to begin with "nature" but which had a more constraining theoretical form: "They learned that reason has insight only into that which it produces after a plan of its own, and that it must not allow itself to be kept, as it were, *in nature's leading strings*, but must itself strew the way with principles of judgement based upon fixed laws, *constraining nature to give answer to questions of reason's own determining*" (my emphasis).

19 See Franklin, *Discoverers, Explorers, Settlers*, p. 214; with Edmundo O'Gorman, *The Invention of America* (Bloomington, 1961).

20 William Wood's *New Englands Prospect* (London, 1634), quoted in Franklin, *Discoverers, Explorers, Settlers*, p. 38.

21 See, respectively, *The Original Writings and Correspondence of the Two Richard Hakluyts*, vol. II, pp. 333 ff.; Stephen Greenblatt, "Invisible Bullets: Renaissance Authority and its Subversion," *Glyph*, 8 (Baltimore, 1981), p. 48; and Thomas Harriot, *A Briefe and True Report of the New Found Land of Virginia* (London, 1588).

22 All parenthetical references to George Alsop's *A Character of the Province of Mary-Land* are from the original London (1666) edition, printed by T.J. for Peter Dring.

23 See *Letters of Christopher Columbus, with Other Original Documents Relating to his Four Voyages to the New World*, trans. R. H. Major, Hakluyt Society (London, 1947), pp. 18–103.

24 See Franklin, *Discoverers, Explorers, Settlers*, p. 5.

25 Hernan Cortés, *Letters from Mexico*, ed. and trans. A. R. Pagden (New York, 1971), p. 109, quoted in Franklin, *Discoverers, Explorers, Settlers*, p. 3.

26 See, respectively, Arthur Barlowe's account in *The Roanoke Voyages 1584–1590*, ed. David B. Quinn, Hakluyt Society, 2nd series, nos 104–5 (London, 1955), vol. I, p. 108; Carleill's discussion of the advantages of the American trade in *A Briefe and Summary Discourse*, in Hakluyt, *Voyages*, vol. VI; and Alsop, *Character*, p. 3.

27 Franklin, *Discoverers, Explorers, Settlers*, pp. 89–90.

28 See *The Original Writings and Correspondence of the Two Richard Hakluyts*, vol. II, pp. 322–4. For an indication of the link between *distributio* in rhetoric and the "distribution" of social and economic positions, see, for example, Thomas Wilson's *Arte of Rhetorique*, fol. 98. The distribution of tasks in

Hakluyt's later text is the older language of distributed and static "vocacions" transformed into the division of labour in an active and appropriating enterprise.

29 Thomas Hobbes, *Leviathan*, ed. C.B. Macpherson (Harmondsworth, 1968), part II, ch. xxiv, p. 295.

30 For this view from above and the metaphor of "prospect" which dominates the literature of New World discovery, see, for example, the text of the mapper of the New England plantations, William Wood's *New Englands Prospect*, esp. A4r and its title page; and Franklin, *Discoverers, Explorers, Settlers*, p. 38. A prefatory poem by one "S.W." in Wood's text conflates the text itself with that high place, or "prospect," speaking of it as a *"Mount"* from "whence we may New England's Prospect take."

31 See *The Comedy of Errors*, III.i and chapter 2, "Literary Fat Ladies," pp. 17–18, above. Peter Stallybrass, in "Patriarchal Territories," p. 129, also notes the Dutch engraving of 1598 in which Elizabeth's body encompasses all of Europe, with different parts distributed over different countries, reproduced in Roy Strong, *Portraits of Queen Elizabeth I* (Oxford, 1963), plate E32. The exchange between the intact virgin body of Elizabeth/England and the Virginia, named after her, "opened" to see "what commoditie by industrie of man" the region might be made to "yield" produces a chiasmic structure of incorporation in which Elizabeth's body is both monarch and colony at once.

32 See Jonathan Carver, *Travels* (1778), 3rd edn (1781; repr. Minneapolis, 1956), p. 531.

33 See, respectively, Daniel Denton's *Brief Description of New-York* (1670), ed. Gabriel Furman (New York, 1845), p. 21; Nathaniel Ames, "America, Past, Present, and Future," in Ola Elizabeth Winslow (ed.), *Harper's Literary Museum* (New York, 1927), pp. 31–3; Ralph Waldo Emerson's "so shall the dumb abyss be vocal with speech. I pierce its order; I dissipate its fear; I dispose of it within the circle of my expanding life ... so far have I extended my being, my dominion" in "Nature"; and Walt Whitman, *Leaves of Grass*.

34 See John Bartram's *Observations on the Inhabitants, Climate, Soil, Rivers, Productions, Animals, and Other Matters Worthy of Notice* (London, 1751), pp. 29–30; and Bartram's letter to Collinson of November 11, 1763, cited in Franklin, *Discoverers, Explorers, Settlers*, p. 54. An earlier letter to Collinson in September 1763, cited by Franklin on p. 53, makes more explicit the gender anxieties involved in this control of alien elements: "the most probable and only method to establish a lasting peace with the barbarous Indians, is to bang them stoutly, and make them sensible that we are men, whom they for many years despised as women."

35 It is important to note that though the fallen Adam's survey of his prospects forms part of the ongoing critique of Virgilian and other secular models of empire in Milton's Christian epic, the appropriation of *Paradise Lost* not just in eighteenth-century landscape poetry but in continuing New World echoings of the Adamic prospect largely efface the Miltonic irony. Both Miltonic and Virgilian epic texts in this sense lent themselves to the imperial motivations of a larger textual and cultural history.

36 Among the texts collected in John Dixon Hunt and Peter Willis (eds), *The Genius of the Place: The English Landscape Garden 1620–1820* (London, 1975), are a number of passages which speak of the "disposing" and "dressing"

of the garden, the "Disposition and Order" and "Harmony to the Eye" of the scene, the "disposing without crowding ... the several varieties of nature"; see pp. 124, 244–5, 252. Stephen Switzer, in *Iconographia Rustica*, 2nd edn (1742), vol. I, pp. i–xiv, writes of the motives of both "pleasure" and "profit" in the proper disposition of the landscape. See Fabricant, "Binding and Dressing Nature's Loose Tresses," p. 117.

37 See Hunt and Willis (eds), *The Genius of the Place*, pp. 152 and 123 respectively.

38 For this description of Twickenham, see ibid., p. 252.

39 See William Shenstone's "Account of an Interview between Shenstone and Thomson" (1746), in ibid., pp. 244–5.

40 For these citations from Addison and the importance of the "eye" in these discussions of both landscape and women, see Fabricant, ibid., pp. 116–17. Beside descriptions of property in landscape might be placed Dr Johnson's description of female chastity ("upon that all the property in the world depends"), in Boswell's *Life of Johnson*, ed. G.B. Hill and L.F. Powell (Oxford, 1934–50), vol. V, p. 209; and evidence of the continuation of the association of adultery with theft in a later text such as *The Whole Duty of Man* (London, 1804), p. 152: "The corrupting of a man's wife, enticing her to a strange bed ... is by all acknowledged to be the worst sort of theft."

41 See, for Pope's reference to the garden of Alcinous, *The Guardian*, 173; for the "Epistolary Description of Twickenham," Hunt and Willis (eds), *The Genius of the Place*, pp. 250–1; and Fabricant, ibid., p. 113, and pp. 117–18 on Pope's advice to Bathurst to "Enclose whole Downs in Walls" (Epistle II.ii.261) in part to protect Pope's own financial investment in the latter's improvement of his land; on Switzer's support of "the Fencing and Enclosing [of] Large and Waste Lordships, Commons, etc."; and on the vogue of the "ha-ha" or sunken fence as a means of "contributing to a sense of expansiveness" (since it in no way interfered with open-prospect views) while yet establishing definite boundaries.

42 Edward Said, *Orientalism* (New York, 1978).

8 The (Self-)Identity of the Literary Text: Property, Proper Place, and Proper Name in *Wuthering Heights*

This essay incorporates portions of two previously published essays, "The (Self-) Identity of the Literary Text: Property, Propriety, Proper Place, and Proper Name in *Wuthering Heights*," in O. J. Miller and Mario Valdés, eds, *Identity of the Literary Text* (Toronto, 1985) and "Anagogic Metaphor: Breaking Down the Wall of Partition," in Eleanor Cook *et al.*, eds, *Centre and Labyrinth: Essays in Honor of Northrop Frye* (Toronto, 1983). I am grateful to Graham Falconer, Cyrus Hamlin, and Mary Nyquist for their reading of it when it was first presented in 1982, and to Heather Jackson, David Simpson, and Mieke Bal for comments helpful in preparing the final versions.

1 Ian Watt, *The Rise of the Novel* (1957; repr. Harmondsworth, 1963), p. 22, citing Locke's *Essay Concerning Human Understanding*, Book III, ch. 3, sect. 6.

2 See Locke, *Essay*, III, 3, 2–5; Hobbes, *Leviathan*, part I, ch. 4; and C. B. Macpherson, *The Political Theory of Possessive Individualism: Hobbes to Locke* (Oxford, 1962).

3 Watt, *Rise of the Novel*, pp. 18–19; Michel Foucault, *Les Mots et les choses*, trans. as *The Order of Things* (New York, 1973), esp. pp. 104 ff.; Emily Brontë, *Wuthering Heights*, ed. David Daiches (Harmondsworth, 1965), ch. III, p. 66. All subsequent parenthetical references to the novel are to chapter and page in this edition.

4 See Patricia Drechsel Tobin, *Time and the Novel* (Princeton, NJ, 1978), introduction; Roland Barthes, "An Introduction to the Structural Analysis of Narrative," trans. Lionel Duisit, *New Literary History*, 6, 2 (Winter 1975), pp. 237–72; Jacques Derrida, *Of Grammatology*, trans. Gayatri Spivak (Baltimore, 1976), pp. 85, 332; Foucault, *The Order of Things*, pp. 82–92; Eleanor N. Hutchens, "The Novel as Chronomorph," *Novel* (Spring 1972), pp. 215–24; and Harold Toliver on "Linear Logic" in *Animate Illusions* (Lincoln, Neb., 1974). See also, on the ideological implications of form, Pierre Macherey, *A Theory of Literary Production*, trans. Geoffrey Wall (London, 1978). The description of this "linear logic" does not imply unawareness of writing in the Enlightenment which parodies or undermines it (the case of Sterne or Swift, for example). For a critique of the Foucauldian characterization of an earlier Renaissance *episteme* and assertion of a rupture with it, see chapter 1, "Retrospective Introduction," above, p. 6.

5 Foucault, *The Order of Things*, p. 114. See also Hugh Blair, *Lectures on Rhetoric and Belles Lettres* (1783), lectures XIV and XV, with Dumarsais's *Les Tropes* (1729), part I and part II, i, on catachresis, and Rousseau's *Essai sur l'origine des langues*. For the relation between metaphor and the "improper," "alien," and "out of place," see "The Metaphorical Plot," chapter 3 above, pp. 36–42, an essay which contains an earlier version of the argument developed here in relation to *Wuthering Heights*. It still remains an open question whether Foucault's characterization of the linear logic of Enlightenment thought can be said to fit all the texts of which he treats—or can be transported *tel quel* from a French to an English context. It can be observed, however, that many of the influential texts of the period we still refer to as the English Enlightenment have strategic recourse to a sequential narrative or genealogical history—in two cases, indeed, specifically in relation to property and the development of proper names. William Blackstone, for instance, in the lengthy chapter on "Property" in his *Commentaries on the Laws of England* (1765–9), begins his discussion by raising an anxiety about an owner's right to an exclusively private property when land was originally granted in common to all, but quickly proceeds to still that anxiety—or potential instability—by recourse to a sequential history, which moves from the fluidity of common property to the stability of private property, a property secured first by the institution of the "house," or permanent dwelling. Hugh Blair, in the *Lectures on Rhetoric and Belles Lettres*, provides a sequential narrative of the movement from figurative instability to the provision of "proper" names, a history of progress away from the mobility of tropes like metaphor which his French authority Dumarsais had defined as living in a "borrowed home" (*Les Tropes*, X). The discourse of rhetoric, concerned with proper names, and that of

economics, concerned with property, are here both in their generation of sequential histories and in their progress towards stability—a place for everything, and everything in its place—strikingly similar. And both as well, in their common concern for placing and for partitions, seem particularly vulnerable to a specifically gothic plot, to a threat to the stability or inviolability of a "house."

6 Foucault, *The Order of Things*, pp. 119–20, 303, 298, and 304 respectively.

7 On identity understood as "self-identity," see the discussion of two differing conceptions of identity (as permanence amid change and as unity amid diversity) in Paul Edwards (ed.), *An Encyclopedia of Philosophy* (New York, 1967), under "Identity"; "Almost all the writers of the period under discussion, from Descartes to Kant, took the term 'identity' to mean that an object 'is the same with itself' (Hume)." The more particular sense of self-identity (*identité à soi*) as used by Derrida involves as well the notion of self-presence. For readings of other nineteenth-century texts in relation to the question of a unified identity and narratorial mastery, see, for example, Shoshana Felman on Henry James's *The Turn of the Screw* in "Turning the Screw of Interpretation," and Peter Brooks's "Freud's Masterplot: Questions of Narrative," *Yale French Studies*, nos 55–6 (1977); Cynthia Chase, "The Decomposition of the Elephants: Double-Reading *Daniel Deronda*," *PMLA*, 93, 2 (March 1978), pp. 215–27; J. Hillis Miller, *Fiction and Repetition* (Cambridge, Mass., 1982); and Maria M. Tatar, "The Houses of Fiction: Toward a Definition of the Uncanny," *Comparative Literature*, 33, 2 (Spring 1981), pp. 167–82.

8 Maurice Blanchot, "L'Absence de livre," in *L'Entretien infini* (Paris, 1969), pp. 564–6. The translations from it here are taken from Derrida's discussion of Blanchot's terms in "LIVING ON: Border Lines," in Harold Bloom *et al.* (eds), *Deconstruction and Criticism* (New York, 1979), pp. 104–7.

9 Derrida, *Of Grammatology*, p. 86.

10 Jacques Derrida, *Dissemination*, trans. Barbara Johnson (Chicago, 1981), p. 86. See also pp. 103–4.

11 See respectively Derrida, *Dissemination*, p. 103; Nietzsche, *Zur Genealogie der Moral*, First Essay, II; and, on ghost/host/guest, J. Hillis Miller, "The Critic as Host," in Bloom *et al.* (eds), *Deconstruction and Criticism*, pp. 220 ff. In addition to the juxtaposition of "guest," "host," and "ghost" in chapter III, we are told at the end of chapter XVII, "The *guest* was now the *master* of Wuthering Heights" (p. 222; my emphasis).

12 For the complex of terms related to "proper," see, *inter alia*, Derrida, *Of Grammatology*, pp. 26, 107–12, 244, and Derrida's long footnote on Marx's critique of the linguistic association of "proper" and "property" in *The German Ideology*, in "White Mythology: Metaphor in the Text of Philosophy," trans. F. C. T. Moore, *New Literary History*, 6, 1 (Autumn 1974), p. 15. For a survey of Marxist criticism of Brontë's novel, including the work of Arnold Kettle, Raymond Williams, and Terry Eagleton, see Ronald Frankenberg, "Styles of Marxism: Styles of Criticism. Wuthering Heights: A Case Study," in Diana Laurenson (ed.), *The Sociology of Literature* (Keele, 1978). This survey necessarily omits Frederic Jameson's provocative short discussion in *The Political Unconscious* (Ithaca, NY, 1981), pp. 126–9.

13 Joseph J. Scaliger, *Poetices Libri Septem* (Lyon, 1561), IV, xxxviii.

14 These have been discussed in, respectively, Tobin, *Time and the Novel*, p. 41, and Mark Schorer, "Fiction and the 'Analogical Matrix,'" *Kenyon Review*, 11 (Autumn 1949).

15 See the discussions of proper names in, for example, Michel Butor, *Répertoire: Etudes et conférences 1948–59* (Paris, 1960), p. 252; Jacques Lacan, "L'instance de la lettre dans l'inconscient," *Ecrits*, I (Paris, 1966), p. 252; Charles Grivel, *Production de l'intérêt romanesque* (Paris, 1973), pp. 128–44; and Derrida, *Of Grammatology*, pp. 107–13.

16 On nominative and accusative, see Geoffrey Hartman, "Psychoanalysis: The French Connection," in Geoffrey Hartman (ed.), *Psychoanalysis and the Question of the Text* (Baltimore, 1978), pp. 94 ff.

17 Foucault, *The Order of Things*, pp. 82–3.

18 Frank Kermode, *The Classic* (New York, 1975), p. 123.

19 Barthes, "An Introduction to the Structural Analysis of Narrative," pp. 251–4. We might remember, in relation to this markedly genealogical novel, the characterization of genealogy itself as a form of spacing in Nietzsche's *Zur Genealogie der Moral*.

20 Kermode, *The Classic*, p. 120. Other readings which have contributed to my argument here include, in addition to those of Hillis Miller and Fredric Jameson already noted, Dorothy Van Ghent's pioneering study in *The English Novel* (New York, 1953); Terry Eagleton's in *Myths of Power: A Marxist Study of the Brontës* (London, 1975), pp. 97–121; Carol Jacobs's "*Wuthering Heights*: At the Threshold of Interpretation," *Boundary*, 2, 7, 3 (1979), pp. 49–71; David Musselwhite, "*Wuthering Heights*: The Unacceptable Text," in Francis Barker *et al.* (eds), *Literature, Society and the Sociology of Literature*, Proceedings of the Conference held at the University of Essex (July 1976), pp. 154–60; and Margaret Homans, "Repetition and Sublimation of Nature in *Wuthering Heights*," *PMLA*, 93, 1 (January 1978), pp. 9–19. Musselwhite speaks of the "bracketting of Lockwood" which characterizes readings as otherwise divergent as those of Q.D. Leavis, "A Fresh Approach to *Wuthering Heights*," in *Lectures in America* (New York, 1969), and Eagleton's chapter. We might add to this the reading of the ending of the novel as Brontë's capitulation to the conventional "novelistic tradition" in Leo Bersani's *A Future for Astyanax* (Boston, Mass., 1976), p. 221.

21 For this temporal form of copular metaphor ("A *is* B"), see Northrop Frye, *Anatomy of Criticism* (1957; repr. New York, 1966), p. 124, on the phenomenon of the grown man's feeling "identical" with himself as a child. The Wordsworthian atmosphere of an episode such as Nelly's experience in chapter 11 also brings to mind Wordsworth's preoccupation with those fearful "vertical" moments when the boundaries vanish and a distancing "space" of years drops away. The late Paul de Man once remarked in conversation that what he referred to as "aberrance" in *The Prelude* was like a grown man's saying of a picture of himself as a child, "That's me" (or "I")—Frye's principal instance of this copula.

22 George Puttenham, *The Arte of English Poesie* (1589), ch. 12. See also Derrida on the "*hysteron proteron* of the generations" in Freud's *Beyond the Pleasure Principle*, in his "Coming into One's Own," in Hartman (ed.), *Psychoanalysis and the Question of the Text*, pp. 136–46.

23 W. J. Harvey, *Character and the Novel* (London, 1965), p. 187.
24 See Charlotte Brontë's Preface to the 1850 edition of *Wuthering Heights*,
    reprinted in the Daiches edition, p. 40.

9 Coming Second: Woman's Place

 1 See Mary Nyquist, "Gynesis, Genesis, Exegesis, and the Formation of Milton's
    Eve," in Marjorie Garber, ed., *Cannibals, Witches, and Divorce: Estranging
    the Renaissance* (Baltimore, 1987), pp. 147 ff. Northrop Frye has long taught
    a course on the Bible, including the Genesis creation stories and the almost
    effaced sense of struggle at its opening, which also informed my thinking about
    structures of a first and second time, and of reversal in the biblical text. All cita-
    tions from the Bible, unless otherwise noted, are from the King James version.
 2 Louis Ginzberg, *The Legends of the Jews*, trans. Henrietta Szold (Philadelphia,
    1913), vol. I, p. 65.
 3 On "sequence," "consequence," following, and the "preposterous" reversal of
    earlier and later, original and derivative, see the discussion of the Miltonic
    problematic of a sequential narrative which, like the hexameron of Genesis,
    depends on "Process of Speech," in my *Inescapable Romance* (Princeton,
    NJ, 1979), p. 126 and pp. 133 ff. On the reversal of Jacob and Esau, first- and
    second-born, in the biblical narrative and its relation to a structure of
    preposterous reversals, including the New and Old Testaments, see also
    chapter 5, "Transfigurations: Shakespeare and Rhetoric," pp. 68–9 above.
 4 This is the quotation, from 1 Timothy 2:11–14, which begins Mieke Bal's
    critique of the misogynist reading of the Genesis 2 creation story, in "Sexuality,
    Sin, and Sorrow: The emergence of the Female Character (A Reading of
    Genesis 1–3)," *Poetics Today* [Special Issue: The Female Body in Western
    Culture: Semiotic Perspectives, ed. Susan Rubin Suleiman], 6, 1–2 (1985), pp.
    21–42; Bal's essay, and its basis in Phyllis Trible's *God and the
    Rhetoric of Sexuality* (Philadelphia, 1978), is subjected to a critique of its
    ahistoricism by Nyquist, in "Gynesis, Genesis, Exegesis," pp. 153 ff., who
    points out the abandonment of the initial logic in the second part of the oft-
    quoted verses from 1 Timothy 2. I have been happy to share my own work on
    "preposterous" structures of reversal in the biblical text with Professor
    Nyquist, together with the sequential spacing of narrative distribution and
    amplificatio, in Renaissance rhetoric, as a model for Reformed attempts to
    relate the first and second creation stories of male and female in Genesis as
    epitome and enlargement. Professor Nyquist's citing of the Bible within a
    general principle of "phallogocentric thought" (p. 158) — the priority of the
    temporally first — omits awareness of the strong biblical counter-instance of
    the reversal of first and second-born sons (as in the case of Jacob and Esau, for
    example), a motif which radically calls into question the imperatives and first
    principles of other traditions. However, the importance granted to Adam's
    priority in creation, within the New Testament and beyond, strongly suggests
    that in respect of gender, its construing of the significance of first-coming
    complicates its radical difference in this particular regard.
 5 This phrase, which begins Antonia Fraser's *The Weaker Vessel: Woman's Lot*

in Seventeenth-Century England (London, 1984), occurs already in Shakespeare's *Love's Labours Lost, As You Like It, Romeo and Juliet,* and elsewhere.

6 Ian Maclean, *The Renaissance Notion of Woman* (Cambridge, 1980), p. 13. Maclean's illuminating discussion comprehends both the attempt to deal with the combination of the Genesis 1 and 2 creation narratives of male and female and the long history of consolidating the Genesis tradition with the Aristotelian legacy described below. For further discussion of the problem of combining the two creation narratives, see Nyquist, "Gynesis, Genesis, Exegesis, and Milton's Eve," pp. 155 ff.

7 For this table of opposites, see Aristotle's *Metaphysics,* trans. in *The Basic Works of Aristotle* (New York, 1941), 986a, 22–5. Subsequent references are to this text of Aristotle's *Works.* For the explication of its implications, see Maclean, *The Renaissance Notion of Woman,* pp. 2–3, 8, who cites G.E.R. Lloyd's *Polarity and Analogy: Two Types of Argumentation in Early Greek Thought* (Cambridge, 1971); and Prudence Allen, RSM, *The Concept of Woman: The Aristotelian Revolution 750 BC–AD 1250* (Montreal, 1985), pp. 19–20, with the general discussion in ch. 2.

8 For the above, see *The Generation of Animals,* 838a, 27, and 775a, 15f; and the discussion in Allen, *The Concept of Woman,* pp. 83–122, and Maclean, *The Renaissance Notion of Woman,* p. 8. For the relation of the Aristotelian tradition to questions of female silence and female speech in particular, see chapter 6, "Motivated Rhetorics," pp. 104–5 above.

9 The other relevant tradition here is, of course, Philo's synthesis of Genesis and Jewish commentary with Platonic and Stoic influences, particularly notions of the feminine as passive and material and the male as active and rational. This history would include the repression of "Sophia" or Wisdom (echoed, as we shall see, in the name given to the secondary "Woman" in Rousseau's *Emile*), and the substitution of a masculine Logos for this pre-existent feminine figure (Proverbs 8). On Philo's preference for Logos over the Sophia of Jewish tradition, see Joan Chamberlain Engelsman, *The Feminine Dimension of the Divine* (Philadelphia, 1979), chapter 5 ("The Expression and Repression of Sophia") and Harry Austryn Wolfson, *Philo: Foundations of Religious Philosophy in Judaism, Christianity, and Islam,* 4th printing, rev. Structure and Growth of Philosophic Systems from Plato to Spinoza, no. 2 (Cambridge, Mass., 1962), vol. I, pp. 188 ff. Engelsman (p. 103) quotes the following passage from Philo on Sophia and the female as second and therefore inferior: "For that which comes *after God,* even though it were the chiefest of all other things, occupies a *second place,* and therefore was termed feminine to express its contrast with the Maker of the Universe who is masculine, and its affinity to every thing else. For *pre-eminence always pertains to the masculine, and the feminine always comes short of and is lesser than it"* (Fuga, 50–2, my emphasis).

10 Aquinas, *Summa Theologica,* Ia, 92, 1. For Aquinas's discussion and the scholastic synthesis of Aristotle and Genesis, see Maclean, *The Renaissance Notion of Woman,* pp. 8–9, together with the more general reference to the assimilation of Aristotelian and biblical, and the later influence of Aristotelian theory in Linda Woodbridge, *Women and the English Renaissance* (Urbana, 1984), pp. 15, 56 and 68. For the following citations and translations from the

commentary of Thomas de Vio, Martin Luther, and Cornelius a Lapide, as well as the more general issues raised in the rest of this section, see Maclean, *The Renaissance Notion of Woman*, pp. 8–13.

11 Thomas de Vio, Cardinal Cajetan (1469–1534), *Commentarii in Quinque Mosaicos Libros* (Paris, 1539), p. 25.

12 See Maclean, *The Renaissance Notion of Woman*, p. 10.

13 See Martin Luther, *Werke: Kritische Gesamtausgabe* (Weimar, 1883–), XLII, 51–2, and *Tischreden*, no. 55 (Weimar, 1912–21), I, 19; as described in Maclean, *The Renaissance Notion of Woman*, p. 10.

14 Cornelius a Lapide, *In Omnes Divi Pauli Epistolas Commentaria* (Paris, 1638), pp. 284–5.

15 Mary Wollstonecraft, *A Vindication of the Rights of Woman*, ed. Carol H. Poston (New York, 1975), p. 81.

16 It is at such junctures, having to do with narrative sequence and with spacing, that Jacques Derrida on "logocentrism" and "phallogocentrism" would be most profitably juxtaposed with Kenneth Burke's notion of the "logological" in *The Rhetoric of Religion: Studies in Logology* (1961; rpt. Berkeley, 1970).

17 My emphasis. The anonymous piece from 1705 appears in a gathering of passages out of the popular *Ladies Diary* in 1775. See *The Diarian Miscellany: Consisting of All the Useful and Entertaining Parts ... extracted from the Ladies Diary, 1704–1773 by Charles Hutton*, 5 vols (London, 1775), vol. IV, pp. 14 ff. This different construing of the Genesis sequence was already played with in Cornelius Agrippa, for example. On Agrippa, see Theodor Reik, *The Creation of Woman: A Psychoanalytic Inquiry into the Myth of Eve* (New York, 1960), along with the reading of his arguments for women in Woodbridge, *Women and the English Renaissance*, pp. 38–44. On the different construing more generally, including its appearance in the recent work of Phyllis Trible, see Nyquist, "Gynesis, Genesis, Exegesis, and Milton's Eve," pp. 160 ff. I would add that Trible is in this respect a recent version of the tradition of Rachel Speght and other early reversals of the misogynist argument from Genesis 2. See below.

18 See Rachel Speght, *A Mouzell for Melastomus* (London, 1617), p. 2; and Joseph Swetnam, *The Arraignment of lewd, idle, froward and unconstant women* (London, 1615). Speght's different construing of the sequence of Genesis 2 joins the figuring of last as best in *Jane Anger her Protection for Women* (London, 1589) and in *Ester hath hang'd Haman* (London, 1617) by the equally appropriately named "Ester Sowernam."

19 For Tiamat, *těhōm* and on later allusions in the Hebrew Bible to creation as a struggle with a dragon or sea-monster several times identified as "Rahab," see Northrop Frye, *The Great Code: The Bible and Literature* (New York and London, 1982), pp. 146, 188–92; *Peake's Commentary on the Bible*, ed. Matthew Black and H. H. Rowley (London, 1962), on the "P" account of creation, p. 178; and especially Nyquist, "Gynesis, Genesis, Exegesis," p. 149. Nyquist's general discussion, in "Gynesis, Genesis, Exegesis," pp. 148 ff., stresses the effacement of Tiamat and of the feminine, both in the "P" text and in the tradition of commentary on this passage; and *Peake's Commentary* similarly stresses the note of conflict involved, and the effacement of this

conflict by commentary which insists on creation *ex nihilo*.

20 *Peake's Commentary*, p. 179.

21 See J. J. Bachofen, *Mutterrecht und Urreligion*, a selection of his writings translated by Ralph Manheim, *Myth, Religion and Mother Right*, Bollingen Series LXXXIV (Princeton, NJ, 1967), pp. 69–207. For the description and critique of historical conceptions of matriarchy, see Joan Bamburger, "The Myth of Matriarchy," in M. Z. Rosaldo and L. Lamphere (eds), *Woman, Culture, and Society* (Stanford, 1974), pp. 263–80. For this opposition in the context of the reading of the *Oresteia* put forward here, I am indebted to Froma I. Zeitlin, "The Dynamics of Misogyny: Myth and Mythmaking in the *Oresteia*," *Arethusa*, 11 (1978), 149–84.

22 See Zeitlin, "The Dynamics of Misogyny," pp. 154–60 and *passim*.

23 See Bachofen, *Myth, Religion and Mother Right*, pp. 157–65.

24 For the linear aspect of the *Oresteia* and the link between the ending of the trilogy and the new "scientific" theories of generation which privileged the father over the mother, see Zeitlin, "The Dynamics of Misogyny," pp. 152, 162–74. For the relation between theogony and embryology as the "*logos* of beginnings," discussed below, see J. Hillman, *The Myth of Analysis* (Evanston, Ill., 1972), pp. 224–5, with Zeitlin, pp. 169–70.

25 See Reik, *Creation of Woman*, p. 131, cited in Zeitlin, p. 179, who notes the similarity between the creation of Eve and the birth of Athena, in the context of the usurpation and reversal involved in the transfer to the male as begetter of the female.

26 Henry Sumner Maine, *Ancient Law* (1861), introduced by J. H. Morgan (London and New York, 1917). See Bamburger, "The Myth of Matriarchy," p. 264.

27 The connections between these texts have already been woven in various directions. Sarah Kofman links Freud on female sexuality with the Genesis 2 tradition of the creation of woman in the fable which ends *L'Enigme de la femme* (Paris, 1980), and Rousseau, Freud, and Aristotle with the Derridean logic of the supplement from *De la grammatologie*, in *Le respect des femmes* (Paris, 1982), especially pp. 73–4; Froma Zeitlin links the *Oresteia*, Aristotle, and Bachofen's *Das Mutterrecht* to Freud; Cleanth Brooks, in an essay I first came across in treating of Eve's narcissistic self-reflection and the "fiat lux" of Genesis in *Inescapable Romance*, assimilates Eve's Narcissism to Freud on the development of the female, in "Eve's Awakening," *Essays in Honor of Walter Clyde Curry* (Nashville, 1954), p. 285. The link between Milton's Eve, Freud's "On Narcissism," and Kofman's reading of the latter is discussed in Mary Jacobus's "Is There a Woman in This Text?", *New Literary History*, 14, 1 (Autumn 1982), pp. 134–7. Nyquist, in "Gynesis, Genesis, Exegesis, and the Formation of Milton's Eve," treats primarily of the Genesis 2 story and Milton's relation to it, but refers more elliptically to Freud and to Zeitlin's study.

28 *Paradise Lost*, IV.288–311. The edition used for this and all subsequent citations of *Paradise Lost* is *The Poems of John Milton*, ed. John Carey and Alastair Fowler (New York, 1972), henceforth referred to as Carey/Fowler. Unless otherwise indicated, all italicization in quotations from Milton is my own.

29 See *Tetrachordon*, in *Complete Prose Works of John Milton*, ed. Ernest
   Sirluck (New Haven, Conn., 1959), vol. II, p. 589, with Nyquist, "Gynesis,
   Genesis, Exegesis," p. 181, who goes on to discuss Eve's turning to the man
   "whose image" she is, and to invoke the Derridean logic of supplementarity in
   the context of Adam's lack.

30 I have discussed Eve's narcissistic moment and its conscription to an ultimate
   teleology, in the context of the commentaries on the separation of light from
   darkness in Genesis which lie behind Eve's turning to "light" and its relation to
   the hierarchy of "Hee for God only, shee for God in him" (IV. 229) in
   Inescapable Romance: Studies in the Poetics of a Mode (Princeton, NJ, 1979),
   pp. 114 ff. See also the reference there to the notion of loops in time — and of a
   whole progression seen from the perspective of a *telos*—in a marvelous essay
   by H. R. MacCallum, "Milton and Sacred History: Books XI and XII of
   Paradise Lost," in Millar MacLure and F. W. Watt (eds), *Essays in English
   Literature from the Renaissance to the Victorian Age Presented to A. S. P.
   Woodhouse* (Toronto, 1964), pp. 166–7.

31 See Carey/Fowler, p. 836, on *Paradise Lost*, VIII. 416–19, and Leon Howard,
   "'The Invention' of Milton's 'Great Argument': A Study of the Logic of 'God's
   Ways to Men,'" *Huntington Library Quarterly*, 9 (1945), p. 160.

32 For this tradition, see chapter 2, "Literary Fat Ladies," pp. 16–17 above, and
   my "Deferral, Dilation, Différance: Shakespeare, Cervantes, Jonson," in
   Patricia Parker and David Quint (eds), *Literary Theory/Renaissance Texts*
   (Baltimore, 1986), pp. 186–8, with Lee W. Patterson, "'For the Wyves Love of
   Bathe': Feminine Rhetoric and Poetic Resolution in the *Roman de la Rose* and
   the *Canterbury Tales*," *Speculum*, 58 (July 1983), pp. 656–95.

33 See Nyquist, "Gynesis, Genesis, Exegesis," p. 178.

34 See the Carey/Fowler gloss here, p. 972.

35 I have treated this Miltonic problem of sequence, syntax, and narrative more
   fully in *Inescapable Romance*, pp. 125–38.

36 *The Standard Edition of the Complete Psychological Works of Sigmund
   Freud*, ed. James Strachey, 24 vols (London, 1953–74), vol. 19, p. 249. Unless
   otherwise noted, all subsequent parenthetical citations from Freud are to
   volume and page numbers in this translation, cited as *SE*.

37 Jean-Jacques Rousseau, *Emile, or On Education*, with introduction, translation and notes by Allan Bloom (New York, 1979), pp. 23, 357. English
   translations from *Emile* are provided, for convenience of reference, from this
   edition, to which page numbers in the text refer, unless otherwise indicated.
   Citations of the text of Rousseau are, with original orthography preserved, to
   volume and page number of the Pléiade edition of the *Œuvres complètes*, ed.
   Bernard Gagnebin and Marcel Raymond (Paris, 1959), abbreviated throughout as *OC*. Unless otherwise indicated, all italicization is my own.

38 For this formulation, see Nannerl O. Keohane, "'But for Her Sex ...': The
   Domestication of Sophie," in the *Trent Rousseau Papers*, ed. Michael
   Neumann *et al.* (Ottawa, 1980), p. 139, an essay to which I am indebted in my
   own discussion of *Emile*'s final Book. For other discussions of the contradic-
   tory appearances of "woman" in the text of Rousseau, see, among others,
   Victor G. Wexler, "'Made for Man's Delight': Rousseau as Antifeminist,"

American Historical Review, 81, 1 (1976), pp. 266–91; Pierre Burgelin, "L'Education de Sophie," *Annales de la Société Jean-Jacques Rousseau*, 35 (1959–62), pp. 113–37; Joel Schwartz, *The Sexual Politics of Jean-Jacques Rousseau* (Chicago, 1984); and Sarah Kofman, *Le Respect des femmes* (Paris, 1982), pp. 57–150, who cites, on p. 80, a specific relation to Aristotle. The contradictory force of texts such as "Sur les femmes" and "Lettre à d'Alembert" notwithstanding, I would argue that it is the traversing of Book V of *Emile* by the logic of Genesis 2 and to a lesser and more subtle extent of Aristotle which allows a reading of it in the terms of sequence and reversal suggested here. Rousseau was, among other things, a frequent reader both of the Bible and of the Protestant tradition of commentary in particular.

39 The text of Rousseau reads as follows: "la seule chose que nous savons avec certitude est que tout ce qu'ils ont de commun est de l'espéce, et que tout ce qu'ils ont de différent est du sexe. ... Ces rapports et ces différences doivent inflüer sur le moral; cette conséquence est sensible ... et montre la vanité des disputes sur la préférence ou l'égalité des sexes; comme si chacun des deux allant aux fins de la nature selon sa destination particuliére n'étoit pas plus parfait en cela que s'il ressembloit davantage à l'autre! En ce qu'ils ont de commun ils sont égaux; en ce qu'ils ont de différent ils ne sont pas comparables: une femme parfaite et un homme parfait ne doivent pas plus se ressembler d'esprit que de visage, et la perfection n'est pas susceptible de plus et de moins" (*OC*, IV, 693).

40 *OC*, IV, 693: "Si la femme est faite pour plaire et pour être subjuguée, elle doit se rendre agréable à l'homme au lieu de le provoquer: sa violence à elle est dans ses charmes; c'est par eux qu'elle doit le contraindre à trouver sa force et à en user. L'art le plus sur d'animer cette force est de la rendre nécessaire par la résistance. Alors l'amour-propre se joint au desir, et l'un triomphe de la victoire que l'autre lui fait remporter. De là naissent l'attaque et la deffense, l'audace d'un sexe et la timidité de l'autre, enfin la modestie et la honte dont la nature arma le foible pour asservir le fort."

41 See Keohane, "'But for Her Sex...,'" p. 144, and Thomas Laqueur, "Orgasm, Generation, and the Politics of Reproductive Biology," *Representations*, Special Issue, *Sexuality and the Social Body in the Nineteenth Century*, 14 (Spring 1986), pp. 20–1.

42 *OC*, IV, 695: "Voici donc une troisiéme consequence de la constitution des séxes; c'est que le plus fort soit le maitre en apparence et dépende en effet du plus foible; et cela non par un frivole usage de galanterie, ni par une orgueilleuse générosité de protecteur, mais par une invariable loi de la nature, qui, donnant à la femme plus de facilité d'exciter les desirs qu'à l'homme de les satisfaire, fait dépendre celui-ci malgré qu'il en ait du bon plaisir de l'autre, et le contraint de chercher à son tour à lui plaire pour obtenir qu'elle consente à le laisser être le plus fort. Alors ce qu'il y a de plus doux pour l'homme dans sa victoire est de douter si c'est la foiblesse qui céde à la force ou si c'est la volonté qui se rend, et la ruse ordinaire de la femme est de laisser toujours ce doute entre elle et lui."

43 *OC*, IV, 766: "Je m'attends que beaucoup de lecteurs, se souvenant que je donne à la femme un talent naturel pour gouverner l'homme, m'accuseront ici de contradiction; ils se tromperont pourtant. Il y a bien de la différence entre

s'arroger le droit de commander, et gouverner celui qui commande. L'empire
de la femme est un empire de douceur, d'addresse et de complaisance, ses
ordres sont des caresses, ses menaces sont des pleurs. Elle doit régner dans la
maison comme un ministre dans l'Etat, en se faisant comander ce qu'elle veut
faire. En ce sens il est constant que les meilleurs ménages sont ceux où la femme
a le plus d'autorité. Mais quand elle méconoit la voix du chef, qu'elle veut
usurper ses droits et commander elle-même, il ne résulte jamais de ce desordre
que misére, scandale et deshoneur."

44 See *Emile*, p. 36.
45 *OC*, IV, 249: "L'homme naturel est tout pour lui: il est l'unité numérique,
l'entier absolu qui n'a de rapport qu'à lui-même ou à son semblable. L'homme
civil n'est qu'une unité fractionnaire qui tient au dénominateur, et dont la
valeur est dans son rapport avec l'entier, qui est le corps social. Les bonnes
institutions sociales sont celles qui savent le mieux dénaturer l'homme, lui ôter
son existence absolue pour lui en donner une relative, et transporter le *moi*
dans l'unité commune; en sorte que chaque particulier ne se croye plus un, mais
partie de l'unité, et ne soit plus sensible que dans le tout."
46 "Commençons par distinguer le moral du Physique dans le sentiment de
l'amour. Le Physique est ce désir général qui porte un séxe à s'unir à l'autre; Le
moral est ce qui détermine ce désir et le fixe sur un seul objet exclusivement, ou
qui du moins lui donne pour cet objet préféré un plus grand dégré d'énergie. Or
il est facile de voir que le moral de l'amour est un sentiment factice: né de
l'usage de la société, et *celebré par les femmes* avec beaucoup d'habilété et de
soin *pour établir leur empire* et rendre *dominant le séxe qui devroit obéir*"
(*OC*, III, 158, my translation).
47 See the *Discours* in *OC*, III, 158, and the accompanying note, p. 1335.
48 "quoi qu'elle ordone, il ne réplique point, et souvent, en partant pour obéir il
me regarde avec des yeux pleins de joye qui me disent: vous voyez qu'elle a pris
possession de moi. Cependant, l'orgueilleuse l'observe en dessous, et sourit en
secret de la fierté de son esclave" (*OC*, IV, 790); "Ô Emile ... Combien je te
vois déchu! Où est ce jeune homme formé si durement, qui ne cédoit qu' à la
raison, et ne tenoit à rien de ce qui n'étoit pas lui? Maintenant amolli dans une
vie oisive il se laisse gouverner par des femmes" (*OC*, IV, 799).
49 Bloom, *Emile*, p. 22.
50 *OC*, 709: "Justifiez toujours les soins que vous imposez aux jeunes filles, mais
imposez-leur en toujours. L'oisieté et l'indocilité sont les deux défauts les plus
dangereux pour elles et dont on guérit le moins quand on les a contractés. Les
filles doivent être vigilantes et laborieuses ... elles doivent être génées de bonne
heure. Ce malheur, si c'en est un pour elles, est inséparable de leur séxe, et
jamais elles ne s'en délivrent que pour en souffrir de bien plus crüels. Elles
seront toute leur vie asservies à la gêne la plus continüelle et la plus sévère, qui
est celles des bienseances: il faut les exercer d'abord à la contrainte, afin qu'elle ne
leur coûte jamais rien, à dompter toutes leurs fantaisies pour les soumettre aux
volontés d'autrui. ... La dissipation, la frivolité, l'inconstance, sont des défauts
qui naissent aisément de leurs prémiers gouts corrompus et toujours suivis. Pour
prévenir cet abus aprenez-leur surtout à se vaincre. Dans nos insensés établis-
semens la vie de l'honnête femme est un combat perpétuel contre elle même; il
est juste que ce séxe partage la peine des maux qu'il nous a causés."

51 See Ernest Jones, *The Life and Work of Sigmund Freud*, 3 vols (New York, 1955), vol. III ("The Last Phase: 1919–1939"), p. 422.

52 For Freud's remark on the creation of Eve and his further reference to Otto Rank's suggestion of a reversal, in the story of Eve born from Adam, of Eve as Adam's mother, see his letter to C. G. Jung, dated December 7, 1911, quoted by Ernest Jones, *The Life and Work of Sigmund Freud* (New York, 1955), vol. II, p. 452; for the anecdote from *The Interpretation of Dreams*, see Reik, *Creation of Woman*, pp. 36–7.

53 For this model and its textual instances, see Sarah Kofman, *L'Enigme de la femme: la femme dans les textes de Freud* (Paris, 1980), trans. Catherine Porter as *The Enigma of Woman: Woman in Freud's Writings* (Ithaca, NY, 1985), esp. pp. 37–9, and Luce Irigaray, *Ce Sexe qui n'en est pas un* (Paris, 1977), trans. Catherine Porter, with Carolyn Burke, as *This Sex Which is Not One* (Ithaca, NY, 1985), esp. pp. 23, 30, 35 ff. Irigaray's remarks here elaborate on the discussion of Freud in her *Speculum de l'autre femme* (Paris, 1974), trans. Gillian C. Gill as *Speculum of the Other Woman* (Ithaca, NY, 1985).

54 The tradition of the originally hermaphrodite Adam, developed from Genesis 1, also leaves its traces in Freud's notions of sexuality and gender difference, but again in a way which makes clear that the starting point of this separating out is male. See Kofman, *Enigma of Woman*, pp. 122 ff., on this original bisexuality.

55 See Kofman, *Enigma of Woman*, pp. 101 ff.

56 See, for example, Charles Bernheimer's introductory remarks to Charles Bernheimer and Claire Kahane (eds), *In Dora's Case: Freud—Hysteria—Feminism* (New York, 1985), pp. 10–11.

57 See Kofman's critique of Luce Irigaray's cruder formulations of a Freudian Aristotelianism, in *Enigma of Woman*, p. 104.

58 Irigaray, *This Sex Which is Not One*, p. 65.

59 For a gathering of studies of Dora's case, see Bernheimer and Kahane (eds), *In Dora's Case, passim*; for the figure of "Anna O."—Bertha Pappenheim, the patient of Breuer who later became a major figure in the German Jewish women's movement—see Dianne Hunter, "Hysteria, Psychoanalysis, and Feminism: The Case of Anna O.," in Shirley Nelson Garner *et al.* (eds), *The (M)other Tongue: Essays in Feminist Psychoanalytic Interpretation* (Ithaca, NY, 1985), pp. 89–115. For the linkages between Milton's Eve, Freud's "On Narcissism," and its reading by Kofman, see Mary Jacobus, "Is There a Woman in this Text?", *New Literary History*, 14, 1 (Autumn 1982), 134–7.

60 See Kofman, *Enigma of Woman*, pp. 50 ff.

61 See ibid., pp. 68–71; and the letter of Lou Andreas-Salome to Freud, January 30, 1919, in Ernst Pfeiffer (ed.), *Sigmund Freud and Lou Andreas-Salome Letters*, trans. William and Elaine Robson-Scott (New York, 1972), p. 89.

62 Herbert Marks, of Indiana University, in an exchange on the differing interpretations of Genesis 2: 18, has pointed out to me the development of "neged" as "opposite to," in a neutral spatial sense, into the sense of "against."

Index